D0999339

BASIC & INTERMEDIATE LEVEL

español Santillana

COMPLETE SPANISH for Americans

Be a proficient Spanish speaker in no time!

Learn more than 4500 vocabulary words used in real-life situations!

More than 1,500 practical exercises!

SPEED UP! Learn Spanish Really Fast!

Published in the United States of America

This program was conceptualized by Trialtea USA, P.O.Box 454402, Miami, FL 33245-4402.
Tel: 1-800-210-0344

The participation and contributions of the following educators in the development of this series is gratefully acknowledged:

Maripaz García, Ph.D.
Yale University

Anna M. Nogar, Ph.D.
University of New Mexico

ISBN-10: 1-60396-215-8
ISBN-13: 978-1-60396-215-5

Santillana USA Publishing Company, Inc.
2105 N.W. 86th Avenue
Doral, FL 33122
Tel.: 1-800-2458584
www.santillanausa.com

Graphic Design: Marina García

Cover photo: Getty Images

Printed in the USA.

INTRODUCCIÓN

Welcome

The book that you have in your hands has been developed by experts in the field of Foreign Language Education with experience in teaching Spanish to adults. The content, structure, and sequence of instruction is based on Second Language Acquisition (SLA) research findings. We hope that using Complete Spanish for Americans is pleasurable and rewarding.

Purpose

This book is designed with ACTFL's (the American Council on the Teaching of Foreign Languages) 5 Cs in mind: *Communication, Cultures, Connections, Comparisons, and Communities*. Given the restrictions inherent in any instructional method that is not face-to-face or teacher-guided, this book is designed to teach the learner basic, communicative grammar and vocabulary, as well as linguistic and cultural strategies to improve communication. Via connections and comparisons between the first language (English) and the target language (Spanish), the learner's understanding of new information is anchored in his or her previous linguistic knowledge, resulting in better retention of the target language.

In the cultural sections of each chapter, the learner will find descriptions of various facets of pan-Hispanic life, and commentary highlighting the differences and similarities between Hispanic and non-Hispanic cultures. Through connections and comparisons of these communities, the learner will broaden his or her view; understand the practices, perspectives and products of different Hispanic cultures; and relate this knowledge to the Spanish language he or she is learning.

General Features

This book features the following language functions: describing, comparing, narrating in the present, asking questions, expressing likes and dislikes, requesting, wishing, recommending, and narrating in the past. These basic functions determine the sequence of instruction for grammar, creating a logical and functional syllabus rather than a series of unrelated grammar points. This instructional structure was chosen with a communicative purpose in mind: guiding the learner towards proficiency in accomplishing specific daily tasks. The sequence of instruction for grammar points follows the recommendation of SLA research findings and keeps in mind that the learner's first language is English. Since the level of this book is basic-intermediate, covering about two semesters of college foreign language instruction, most explanations are concise and do not delve into the numerous possible exceptions and nuances learned at a more advanced level. Reading and writing are emphasized, but the book can also be purchased with an audio CD that aids in developing listening and speaking skills. The use of English in the book diminishes progressively as the learner advances in proficiency. By the end of the book, English is used sparingly, encouraging the learner to use Spanish as often as possible.

Contents

This book has 32 units. Each unit ('unidad') features sections on vocabulary, grammar, culture, and additional recommendations. Units 8, 16, 24, and 32 are self-exams that present exercises on the previous seven units. These exams challenge the learner to remember, review, and synthesize the information learned up to that point. The purpose of these exams is not only to review and practice, but also to self-evaluate, so that the learner can make conscious decisions about his or her progress.

Vocabulary and grammar are presented in a natural, contextualized setting accompanied by illustrations that promote visual memory for a more comprehensive learning experience. Contextualization is achieved through the presentation of specific characters that repeatedly interact with each other in different scenarios, and also through the thematic organization of the units. The learner is constantly encouraged to guess meaning from context and from linguistic features, expanding his or her ability to read in a foreign language without having to depend on rote memorization. Although this method is more challenging, it will eventually help the learner to face real-life linguistic needs. The vocabulary is presented in standard Spanish with an inclination towards peninsular Spanish (Castilian), since the characters are living in Spain. However, other regional variations are also included to expand the

learner's lexicon and linguistic awareness. Vocabulary and reading comprehension exercises (and answers) end this section.

Following the vocabulary section, each unit features a grammar explanation that uses a deductive approach. We believe that this approach is better suited to an adult learner who is learning on his or her own. Grammar exercises increase in difficulty from recognition to production. Translation is used extensively as a way to enhance vocabulary and grammar learning, while discouraging too-literal translation. Grammar exercises and their answers end this section.

Following the grammar section, there is a Spanish-only vocabulary list with the most important words learned in that specific unit. Rather than having a bilingual vocabulary list that promotes passive learning, we encourage the learner to become more active by providing the English equivalents of the words listed.

After this section, the units include cultural readings that cover different Spanish-speaking countries. These cultural sections further develop the themes of each unit, creating a natural connection between language and culture, and expanding the learner's knowledge of different issues directly connected to Hispanics/Latinos in and out of the United States. The readings increase in difficulty as the learner advances in proficiency. The data on which these readings are based were taken from various sources, referenced and credited in each instance. The information provided in these sections includes 'small c culture' (famous people, food, traditions, etc.) and 'big c culture' (politics, values, literature, etc.) to fit the needs of the adult learner.

At the end of the each unit, we have included recommendations that encourage the learner to take appropriate steps to expand his or her knowledge of the subject. These suggestions promote active learning, specifically the exploration of other venues (films, radio, newspapers, etc.) that will complement his or her learning experience.

Acknowledgements

We would like to thank María de la Paz García and Anna M. Nogar for the invaluable guidance on the writing of this book. Ms. García has a Ph.D. in foreign language education from The University of Texas at Austin and has taught Spanish for more than a decade. She currently teaches Spanish at Yale University. Ms. Nogar has a Ph.D. in Spanish from the University of Texas at Austin, has also experience teaching Spanish to adults, and is currently teaching Latin American literature at the University of New Mexico.

The Future

We believe this book will provide you with the tools necessary to learn the basics of Spanish in a pleasant and gratifying way. We encourage you to continue studying Spanish with our next books, that will be published shortly. If you have comments, suggestions or any kind of feedback, we would love to hear from you. You can contact us at:

Santillana USA
2105 NW 86 Ave
MIAMI FL 33122
Tel. 1-800-245-8584
www.santillanausa.com
sales@santillanausa.com

ÍNDICE

UNIDADES

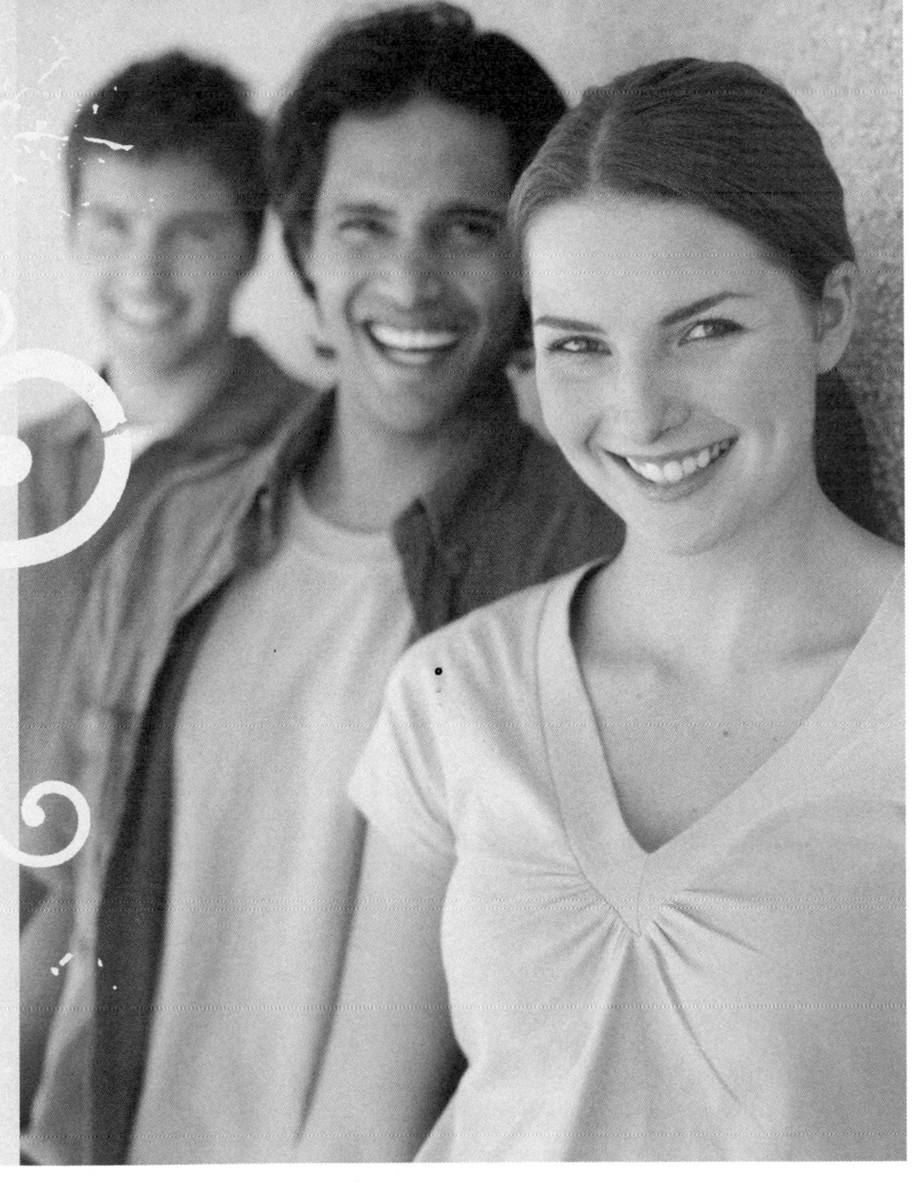

UNIDAD 1 CONTENIDO

In this unit, you will learn:

1 - How to greet people in different ways

2 - Some 'survival' expressions

3 - A basic guideline for pronunciation

4 - Cultural information about informal greetings and the so-called Spanish lisp

los saludos

LOS SALUDOS
(Greetings)

Meet your new friend.

Hola, amigos. Me llamo Peter McPherson y ésta es mi nueva oficina.

(Hello, my friends. My name is Peter McPherson and this is my new office)

Peter is an American business man working in Spain. Today is his first day at the office. Read the dialogue between Peter, his new boss, and another co-worker, Ana.

Antonio Pérez:	Hola, buenos días. ¿Cómo se llama usted? *(Hello, good morning. What's your name?)*
Peter:	Buenos días. Soy Peter McPherson. *(Good morning, I am Peter McPherson)*
Antonio Pérez:	Bienvenido. Yo soy su jefe, Antonio Pérez. Mucho gusto. *(Welcome. I am your boss, Antonio Pérez. Pleased to meet you)*
Peter:	El gusto es mío, señor Pérez. *(The pleasure is mine, Mr. Pérez)*
Antonio Pérez:	Permítame presentarle a Ana, otra empleada. *(Let me introduce you to Ana, another employee)*
Ana:	Hola. Me llamo Ana Gómez Rivera. ¿Cómo te llamas? *(Hello. My name is Ana Gómez Rivera. What's your name?)*
Peter:	Me llamo Peter McPherson. Encantado. *(My name is Peter McPherson. Pleased to meet you)*
Ana:	Ah, ¿el nuevo empleado americano? Hablas español muy bien. (Ah, the new American employee? You speak Spanish very well)
Peter:	Gracias, lo aprendí en la universidad. (Thanks, I learned it in college)

[Footnotes]

[1] *Even though this is an Italian word, it is used in some Spanish-speaking countries as an informal 'goodbye' it can have other spellings, such as chau or chao.*

Ana:	¿Y cómo estás? ¿Todo bien en tu primer día de trabajo? *(And how are you? Is everything OK on your first day of work?)*
Peter:	Muy bien, gracias. Sin problemas. Y tú, ¿qué tal? *(Very well, thanks. No problems. And you, how is everything?)*
Ana:	Bien, gracias. Mira, ésta es tu oficina. Luego regreso y te ayudo con tus cosas, eh? Ciao[1]. *(Fine, thanks. Look, this is your office. I will return later and help you with your things, OK? See you)*
Peter:	Hasta luego. *(See you later)*
Antonio Pérez:	Adiós. *(Goodbye)*

Ejercicio A

Read the dialogue again and try to answer these questions.

1) How do you say 'How are you?' 'Is everything OK' and 'How is everything'?

____

2) What are three ways to say 'nice meeting you' or something similar?

____

3) What are two ways to ask 'What's your name?'?

____

4) What are three ways to say 'My name is….' or 'I am ….'?

____

5) What are three ways to say goodbye or something similar?

____

Answers A: **1)** ¿Cómo estás? - ¿Todo bien? - ¿Qué tal? / **2)** Mucho gusto - El gusto es mío - Encantado **3)** ¿Cómo se llama usted? - ¿Cuál es tu nombre? / **4)** Soy…. - Me llamo…. - Mi nombre es…. / **5)** Ciao - Hasta luego - Adiós

Ejercicio B

Now, with the vocabulary that you have learned, complete this version of our friends' conversation.

Peter:	**(1)** ____________ días. ¿Es usted el señor Pérez?
Antonio Pérez:	Sí, soy yo. **(2)** ¿______________________________?

Peter:	Soy Peter McPherson. Mucho (**3**) __________.
Antonio Pérez:	Encantado. ¿Qué tal le va en su primer día de trabajo?
Peter:	Muy (**4**) ________, señor. Sin (**5**) _____________.
Antonio Pérez:	Permítame presentarle a una compañera de trabajo *(co-worker)*, Ana Gómez Rivera.
Peter:	(**6**) ___________ gusto, Ana. ¿Qué (**7**) ________?
Ana:	Todo bien, (**8**) ___________. ¿Cómo (**9**) ________?
Peter:	(**10**) ________, gracias. El primer día...ya sabes *(you know)*.
Ana:	Sí, lo comprendo *(I understand)*. Pues, nos vemos luego *(Then, I will see you later)*, eh? Bienvenido.
Peter:	Gracias. Mucho gusto en conocerte *(Nice meeting you)*.
Ana:	Igualmente *(Same here)*.

Answers B: **1)** Buenos / **2)**¿Cómo se llama usted? - ¿Cuál es tu nombre? / **3)** gusto / **4)** bien / **5)** problemas / **6)** Mucho / **7)** tal? / **8)** *gracias* / **9)** *estás?* / **10)** *Bien*

OTROS SALUDOS

(Other greetings)

There are many ways to greet a person and the expressions vary from country to country. Here are some more useful expressions used to greet people:

¿cómo va todo? / ¿cómo le va? / ¿cómo te va?	*(how is everything?)*
¿qué hay? / ¿qué pasa? / ¿qué pasó? / ¿qué onda?	*(what's up? what's going on?)*
buenas	*(morning)*
buenas tardes	*(good afternoon / good evening)*
buenas noches	*(good evening / good night)*
nos vemos	*(see you)*
nos vemos luego / hasta luego / hasta la vista	*(see you later)*
hasta mañana	*(see you tomorrow)*
hasta pronto / nos vemos pronto	*(see you soon)*

Responses to the previous greetings

muy bien *(very well)*	bien *(fine)*
más o menos *(so-so)*	mal *(bad)*
regular *(so-so)*	fatal *(horrible)*
no mucho *(nothing much)*	Sí, gracias. Todo bien *(Yes, thanks. Everything is OK)*

Ejercicio C

Select the most appropriate response to the following greetings.

1) ¡Mucho gusto!
- a) mi nombre es…
- b) buenas tardes
- c) el gusto es mío

2) ¡Hola!
- a) hola
- b) adiós
- c) soy…

3) Buenas noches
- a) buenos días
- b) el gusto es mío
- c) buenas noches

4) ¿Cómo estás?
- a) no mucho
- b) bien, gracias
- c) ¿cuál es tu nombre?

5) Hasta luego
- a) hasta la vista
- b) hola
- c) soy….

Answers C: **1)** - c) / **2)** - a) / **3)** - c) / **4)** - b) / **5)** - a)

EXPRESIONES ESENCIALES

(Essential expressions)

Here are some useful expressions for beginners:

gracias / muchas gracias *(thanks / thanks a lot)*	por favor *(please)*
de nada *(you're welcome)*	no comprendo *(I don't understand)*
¿habla usted español? *(do you speak Spanish?)*	lo siento *(I am sorry)*
no hablo español *(I don't speak Spanish)*	repita, por favor *(repeat, please)*
¿habla usted inglés? *(do you speak English?)*	¿qué significa….? *(what does …. mean?)*
soy americano/a *(I am American)*	¿cómo se dice… en español? *(how do you say…..in Spanish?)*
hable más despacio *(speak slowly)*	un momento, por favor *(one moment, please)*

Ejercicio D

Select the most appropriate response for the following situations.

1) Someone is speaking very fast.

a) de nada	b) lo siento	c) más despacio, por favor

2) Someone is speaking Spanish thinking you can understand it all.

a) no comprendo	b) muchas gracias	c) el gusto es mío

3) Someone said something you did not quite understand.

a) de nada	b) repita, por favor	c) mucho gusto

4) Someone said 'gracias'.

a) de nada	b) el gusto es mío	c) ¿habla usted inglés?

5) Someone just asked you '¿hablas español?'

a) repita, por favor	b) no hablo español	c) muchas gracias

6) Someone asked you where you are from

a) ¿qué significa...?	b) soy americano	c) no hablo español

7) Someone just said 'mucho gusto'

a) bien, gracias	b) mal	c) el gusto es mío

Answers D: **1)**-c) / **2)**-a) / **3)**-b) / **4)**-a) / **5)**-b) / **6)**-b) / **7)**-c)

GUIA DE PRONUNCIACIÓN *(Pronunciation guidelines)*

The following is a set of guidelines that you will have to review several times. We do not expect that you will learn everything written here right away, but we hope that it will help a little with pronunciation. Also, remember that Spanish is spoken in many countries, so there is a good chance that some sounds will be slightly different from country to country, just like some sounds are different in the United States than they are in Great Britain. In Spanish, most vowels and consonants do not sound exactly the same as in English.

Vocales *(Vowels)*

Let's take a look at some differences between Spanish and English. In English, vowels have different sounds depending on the letters before and after the vowel. For example, the letter 'a' is not pronounced the same in the word 'man' as in the word 'mane.' But in Spanish, vowels always have the same sound, regardless of the surrounding letters. This feature makes Spanish a very easy language to pronounce.

In Spanish, vowels are pronounced with a single, crisp sound (not a combination of two sounds). For example, the English word 'no' sounds like /nou/ with a u sound at the end. In contrast, the Spanish no has only the o sound without the u sound. Try it!

Consonantes *(Consonants)*

Consonants are also different in English and Spanish. Sometimes the difference is minimal and sometimes it is noticeable.

LAS VOCALES			
A	Similar to 'f**a**ther'	Ana	oficina *(office)*
E	Similar to 'b**e**d' or 't**e**n'	jefe *(boss)*	encantado *(nice meeting you)*
I	Similar to 's**ee**d' or 't**ee**n'	día *(day)*	apellido *(last name)*
O	Similar to 'c**o**ld'	hola *(hello)*	nombre *(name)*
U	Similar to 'l**oo**p' or 'm**oo**n'	mucho gusto *(pleased to meet you)*	

LAS CONSONANTES		
B	Pronounced like the letter 'b' in the word 'boat'	buenos, bien
C	-Pronounced like the letter 'c' in the word 'cat' when followed by 'a,' 'o' or 'u'	encantado, cómo, cuál
	-Pronounced like the letter 's'[2] in 'sigh' when followed by 'e' or 'i'	dice, gracias
CH	Pronounced like 'ch' in the word 'much'	mucho, chau
D	Pronounced like the letter 'd' in the word 'door'	dice, todo
F	Pronounced like the letter 'f' in the word 'fake'	jefe, oficina
G	-Pronounced like the letter 'g' in the word 'go' when followed by 'a,' 'o' or 'u'	gato, amigo, gusto
	-Pronounced like 'gu' in the words 'guest' and 'guilty' when followed by 'ue' or 'ui'(if it has two dots over the 'u' then pronounce the actual sound 'u')	guerra, guitarra
		güero, vergüenza
	-Pronounced like the letter 'h' in the word 'hello' when followed by 'e' and 'i'	gente, gitano
H	Always silent (don't pronounce it at all) (thus, 'hola' sounds like 'ola')	hola, hasta
J	Pronounced like the letter 'h' in the word 'hello'[3] (thus, 'ge' sounds like 'je,' and 'gi' sounds like 'ji')	jefe, ejercicio

K	Pronounced like the letter 'k' in the word 'fake'(this letter only exists in a few foreign words)	kilo, kimono
L	Pronounced like the letter 'l' in the word 'letter'	hola, presentarle
LL	Pronounced like the letter 'j' in jail[4]	llamo, apellido
M	Pronounced like the letter 'm' in 'mom'	me llamo
N	Pronounced like the letter 'n' in 'never'	no, encantado
Ñ	Pronounced like 'gn' in the word 'cognac'	año, español
P	Pronounced like the letter 'p' in 'Napa'	empleada, español
Q	Pronounced like the letter 'k' in 'kilo'(it is always followed by 'ue' or 'ui')	que, quien
R	-Pronounced like 'tt' in the word 'butter' -Pronounced as a 'rolling r' at the beginning of a word -Pronounced as a 'rolling r' when double (rr)	Pérez, conocerte Rivera, Rodríguez carro
S	Pronounced like the letter 's' in the word 'seat'	estás, es
T	Pronounced like 'ed' in the word 'passed'	estás, todo
V	Pronounced like the letter 'b' in the word 'boy'[5](thus, ballenato is pronounced like vallenato)	Rivera, va
X	-Pronounced like the letter 'x' in the word 'sex' -Pronounced like the letter 'h' in the word 'hotel'	México, sexo Ximena
Y	-Pronounced like the letter 'll' (see above)(thus, 'cayó' sounds like 'calló') -Pronounced like 'ee' when by itself or part of a diphthong	yo, ya soy, y
Z	-Pronounced like the letter 's' in the word 'sigh' (Latin America) -Pronounced like 'th' in the word 'thanks' (Spain)(There is no 'ze' or 'zi' combination. When needed, you have to write 'ce' or 'ci')	Pérez, zapato Gómez, zapato

[Footnotes]

[2] *In Spain, 'c' followed by 'e' or 'i' is pronounced like the letter 'th' in 'thanks.'*
[3] *This 'j' sound (/h/) is harder (more guttural) in Spain than in Latin America.*
[4] *In some countries, like Argentina and Uruguay, it sounds harder (almost like the 'ch' in 'Chicago'); but in some other countries, like those in the Caribbean, it sounds softer (almost like the letter 'y' in 'yam').*
[5] *In some regions, the letters 'v' and 'b' are pronounced differently (as they are pronounced in English).*

MI LISTA DE VOCABULARIO

This is a list of the words that you have learned in this unit. Can you remember what all these words mean? Give it a try. If there is a word that you do not know, look for it in the unit. At the bottom of this list, there is room for you to add additional words.

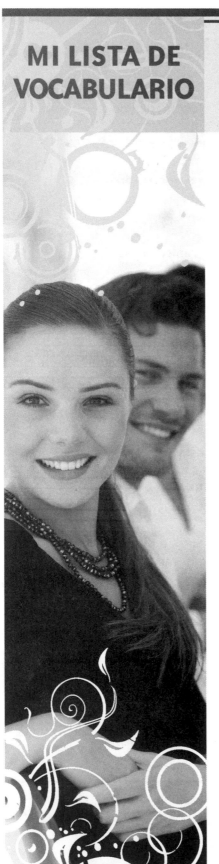

adiós
bien
bienvenido
bueno
buenas
buenas noches
buenas tardes
buenos días
ciao o chau o chao
¿cómo está? ¿cómo estás?
¿cómo le va? ¿cómo te va?
(el) compañero de trabajo
de nada
despacio
(el) día
(el) empleado
encantado
fatal
(las) gracias
el gusto es mío
hasta la vista
hasta luego
hasta mañana
hasta pronto
hola

igualmente
lo siento
mal
más o menos
(el) momento
muchas gracias
mucho gusto
no mucho
no comprendo
(la) noche
¿qué hay?
¿qué significa….?
¿qué tal?
regular
repita
(el) saludo
soy….
(la) tarde
¿todo bien?
(el) vocabulario

UN POCO DE CULTURA

Informal Greetings

Many Spanish-speaking people in general use an informal greeting that involves kissing the person they are meeting on the cheek, whether they are meeting the person for the first time, or it friend they have not seen in a while. In Spain, two kisses are the norm, but in Latin America one kiss is more typical. The kiss is usually a little peck on the right cheek rather than a full kiss. Generally, the motion of touching cheeks (or kissing 'in the air') is sufficient.

In most countries, this greeting occurs between two women or between a man and a woman, but never between two men (with the exception of metrosexual crowds, close relatives, and some gay men). However, in Argentina and Uruguay, this type of greeting is acceptable between two men.

In business settings, where shaking hands is more common, this informal greeting is not very appropriate. However, it is often seen in some informal business environments or when the people involved are young. A general recommendation would be to wait and see how the native Spanish speaker approaches you, and then to do tas he or she does. Otherwise, you might extend your hand to a person who is approaching with the intention of kissing you on the cheek, causing you too find yourselves in an awkward situation. Something else to remember is that there is no hug involved in the greeting, just the kiss(es) and maybe a hand on the shoulder or arm to position yourself correctly. This is helpful to keep you from kissing the person somewhere other than the cheek. Oops!

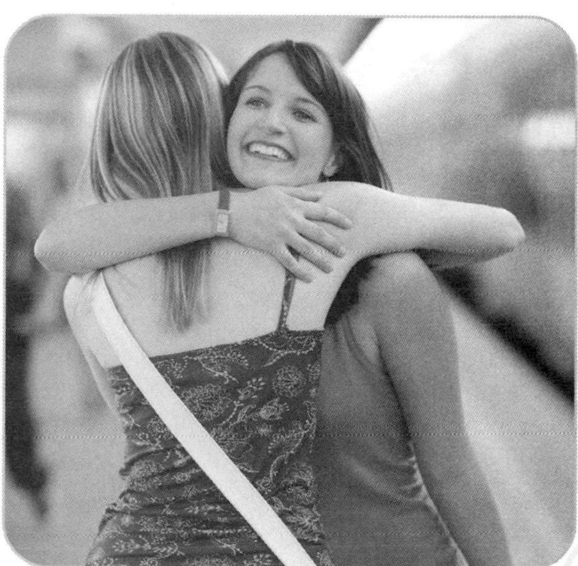

The So-called Spanish Lisp

Another curious thing that you will notice in Spanish speakers is that they have different accents if they are from different countries, just as American English sounds different than British English. One of the most noticeable aspects of Spaniards' accent is the so-called Spanish lisp. A lisp is defined as a speech impediment or a speech disorder in which one cannot produce s-sounds correctly, pronouncing them like the /th/ sound in 'thanks'. (Tho, a perthon with a lithp would thpeak like thith.) The cause of this disorder is unknown.

Have you ever heard that Spaniards have a lisp? This is not true, nor is there a lisping king in their history, either! Spaniards and Latin Americans differ in their pronunciation of certain sounds because their languages evolved separately throughout the centuries. Like the English spoken in the United States versus that of Australia or Great Britain, the language is the same, but pronunciations, as well as some words and expressions, are different.

In Spain, people who speak castellano (Castilian) pronounce 'za,' 'ce,' 'ci,' 'zo,' and 'zu' (there is no 'ze' or 'zi') with the sound /th/ that we mentioned before, but they pronounce 'sa,' 'se,' 'si,' 'so' and 'su' with the sound /s/, like in English. Accordingly, the word 'gracias' is pronounced /grathias/. This phenomenon is called the 'ceceo.'

In Latin America, on the other hand, people pronounce 'za,' 'ce,' 'ci,' 'zo' and 'zu' with the sound /s/, just like 'sa,' 'se,' 'si,' 'so' and 'su'. Therefore, the word 'gracias' is pronounced /grasias/. This is called the 'seseo.' The use of the 'seseo,' however, makes spelling a little more complicated for a Latin American than for a Spaniard, as the 'z' and 's' are indistinguishable.

Not all Spaniards use the 'ceceo.' For example, in many areas of Andalucía (Southern Spain), people speak with the 'seseo,' like in Latin America.

Dialectal differences in the pronunciation of Spanish make this language rich and interesting. Although these varieties might confuse a learner at first, the more he or she is exposed to different accents, the more proficient he or she will become in listening to and understanding Spanish.

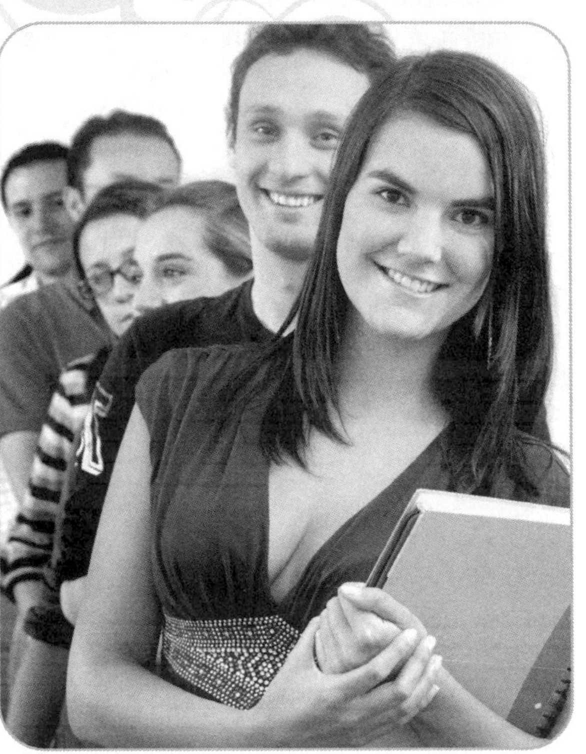

RECOMENDACIÓN PARA ESTA UNIDAD

To finish this unit, we recommend that you check out the following website, where you can hear how vowels and consonants are pronounced in Spanish:

http://www.uiowa.edu/~acadtech/phonetics/spanish/frameset.html

You can also practice pronunciation by listening to Spanish music while reading the lyrics, by watching Spanish movies with subtitles, and by trying to imitate the Spanish words you hear on television or on the radio.

UNIDAD 2

CONTENIDO

In this unit, you will learn:

1 - How to provide personal information

2 - Vocabulary related to the office

3 - About definite and indefinite articles

4 - About gender and number

5 - Cultural information about names and last names

DATOS PERSONALES

(Personal information)

Now Peter is in Human Resources office, where Ana works. He has to fill out some paperwork for payroll and Ana is helping him with it. By looking at his answers, try to predict what some of her questions mean.

Ana:	Hola, otra vez. *(Hello, again)*
Peter:	Hola. ¿Qué tal? Vine a completar unos formularios para la nómina. *(Hello, how are you? I came to fill out some forms for payroll)*
Ana:	Ah, sí. Pues ése es mi trabajo. Déjame hacerte unas preguntas. *(Oh, OK. Well, that's my job. Let me ask you a few questions.)*
Peter:	¡Por supuesto!
Ana:	¿Nombre y apellidos?
Peter:	Peter McPherson.
Ana:	¿Domicilio?
Peter:	Calle Luna, número 25, sexto B[1].
Ana:	¿Ciudad, provincia[2] y código postal?
Peter:	Madrid, Madrid, 28022.
Ana:	¿Número de teléfono?
Peter:	345-7804
Ana:	¿y el código de área?
Peter:	Ah, sí, perdón. El código de área es 91, de Madrid.
Ana:	Muy bien.... ¿Sexo? Masculino... ¿Fecha de nacimiento?

[Footnotes]

[1] Note that the order of these elements (street, number, and apartment number) is very different in Spanish than in English.
[2] In Spain, internal political divisions are called 'provincias' (provinces) and 'comunidades,' but in Mexico, they are called 'estados' (states), and in Colombia, 'departamentos.' You should learn the appropriate term wherever you go.

[Footnotes]

[3] *Job application forms in other countries frequently request personal information that would seem irrelevant and even illegal for an American, such as your date of birth or marital status.*

[4] *Every country uses a different form of identification. In the United States, the driver's license is the most common. In many Spanish-speaking countries, the DNI (Documento Nacional de Identidad) is the card that you show for identification, but it is separate from a driver's license. Some words for 'card' or 'license' are: carnet, tarjeta, documento, licencia, and cédula.*

Peter: 13 de marzo de 1965.

Ana: ¿Estado civil?[3]

Peter: Soltero. *(Single)*

Ana: ¿Número del DNI?[4]

Peter: 51687904

Ana: Perfecto. ¿Me firmas aquí, por favor? Y me pones la fecha de hoy.
(Perfect. Would you sign here for me, please? And could you write today's date?)

Peter: ¡Claro!

Ejercicio A

Let's take a look at the dialogue and figure out what Ana is asking. Try to keep in mind the type of information requested in forms like these.

1) According to Peter's response, what do you think the word 'apellido' means?

____

2) If 'calle' means 'street,' what is Ana asking for with the word 'domicilio'?

____

3) When Peter provides his telephone number, he forgets 'el prefijo.' What is 'el prefijo'?

____

4) If Ana was asking these questions to a woman, what would she fill out for 'sexo'? Look it up in a dictionary.

____

5) What do you think '13 de marzo de 1965' refers to?

____

6) When Peter answers 'soltero,' other options would be 'casado,' 'divorciado' or 'viudo.' Looking closely at those words, can you guess what they mean?

____

7) Peter uses two different expressions/words to say 'Of course!' Can you find them?

____

Answers A: **1)** Last name / **2)** Address / **3)** Area code / **4)** Mujer / **5)** His date of birth / **6)** Casado *(married)* - Divorciado *(divorced)* - Viudo *(widower)* / **7)** Claro - Por supuesto

Ejercicio B

Now, let's fill out a similar form with your own information.
Watch out for the order of the elements in your address, date of birth, and today's date.

Nombre(s): ______________________________

Apellido(s): ______________________________

Domicilio: ______________________________

Ciudad, estado/provincia, código postal: ______________________________

Número de teléfono: (____)______________ DNI: ______________

Sexo: M F Fecha de nacimiento: ______________

Estado civil: ______________________________

Firma: ______________ Fecha de hoy: ____/____/____

Correo electrónico: ______________@[5]______________ .com

[Footnotes] [5] *When you are telling somebody your e-mail address, the symbol @ is called an 'arroba' and the period is called a 'punto.' Example: John.Doe@yahoo.com would be: 'John punto Doe arroba Yahoo punto com.'*

EN LA OFICINA

(At the office)

Mr. Pérez is showing Peter his new office. Though most of the words are not translated into English, try to figure out the definitions of those that look like their English equivalents.

Antonio Pérez: Bueno *(Well)*, señor McPherson, ésta *(this)* es su nueva oficina. Tiene *(It has)* una ventana grande con buena vista, un ordenador[6] *(computer)* en su escritorio *(desk)*, una lámpara, unos bolígrafos *(pens)*, unos lápices *(pencils)*, un archivador, una impresora y una estantería para sus *(for your)* libros y sus cosas *(your things)*.

Peter: Muchas gracias, señor Pérez. Todo es perfecto. Voy a traer *(I am going to bring)* mis cosas más tarde *(later)*.

[Footnotes]

[6] *In Latin America, the word for computer is 'computadora.'*

Ejercicio C

In the dialogue, several items are named and some look like certain English words. Try to match those first and then figure out the rest by elimination and with the help of the translations in the dialogue.

1) ventana *(related to 'viento' = wind)*	a) things
2) lámpara	b) file cabinet
3) estantería	c) window
4) libros *(related to library)*	d) book shelf
5) cosas	e) printer
6) impresora	f) desk
7) ordenador / computadora	g) lamp
8) archivador *(related to archiving)*	h) books
9) escritorio *(related to 'escribir' = to write)*	i) computer
10) bolígrafos *(-grafo = -graph, related to writing)*	j) pens

Answers C: **1** - c) / **2** - g) / **3** - d) / **4** - h) / **5** - a) / **6** - e) / **7** - i) / **8** - b) / **9** - f) / **10** - j)

MÁS COSAS EN LA OFICINA

(More things in the office)

Hola, amigos. Voy a mostrarles algunas de mis cosas.

(Hello, my friends. I am going to show you some of my things)

Peter just brought some things to his office and is showing us what the office now has.

Ésta es mi nueva oficina. Aquí hay *(Here are)* unos libros de negocios *(business)*, un libro de alemán *(German)*, y unos recuerdos *(souvenirs)* de Sudamérica *(from South America)*. En el escritorio tengo una fotografía de mis padres *(my parents)*. Son muy simpáticos *(They are very nice)*. También tengo *(I also have)* una cámara para la computadora, unas revistas *(magazines)*, unos cuadernos *(notebooks)*, una calculadora, un teléfono, y una lámpara de Francia. En la pared *(On the wall)* tengo un mapa del mundo *(world)* muy bonito *(beautiful)*. Y ésta es mi silla *(chair)* de cuero *(leather)*. Es muy cómoda *(It is very comfortable)*. Por la *(Through the)* ventana podemos ver mi coche *(we can see my car)*. Es muy rápido.
En esta otra oficina hay *(there is)* una fotocopiadora para hacer *(to make)* fotocopias, una máquina de fax, papel, unos sobres *(envelopes)*, una grapadora/engrapadora *(stapler)* y otras *(and other)* cosas.

Ejercicio D

Translate the following words from the dialogue.

1) un mapa del mundo

____

2) papel

____

3) una fotografía

____

4) una máquina de fax

____

5) una cámara

____

6) rápido

____

7) una fotocopiadora

____

Answers D: **1)** a world map / **2)** paper / **3)** a photograph / **4)** a fax machine / **5)** a camera / **6)** fast / **7)** a copier

Ejercicio E

Using the previous dialogue, write down the article that accompanies these nouns. Example: una ventana.

1) __________ libro, teléfono, mapa

2) __________ fotografía, cámara, calculadora, lámpara, fotocopiadora, máquina, grapadora

3) __________ libros, recuerdos, cuadernos, sobres

4) __________ revistas

Answers E: **1)** un / **2)** una / **3)** unos / **4)** unas

EL ARTÍCULO

(The article)

The article that you just saw in the previous dialogue (un, una, unos, unas) is called the 'indefinite' article because it is not very specific. Its translation is 'a' (un libro/a book), or 'some' (unos libros/some books). If the accompanying noun is masculine and plural, then you need 'unos;' if feminine and singular, then you need 'una,' and so on.

artículo indefinido		
	masculino	femenino
singular	un	una
plural	unos	unas

Another type of article is the 'definite' article (el, la, los, las), which is more specific than the indefinite article. It translates as 'the' (el libro/the book; los libros/the books). In order to place the appropriate article in front of a noun, you must know the gender and number of the noun.

artículo definido		
	masculino	femenino
singular	el	la
plural	los	las

EL NÚMERO (Noun)

It is easy to make nouns and adjectives plural:

Add -s to a word ending in vowel:
libr**o** / libr**os**

Add -es to a word ending in consonant:
pare**d** / pared**es**

There are some nouns that are always used in the plural, such as 'las gafas'/'los anteojos' *(glasses)*, or 'las vacaciones' *(vacations)*.

There are some nouns that are singular even though they refer to something plural, such as 'la gente' *(people)*, or that are singular because they are non-countable, such as 'la leche' *(milk)*, or that are singular even though they look like plural, such as 'el cumpleaños' *(birthday)*.

The plural of a word that ends in -y is 'es'
ley / leyes *(law/laws)*

The plural of a word that ends in -z is 'ces'
lápiz / lápices *(pencil/pencils)*

EL GÉNERO (Gender)

A noun's gender is a little bit more complicated. All nouns in Spanish are either masculine or feminine. When you learn a noun, learn it with its article, because the article will give you a clue about the noun's gender. Although there are exceptions, these general rules will help you:

Masculine nouns

-nouns referring to males: el hombre *(man)*
-nouns ending in -o: el libro, el teléfono
-most nouns ending in -e: el coche
-nouns ending in -ema (from Greek): el problema
-geographical names, days of the week, months, seasons (except spring), numbers, and cardinal points (north, south, east, west)

[**Exceptions**: la mano *(hand)*, la moto *(motorcycle)*, la foto *(photograph)*, la noche *(night)*, la calle *(street)*, la tarde *(afternoon)*, la gente *(people)*, etc.]

Feminine nouns

-nouns referring to females: la mujer *(woman)*
-nouns ending in -a: la máquina, la lámpara
-nouns ending in -ez, -dad, -ud, -umbre:
la univer-sidad, la niñez *(childhood)*
-nouns ending in -tad, -ión, -sis, -triz:
la actriz *(actress)*, la libertad *(liberty)*
-the alphabet letters, one season (spring)

[**Exceptions**: el mapa *(map)*, el día *(day)*, el clima *(climate)*, el cometa *(comet)*, el idioma *(language)*, el poema *(poem)*, el ajedrez *(chess)*, etc.]

Other nouns can be masculine or feminine depending on the person to whom they refer. The article will tell you the noun's gender.

el estudiante *(male student)*
la estudiante *(female student)*
el taxista *(male taxi driver)*
la taxista *(female taxi driver)*

Other nouns can be masculine or feminine by changing their form slightly.

el doctor / la doctora
el león *(lion)* / la leona *(lioness)*
el señor / la señora
el americano / la americana
el niño *(boy)* / la niña *(girl)*

If you have a plural noun that contains both masculine and feminine items, the masculine plural article is used:

los padres *(parents = father and mother)*
los niños *(children = boys and girls)*

Adjectives must agree in gender and number with the noun they modify:

el niño triste *(the sad boy)*
los niños tristes *(the sad boys)*
el niño malo *(the bad boy)*
los niños malos *(the bad boys)*

UNIDAD 2

Ejercicio F

According to the previous rules (and exceptions), let's try to figure out the definite article (el, la, los, las) for each of the following nouns.

1) _____ teléfono **2)** _____ ventanas **3)** _____ noche **4)** _____ lámparas
5) _____ estado **6)** _____ fecha **7)** _____ pantalones **8)** _____ hombres
9) _____ sexo **10)** _____ firma **11)** _____ cosas **12)** _____ computadoras
13) _____ prefijo **14)** _____ nombres **15)** _____ libros **16)** _____ padres
17) _____ tarde **18)** _____ tijeras **19)** _____ oficina **20)** _____ cámaras
21) _____ apellido **22)** _____ gente **23)** _____ gusto **24)** _____ día
25) _____ domicilio **26)** _____ escritorios **27)** _____ mujer **28)** _____ paredes

Answers F: **1)** el / **2)** las / **3)** la / **4)** las / **5)** el / **6)** la / **7)** los / **8)** los / **9)** el / **10)** la / **11)** las / **12)** las / **13)** el / **14)** los / **15)** los / **16)** los / **17)** la / **18)** las / **19)** la / **20)** las / **21)** el / **22)** la / **23)** el / **24)** el / **25)** el / **26)** los / **27)** la / **28)** las

MI LISTA DE VOCABULARIO

This is a list of the words that you have learned in this unit. Can you remember what all these words mean? Give it a try. If there is a word that you do not know, look for it in the unit. At the bottom of this list, there is room for you to add additional words.

americano	(la) fotocopia
(el) apellido	(la) fotocopiadora
(el) archivador	(la) fotografía o (la) foto
(el) bolígrafo o (la) pluma	Francia
(la) calculadora	(las) gafas / (los) anteojos
(la) calle	(la) gente
(la) cámara	(la) grapa
(la) ciudad	(la) grapadora/engrapadora
¡claro!	(el) hombre
(el) coche	(la) impresora
(el) código de área	(la) lámpara
(el) código postal	(el) lápiz
cómodo	(el) león / (la) leona
(la) computadora	(la) ley
(la) cosa	(el) libro
(el) cuaderno	(la) mano
(el) cuero	(el) mapa
(los) datos	(la) máquina
(el) D.N.I.	(la) mujer
(el) doctor / (la) doctora	(el) mundo
(el) domicilio	(los) negocios
(el) escritorio	(la) niñez
(el) estado civil	(el) niño / (la) niña
(la) estantería	(el) nombre
(el / la) estudiante	(el) número

(la) oficina	(el) señor / (la) señora	(las) vacaciones
(los) padres	(el) sexo	(la) ventana
(el) papel	(la) silla	(la) vista
(la) pared	simpático/a	
¡por supuesto!	(el) sobre	
(el) problema	soltero	
(la) provincia	(la) tarde	
rápido	(el / la) taxista	
(el) recuerdo	(el) teléfono	
(la) revista	(la) universidad	

UN POCO DE CULTURA

Nombres y apellidos

In Spanish-speaking countries, people use two last names: the first comes from their father and the second from their mother (since women do not change their last name when they marry). Eventually, both men and women pass on their father's last name to their children. Therefore, if *Antonio Rodríguez Benítez* married *Yolanda Acaso Salvador*, his son's name would be *Ricardo Rodríguez Acaso*. This system has the advantage of letting you trace your family history on both sides (e.g., *Ricardo Rodríguez Acaso Benítez Salvador etc.*). Your last names might also indicate where your ancestors came from and whether you have non-Hispanic roots.

Some women unofficially drop their second last name and take their husband's. For example, Yolanda might call herself *Yolanda Acaso de Rodríguez*. This custom is disappearing, because the word 'de' (which means 'of') suggests possession, a concept not in keeping with modern perspectives on marriage.

As in English, there are certain last names that mean 'son of –' (Johnson = son of John). In Spanish, these last names end in –ez; so, Rodríguez would mean 'son of Rodrigo,' and

'Martínez,' son of Martín. These names have been recorded in manuscripts as early as the 11th century.

Spanish speakers can have one, two, and even three names before their first last name. Because of the strong influence of the Catholic Church, names are usually biblical (e.g., Jesús, José, María, Raquel, Ruth, etc.) or are saints' names (e.g., Tomás, Ignacio, etc.). The name María is so common, that most parents either add another name to it (e.g., María Teresa), or choose one of the different versions of the Virgin Mary's name (e.g., María del Sol, María de la Paz, María de la Luz, etc), which are often shortened (e.g., Marisol, Maripaz, Mariluz, etc). Other common shortened versions of names include: Ignacio - Nacho / María Teresa - Maite / José María - Chema / Catalina - Cati / Francisco - Paco / Pilar - Pili / Javier - Javi / Concepción - Concha or Conchita / José - Pepe / Cristina - Cristi / Manuel - Manolo / Dolores - Lola

In the last decades, naming practices have changed, likely as a result of the reduced influence of the Catholic Church and the increase of globalization. Now, children frequently have non-Spanish names, like Amanda, Jennifer or Jonathan. However, the tradition of using initials (e.g., J.J.) or suffices like 'III' or 'junior' are not common in Hispanic culture (except in the case of royalty).

Do you know where you last name comes from?

RECOMENDACIÓN PARA ESTA UNIDAD

To finish this unit, we recommend that you label each item in your office with its Spanish name (on an inconspicuous sticky note), so that you 'study' your first words while at work. If you find an item for which you do not know the word, look it up in the dictionary, label the item, and add the word to your list. After a week, remove all labels. After one more week, test yourself to see how many of these words you remember. For those words that you do not remember, repeat the process.

UNIDAD 3

CONTENIDO

In this unit, you will learn:

1 - About describing people in the world and names of countries
2 - About agreement
3 - About the verb 'ser'
4 - Vocabulary related to different foreign languages
5 - About cognates
6 - Cultural information about Spanglish

describir a la gente del mundo

DESCRIBIR A LA GENTE DEL MUNDO

(Describing people in the world)

Read this conversation between Ana and Peter while they are in Peter's office looking at the world map he has hung on the wall.

Ana:	Peter, ¿qué son estas marcas en el mapa? *(Peter, what are these marks on the map?)*
Peter:	¿Dónde? *(Where?)*
Ana:	Aquí, allí, más allá... por toda Sudamérica *(Here, there, over there... all over South America.)*
Peter:	Ah, ésos son los países que he visitado. *(Ah, those are the countries that I have visited.)*
Ana:	¡Son muchos países! ¿Tienes amigos *(Do you have friends)* allá?
Peter:	Sí, aquí hay *(here are)* unas fotos. Mi amigo *(My friend)* Federico es colombiano[1], Gabriela y Damián son *(are)* ecuatorianos, Cristina es peruana, y mis amigos Ricardo y María del Carmen son argentinos.
Ana:	¡Qué internacional! Mi amiga Marisol es chilena. Es muy simpática *(nice)*. Y su esposo *(her husband)*, Leopoldo, es uruguayo. Ahora viven *(They now live)* en Nueva York.
Peter:	Ah, sí, en Nueva York hay *(there are)* muchas personas de América del Sur.

[Footnotes]

[1] Nationality adjectives are not capitalized in Spanish.

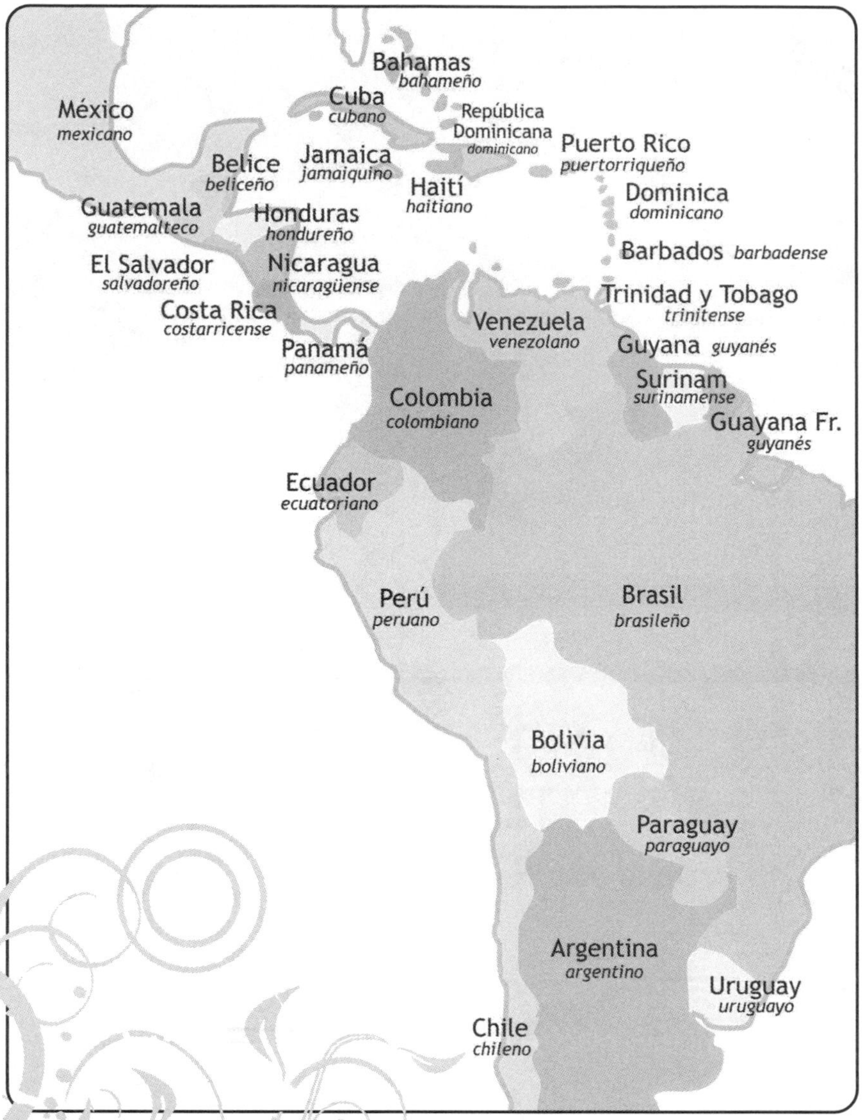

México *mexicano*
Bahamas *bahameño*
Cuba *cubano*
República Dominicana *dominicano*
Puerto Rico *puertorriqueño*
Belice *beliceño*
Jamaica *jamaiquino*
Haití *haitiano*
Dominica *dominicano*
Guatemala *guatemalteco*
Honduras *hondureño*
Barbados *barbadense*
El Salvador *salvadoreño*
Nicaragua *nicaragüense*
Trinidad y Tobago *trinitense*
Costa Rica *costarricense*
Venezuela *venezolano*
Guyana *guyanés*
Panamá *panameño*
Surinam *surinamense*
Colombia *colombiano*
Guayana Fr. *guyanés*
Ecuador *ecuatoriano*
Perú *peruano*
Brasil *brasileño*
Bolivia *boliviano*
Paraguay *paraguayo*
Argentina *argentino*
Uruguay *uruguayo*
Chile *chileno*

Ejercicio A

Complete these sentences with the appropriate country. The first one is done for you.

1) Marisol es de *(from)* Chile

2) Federico es de ____________

3) Leopoldo es de ____________

4) Gabriela y Damián son de ____________

5) Cristina es de ____________

Answers A: **2)** Colombia / **3)** Uruguay / **4)** Ecuador / **5)** Perú

LA CONCORDANCIA *(Agreement)*

Like articles, adjectives also agree in gender and number with the noun they modify. In English, this kind of agreement does not exist and that is why this concept might be a little bit difficult at first. Keep practicing!

Verónica es <u>chilena</u> *(Veronica is Chilean)*

Gerardo es <u>chileno</u> *(Gerardo is Chilean)*

Verónica y Gerardo son <u>chilenos</u>
(Veronica and Gerardo are Chilean)

Did you notice that the verb also changed? That's because there is also agreement between the subject and the verb, like in English (Veronica is... / Veronica and Gerardo are...).

In Spanish, when the adjective and noun are right next to each other, the adjective generally follows the noun (el chico <u>alto</u>), unlike in English (the <u>tall</u> boy).

Ejercicio B

Complete these sentences with the missing adjectives. Look at the previous map to figure out the right adjective for each nationality and then apply the adjetives to the situations below, matching gender and number.

Follow the example.

1) Marisol es ___chilena___ (Chile)

2) Carlos y Andrés son ______________ (Paraguay)

3) Felipe es ______________ (Venezuela)

4) Federico es ______________ (Colombia)

5) Gabriela y Damián son ______________ (Ecuador)

6) Ricardo y Mari Carmen son ______________ (Argentina)

7) Leopoldo es ______________ (Uruguay)

8) Eva es ______________ (Bolivia)

9) Cristina e Inés son ______________ (Perú)

Answers B: **2)** paraguayos / **3)** venezolano / **4)** colombiano / **5)** ecuatorianos / **6)** argentinos / **7)** uruguayo / **8)** boliviana / **9)** peruanas

EL VERBO 'SER' *(The verb 'to be')*

The verb 'ser' is used to talk about somebody's nationality, but also for descriptions in general. Let's take a look at its conjugation.

VERBO 'SER'	*VERB 'TO BE'*
(yo) **soy**	*I am*
(tú[2]) **eres**	*you are*
(él, ella) (usted) **es**	*he, she is/you are*
(nosotros, -as) **somos**	*you are*
(vosotros, -as[3]) **sois**	*we are*
(ellos, ellas) (ustedes) **son**	*you are/they are*

In Spanish, every person (I, you, she, etc.) requires a different verb conjugation. For this reason, it is usually not necessary to write out the subject pronoun (yo, tú, él, etc.). This does not happen in English, because most conjugation forms are the same regardless of the subject. For example, since 'you,' 'we,' and 'they' all go with the verb 'are,' it is necessary to specify the subject in English (you are, we are, etc.). In Spanish, stating the subject can seem repetitious and unnecessary (unless it is done for emphasis). Example:

Soy Antonio (*versus* Yo soy Antonio)

¿Eres inteligente? (*versus* ¿Eres tú inteligente?)

The verb SER is also used for:

physical appearance	Peter es alto	*(Peter is tall)*
personality	Ana es simpática	*(Ana is nice)*
race	Yo soy blanco	*(I am white)*
ethnicity or cultural background	Tú eres hispano	*(You are Hispanic)*
religion	Isabel y Fernando son católicos	*(I. and F. are Catholic)*
city or country of origin	Nosotros somos de España	*(We are from Spain)*
professions	Francisco es abogado	*(Francisco is a lawyer)*
name	Él/éste es Antonio	*(He/This is Antonio)*
classifications / definitions	Esto es una silla	*(This is a chair)*
materials	La silla es de madera	*(The chair is made of wood)*
possession	Esto es de Ramón	*(This is Ramon's)*

[Footnotes]

[2] 'Tú' is the informal 'you,' and 'usted' is the formal 'you.' We will learn more about these pronouns at a later time.
[3] 'Vosotros/as' is the informal plural 'you,' and 'ustedes' is the formal plural 'you.'

Ejercicio C

Now looking at the maps of Central America, North America, and Spain, select the right adjective for each nationality.

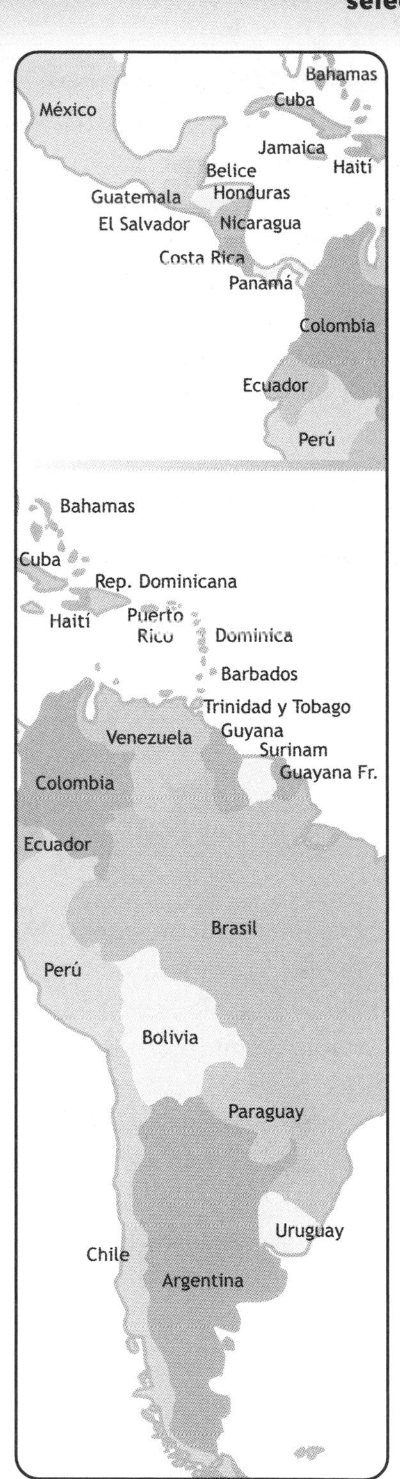

1) Margarita es (Guatemala)
a) guatemaleña b) guatemalena c) guatemalteca

2) Pablo y Graciela son (Panamá)
a) panameños b) panamianos c) panamenses

3) Juan Esteban es (Costa Rica)
a) costarricano b) costarricense c) costarricalense

4) Yolanda y Juan son (Nicaragua)
a) nicaragüenses b) nicaraguanos c) nicaragualenses

5) Teresa y Sonia son (Honduras)
a) honduranos b) hondurenses c) hondureños

6) Nosotros somos (El Salvador)
a) salvadorenos b) salvadoranos c) salvadoreños

7) Yo soy (Estados Unidos)
a) estadounidense b) estadounidano c) estadounidol

8) Usted es (México)
a) mexicalense b) mexicalana c) mexicana

9) Óscar es (Puerto Rico)
a) puertorriquense b) puertorriqueño c) puertoricano

10) Pablo y Jazmín son (República Dominicana)
a) dominicanos b) dominicalenses c) dominiqueños

11) Fidel es (Cuba)
a) cubense b) cubano c) cubañol

12) Tú eres (España)
a) hispano b) espanilense c) español

Answers C: **1)** - c) / **2)** - a) / **3)** - b) / **4)** - a) / **5)** - c) / **6)** - c) / **7)** - a) / **8)** - c) / **9)** - b) / **10)** - a) / **11)** - b) / **12)** - c)

Ejercicio D

Complete these simple sentences about yourself, selecting the most appropriate words from the list (if they apply to you). Remember: If you are a woman, your adjectives should be feminine; if you are a man, masculine. If the word you need is not here, look it up.

1) Yo soy ______________________
[(un) hombre/(una) mujer]

2) Yo soy ______________________
[americano, británico, australiano, ...]

3) Yo soy de ______________________
[city of origin] [state] [country]

4) Yo soy ______________________
[alto, bajo *(short)*, gordo *(fat)*, delgado *(thin)*]

5) Yo soy ______________________
[simpático, antipático *(unpleasant)*]

6) Yo soy ______________________
[blanco, negro, asiático, mestizo *(mixed)*]

7) Yo __ soy ______________________
[hispano, no hispano] *(the 'no' goes before 'soy')*

8) Yo soy ______________________
[católico, cristiano, protestante, budista, musulmán]

9) Yo soy ______________________ [your name]

LOS IDIOMAS *(Languajes)*

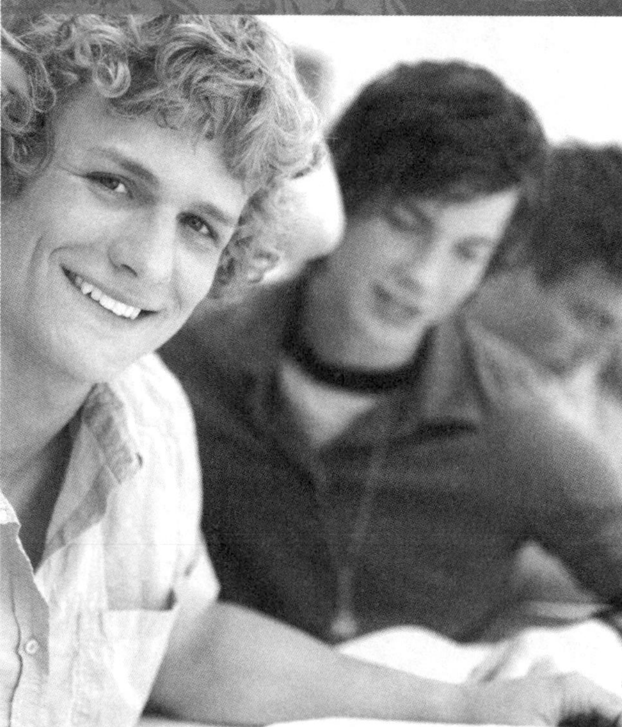

The name of a language sometimes coincides with the adjective of nationality, but sometimes it does not. For example, a man from Spain (español) speaks Spanish (español), but a man from Brazil (brasileño) speaks Portuguese (portugués).
In addition, the name of a language may refer to the historical region out of which it appeared, like árabe/Arabia. The names of languages (which are not capitalized in Spanish) are easy to learn, because they are very similar to their English counterparts (latín = Latin, griego = Greek, etc.).

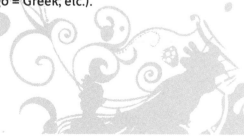

Ejercicio E

Look at the map and answer these questions.

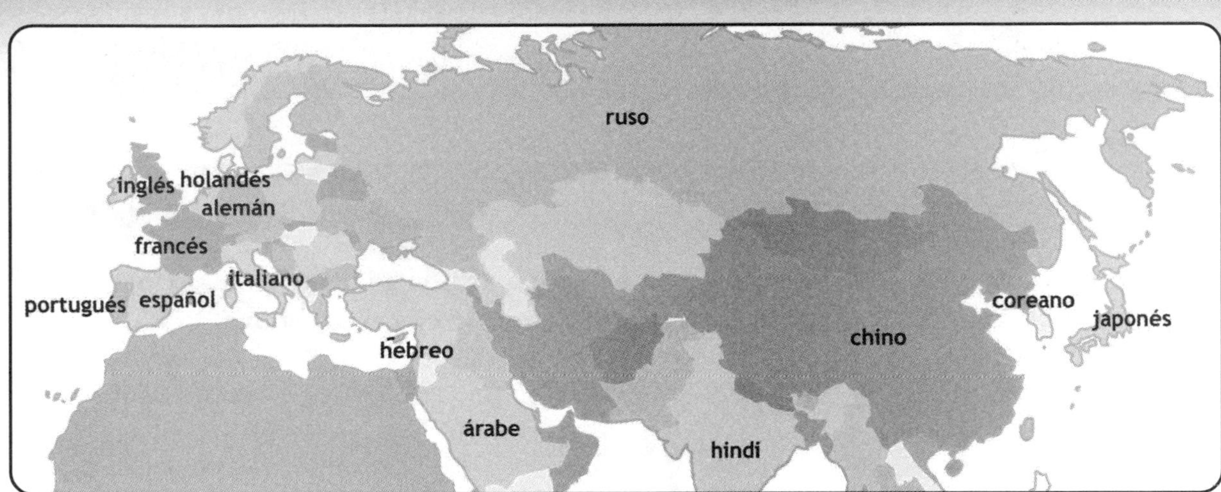

1) ¿Qué idioma se habla[4] en Holanda?

En Holanda se habla holandés

2) ¿Qué idioma se habla en India?

3) ¿Qué idioma se habla en Japón?

[Footnotes] [4] *The construction 'se + verb' can be translated here as 'people speak.' We will see more on this construction at a later time.*

4) ¿Qué idioma se habla en Alemania *(Germany)?*

5) ¿Qué idioma se habla en Grecia?

6) ¿Qué idioma se habla en Francia?

7) ¿Qué idioma se habla en China?

Answers E: **2)** hindi / **3)** japonés / **4)** alemán / **5)** griego / **6)** francés / **7)** chino

LOS COGNADOS *(Cognates)*

A cognate is a word that has the same origin (Latin, Greek, etc.) as another word in your native language. This is evident in the root of the word.

información = information
hispano = Hispanic
aeropuerto = airport

Cognates are very useful when trying to understand what we read in Spanish or when translating documents. If the cognate has changed in meaning overtime, however, then it is considered a 'false friend' (falso amigo/calco léxico).

simpático *(nice)* — sympathetic *(understanding)*

When there is a word in another language that looks similar to a word in your native language, but they does not share the same origin, this is a 'false cognate' *(falso cognado)*. Be careful with these!

actualmente *(currently)* — actually *(in fact)*

Words are also sometimes taken directly from another language (as is, or slightly changed) for multiple reasons. A word borrowed from another language is a 'loan' *(préstamo)*.

Spanish speakers say *líder* (from English, 'leader')

English speakers say *patio* (from Spanish, 'patio')

Ejercicio F

Did you notice any words in the dialogue of this unit that might be cognates or loans? Write some here (do not include words referring to places or nationalities).

______________ ______________ ______________

______________ ______________ ______________

______________ ______________ ______________

Possible answers F: marcas, mapa, visitado, foto, internacional, simpática, esposo, persona

MI LISTA DE VOCABULARIO

This is a list of the words that you have learned in this unit.

ahí / allí / más allá

alemán

alto

americano (América)

antipático

aquí

árabe

argentino (Argentina)

asiático

australiano

bajo

blanco

boliviano (Bolivia)

británico

budista

católico

chileno (Chile)

chino

(el) cognado

colombiano (Colombia)

coreano

costarricense (Costa rica)

cristiano

cubano (Cuba)

delgado	hispano	nicaragüense (Nicaragua)
¿dónde?	holandés	(el) país
dominicano	hondureño (Honduras)	panameño (Panamá)
(República Dominicana)	(el) idioma	paraguayo (Paraguay)
ecuatoriano (Ecuador)	inglés	peruano (Perú)
español (España)	inteligente	portugués
estadounidense (Estados Unidos)	italiano	protestante
francés	japonés	puertorriqueño (Puerto Rico)
(la) gente	latín	ruso
gordo	(la) marca	salvadoreño (El Salvador)
hebreo	mestizo	ser
griego	mexicano (México)	simpático
guatemalteco (Guatemala)	musulmán	uruguayo (Uruguay)
hindi	negro	venezolano (Venezuela)

UN POCO DE CULTURA

Spanglish

The term *Spanglish* usually refers to a variation of Spanish spoken by Hispanics and Latinos living in the United States, Puerto Rico, and Canada. It is distinguished from other Spanish dialects by the heavy influence of the English language on it. Language purists see Spanglish as a language spoken by people who do not know either language perfectly and have to compensate by mixing the two. Advocates of Spanglish defend its existence as a fact of life and adamantly claim that people who speak Spanglish are bilingual individuals who have mastered both languages and choose to combine them in different ways. *Spanglish* is the result of a multitude of phenomena that are brought about by the close contact of Spanish with English. Spanglish is prevalent in places where there is a large population of Hispanics and Latinos in English-speaking areas, such as Miami, Chicago, Los Angeles, and New York, and in regions with a long history of contact between English and Spanish speakers, such as Puerto Rico, Gibraltar, and Panama. This combining of languages is not limited to Spanish and English: it also occurs with other languages in close contact, such as French and English in Canada (Frenglish) or Hindi and English in India (Hinglish).

One typical characteristic of Spanglish is switching back and forth from one language to the other. This is called code-switching (e.g., I am tired, so *te llamo más tarde.*)

Another manifestation is borrowing a word directly from the other language (e.g., *Te mando un e-mail mañana*) on a frequent basis. A completely different example is using an English word with a certain ending added, so that it looks like a Spanish word (e.g., ***mopear*** *(to mop)*, ***chequear*** *(to check)*, ***troca*** *(truck)*, *lonche (lunch)*). This type of lexical change is what language purists most frequently attack.

A final example is using a word or expression in Spanish that looks like a similar word in English, even though the Spanish word has a completely different meaning. Example: using 'vacunar la carpeta' to mean 'vacuum the carpet,' though you are actually saying 'vaccinate the folder.' Another example: using 'deliberar groserías' to mean 'deliver groceries,' when you are actually saying 'to debate rude words/acts.'

RECOMENDACIÓN PARA ESTA UNIDAD

To finish this unit, we recommend you to paying extra attention to the roots of words from now on, so that you can take advantages of similarities among languages in order to learn Spanish. According to Ethnologue, an encyclopedic research institution that catalogues world languages, a language family is defined as a group of languages of common origin. The common language from which these languages originate can also be part of a larger family. For example, Spanish and Italian are sister languages because they both descend from Romance (vulgar Latin) and Romance is one of the Indo-European languages, like English.

Indo-European languages

- Germanic languages
  - English
  - German
- Italic languages
  - Romance
    - -Italian
    - -Portuguese
    - -Spanish, etc.
  - etc.
- etc.

Although related languages have many similarities, they have developed independently to the point that they are considered distinct systems. A dialect, on the other hand, is a regional variety of a language spoken by a group of people from a specific area. It is characterized by a unique accent and some different vocabulary. A dialect, therefore, is not a language, as it is similar enough to an existing language to be considered a variation of that language rather than a new language. However, the distinction between language and dialect can change and is often subject to political and social agendas.

English and Spanish share many common features, not only because they are cousin languages, but also because of the centuries-long contact they have had with each other and with other languages, such as Greek and French. English speakers learning Spanish can take advantage of these shared features, but they must pay attention to the roots of words. Both cognates and loans can help you learn vocabulary and make connections between languages.

UNIDAD 4

CONTENIDO

In this unit, you will learn:

1 - How to describe a person's physical appearance and personality

2 - About the verb 'estar'

3 - How to describe temporary physical, mental or emotional conditions

4 - Cultural information about the terms 'hispano' and 'latino'

describir la apariencia y personalidad

DESCRIBIR LA APARIENCIA Y LA PERSONALIDAD

(Describing appearance and personality)

Ana took Peter to lunch today to celebrate his first day in the office. During lunch, Peter talks a little bit more about his friends from South America and shows Ana some pictures he carries in his wallet.

Peter: Mira, éste es Federico. Como ves, es bajo, moreno y guapo. Es muy popular con las mujeres porque es muy generoso.
(Look, this is Federico. As you see, he is short, dark-haired and handsome. He is very popular with women because he is very generous)

Ana: Ya veo. ¿Y éstos? *(I see. And these?)*

Peter: Son Ricardo y Mari Carmen, mis amigos argentinos. Son muy diferentes: él es rubio, fuerte y alto, y muy serio. En cambio, ella es pelirroja, baja, y muy cómica. Los dos son muy agradables.
(They are Ricardo and Mari Carmen, my Argentinian friends. They are very different: he is blond, strong and tall, and very serious. In contrast, she is red-haired, short, and very funny. Both are very pleasant)

Ana: ¿Y esta chica tan atractiva?
(And this very attractive girl?)

Peter: Es Cristina, de Perú. Es actriz, por eso es tan delgada. Es muy locuaz.
(She is Cristina, from Peru. She is an actress, that's why she is so thin. She is very talkative)

Ana: ¿Sí? *(Really?)*

Peter: Este gordo y feo de aquí es mi mejor amigo. Se llama Damián y es de Ecuador. Y la mujer que está a su lado es su esposa, Gabriela. Ella es muy inteligente y muy humilde. Son muy simpáticos.
(This fat and ugly one here is my best friend. His name is Damian and he is from Ecuador. And the woman who is next to him is his wife, Gabriela. She is very intelligent and humble. They are very nice)

Ejercicio A

Make a list of all adjectives corresponding to the people they talk about. Be careful with your gender agreement.

Federico: bajo ____________

Mari Carmen: ____________

Damián: ____________

Ricardo: ____________

Cristina: ____________

Gabriela: ____________

Answers A: Federico: moreno, guapo, popular, generoso / Ricardo: rubio, fuerte, alto, serio, agradable / Mari Carmen: pelirroja, baja, cómica, agradable / Cristina: atractiva, delgada, locuaz / Damián: gordo, feo, simpático / Gabriela: inteligente, humilde, simpática

MÁS ADJETIVOS DE DESCRIPCIÓN FÍSICA

Here are some adjectives that describe the physical appearance of a person.

alto *(tall)*
bajo[1]/mediano *(short/average)*
fuerte[2] *(strong)*
débil *(weak)*
gordo[3] *(fat)*
delgado, flaco *(thin)*
grande *(big)*
pequeño *(small/petite)*
guapo[4] *(handsome/beautiful)*

[Footnotes]

[1] A popular word in Mexico is 'chaparro,' which means 'short.'
[2] Remember that adjectives that end in -o make their feminine counterpart by dropping the -o and adding -a and the plurals by adding -os or -as (e.g., grosero, grosera, groseros, groseras). Those adjectives that end in -e have the same form for the feminine, and then -es for both plurals (e.g., inteligente, inteligente, inteligentes, inteligentes).

[Footnotes]

[3] Sometimes, in order not to offend people, the diminutive -ito is used. Example: gordo = gordito, viejo = viejito.
[4] 'Bonita,' 'bella,' and 'linda' are other adjectives that mean beautiful, but they are usually reserved for women.
[5] In some countries, 'moreno' means black (black race). In some countries, the word 'prieto' is used for dark-skinned people.
[6] Another popular word in Mexico is 'güero' for a light-skinned person.

feo *(ugly)*
joven *(young)*
viejo *(old)*
moreno *(dark-haired)*
rubio/pelirrojo/calvo *(blond/red-haired/bald)*
moreno[5] *(dark-skinned)*
blanco[6] *(light-skinned/white)*

MÁS ADJETIVOS PARA DESCRIBIR LA PERSONALIDAD

Here are some adjectives that describe personality traits.

agradable *(pleasant)*
cómico, gracioso, chistoso *(funny)*
generoso *(generous)*
locuaz *(talkative)*
honesto/franco/sincero *(honest)*
humilde *(humble)*
inteligente, listo *(intelligent, smart)*
interesante *(interesting)*
optimista *(optimist)*
organizado *(organized)*
práctico *(practical)*
simpático *(nice)*
trabajador *(hard-working)*

desagradable, grosero *(unpleasant, nasty/rude)*
serio *(serious)*
egoísta *(selfish)*
callado *(quiet)*
deshonesto, mentiroso *(dishonest, liar)*
orgulloso *(proud)*
ignorante, tonto, estúpido *(ignorant, silly, stupid)*
aburrido *(boring)*
pesimista *(pessimist)*
desorganizado *(disorganized)*
idealista *(idealist)*
antipático *(unpleasant/nasty)*
perezoso/vago/flojo *(lazy)*

Ejercicio B

Using some of the adjectives listed previously, describe the physical appearance of Peter and Ana. Don't forget the agreement.

Peter es: ______________________

____

____

Ana es: ______________________

____

____

Possible answers B: Peter es alto, moreno, fuerte y un poco gordo / Ana es baja, rubia, delgada y guapa

Ejercicio C

Now describe your physical appearance and then your personality.

Soy ______________________ y también *(and also)* ______________________

______________________ ______________________

______________________ ______________________

______________________ ______________________

Ejercicio D

Find 6 adjectives from the personality adjective list.

A	B	E	R	I	C	U	P	O	M
P	G	L	O	P	N	J	P	R	A
A	E	R	T	M	O	T	R	T	T
R	Z	R	S	F	T	M	A	S	S
R	E	P	E	O	A	L	C	E	I
E	Y	Z	N	Z	F	J	T	P	O
N	G	T	O	P	O	D	I	D	G
E	O	N	H	P	A	S	C	I	E
G	E	N	E	R	O	S	O	N	Z
A	U	C	I	R	A	P	E	R	O

Answers D:

P			O				P		A
	E		T				R		T
		R	S		T		A		S
			E	O			C		I
			N	Z			T		O
		T	O		O		I		G
	O		H			S	C		E
G	E	N	E	R	O	S	O		

Ejercicio E

Using some of the adjectives for personality and physical appearance listed previously, describe these famous people. Remember to make sure that the gender and number of adjectives agree with the noun(s) they modify (in this case, the subject).

Bill Clinton y Hillary Clinton son

____

____

____

Bart Simpson es

____

____

____

Las hermanas Hilton son

____

____

____

Ejercicio F

Translate the following items using some of the adjectives you have learned. Remember that adjectives, when directly accompanying a noun, go AFTER the noun, not before as they do in English.

1) The White House is big. ______________________

2) The Ecuadorian boy is nice. ______________________

3) The old man is very thin. ______________________

4) Red-haired women are strong. Las ______________________

5) Young children are talkative. Los ______________________

Answers F: **1)** La Casa Blanca es grande / **2)** El niño ecuatoriano es simpático / **3)** El hombre viejo es muy delgado / **4)** Las mujeres pelirrojas son fuertes / **5)** Los niños jóvenes son habladores

ESTADOS DE ÁNIMO

(Temporary feelings or emotional states)

Ana and Peter are back in Peter's office.

Ana:	Entonces, *(So)* ¿cómo estás, ahora que *(now that)* tus cosas están *(are)* en la oficina?
Peter:	Estoy tranquilo y contento, pero también estoy muy cansado. *(I am calm and happy, but I am also very tired)*
Ana:	Sí, lo comprendo. ¿Estás también nervioso? *(Yes, I understand. Are you nervous too?)*
Peter:	Ya no. Pero ahora estoy preocupado, porque tengo que hablar con el jefe después. *(Not anymore. But now I am worried, because I have to talk to the boss later)*
Ana:	¿Por qué no hablas con él ahora? *(Why don't you talk to him now?)*
Peter:	Ahora está ocupado. Está hablando con otro empleado. *(He is busy now. He is talking to another employee)*
Ana:	Bueno, mañana estarás más relajado, ya verás. *(Well, tomorrow you will be more relaxed, you'll see)*
Peter:	¡Eso espero! *(I hope so!)*

Ejercicio G

Peter is experiencing various feelings. Write down all the adjectives that describe how Peter is feeling along with their translations in English.

1) ________________ significa calm

2) ________________ significa ________________

3) ________________ significa ________________

4) ________________ significa ________________

5) ________________ significa ________________

6) ________________ significa ________________

Answers G: **1)** tranquilo - calm / **2)** contento - happy / **3)** cansado – tired / **4)** nervioso – nervous / **5)** preocupado – preocupied/worried / **6)** relajado - relaxed

EL VERBO 'ESTAR' *(Verb 'to be')*

As you noticed in the previous dialogues, the verb 'estar' means 'to be,' but the verb 'ser' also means 'to be.' However, they have different uses. We will examine these differences in greater detail in the next unit. For now, let's take a look at the conjugation of 'estar.'

VERBO 'ESTAR'	*VERB 'TO BE'*
(yo) **estoy**	*I am*
(tú) **estás**	*you are*
(él, ella) (usted) **está**	*he, she is/you are*
(nosotros, -as) **estamos**	*we are*
(vosotros, -as) **estáis**	*you are*
(ellos, ellas) (ustedes) **están**	*they are/you are*

'Estar' is used:

a) for temporary physical, mental or emotional conditions:

estoy tranquilo / estoy nervioso

b) for certain other conditions (especially those described with past participles):

ella está muerta *(she is dead)*
están casados *(they are married)*

c) for location:

las cosas están en la oficina

d) for company:

él está con nosotros *(he is with us)*

e) as an auxiliary verb:

él está hablando *(he is talking)*

In this unit, we will focus on the first use of 'estar:' adjectives of temporary physical, mental or emotional conditions. Here are more adjectives for your list:

calmado, tranquilo *(calm, quiet)*	nervioso *(nervous)*
contento *(happy)*	triste *(sad)*
interesado *(interested)*	aburrido *(bored)*
libre[7] *(free)*	ocupado *(busy/occupied)*
orgulloso *(proud)*	decepcionado *(disappointed)*
relajado/renovado *(relaxed)*	cansado, agotado *(tired, exhausted)*
sano *(healthy)*	enfermo *(sick)*
satisfecho *(satisfied)*	frustrado *(frustrated)*

[Footnotes]

[7] *This adjective refers to a personal or political state, not to money. When you don't have to pay for something, the adjective used is 'gratis.'*

Ejercicio H

How do these people feel in the following situations? Use some of the adjectives you just learned. Make sure you conjugate the verb 'estar' correctly and that the adjectives agree with their nouns or pronouns (in this case, subjects).

1) Cuando yo estoy en el cine *(When I am in the movies)*

Yo ___________ ______________________________

2) Cuando Peter habla con el jefe *(When Peter speaks with his boss)*

Peter ___________ ______________________________

3) Cuando nosotros no sabemos las respuestas *(When we do not know the answers)*

Nosotros ___________ ______________________________

4) Cuando Ana visita al doctor *(When Ana visits the doctor)*

Ana ___________ ______________________________

5) Cuando mis padres caminan muchas millas *(When my parents walk many miles)*

Mis padres ___________ ______________________________

Possible answers H: **1)** estoy contento/interesado/aburrido / **2)** está nervioso/preocupado / **3)** estamos frustrados/ tristes / **4)** está enferma / **5)** están cansados/agotados

UNIDAD 4

Ejercicio I

Translate the following sentences into Spanish. Pay attention to subject-verb agreement and to noun-adjective agreement.

1) Diana is sick ______________________

2) The boss is busy now ______________________

3) Peter is nervous in the office ______________________

4) We are very proud ______________________

5) Juan y Nacho are satisfied ______________________.

Answers I: **1)** Diana está enferma / **2)** El jefe está ocupado ahora / 3) Peter está nervioso en la oficina / **4)** Nosotros estamos muy orgullosos / **5)** Juan y Nacho están satisfechos

MI LISTA DE VOCABULARIO

This is a list of the words that you have learned in this unit.

- aburrido
- agradable
- ahora
- alto
- antipático
- atractivo
- bajo
- calmado
- callado
- cansado
- chistoso
- cómico
- contento
- débil
- decepcionado
- delgado
- desagradable
- deshonesto
- desorganizado
- diferente
- egoísta
- enfermo
- ¡eso espero!
- (el) estado de ánimo
- estúpido
- feo
- franco
- frustrado
- fuerte
- generoso
- gordo
- gracioso
- grande
- grosero

guapo	muerto	renovado
inteligente	nervioso	rubio
honesto	ocupado	sano
humilde	optimista	satisfecho
idealista	organizado	serio
ignorante	orgulloso	sincero
interesado	pelirrojo	tonto
interesante	pequeño	trabajador
joven	perezoso	tranquilo
libre	pesimista	triste
listo	popular	vago
locuaz	práctico	viejo
mentiroso	preocupado	
moreno	relajado	

UN POCO DE CULTURA

¿Hispano o latino?

According to the United States Census Bureau, the terms *Hispanic* ('hispano' in Spanish) and *Latino* ('latino' in Spanish) refer to individuals who consider themselves Mexican, Puerto Rican, Cuban, or any of the other Spanish-speaking subgroups that the Census provides, regardless of race, place of birth, or years living in the U.S. The Census Bureau clearly considers *Hispanic* and *Latino* synonyms, and they classify people of many different nationalities and races under this category.

However, many people see a real distinction between the terms *Hispanic* and *Latino* that goes beyond simple preference. For some, a Hispanic is a person born and mostly raised in a Spanish-speaking country (e.g., Chile, Ecuador, etc), whereas a Latino is a person of Hispanic ancestry born and/or raised in the U.S. According to this definition, a Hispanic speaks Spanish but a Latino does not necessarily. These groups have major cultural differences, as Hispanics grow up in Spanish-speaking countries where their cultural practices dominate, whereas Latinos grow up in the U.S., where the mainstream culture is non-Hispanic. Some examples of Latinos would be Chicanos (*Mexican-Americans*), Nuyoricans (*Puerto Ricans* living in New York City), and Cuban-Americans.

Another definition of the term *Hispanic* refers to a person either from Spain or a country conquered by Spain, whereas the term *Latino* refers to a person from a country conquered by the Roman Empire (in which Latin was the official language). Because Spain was conquered by the Romans, all Hispanics (e.g., Mexicans, Argentineans, Dominicans, etc) are also Latinos; however, people from Italy, Portugal or France are Latinos, but they are not Hispanics. In fact, when one thinks of a 'Latin lover,' an Italian (like Casanova) or a French character (like Pepe le Peu) usually comes to mind. None of these terms is derogatory, pejorative, or offensive per se. However, you must use them with caution, because certain people might think diferently.

RECOMENDACIÓN PARA ESTA UNIDAD

To finish this unit, we are going to give you some tips for remembering vocabulary, which is usually one of the most daunting parts of learning a foreign language. Because human memory has a limited capacity and because one often must learn a lot of words at a time, the foreign language learner should prioritize vocabulary learning.

Traditional methods of acquiring vocabulary, such as flipping flash cards and reading long bilingual lists of vocabulary, are obsolete. These techniques are based on old-fashioned theories of language learning that depend exclusively on rote memorization. New theories suggest that the human brain functions like a computer network in which connections between new information and old information must be made; the more connections, the easier it is to remember, retrieve, and eventually acquire new vocabulary.

OLD METHOD

Hand = (la) mano
Head = (la) cabeza
Arm = (el) brazo

With this system, you depend exclusively on memory to learn these words. Learning three words is not complicated, but when you must learn 70 words in one sitting, it can be overwhelming. If the link between the English word and the Spanish word is lost, you will not be able to think of and use the Spanish word, though you might recognize it if you see it.

NEW METHOD

New methods use different techniques for learning vocabulary.

-Create visual connections either with illustrations or with your own drawings and sketches.

mano cabeza brazo

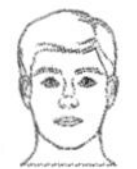

-Create an inter-linguistic connection by searching for words that have linguistic similarities.

Lung = pulmón (like in pulmonary system)
Hand = mano (like in manicure)
Tongue = lengua (like in languages)

-Create a meaningful connection by making up sentences that contain the vocabulary to be learned, or by asking questions that require you to answer using the new vocabulary.

-¿De qué color es tu pelo? Lo siento, pero yo no tengo pelo en la cabeza. *(What color is your hair? I am sorry, but I have no hair on my head)*

-Create other sensory connections besides sight.

-Write or type sentences created with the new vocabulary; label the items in an illustration, label the items around your office or bedroom.

-Listen to the radio or television, listen to music and try to repeat aloud the words that you hear.

-If the vocabulary is related to food or drink, eat and drink those products.

-Recycle old vocabulary

-Make sure you re-use the vocabulary that you learn.

With this system, you create many connections to a particular word, making it easier to retrieve it from your memory when you need it (and less likely that you will forget it). Mechanical practice (e.g., rote memorization) can supplement the learning process, but it should not be the principal technique.

UNIDAD 5 CONTENIDO

In this unit, you will learn:

1 - How to describe basic places and things
2 - About 'hay'
3 - The colors
4 - About the differences between 'ser' and 'estar'
5 - How to compare
6 - Linguistic cultural information about the terms 'español' and 'castellano'

describir lugares y cosas

DESCRIBIR LUGARES Y COSAS

(Describing places and things)

From the office window Peter and Ana can see the parking lot, where Peter's car is parked.

Ana: ¿Es ése tu coche[1]?
(Is that your car?)

Peter: Sí, es un Toyota. Es muy grande, cómodo, y rápido. ¿Qué coche tienes tú?
(Yes, it is a Toyota. It is very large, comfortable and fast. What kind of car do you have?)

Ana: Un pequeño Seat[2]. No es muy rápido, pero es económico.
(A little Seat. It is not very fast, but it is economical)

Peter: Ya veo. Y tu casa.... ¿está cerca de la oficina?
(I see. And your house.... is it close to the office?)

Ana: Sí, muy cerca. Es una vieja casa muy grande y acogedora. Es un poco cara porque está en un barrio muy bueno.
(Yes, very close. It is a very large and cozy old house. It is a little expensive because it is in a very good neighborhood)

Peter: ¿Sí? Mi apartamento no está muy cerca de la oficina, pero está al lado del cine y del centro comercial.
(Oh, yeah? My apartment is not very close to the office, but it is next to the movie theater and the mall.)

Ana: ¿Y cómo es tu apartamento?
(And how is your apartment?)

[Footnotes]

[1] Other common words for 'coche' are 'auto', 'carro,' and 'vehículo.'
[2] Seat (Sociedad Española de Automóviles de Turismo S.A.) is a Spanish car company founded in 1950.

Peter: Es muy nuevo. Es espacioso y barato. Es muy tranquilo porque está lejos de la autopista. Hay muchas plantas.
(It is very new. It is spacious and cheap. It is very quiet because is far from the highway. There are lot of plants.)

Ana: Ah, ¡qué suerte! Mi casa es un poco ruidosa porque está cerca de una escuela.
(Ah, how lucky! My house is a little bit noisy because it is close to a school.)

Ejercicio A

Using the adjectives you just saw in the dialogue, describe the following objects and places by selecting the best option.

1) La silla es
- a) rápida
- b) cómoda
- c) ruidosa

2) El coche es
- a) tranquilo
- b) acogedor
- c) grande

3) La oficina es
- a) espaciosa
- b) barata
- c) mala

4) La escuela es
- a) cómoda
- b) rápida
- c) buena

5) El barrio es
- a) tranquilo
- b) cómodo
- c) espacioso

6) Las plantas son
- a) rápidas
- b) cómodas
- c) grandes

Answers A: **1)** - b) / **2)** - c) / **3)** - a) / **4)** - c) / **5)** - a) / **6)** - c)

Ejercicio B

Did you notice that Peter and Ana used the verb 'estar' to describe location (close to, far from, etc)? Let's see if you can complete the following translations using expressions from the dialogue.

1) La casa está ______________________ oficina.

2) La casa está ______________________ escuela.

3) El apartamento está ______________________ cine[3] y del centro comercial.

4) El apartamento está ______________________ autopista.

[Footnotes]

[3] *When 'de' is followed by 'la,' you just write 'de la,' but when 'de' is followed by 'el,' you write 'del.'*

Answers B: **1)** cerca de la / **2)** cerca de una / **3)** al lado del / **4)** lejos de la

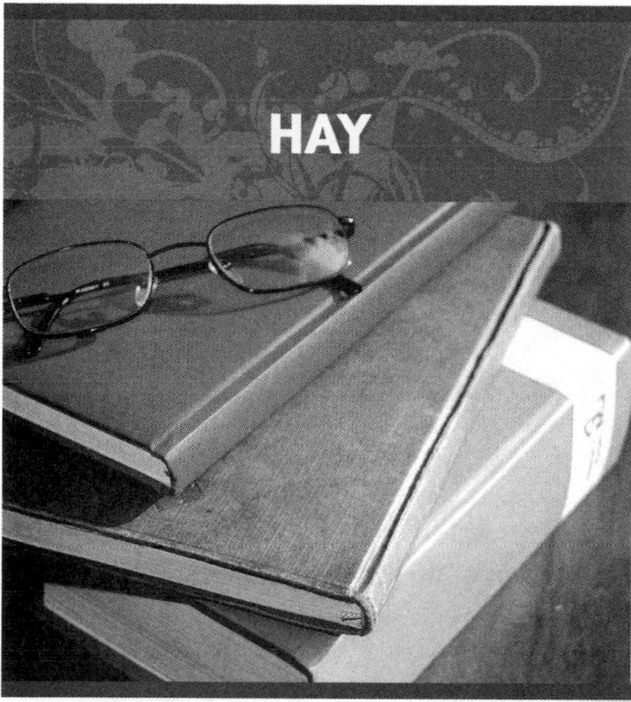

HAY

(There is, there are)

Pronounced exactly like the word 'eye' in English, 'hay' means both 'there is' and 'there are.' It comes from the verb 'haber':

Hay un libro en la mesa.
(There is a book on the table.)

Hay muchos libros en la mesa.
(There are many books on the table.)

¿Hay algo de comer?
(Is there anything to eat?)

Ejercicio C

Complete the following sentences using the places listed in the table.

patio
cine
escuela
autopista
centro comercial
edificio *(building)*
coche
casa

1) Hay muchos libros en la ____________________

2) Hay muchos coches en la ____________________

3) Hay muchos muebles *(furniture)* en la ____________________

4) Hay muchos apartamentos en el ____________________

5) Hay muchas plantas en el ____________________

6) Hay muchos discos compactos *(CDs)* en el ____________________

7) Hay muchas películas *(movies)* en el ____________________

8) Hay muchas tiendas *(stores)* en el ____________________

Answers C: **1)** escuela / **2)** autopista / **3)** casa / **4)** edificio / **5)** patio / **6)** coche / **7)** cine / **8)** centro comercial

LOS COLORES

(Colors)

rojo

amarillo

verde

naranja/anaranjado

azul

blanco

negro

marrón/café

gris

rosa/rosado

morado/violeta

dorado *(golden)*

Ejercicio D

Complete the following descriptions by matching the items in column A with their colors in column B.

A	B
1) El cielo *(sky)* es	a) blanco
2) La autopista es	b) roja
3) La planta es	c) dorado
4) El jugo de naranja *(orange juice)* es	d) negra
5) El oro *(gold)* es	e) gris
6) El chocolate es	f) naranja
7) El papel es	g) verde
8) El sol *(sun)* es	h) azul
9) La sangre *(blood)* es	i) marrón
10) La noche es	j) amarillo

Answers D: **1)** - h) / **2)** - e) / **3)** - g) / **4)** - f) / **5)** - c) / **6)** - i) / **7)** - a) / **8)** - j) / **9)** - b) / **10)** - d)

Ejercicio E

Try to find 10 colors in this word search game.

U	Z	A	U	B	L	A	N	C	O
T	E	J	L	V	E	R	D	R	U
O	R	N	L	S	I	R	G	O	J
L	P	A	O	R	T	E	N	J	B
N	A	R	R	G	N	D	N	O	L
E	Z	A	O	D	A	R	O	M	A
G	U	N	E	J	L	E	R	O	R
R	L	R	V	E	U	V	R	R	O
T	S	A	S	S	U	Z	A	A	J
Z	O	L	L	I	R	A	M	A	E

Answers E:

		A		B	L	A	N	C	O
		J						R	
		N		S	I	R	G	O	
		A				E		J	
	A	R			N	D	N	O	
	Z	A	O	D	A	R	O	M	
	U	N				E	R		
	L					V	R		
							A		
	O	L	L	I	R	A	M	A	

UNIDAD 5

DIFERENCIAS ENTRE 'SER' Y 'ESTAR'

(Ser vs. Estar)

We already learned that both 'ser' and 'estar' mean 'to be,' but they are used for different things. Here is a list of some of their uses.

SER
Description (profession, religion, name, physical appearance, personality, race, ethnicity, nationality, composition, color, etc) -Nicolás es francés -Yo soy alto[4]
Possession -Esta silla es de Ana *(This chair is Ana's)*

ESTAR
Temporary physical, emotional and mental conditions -Juan está enfermo *(sick)* -Paco está enojado *(angry)* -Irene está loca *(crazy)*
Other conditions (especially those described with past participles) -Nuria está casada[5] *(married)* -La tienda está cerrada *(closed)*
Location -La escuela está aquí *(here)*
Company -Daniel está con Inés *(Daniel is with Inés)*
Auxiliary verb (with the progressive form) -Yo estoy cantando *(I am singing)*

[Footnotes]

[4] For physical description, both 'ser' and 'estar' can sometimes be used, but the expression with 'estar' will have a connotation of non-permanence. For example: Ana es elegante (Ana is an elegant person in general) vs. Ana está elegante (Ana looks elegant today with that new dress).

[5] Depending on the country, 'single,' 'married,' 'widowed' and 'divorced' can go with either 'ser' or 'estar.'

Ejercicio F

Circle the best option for the following sentences with 'ser' or 'estar'.

1)	La casa	(es/está)	grande.
2)	La librería	(es/está)	cerrada *(closed)*
3)	El patio	(es/está)	pequeño.
4)	El parque *(park)*	(es/está)	cerca de la escuela.
5)	Yo	(soy/estoy)	hablando en español.
6)	Jenaro y Rocío	(son/están)	frustrados.
7)	Tú	(eres/estás)	rubia.

Answers F: **1)** es / **2)** está / **3)** es / **4)** está / **5)** estoy / **6)** están / **7)** eres

Ejercicio G

Complete the following sentences with the correct conjugation of either 'ser' or 'estar.'

1) Mi esposo ________ fuerte.		**6)** Mariano y Raúl ________ cansados.	
2) La escuela ________ lejos.		**7)** Tú ________ muy simpática.	
3) Ustedes ________ guapos.		**8)** Nosotros ________ nerviosos hoy *(today)*.	
4) Las casas ________ blancas.		**9)** Ellos no ________ hablando de política.	
5) Elena ________ triste.		**10)** Yo ________ con mis amigos.	

Answers G: **1)** es / **2)** está / **3)** son / **4)** son / **5)** está / **6)** están / **7)** eres / **8)** estamos / **9)** están / **10)** estoy

LAS COMPARACIONES *(Comparisons)*

Comparisons of equality

-tan.....como.... *(as... as....)*
[make sure the adjective in between agrees with the subject]

-Paloma es tan *alta* como Fernando
(Paloma is as tall as Fernando)

-Estos coches son tan *rápidos* como ésos
(These cars are as fast as those)

-tantos/as…. como…. *(as many…. as…)*
[make sure the 'tantos/as' agrees with the plural noun in the middle]

-Hay tantos *libros* aquí como allá
(There are as many books here as there)

-Tengo tantas *plantas* como tú
(I have as many plants as you)

-tanto/a…. como…. *(as much… as…)*
[make sure the 'tanto/a' agrees with the noun in the middle, if any]

-Tengo tanto *dinero* como tú
(I have as much money as you)

-Tengo tanta *paciencia* como Carlos
(I have as much patience as Carlos)

-Trabajo tanto como tú *(I work as much as you)*

Ejercicio H

Translate the following sentences using the comparison structures that you just learned.

1) The school is as big as the movie theater.

2) The apartments are as small as the houses.

3) There are as many cars in Spain as in France.

4) There is as much pollution *(contaminación)* in Madrid as in Barcelona.

Answers H: **1)** La escuela es tan grande como el cine / **2)** Los apartamentos son tan pequeños como las casas / **3)** Hay tantos coches en España como en Francia / **4)** Hay tanta contaminación en Madrid como en Barcelona

MAS COMPARACIONES *(More comparisons)*

Comparisons of inequality

-más… que…. *(more… than….)*

-menos…. que…. *(less/fewer… than….)*

[if you have an adjective in the middle, make sure it agrees with the subject]

-Hay más *libros* que coches
(There are more books than cars)

-Jesús es más *inteligente* que Carla
(Jesús is more intelligent than Carla)

-Mi esposa es menos *práctica* que yo
(My wife is less practical than I)

-Estudio menos que tú *(I study less than you)*

-mejor que... *(better than...)*

-Mi casa es mejor que tu apartamento
(My house is better than your apartment)

-peor que... *(worse than...)*

-Mi escuela es peor que tu escuela
(My school is worse than your school)

-mayor que... *(older[6] than...)*

-Mi hermano es mayor que yo
(My brother is older than I)

-menor que... *(younger than...)*

-Mi prima es menor que tú
(My cousin is younger than you)

The superlative

-el/la/los/las (....) más/menos....de...
(the most.... in the....)

-Verónica es la (chica) más guapa de la clase
(Veronica is the most beautiful (girl) in the class)

-Nacho es el (policía) más valiente del país
(Nacho is the most brave (policeman) in the country)

[Footnotes] [6] *'Mayor' and 'menor' are used when comparing people only. When comparing things, use 'más viejo que,' 'más nuevo que'.*

Ejercicio I

Translate the following sentences using the comparison structures you just learned.

1) There are more houses than apartments.

____

____

2) There are fewer desks than lamps.

____

____

3) Ariadna is more tired than Nick.

____

____

4) I am less tall than you (usted).

____

____

5) You (Tú) are better than I.

____

____

6) Your (Tu) brother is younger than my sister.

____

____

7) Alberto is the most intelligent boy in the class.

____

____

8) You (Ustedes) are the best students.

____

____

Answers I: **1)** Hay más casas que apartamentos / **2)** Hay menos escritorios que lámparas / **3)** Ariadna está más cansada que Nick / **4)** Yo soy menos alto/a que usted / **5)** Tú eres mejor que yo / **6)** Tu hermano es menor que mi hermana / **7)** Alberto es el (chico) más inteligente de la clase / **8)** Ustedes son los mejores estudiantes

MI LISTA DE VOCABULARIO

This is a list of the words that you have learned in this unit.

acogedor
al lado (de)
amarillo
anaranjado
(el) apartamento
(la) autopista
azul
barato
(el) barrio
bueno
café
cansado
(la) casa
casado
caro
(el) carro o (el) coche
(el) centro comercial
cerca (de)
cerrado
(el) cielo
(el) cine
cómodo
(el) disco compacto
dorado
económico
(el) edificio
enojado
(la) escuela
espacioso
lejos (de)
loco
gris
hay
(el) jugo
marrón
más… que….
mayor
mejor
menor
menos… que…
(la) mesa
morado
(el) mueble
naranja
(la) nube
nuevo
(el) oro
(el) parque
(el) patio
(la) película
peor
¡qué suerte!
rápido
rojo
rosa, rosado
ruidoso
(la) sangre
(el) sol
tan… como….
tanto/a…. como….
tantos/as…. como…
(la) tienda
verde
violeta

UN POCO DE CULTURA

¿Español o castellano?

Ever since the 1978 Spanish Constitution declared that the official language of Spain was 'el castellano' *(Castilian)*, the terms '*español*' *(Spanish)* and '*castellano*' have become synonyms for many people. Accordingly, when someone asks '¿Hablas castellano?' *(Do you speak Castilian?)* you can assume they mean '¿Hablas español?' *(Do you speak Spanish?)*.

Others believe that 'castellano' refers to the dialect of Spanish spoken in the province of Castilla (from which the Spanish language originated), whereas *español* refers more generally to the modern language used in all Spanish-speaking countries. According to this second definition, a person from Madrid (located in Castilla) would speak *castellano* but a person from Chile would not; both, however, would speak *español*.

Spanish was not born at a particular moment -it developed over hundreds of years. Modern Spanish is the result of the mixing that took place between the various languages and cultures that occupied the Iberian peninsula. When the Romans conquered what they called 'Hispania' in 206 A.D., bringing with them Romance (vulgar Latin), they found a language there that arose from the Celts, Greeks, Phoenicians, Basques, and Iberians that already lived there. Though Spanish derives its grammatical basis from Latin, subsequent invasions by the Visigoths and Arabs, as well as influence from other languages (French, English, American indigenous languages, etc.) also contributed to the development of this language. Let's take a look at some examples of loans from these various groups.

- From other Indo-European languages: madre *(mother)*, padre *(father)*, and Dios *(God)*
- From Greek: atleta *(athlete)*, matemáticas *(mathematics)*, política *(politics)*, Biblia *(Bible)*, and programa *(program)*
- From the Visigoths: guerra *(war)*, ropa *(clothes)*, and guardián *(guardian)*
- From Arabic: alfombra *(carpet)*, alcohol *(alcohol)*, almohada *(pillow)*, álgebra *(algebra)*, café *(coffee)*, tabaco *(tobacco)*, Andalucía, Madrid, asesino *(assassin)*, and ajedrez *(chess)*
- From Native American languages: canoa *(canoe)*, chocolate, papa *(potato)*, puma, huracán *(hurricane)*, maíz *(corn)*, Caribe *(Caribbean)*, cacao, and caníbal *(cannibal)*
- From English: cocktail, radar, hockey, e-mail, and whiskey

- From Italian: piano, soneto *(sonnet)*, novela *(novel)*, and charlar *(to chat)*
- From French: bebé *(baby)*, chofer *(driver)*, boutique *(shop)*, fresa *(strawberry)*, croissant, chaqueta *(jacket)*, and jardín *(garden)*
- From Euskera (Basque language): perro *(dog)*, izquierda *(left)*, carro *(carriage/car)*, and mochila *(backpack)*

The Real Academia de la Lengua Española, an institution created to protect, preserve and determine the quality of the Spanish language, was established in 1713. This scholarly entity has been criticized for its rejection of certain non-canonical varieties of Spanish, as well as of particular vocabulary borrowed or modified from other languages.

What do you think? Do you think an institution should determine what a language should look like and sound like, so that it can be preserved and protected? Or should the natural development of a language be determined by the people who speak it and by their environment? Is there a similar institution that protects and preserves the English language?

RECOMENDACIÓN PARA ESTA UNIDAD

To finish this unit, we recommend you visit the webpage http://www.etymonline.com/ where you can enter any word in English and find out its origin. This information will also help you learn Spanish indirectly.

If you need an online dictionary, you can try http://www.wordreference.com/

UNIDAD 6

CONTENIDO

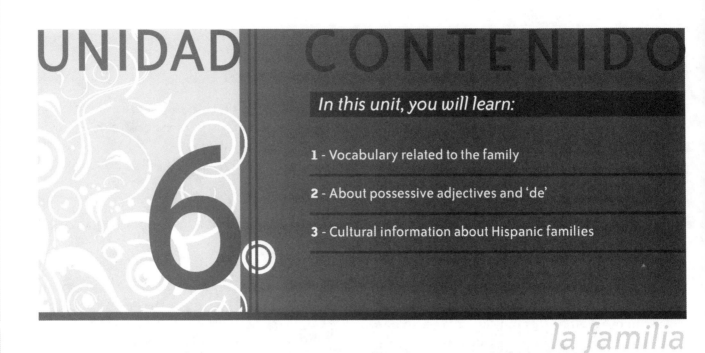

In this unit, you will learn:

1 - Vocabulary related to the family

2 - About possessive adjectives and 'de'

3 - Cultural information about Hispanic families

la familia

LA FAMILIA

(The family)

Peter is now visiting Ana's office to pick up some paperwork. On her desk, there are some family pictures.

Peter: ¡Qué niña tan guapa! ¿Es tu hija?
(What a beautiful girl! Is this your daughter?)

Ana: Sí, es mi hija mayor, Sofía, y ésta es mi hija menor, Rosa.
(Yes, she is my eldest daughter, Sofía, and this is my youngest daughter, Rosa)

Peter: Parecen gemelas. *(They look like twins)*

Ana: Sí, son muy parecidas, pero se llevan cinco años. En esta foto estamos los cuatro.
(Yes, they are very similar, but they are five years apart. The four of us are in this picture)

Peter: Ah, ¡qué familia tan bonita! ¿Qué hace tu marido?
(Ah, what a beautiful family! What does your husband do?)

Ana: Es abogado. Trabaja cerca de aquí.
(He is a lawyer. He works nearby)

Peter: Yo no estoy casado, pero tengo una familia muy grande. Mira esta foto….
(I am not married, but I have a very big family. Look at this picture…)

Ana: ¡Uy, cuántas personas! ¿Éstos son tus padres?
(Wow! How many people! These are your parents?)

Peter: Sí, y aquéllos son mis tíos y sus esposas. Thomas y Brandon son los hermanos de mi padre y viven en Miami. Esta señora de aquí es mi tía Rose, la hermana de mi madre.

(Yes, and those over there are my uncles and their wives. Thomas and Brandon are my father's brothers and they live in Miami. This lady here is my Aunt Rose, my mother's sister)

Ana: ¿Y esos niños? *(And those children?)*

Peter: Son los hijos de mi tío Thomas. Éste es mi primo Josh y el pequeño se llama Alex. Es muy travieso. El bebé de ahí es mi prima Lucy.
(They are my Uncle Thomas's children. This one is my cousin Josh and the little one is Alex. He is very mischievous. This baby here is my cousin Lucy.)

Ana: Entonces, ¿eres hijo único? ¿No tienes hermanos?
(So, are you an only child? You don't have siblings?)

Peter: Sí, sí, tengo dos hermanos. Mi hermano mayor se llama Chris y mi hermana se llama Ruth. Mira esta otra foto.... Aquí está Chris con su esposa y mis sobrinos, Brian y Daniel. Viven en Chicago. Ruth no está casada y no tiene hijos.
(Yes, yes, I have two siblings. My oldest brother's name is Chris and my sister's name is Ruth. Look at this other picture... Here is Chris with his wife and my nephews, Brian and Daniel. They live in Chicago. Ruth is not married and does not have children)

Ana: ¿Dónde viven tus padres? *(Where do your parents live?)*

Peter: En Miami *(In Miami)*

Ana: Entonces, ¿tu madre y tu padre no ven mucho a sus nietos? *(So, your mother and father don't see their grandchildren much?)*

Peter: Oh, sí, los ven de vez en cuando. Como están jubilados, viajan a Chicago cuatro o cinco veces al año.
(Oh, yes, they see them occasionally. Since they are retired, they travel to Chicago four or five times a year)

UNIDAD 6

Ejercicio A

Try to draw Peter's family tree according to the description from the dialogue.

Ejercicio B

Translate the following words and expressions. If you need help, look for them in the dialogue.

1) children ______

2) siblings ______

3) parents ______

4) oldest daughter ______

5) youngest daughter ______

6) twins[1] ______

7) baby ______

8) only child ______

9) she is not married ______

10) she doesn't have children ______

11) they are X years apart ______

12) my father's brothers ______

13) my mother's sister ______

14) my parents are retired ______

15) four times a year ______

[Footnotes] [1] *The word 'twin' can be a noun (mi gemelo llamó hoy = my twin called today) and also an adjective (mi hermano gemelo = my twin brother). Either way, it takes feminine ending -a and plural endings -os, -as, just like any other noun that ends in -o.*

Answers B: **1)** hijos / **2)** hermanos / **3)** padres / **4)** hija mayor / **5)** hija menor / **6)** gemelos/as / **7)** bebé / **8)** hijo/a único/a / **9)** no está casada / **10)** no tiene hijos / **11)** se llevan X años / **12)** los hermanos de mi padre / **13)** la hermana de mi madre / **14)** mis padres están jubilados / **15)** cuatro veces al año

Ejercicio C

Now draw your own family tree. Include your spouse and children, your parents, your siblings and their children. Under each person's name (e.g., Anthony) write the name of the relationship they have to you (e.g., hermano).

MAS VOCABULARIO DE LA FAMILIA

suegro *(father-in-law)*
suegra *(mother-in-law)*
nuera *(daughter-in-law)*
yerno *(son-in-law)*
cuñado/a *(brother/sister-in-law)*
padrastro *(stepfather)*
madrastra *(stepmother)*
hijastro/a *(stepson/stepdaughter)*
medio hermano/a *(half-brother)*
media hermana *(half-sister)*
bisabuelo/a *(great-grandfather/mother)*
bisnieto/a *(great-grandson/daughter)*
tatarabuelo/a *(great-great-grandfather/mother)*
madre soltera *(single mother)*
tataranieto/a *(great-great-grandson/daughter)*
hijo ilegítimo *(illegitimate child)*
descendencia *(descent/origin)*
ascendencia *(ascendancy)*
antepasados *(ancestors)*
solterón/a *(bachelor/spinster)*
huérfano/a *(orphan)*
madrina *(godmother)*
padrino *(godfather)*
primo segundo *(second cousin)*
pariente *(relative)*
pariente lejano *(distant relative)*
hijo adoptivo *(adopted child)*
benjamín/a *(youngest in the family)*
matrimonio *(marriage)*

Ejercicio D

¿Quiénes son?
(Who are they?)
Write the appropriate family name for the following descriptions. The first one is done for you.

1) My mother's father — Es mi abuela
2) My mother's grandmother — Es mi ____________
3) My second husband's daughter — Es mi ____________
4) My husband's brother — Es mi ____________
5) My daughter's husband — Es mi ____________
6) A mother who is not married — Es una ____________
7) A son without parents — Es ____________
8) A member of my distant family — Es mi ____________
9) My husband's mother — Es mi ____________
10) My grandmother's grandfather — Es mi ____________

Answers D: **2)** bisabuela / **3)** hijastra / **4)** cuñado / **5)** yerno / **6)** madre soltera / **7)** huérfano / **8)** pariente lejano / **9)** suegra / **10)** tatarabuelo

POSESIÓN *(Possession)*

Possession can be expressed in different ways. Here we are going to see two different forms used to express possession.

-The first form involves the use of the preposition 'de' in expressions that in English use an apostrophe plus 's' or in which possession is understood:

-Peter**'s** brother (=the brother of Peter)
El hermano **de** Peter

-my uncle**s'** children (=the children of my uncles)
Los hijos **de** mis tíos

-market value (=the value of the market)
El valor **del**[2] mercado

-farm animals (=the animals of the farm)
Los animales **de** granja

-The second form involves the use of possessive adjectives, which are positioned directly in front[3] of the nouns they modify:

-my uncles / **mis** tíos
-their mother / **su** madre

Here is a list of these possessive adjectives:

ADJETIVOS POSESIVOS	*POSSESSIVE ADJECTIVES*
mi / mis	*my*
tu / tus	*your*
su / sus	*his, her, its*
nuestro /-a /-os /-as	*our*
vuestro /-a /-os /-as	*your*
su / sus	*their*

Possessive adjectives follow the same rules as regular adjectives: they must agree with the noun they modify. In other words, in English, we can say both 'her house' and 'her houses' without changing the word 'her;' in Spanish, we say 'su casa' but 'su**s** casa**s**,' 'nuestr**o** hij**o**' but 'nuestr**a** hij**a**.'

[Footnotes]

[2] When the preposition 'de' is followed by the article 'el', they are combined to form the contraction 'del.'

[3] Possessive adjectives also have another form that goes after the noun (un amigo mío = a friend of mine), but we are not learning this version at this time.

Ejercicio E

Translate the following expressions using 'de' or a possessive adjective. The first one is done for you.

1) Manolo's children Los hijos de Manolo

2) Pepe's only child ______

3) Our mother ______

4) His apartment ______

5) Their son ______

6) My sister's son ______

7) Her nephews ______

8) Your (tu) father ______

9) Her sister's husband's brother ______

10) My brother's wife's sisters ______

Answers E: **2)** El hijo único de Pepe / **3)** Nuestra madre / **4)** Su apartamento / **5)** Su hijo / **6)** El hijo de mi hermana / **7)** Sus sobrinos / **8)** Tu padre / **9)** El hermano del esposo de su hermana / **10)** Las hermanas de la esposa de mi hermano

MI LISTA DE VOCABULARIO

This is a list of the words that you have learned in this unit.

(el) abuelo/(la) abuela
(los) abuelos
(el) antepasado
(la) ascendencia
(el) bebé
(el) benjamín/(la) benjamina
(el) bisabuelo/(la) bisabuela
(los) bisabuelos
(el) bisnieto/(la) bisnieta
(los) bisnietos
casado
(el) cuñado/(la) cuñada
de
(la) descendencia
divorciado
(la) esposa o (la) mujer
(el) esposo o (el) marido
(la) familia
(el) gemelo
(el) hermano/(la) hermana
(los) hermanos
(el) hijastro/(la) hijastra
(los) hijastros

(el) hijo/(la) hija
(el) hijo adoptivo
(el) hijo ilegítimo
(los) hijos
jubilado
(el) matrimonio
(la) madrastra
(la) madre o (la) mamá
(la) madrina
(el) matrimonio
(el) medio hermano/
(la) media hermana
mi
(el) nieto/(la) nieta
(los) nietos
(el) niño/(la) niña
(los) niños[4]
(la) nuera
nuestro
(el) padrastro
(el) padre o (el) papá
(los) padres
parecido

(el) pariente
(la) posesión
(el) primo/(la) prima
se llevan X años
(el) sobrino/(la) sobrina
soltero
(el) solterón/(la) solterona
su
(el) suegro/(la) suegra
(los) suegros
(el) tatarabuelo/
(la) tatarabuela
(los) tatarabuelos
(el) tataranieto/
(la) tataranieta
(los) tataranietos
(el) tío /(la) tía
travieso
tu
único
viudo
vuestro
(el) yerno

[Footnotes]

[4] Both 'hijos' and 'niños' translate as children. 'HIjos' is used to describe somebody's offspring, whereas 'niños' is used when you mean children in general or are discussing a particular group of children. Ex: 'I like children' would go with the word 'niños,' but 'your children are beautiful' would go with 'hijos.'

UN POCO DE CULTURA

The concept of family

Family is very important in the Hispanic culture. Families are made up of a large, tight network of individuals that includes even second cousins and individuals not related by blood, such as godparents or close family friends.

One factor that reinforces these networks is the fact that many Hispanic women do not work outside the home[5]. They often assume the role of caretaker of the elderly and/or of a large number of kids, turning women into important matriarchal figures through which family connections are made and maintained. For many Hispanic families, taking care of the elderly in one's own house is an assumed responsibility. Furthermore, in families with three or more children, the grandmother's help with child care and household chores is necessary. Data from the United States Census Bureau shows that 12% of U.S. Hispanic children live in households with at least one grandparent, compared to 5% of non-Hispanic white children.

Another reason that families tend to be extended is that people often remain where they grow up. Unless job markets permit, moving from one's home to a different city or state/province is not very justifiable, logical or practical. Because most family members remain in the same city or region, it is easier to get together to celebrate and develop relationships with one's relatives and their families, fostering a sense of an extended family.

One more factor that contributes to the tightness of Hispanic families is the fact that poor economic conditions do not allow children over 18 to leave their home right away. Unlike many teenage Americans who leave home after graduating from high school, young Hispanic adults usually stay at home for a few more years until they marry or earn enough to live on their own. Also, in many Hispanic countries, renting a home is not common. Therefore, young people live with their parents until they have saved enough money to start paying for their own mortgage.

As you have probably noticed, Hispanic families generally have more children than the average U.S. non-Hispanic family. This is due to several factors, one of which is the influence of the Catholic Church, which prohibits the use of contraceptives, condemns abortion, and discourages divorce. Another factor is the negative social stigma associated with barren women in Hispanic cultures. A third and very important factor is the educational attainment level of Hispanic women and its effect on childbirth rates. According to the U.S. 2002 National Survey of Family Growth, the number of women with three or more pregnancies, unintended pregnancies, and who do not use contraception is closely correlated with lower levels of education and income, a common feature in Hispanic families in the U. S[6]. For

example, for Hispanic and non-Hispanic women ages 22–44, the NSFG report shows that 47% of women with less than a high school education have three children or more (compared to 12% of college-educated women). Expectations of having no children are also associated with higher levels of education and income.

According to a 2005 Associated Press article[7], nearly 10% of births in the U.S. in 2002 were to women born in Mexico. The article also claims that Hispanics account for almost 60% of all births by immigrants in the U.S. The National Center for Health Statistics reported that in 2004, births among Hispanic women increased, remained unchanged for African American women, and declined for non-Hispanic white women. These data indicate that Hispanics are the fastest growing minority in the U.S., and that their birth rate is higher than that of non-Hispanic whites and African Americans.

Though this information has multiple social implications, it clearly shows that Spanish is not only an important language currently, but that its use will continue to expand in the coming years. Whether you are learning Spanish for social, professional or personal reasons, the knowledge you gain will always be useful.

[Footnotes] [5] *Some of the reasons include poor education level and other social factors, such as traditional gender roles. Women of higher social classes, from more developed Hispanic countries, or with a higher level of education do not tend to follow this pattern. For example, the number of children per woman in Spain is only 1.3 (according to the Instituto Nacional de Estadística de España). Regarding education, in the United States, in 2004, 31% of non-Hispanic white mothers had a BA or higher, compared to 10.1% of non-Hispanic black mothers, and 7.5% of Hispanic mothers, which might explain why Latinas tend to have more children than non Latinas (data from the NCHS, http://www.cdc.gov/nchs/).*

[6] *According to the U.S. Census Bureau, the median income of non-Hispanic whites is $50,784, whereas the median income of Hispanics is $35,967.*

[7] *Article published in the International Herald Tribune on July 8th, 2005.*

RECOMENDACIÓN PARA ESTA UNIDAD

To finish this unit, we recommend that you watch movies that portray Hispanic/Latino families, such as *Tortilla Soup* (2001, USA) by María Ripoll, *Fools Rush In* (1997, USA) by Andy Tennant, *My Family* (1995, USA) by Gregory Nava, and *Like Water for Chocolate* (1992, Mexico) by Alfonso Arau. There are also television series such as *American Family: Journey of Dreams* (2002–2004, USA) by Gregory Nava, and *Resurrection Blvd.* (2000–2002, USA) by Camino Vila and Albert Xavier.

UNIDAD 7

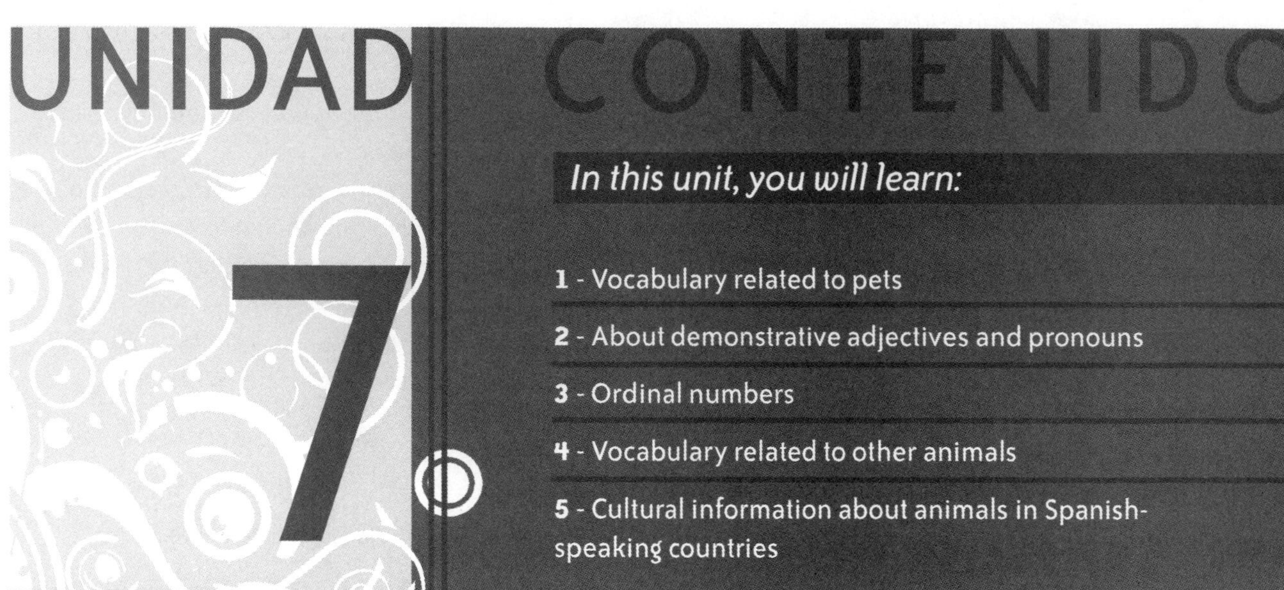

UNIDAD 7 CONTENIDO

In this unit, you will learn:

1 - Vocabulary related to pets

2 - About demonstrative adjectives and pronouns

3 - Ordinal numbers

4 - Vocabulary related to other animals

5 - Cultural information about animals in Spanish-speaking countries

las mascotas

LAS MASCOTAS

(The pets)

Ana also shows Peter a picture of her cat, Arigato. He is part of the family. Peter does not have a cat, but his parents have a dog named Pluto.

perro

gato

conejo

pájaro

caballo

hámster

tortuga

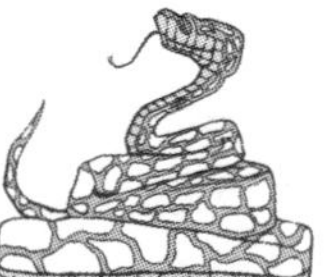
serpiente

pez[1]

araña

[Footnotes]

[1] To make the plural of a word that ends in –z, change the 'z' to 'c' and then add -es (pez = peces).

MAS VOCABULARIO SOBRE MASCOTAS

jaula

juguetes

pecera

acuario

columpio

establo(s)

agua

veterinario

Ejercicio A

Complete these sentences with an appropriate animal.

1) Los _____________ y los perros no son buenos amigos.

2) El perro de Lupe está enfermo *(sick)* y necesita ver a *(it needs to see)* un ____________.

3) Los _____________ son animales muy grandes que viven *(live)* en los establos.

4) El _____________ vive *(lives)* en la pecera.

5) El _____________ juega *(plays)* en su columpio y canta *(sings)*

6) La _____________ no tiene patas *(legs)*.

7) La _____________ tiene ocho (8) patas.

8) Arigato es el _____________ de Ana.

9) En el mar *(sea)* y el océano *(ocean)* hay muchos _____________.

10) Peter no tiene _____________ *(pets)*.

Answers A: **1)** gatos / **2)** veterinario / **3)** caballos / **4)** pez / **5)** pájaro / **6)** serpiente / **7)** araña / **8)** gato / **9)** peces / **10)** mascotas

ADJETIVOS Y PRONOMBRES DEMOSTRATIVOS

(Demonstrative adjectives and pronouns)

Demonstrative adjectives specify which nouns are being referred to and how far they are from the speaker. In English, 'this,' 'these,' 'that,' and 'those' function as demonstrative adjectives when they accompany a noun. The same words act as demonstrative pronouns either when used alone or with the word 'one' (that is mine, that one is mine).

-Estos perros son lindos *(These dogs are cute)* (demonstrative adjective)

-Éstos son lindos *(These (ones) are cute)* (demonstrative pronoun)

-Esos apartamentos son caros *(Those apartments are expensive)* (demonstrative adjective)

-Ésos son caros *(Those (ones) are expensive)* (demonstrative pronoun)

-No quiero aquellas blusas *(I don't want those blouses over there)* (demonstrative adjective)

-No quiero aquéllas *(I don't want those over there)* (demonstrative pronoun)

To differentiate the adjective from the pronoun in Spanish, pronouns have an accent mark[2].

ADJETIVOS DEMOSTRATIVOS	*DEMONSTRATIVE ADJECTIVES*
este/esta/estos/estas	*this/these*
ese/esa/esos/esas	*that/those*
aquel/ aquella/ aquellos/aquellas	*that over there/ those over there*

Spanish also has a demonstrative pronoun of neutral gender (esto, eso, and aquello). It is used to refer to things whose gender we do not know or to general concepts and ideas. In spite of the fact that it is a pronoun, it does not have an accent and it is always used in the singular. Examples:

-¿Por qué hizo eso? *(Why did he do that?)*
-Esto no es fácil de explicar *(This is not easy to explain)*
-¿Qué es eso? *(What is that?)*.

[Footnotes]

[2] *All demonstrative pronouns (except for 'aquél') have the accent on the second to last syllable: éste, ésta, éstos, éstas, ése, ésa, ésos, ésas, aquélla, aquéllos, and aquéllas.*

Ejercicio B

Go back to the dialogue in lesson 6 and find all the demonstrative adjectives and pronouns. Write the sentences they appear in here, in the same order they appear in the dialogue. The first one is done for you.

1) Ésta es mi hija menor, Rosa
2) ______
3) ______
4) ______
5) ______
6) ______
7) ______
8) ______
9) ______

Answers B: **2)** En esta foto estamos los cuatro / **3)** Mira esta foto… / **4)** ¿Éstos son tus padres? / **5)** Aquéllos son mis tíos y sus esposas / **6)** Ésta señora de aquí es mi tía / **7)** ¿Y esos niños? / **8)** Éste es mi primo Josh / **9)** Mira esta otra foto

LOS NÚMEROS ORDINALES *(Ordinal numbers)*

Ordinal numbers indicate order. They can be used as adjectives (el quinto perro = the fifth dog) or as pronouns (el quinto = the fifth one). These are the ordinal numbers from 1 to 20:

	Ordinal numbers from 1 to 20
1.	primero *(first)*
2.	segundo *(second)*
3.	tercero *(third)*
4.	cuarto *(fourth)*
5.	quinto *(fifth)*
6.	sexto *(sixth)*
7.	séptimo *(seventh)*
8.	octavo *(eighth)*
9.	noveno *(ninth)*
10.	décimo *(tenth)*
11.	undécimo/decimoprimero *(eleventh)*
12.	duodécimo/decimosegundo *(twelfth)*
13.	decimotercero *(thirteenth)*
14.	decimocuarto *(fourteenth)*
15.	decimoquinto *(fifteenth)*
16.	decimosexto *(sixteenth)*
17.	decimoséptimo *(seventeenth)*
18.	decimoctavo *(eighteenth)*
19.	decimonoveno *(nineteenth)*
20.	vigésimo *(twentieth)*

The words 'primero' and 'tercero' (masculine form only) drop the -o when they are used as adjectives, but keep it when they function as pronouns:

-mi primer gato *(my first cat)* *(adjective)*
-él es el primero *(he is the first one)* *(pronoun)*
-su tercer cachorro *(her third cub)* *(adjective)*
-éste es el tercero *(this one is the third one)* *(pronoun)*

The word 'primero' is also used to indicate the first day of the month. In some countries, however, 'uno' is preferred. Both use the definite article 'el.'

-el uno de enero es Año Nuevo
(the first of January is New Year's)
-el primero de mayo es fiesta
(the first of May is a holiday)

Ordinal numbers are used to indicate the floors of a building:

-¿a qué piso va? *(what floor are you going to?)*
-voy al tercero *(I am going to the third one)*
-¿en qué piso vive? *(on what floor do you live?)*
-vivo en el quinto piso *(I live on the fifth floor)*

Unlike in the United States, cities in Spanish-speaking countries do not have numbered streets (First Street, Second Avenue, etc).

To indicate the order of events in a story or instructions, you can use the word 'primero' but time adverbs (not ordinal numbers) are used after that to describe the sequence:

-primero, enciende el televisor *(first, turn on the TV)*
-luego, pulsa el botón rojo *(then, press the red button)*
-después, selecciona el programa que deseas
(later, select the program you want)
-y finalmente, presiona 'enter' *(and finally, press 'enter')*

Ejercicio C

Write the appropriate ordinal number to complete this conversation between two people in an elevator. Follow the clues in parentheses.

- Buenos días, ¿a qué piso? *(what floor?)*

- Buenos días, al ____________________ (**3**) piso. ¿Y usted?

- Yo voy al ____________________ (**7**).

- En ese piso está la señora Marcela, ¿verdad?

- Sí, yo soy su primo. Yo también vivo aquí *(I also live here).*

- ¿Ah, sí? ¿En qué piso?

- Yo vivo en el ____________________ (**9**) y mis padres viven en el ____________________ (**4**) piso.

- Ah, qué bien… yo tengo familia en el ____________________ (**1**) piso.

Answers C: **1)** tercer / **2)** séptimo / **3)** noveno / **4)** cuarto / **5)** primer

OTROS ANIMALES *(Other animals)*

Mamíferos

coyote

lobo

zorro

oso

ciervo/venado

ardilla

leopardo

mono

jirafa

cebra

gorila

pantera

camello

tigre

león

canguro

elefante

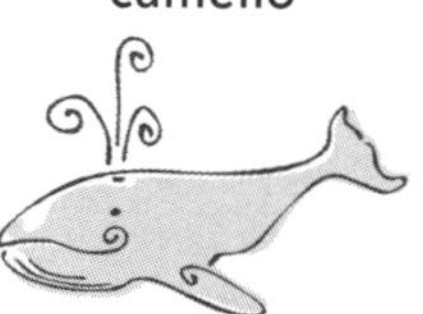
ballena

delfín

rata

UNIDAD 7

Animales de granja

cabra

oveja

burro/asno

vaca

toro

gallina

gallo

mula

buey

cerdo[3]

Pájaros e insectos

pato

águila

búho

paloma

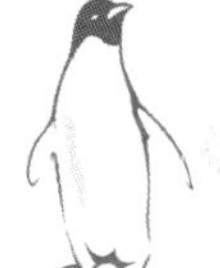
pingüino

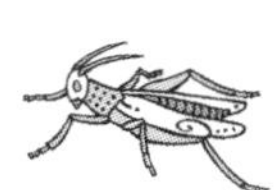
grillo

mosca

escorpión

mariposa

mosquito

avispa

cucaracha

abeja

gusano

Peces, anfibios y reptiles

tiburón

pulpo

cangrejo

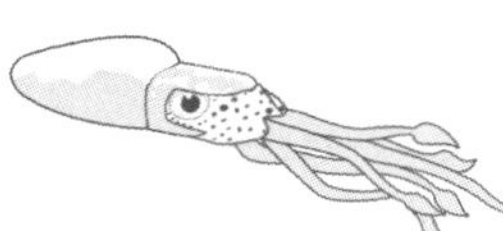
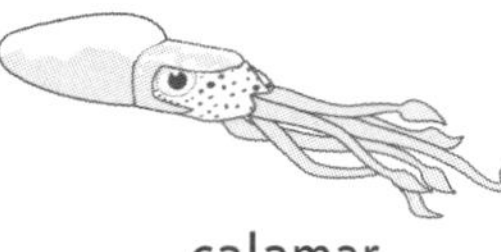
calamar

camarón/gamba

cocodrilo

caimán

sapo

[Footnotes]

[3] Other words for 'cerdo' are 'puerco,' 'cochino,' 'chancho,' and 'marrano.' These words are also used as an insult to describe somebody who is very dirty. The piglet, which is a culinary delicacy, is called 'lechón' or 'cochinillo.'

Ejercicio D

Match the following animals with their description.

1) león	a) es el terror del Mar Caribe
2) lobo	b) duerme *(sleeps)* por el día y trabaja *(works)* de noche
3) elefante	c) es el esposo de la gallina
4) tiburón	d) es el símbolo de los Demócratas de Estados Unidos
5) mariposa	e) es el rey *(king)* de la selva *(jungle)*
6) búho	f) vive *(lives)* en Australia
7) toro	g) es similar al perro
8) burro	h) primero es un gusano feo
9) gallo	i) tiene una trompa *(trunk)* muy larga
10) canguro	j) es el esposo de la vaca

Answers D: **1)** - e) / **2)** - g) / **3)** - i) / **4)** - a) / **5)** - h) / **6)** - b) / **7)** - j) / **8)** - d) / **9)** - c) / **10)** - f)

Ejercicio E

List as many animals as you can remember (including pets) that fulfill the following conditions.

1) Viven *(live)* en el agua solamente *(only)*:

____

____

2) Viven en una jaula:

____

____

3) Viven en el desierto *(desert)*:

____

____

4) Vuelan *(fly)*:

____

____

5) Tienen cuernos *(have horns)*:

____

____

6) Tienen veneno *(poison)*:

____

____

Possible answers E: **1)** pez, ballena, delfín, tiburón, pulpo, cangrejo, calamar, camarón / **2)** pájaro, hámster, conejo, serpiente / **3)** coyote, camello, escorpión, serpiente, araña / **4)** pájaro, águila, pato, búho, mosca, paloma, pingüino, mariposa, mosquito / **5)** toro, vaca, buey, cabra / **6)** araña, serpiente, escorpión, avispa, abeja

MI LISTA DE VOCABULARIO

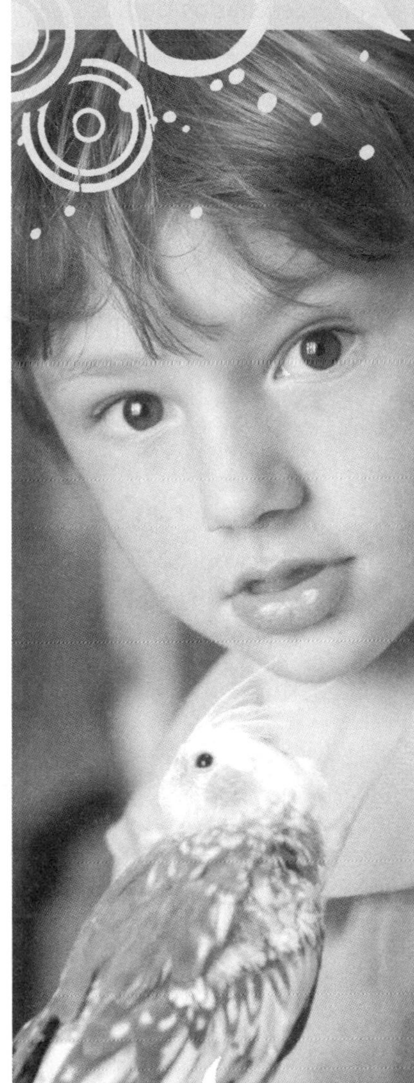

This is a list of the words that you have learned in this unit.

(la) abeja[4]	(el) calamar
(el) acuario	(el) camarón o (la) gamba
(el) agua[5]	(el) camello
(el) águila	(el) cangrejo
(el) anfibio	(el) canguro
(el) animal	(la) cebra
aquel, aquella,	(el) cerdo /(la) cerda
aquellos, aquellas	(el) ciervo /(la) cierva
aquél, aquélla,	(el) cocodrilo
aquéllos, aquéllas	(el) columpio
(la) araña	(el) conejo/(la) coneja
(la) ardilla	(el) coyote
(la) avispa	cuarto
(la) ballena	(la) cucaracha
(el) buey	décimo
(el) búho	decimoprimero, etc
(el) burro o (el) asno	(el) delfín
/(la) burra	después
(el) caballo/(la) yegua	(el) elefante/(la) elefanta
(la) cabra	(el) escorpión
(el) caimán	ese, esa, esos, esas

[Footnotes]

[4] *Many animals only have one form for both male and females. Thus, to specify gender, you might have to add the word 'macho' (male) or 'hembra' (female). Example: la ardilla hembra y la ardilla macho.*

[5] *'Agua' is a feminine noun. However, it takes the masculine article 'el' to break up the long 'a' sound that would occur with 'el agua.' Other words with this characteristic are: el águila, el ánima, el ala, el ama.*

ése, ésa, ésos, ésas
(el) establo
este, esta, estos, estas
éste, ésta, éstos, éstas
esto, eso, aquello
finalmente
(el) gallo/(la) gallina
(el) gato/(la) gata
(el) gorila
(la) granja
(el) grillo
(el) gusano
(la) jaula
(el) hámster[6]
(el) insecto
(la) jirafa
(el) juguete
(el) león/(la) leona
(el) leopardo
(el) lobo/(la) loba

luego
(el) mamífero
(la) mariposa
(la) mascota
(el) mono/(la) mona
(la) mosca
(el) mosquito
noveno
octavo
(el) oso/(la) osa
(la) oveja
(el) pájaro
(el) palomo/(la) paloma
(la) pantera
(el) pato/(la) pata
(la) pecera
(el) perro/(la) perra
(el) pez
(el) pingüino
(el) piso

primero
(la) pulga
(el) pulpo
quinto
(la) rata
(el) reptil
(el) rey/(la) reina
(el) sapo
segundo
(la) selva
séptimo
(la) serpiente
sexto
tercero
(el) tiburón
(el) tigre/(la) tigresa
(el) toro/(la) vaca
(la) tortuga
(la) trompa
(el) veterinario/
(la) veterinaria
vigésimo
(el) zorro/(la) zorra

[Footnotes]

[6] *Although the letter 'h' is never pronounced in Spanish, it is pronounced softly here, because this word is a linguistic loan from German.*

UN POCO DE CULTURA

La llama

The llama is an herbivorous animal that originated in North America and which currently is found in Peru, Bolivia, Argentina, and Chile. It is a mammal from the camel family that was domesticated and used by the Incas for transportation and wool. The llama is usually a docile, curious and social animal, but if it gets angry or if its pack load is too heavy, it might spit in your face. Llamas are known to live up to 20 years or so. There are 3.5 million left in South America.

El jaguar

The jaguar is the third largest of the big cats, after the tiger and the lion. Its habitat extends from Mexico to Argentina and includes everything from jungle to open terrain. Although similar in appearance to the leopard, the jaguar is heavier, has stockier limbs, and has larger and fewer spots. In the Mayan culture (southern Mexico and Guatemala) the jaguar was believed to be a mediator between the living and the dead and a representation of the underworld (which is associated with ancestors and the origin of water and plants). Often, Mayan shamans used the symbol of the jaguar in their religious ceremonies, and many Mayan rulers adopted the name 'jaguar' (Balam) in their own names to denote strength and pride, as shown in the movie *Apocalipto* (2006, USA) by Mel Gibson. In the Aztec culture (Central Mexico) the jaguar was an important symbol of authority and courage for warriors in battle and hunting.

El coquí

The coquí is an amphibian typical of Puerto Rico that also lives on the American continents. It is similar to a frog and its singing (used as a female mating call and to establish territory) rocks *puertorriqueños* to sleep and enchants tourists. Puerto Ricans are very proud and protective of their coquíes, and have created numerous myths and legends about them.

RECOMENDACIÓN PARA ESTA UNIDAD

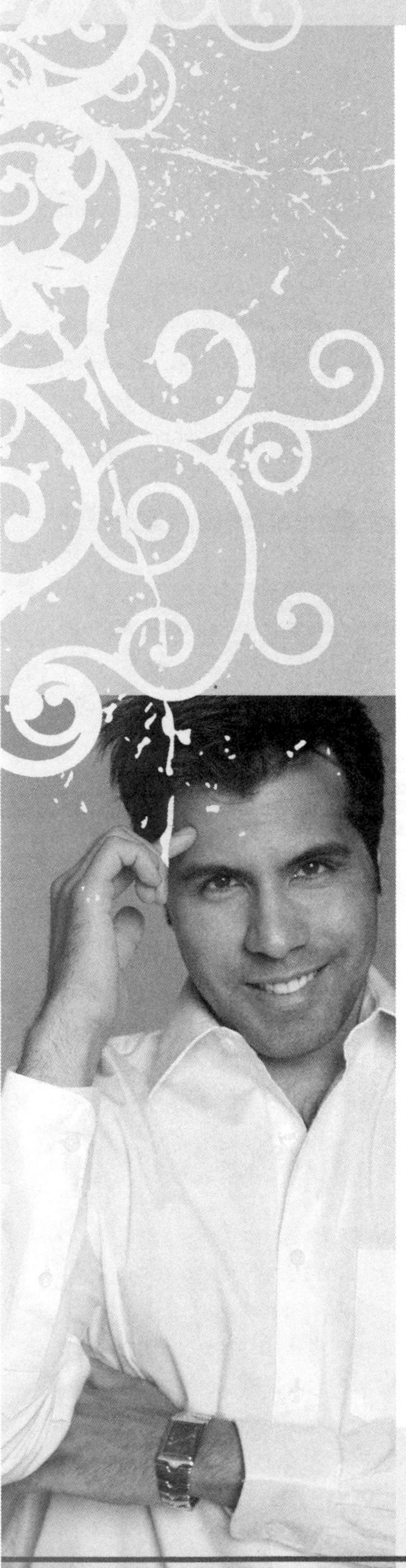

To finish this unit, we give you a recommendation about accent marks (also called 'tildes'):

When learning a word that has an accent mark, make sure you always write this accent mark every time you write the word. Otherwise, it will be difficult to remember which words have accent marks and which ones do not. If you want to know the basic rules about accentuation in Spanish, here is a simple[7] explanation:

1) If the stress is located on the last syllable, and the word ends in -n, -s, or -a vowel, write an accent. If it ends in anything else, do not write an accent.

canción   mamá   universidad   trabajar

2) If the stress is located on the second to last syllable, and the word ends in -n, -s, or -a vowel, do not write an accent. If it ends in anything else, write an accent.

lápiz   útil   ventana   madres

3) If the stress is located on the third to last syllable or before, always write an accent.

música   práctico   rápido   básico

Remember that monosyllables do not have written accents [unless they need to be distinguished from another monosyllable that means something different: tú (you)/tu (your)].

sol   mar   Dios   pez

[Footnotes]

[7] This explanation is very simple, but sufficient for now. The rules have numerous exceptions and other nuances.

UNIDAD 8 CONTENIDO

EXÁMEN 1

exámen 1

EXÁMEN 1

In this unit, you will find several exercises to practice what you have learned in the first seven units. If you do well in this first exam, go ahead and continue studying the following units. If you are not satisfied with the results, we recommend that you review the first seven units again before proceeding.

Ejercicio A

Write the name of the animals that correspond to the following descriptions. Include the article (el, la, los, las). The first one is done for you.

1) Son mamíferos similares al hombre: los monos

2) Este insecto es el amigo de Pinocchio: ____________

3) Es un animal que tiene *(has)* el cuello *(neck)* muy largo *(long)*: ____________

4) Es un felino que acompaña *(goes)* a Dorothy en el Mago de Oz: ____________

5) Es un animal que vive *(lives)* en el agua y es muy amistoso *(friendly)*: ____________

6) Este animal se llama Yogi y vive en los bosques de Estados Unidos: ____________

7) Estos roedores *(rodents)* feos viven cerca de la basura *(garbage)*: ____________

8) Este animal es el mejor amigo del hombre: ____________

Answers A: **2)** el grillo / **3)** la jirafa / la llama / **4)** el león / **5)** el delfín / **6)** el oso / **7)** las ratas / **8)** el perro

Ejercicio B

Select the best translation for these demonstrative adjectives and pronouns.

1) __________ fotografía es muy bonita.

a) Ésta	b) Esta	c) Este	d) Éste

2) En __________ casa viven 7 personas.

a) esa	b) esas	c) ésa	d) ésas

3) __________ son mis padres.

a) Aquellos	b) Aquel	c) Aquéllos	d) Aquél

4) No comprendo __________.

a) esto	b) este	c) estos	d) éstos

5) __________ animales son roedores, pero __________ no.

a) Estos/Esos	b) Éstos/ésos	c) Estos/ésos	d) Éstos/esos

Answers B: **1)** - b) / **2)** - a) / **3)** - c) / **4)** - a) / **5)** - c)

Ejercicio C

Ana is trying to find out on which floor of the mall certain stores are located. Complete the sentences with the appropriate ordinal numbers.

1) El restaurante está en el ____________ *(first)* piso.

2) Los baños públicos están en el ____________ *(third)* piso y en el ____________ *(fifth)* piso.

3) La joyería *(jewelry store)* está en el ____________ *(sixth)*.

4) La tienda de Disney está en el ____________ *(first)* también *(also)*.

5) La tienda de ropa de mujeres está en el ____________ *(fourth)* piso.

Answers C: **1)** primer / **2)** tercer - quinto / **3)** sexto / **4)** primero / **5)** cuarto

Ejercicio D

Write down the word that corresponds to the following family members.

1) El hijo de mi tío es mi ____________

2) Los padres de mis padres son mis ____________

3) La esposa de mi hijo es mi ____________

4) La mamá de mi hermanastro es mi ____________

5) Las hermanas de mi padre son mis ____________

Answers D: **1)** primo / **2)** abuelos / **3)** nuera / **4)** madrastra / **5)** tías

Ejercicio E

Translate these sentences about the family.

1) My parents are retired

____

2) They (masc.) are twins

____

3) They (fem.) do not have children

____

4) John is an only child

____

5) She is the oldest daughter

____

Answers E: **1)** Mis padres están jubilados / **2)** Ellos son gemelos / **3)** Ellas no tienen hijos / **4)** John es hijo único / **5)** Ella es la hija mayor

Ejercicio F

Claudia and Lina are talking about their families. Write the appropriate possessive adjectives so that the conversation makes sense. The first one is done for you.

Claudia:	Mis **(1)** padres se llaman Leonor y Eduardo, ¿y ________ **(2)** padres?
Lina:	Gerardo y Gabriela. Oye, qué foto tan bonita tienes aquí. ¿Estas personas de la foto son ________ **(3)** primos?
Claudia:	Sí, son mis primos. Tengo muchos.
Lina:	¿Cómo se llama este primo tan atractivo?
Claudia:	Éste es ________ **(4)** primo Paco y éstas son ________ **(5)** primas Verónica e Inés, que *(who)* son ________ **(6)** hermanas.
Lina:	¿Y esta persona de aquí es la madre de Verónica, Inés y Paco?
Claudia:	Sí, es ________ **(7)** madre, o sea *(that is)*, ________ **(8)** tía Roberta.

Answers F: **2)** tus / **3)** tus / **4)** mi / **5)** mis / **6)** sus / **7)** su / **8)** mi

Ejercicio G

Write the name of the typical color of these items. Articles are not necessary.

1) __________ **2)** __________ **3)** __________ **4)** __________ **5)** __________

Answers G: **1)** naranja o anaranjado / **2)** verde / **3)** dorado o amarillo / **4)** rojo / **5)** blanco

Ejercicio H

Federico and Juan Carlos are talking about the things they have. Complete their conversation with the appropriate form of 'ser' or 'estar'.

Federico: Mi casa __________ (**1**) más grande que tu apartamento.

Juan Carlos: Sí, pero mi coche __________ (**2**) mejor que tu coche.

Federico: ¿Por qué *(Why)* __________ (**3**) tan orgulloso de tu coche?

Juan Carlos: Porque __________ (**4**) un coche japonés y funciona perfectamente.

Federico: ¿Dónde *(Where)* __________ (**5**) tu coche ahora?

Juan Carlos: Mi coche __________ (**6**) cerca de mi apartamento. Vivo *(I live)* con otras personas. Ellos __________ (**7**) chilenos.

Federico: Ah, qué interesante. Yo __________ (**8**) casado y vivo con mi esposa y mis hijos.

Juan Carlos: Ah, sí….. Tu esposa __________ (**9**) profesora, ¿verdad?

Federico: Sí, y mis hijos __________ (**10**) estudiantes.

Answers H: **1)** es / **2)** es / **3)** estás / **4)** es / **5)** está / **6)** está / **7)** son / **8)** estoy o soy / **9)** es / **10)** son

Ejercicio I

Translate the following sentences using the appropriate comparison structures.

1) My father works as much as your (tu) father.

____

2) Our cousins are as handsome as his cousins. [all male cousins]

____

3) My great-grandmother is older than my great-grandfather.

____

4) I am younger than you (tú).

____

5) You (usted) are more nervous than I.

____

6) My house is your (plural) house.

____

7) They (fem.) have as many cars as we (fem.) do.

____

Answers I: **1)** Mi padre trabaja tanto como tu padre / **2)** Nuestros primos son tan guapos como sus primos / **3)** Mi bisabuela es mayor que mi bisabuelo / **4)** (Yo) soy menor que tú / **5)** Usted está más nervioso que yo / **6)** Mi casa es su casa / **7)** Ellas tienen tantos coches como nosotras

Ejercicio J

Describe these people with a couple of adjectives.
Make sure the agreement is done correctly. The first one is done for you.

Possible answers J: **2)** la mujer es delgada y rubia / **3)** la mujer es vieja y fea / **4)** la niña es guapa - bonita y pequeña / **5)** el hombre es fuerte, bajo, y moreno

Ejercicio K

Write down as many adjectives describing personality as you can remember.

1) Positive adjectives:

____

____

____

____

____

2) Negative adjectives:

____

____

____

____

____

Possible answers K: **1)** agradable, sincero, trabajador, honesto, inteligente, humilde, generoso, cómico, interesante, simpático, etc. / **2)** egoísta, ignorante, orgulloso, aburrido, pesimista, serio, estúpido, desagradable, antipático, vago, etc. [you should know a minimum of 5 in each section]

Ejercicio L

How would you feel in the following situations? Write at least one adjective per sentence (the masculine, singular form is OK).

1) When you are about to take an exam:

____

2) When you are watching a dull movie:

____

3) When you receive good news:

____

4) When you receive bad news:

____

5) When you have many things to do and little time:

____

6) When you are in the hospital:

____

7) When you are getting a massage:

____

Possible answers L: **1)** nervioso / **2)** aburrido / **3)** contento, feliz / **4)** triste, deprimido, enojado / **5)** ocupado, frustrado / **6)** enfermo / **7)** calmado, tranquilo, contento, relajado

Ejercicio M

Complete these sentences with the appropriate adjective denoting nationality. Don't forget the agreement.

1) Vera y Luisa son (Argentina)

____

2) Luis y Juan son (Perú)

____

3) Tomás es (España)

____

4) Roberto es (Venezuela)

____

5) Daniel y Jaime son (Nicaragua)

____

Answers M: **1)** argentinas / **2)** peruanos / **3)** español / **4)** venezolano / **5)** nicaragüenses

Ejercicio N

Write the main language spoken in the following places.

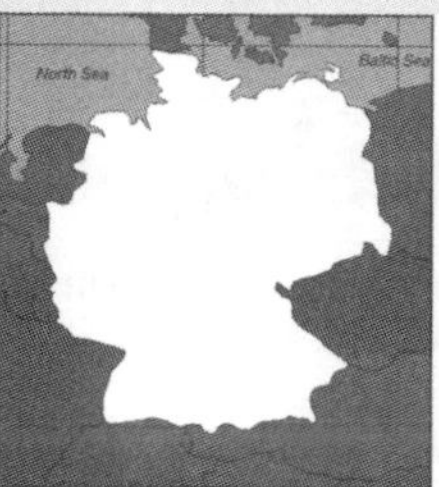

1) ________ **2)** ________ **3)** ________ **4)** ________ **5)** ________

Answers N: **1)** italiano / **2)** japonés / **3)** alemán / **4)** portugués / **5)** árabe/hebreo

Ejercicio Ñ

Provide the following information about your best friend.

1) Domicilio: ____________

2) Nº de teléfono: ____________

3) Apellidos: ____________

4) Correo electrónico: ____________

5) Estado civil: ____________

Answers Ñ: **1)** Provide your address / **2)** your telephone number / **3)** your last name(s) / **4)** your e-mail address / **5)** your marital status (feminine for women, masculine for men)

Ejercicio O

Write the definite article (el, la, los, las) that goes with each of these nouns.

1) ____ noche

2) ____ día

3) ____ ventanas

4) ____ caballo

5) ____ universidad

6) ____ profesores

7) ____ chica

8) ____ bolígrafo

Answers O: **1)** la / **2)** el / **3)** las / **4)** el / **5)** la / **6)** los / **7)** la / **8)** el

Ejercicio P

Write the best response to these greetings.

1) Mucho gusto ____________

2) Buenos días ____________

3) Adiós ____________

4) ¿Cómo está? ____________

5) ¿Qué pasa? ____________

Possible answers P: **1)** mucho gusto - el gusto es mío - encantado / **2)** buenos días - hola **3)** adiós - hasta luego - chau - hasta pronto - etc / **4)** bien, gracias / **5)** no mucho

UNIDAD 9

CONTENIDO

In this unit, you will learn:

1 - The days of the week

2 - About subject pronouns

3 - About regular -AR verbs

4 - The numbers from 0 to 30

5 - Cultural information about the number of Hispanics/Latinos in the United States

los días de la semana

LOS DÍAS DE LA SEMANA

(The days of the week)

Peter is looking at his calendar to figure out the things he needs to do the first week of his new job. On the calendar, there is an explanation about the origin of the Spanish names of the days of the week.

LUNES[1]	de 08:00 a 18:00[2]
MARTES	de 09:00 a 18:00
MIÉRCOLES	de 09:00 a 18:00
JUEVES	de 09:00 a 18:00
VIERNES	de 08:00 a 17:00
SÁBADO	No trabajo
DOMINGO	No trabajo

lunes:	De la luna *(named after the moon)* del planeta Tierra
martes:	Del planeta Marte
miércoles:	Del planeta Mercurio
jueves:	Del planeta Júpiter
viernes:	Del planeta Venus
sábado:	De la fiesta judía *(Jewish holy day)* Shábbath
domingo:	Del latín 'dominicus' (del Señor) *(of God)*

[Footnotes]

[1] The week in the calendar starts on Monday in all Spanish-speaking countries, except for Argentina, where it starts on Sunday, like in the U.S.

[2] Military time is common in Spanish-speaking countries. The abbreviations 'am' and 'pm' are not used.

Here are Peter's notes for this week:

EL **LUNES**

-es el primer día de trabajo *(work)*

-los lunes *(on Mondays)* yo llego temprano *(I arrive early)*, a las 08:00

-hablo con mi jefe y con otros empleados *(I talk to my boss and to other employees)*

EL **MARTES**

-preparo *(I prepare)* unos documentos para el departamento de Recursos Humanos *(department of Human Resources)*

EL **MIÉRCOLES**

-busco *(I look for)* información sobre *(about)* mi trabajo

-converso[3] *(chat)* con mi jefe sobre mis responsabilidades *(my responsibilities)*

EL **JUEVES**

-compro *(I buy)* cosas que necesito *(things that I need)*

-empiezo *(I start)* mi trabajo

EL **VIERNES**

-llego temprano

-trabajo hasta *(I work until)* las 17:00

-la empresa me paga un viernes sí y otro no *(the company pays me every other Friday)*

EL **SÁBADO**

-descanso todo el día *(I rest all day)*

-los sábados por la tarde normalmente *(usually)* mi amigo Juan y yo practicamos *(Juan and I practice)* tenis en el gimnasio *(gym)*

EL **DOMINGO**

-llamo *(I call)* a mis padres, que viven *(who live)* en Miami

-también *(also)* visito *(I visit)* a mi amiga Pilar en el hospital

-tres domingos al mes *(three Sundays per month)* voy a la iglesia *(I go to church)*

[Footnotes]

[3] Another word for 'conversar', especially popular in Mexico, is 'platicar.'

LOS DÍAS DE LA SEMANA

(The days of the week)

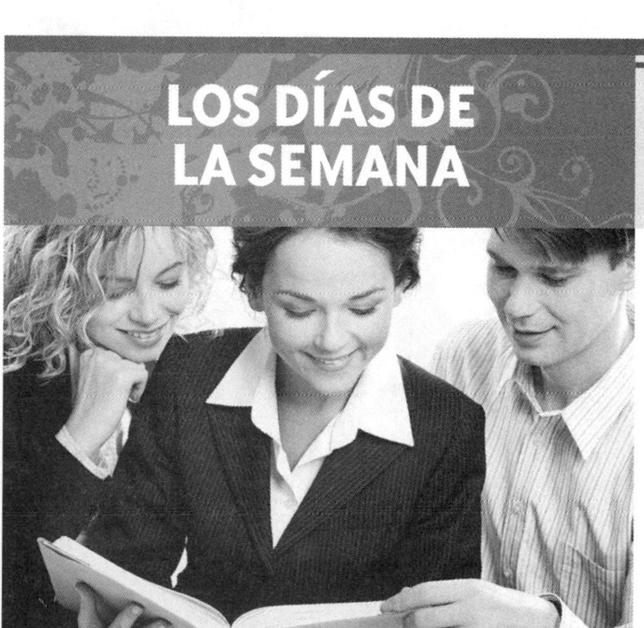

The preposition 'on' (on Monday, on Fridays, etc) turns into the definite article in Spanish (el lunes, los viernes, etc.). The days of the week are not capitalized in Spanish. The plural forms of Monday – Friday are the same as the singular, but the article shows plurality (el lunes, los lunes). However, Saturday and Sunday have regular plural forms (el sábado, los sábados/el domingo, los domingos).

Ejercicio A

According to the previous account, describe what Peter has to do every day of this week. Watch out! Instead of writing in the first person singular (yo), as Peter did, write in the third person (él). To do this, change the ending of the infinitive (-ar) into an -a. The first one is done for you.

El lunes es el primer día de trabajo *(work)*. Los lunes *(on Mondays)* Peter llega (**1**. llegar) temprano, a las 08:00. Él *(He)* ___________ (**2**. hablar) con su jefe y con otros empleados.

El martes Peter _______________ (**3**. preparar) unos documentos para el departamento de Recursos Humanos.

El miércoles, él ________________ (**4**. buscar) información sobre su trabajo y ________________ (**5**. conversar) con su jefe sobre sus responsabilidades.

El jueves, _________________ (**6**. comprar) cosas que ________________ (**7**. necesitar) y empieza su trabajo.

El viernes ____________________ (**8**. llegar) temprano. __________________ (**9**. trabajar) hasta las 17:00. La empresa le paga un viernes sí y otro no.

El sábado Peter ___________________ (**10**. descansar) todo el día. Los sábados por la tarde normalmente su amigo Juan y él practican tenis en el gimnasio.

El domingo él ___________________ (**11**. llamar) a sus padres, que viven en Miami. También ___________________ (**12**. visitar) a su amiga Pilar en el hospital. Tres domingos al mes, Peter va a la iglesia.

Answers A: **2)** habla / **3)** prepara / **4)** busca / **5)** conversa / **6)** compra / **7)** necesita / **8)** llega / **9)** trabaja / **10)** descansa / **11)** llama / **12)** visita

PRONOMBRES PERSONALES *(Subject pronouns)*

As you already saw in the conjugations of 'ser' and 'estar,' there are different subject pronouns with which we need to become familiar.

Tú: In many countries, 'tú' is the direct address used with another person in informal situations (e.g., a friend), with a young person, or with a person of inferior 'status.' In many countries, the word 'vos'[4] is used instead of 'tú':

Tú eres un niño malo (standard Spanish)
Vos sos un niño malo (Costa Rica, Argentina, etc)

Usted: In most countries, 'usted' is the direct address used with another person in formal situations (e.g., a professor), or with an older person, or with a person you do not know. In order to distinguish 'tú' from 'usted,' the 'usted' form uses the third person singular conjugation of any verb. That's why you always see 'usted' on the third line of a conjugation table, right next to él and ella.

Tú eres muy simpático (informal)
Usted es muy simpático (formal)

It: Since everything must be feminine or masculine in Spanish, there is no subject pronoun for 'it.' When you want to translate 'it,' just ignore it.

It is big *(Es grande)*

Vosotros/as[5]: This form is only used in Spain to address a group of people in informal situations. In other countries, the form 'ustedes' is used for both informal and formal situations.

Vosotros sois franceses (Spain) (informal)

Ustedes son franceses (Latin America) (formal & informal)

PRONOMBRES PERSONALES	*SUBJECT PRONOUNS*
yo	*I*
tú / vos *(informal)*	*you (sing.)*
usted *(formal)*	*you (sing.)*
él	*he*
ella	*she*
—	*it*
nosotros	*we (masc. or masc.+ fem.)*
nosotras	*we (fem.)*
vosotros *(informal in Spain)*	*you (plural)*
vosotras *(informal in Spain)*	*you (plural)*
ustedes *(informal and formal in Latin America)*	*you (plural)[6]*
ellos	*they (masc. or masc.+ fem.)*
ellas	they (fem.)

[Footnotes]

[4] Since the pronoun 'tú' is considered standard, we will focus on 'tú' in this book and will not have exercises with 'vos' after this unit.
[5] Since this pronoun is only used in one country (Spain), we will focus on the more general 'ustedes' form and will not use 'vosotros' in exercises after this unit.
[6] You guys, you all.

Ejercicio B

Write the Spanish subject pronoun that corresponds to each group of people.

1) I ____________

2) John & I ____________

3) John & Paul ____________

4) My aunts ____________

5) My parents and you ____________ (Spain) ____________ (Latin Am.)

6) You guys (fem.) ____________ (Spain) ____________ (Latin Am.)

7) Jennifer ____________

8) Jennifer and Eva ____________

9) Alexander ____________

10) You ________ / ________ (informal) ____________ (formal)

Answers B: **1)** yo / **2)** nosotros / **3)** ellos / **4)** ellas / **5)** vosotros - ustedes / **6)** vosotras - ustedes / **7)** ella / **8)** ellas / **9)** él / **10)** tú - vos - usted

LOS VERBOS TERMINADOS EN -AR

(The -AR finished verbs)

In Spanish, all verbs end in either **-ar**, **-er**, or **-ir** in their infinitive form (to sing, to talk, etc). In this unit, we will see the conjugation of regular -AR verbs only.

As you can see, each conjugated form is different; that's why it is not necessary to write out the subject pronoun. To conjugate a verb, you have to drop the infinitive ending (-ar) and add the appropriate conjugated ending (-o, -as, -a, -amos, -áis, -an for present tense):

— Peter works at the office. Later, he talks to his boss.
— Peter trabaja en la oficina.
— Después, (él) habla con su jefe.

HABLAR *(presente)*	***TO TALK*** *(present tense)*
(yo) habl**o**	*I talk*
(tú) habl**as**	*you talk*
(él, ella) (usted) habl**a**	*he, she, it talks*
(nosotros, -as) habl**amos**	*we talk*
(vosotros, -as) habl**áis**	*you (guys) talk*
(ellos, ellas) (ustedes) habl**an**	they talk

Ejercicio C

Match the beginning of these sentences with an appropriate ending. Focus on the verb endings to help you match them up.

1) Yo	a) siempre *(always)* llega tarde
2) Nosotros no	b) preparo la cena esta noche *(tonight)*
3) Mis amigos	c) no trabajáis los domingos
4) Tú	d) buscan *(look for)* buenos restaurantes
5) Lucía	e) hablamos griego
6) Vosotros	f) no descansas de lunes a viernes

Answers C: **1)** - b) / **2)** - e) / **3)** - d) / **4)** - f) / **5)** - a) / **6)** - c)

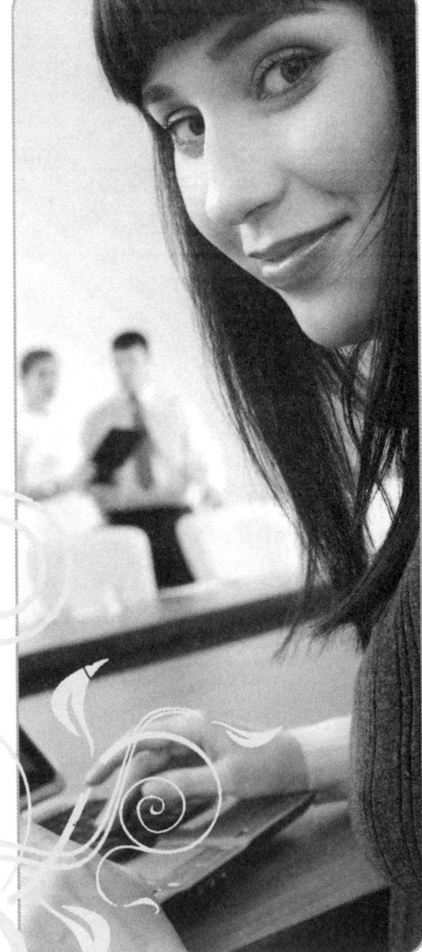

Ejercicio D

Following the model of the conjugation of 'hablar', conjugate the following regular -AR verbs.

	COMPRAR *(to buy)*	LLEGAR *(to arrive)*	TRABAJAR *(to work)*
yo			
tú			
él, ella/usted			
nosotros, nosotras			
vosotros, vosotras			
ellos, ellas/ustedes			

Answers D: **1)** COMPRAR: compro, compras, compra, compramos, compráis, compran / **2)** LLEGAR: llego, llegas, llega, llegamos, llegáis, llegan / **3)** TRABAJAR: trabajo, trabajas, trabaja, trabajamos, trabajáis, trabajan

Ejercicio E

Complete the following sentences with the correct conjugation of the verbs in parentheses. Remember to drop the -ar and add the ending that corresponds to the subject.

1) Juan y yo ________ (practicar) tenis en el gimnasio.

2) Yo ________ (visitar) a mi amiga Pilar.

3) Ustedes ________ (preparar) la comida *(food)*.

4) Sonia ________ (comprar) muchas cosas en las tiendas *(stores)*.

5) Tú no ________ (trabajar) por la noche.

6) Jesús siempre ________ (llegar) tarde.

7) Nosotras no ________ (descansar) mucho.

8) Vosotros ________ (conversar) en español.

9) Usted ________ (hablar) español muy bien.

10) Ustedes ________ (visitar) España en verano *(summer)*.

Answers E: **1)** practicamos / **2)** visito / **3)** preparan / **4)** compra / **5)** trabajas / **6)** llega / **7)** descansamos / **8)** conversáis / **9)** habla / **10)** visitan

OTROS VERBOS REGULARES -AR

ayudar *(to help)*	bailar *(to dance)*
caminar *(to walk)*	cantar *(to sing)*
enseñar *(to teach)*	escuchar *(to listen)*
estudiar *(to study)*	mirar *(to look, to watch)*
necesitar *(to need)*	regresar *(to return)*
tomar *(to take, to drink)*	viajar *(to travel)*

Ejercicio F

Translate the following sentences with the vocabulary that you know and the new verbs that you just learned. Make sure to select the appropriate ending for each verb. You do not need to use 'vos' or 'vosotros/as' from now on.

1) I dance salsa.

2) You (tú) don't sing well.

3) He studies Spanish.

4) She travels a lot.

5) Usually, we return early.

6) You (ustedes) need information.

7) They (fem.) watch television.

8) They (masc.) drink coffee.

9) You (usted) take an exam today *(hoy)*.

10) My father and I travel a lot *(mucho)*.

Answers F: **1)** Yo bailo salsa. / **2)** Tú no cantas muy bien. / **3)** Él estudia español. / **4)** Ella viaja mucho. / **5)** Normalmente, nosotros regresamos temprano. / **6)** Ustedes necesitan información. / **7)** Ellas miran televisión. / **8)** Ellos toman café. / **9)** Usted toma un examen hoy. / **10)** Mi padre y yo viajamos mucho.

NÚMEROS DEL 0 AL 30 *(Numbers from 0 to 30)*

Numbers from 16 to 19 and from 21 to 29 are generally written in one word, but they can also be found in their traditional three-word spelling.

Numbers from 0 to 30

0.	cero[7]	16.	dieciséis (diez y seis)
1.	uno[8]	17.	diecisiete (diez y siete)
2.	dos	18.	dieciocho (diez y ocho)
3.	tres	19.	diecinueve (diez y nueve)
4.	cuatro	20.	veinte
5.	cinco	21.	veintiuno (veinte y uno)
6.	seis	22.	veintidós (veinte y dos)
7.	siete	23.	veintitrés (veinte y tres)
8.	ocho	24.	veinticuatro (veinte y cuatro)
9.	nueve	25.	veinticinco (veinte y cinco)
10.	diez	26.	veintiséis (veinte y seis)
11.	once	27.	veintisiete (veinte y siete)
12.	doce	28.	veintiocho (veinte y ocho)
13.	trece[9]	29.	veintinueve (veinte y nueve)
14.	catorce	30.	treinta
15.	quince		

[Footnotes]

[7] It is believed that the zero was an invention of the Olmec, who lived in Central Mexico, and it was later extensively used by the Maya in their calendars.

[8] When 'uno' accompanies a noun, it drops the -o (un momento). The same happens with 21 31, 41, etc. (veintiún perros).

[9] For Hispanics, the number 13 also represents bad luck, especially if it falls on a Tuesday.

Ejercicio G

Match the following numbers with their correct spelling.

1) 9	a) cinco
2) 17	b) once
3) 5	c) veinte
4) 29	d) tres
5) 20	e) diecisiete
6) 15	f) nueve
7) 17	g) veinticuatro
8) 3	h) veintinueve
9) 11	i) diecisiete
10) 24	j) quince

Answers G: **1)** - f) / **2)** - e) / **3)** - a) / **4)** - h) / **5)** - c) / **6)** - j) / **7)** - e) / **8)** - d) / **9)** - b) / **10)** - g)

Ejercicio H

Write these numbers in Spanish.

1)	25 ________________	**6)**	10 ________________
2)	14 ________________	**7)**	8 ________________
3)	6 ________________	**8)**	26 ________________
4)	28 ________________	**9)**	30 ________________
5)	13 ________________	**10)**	0 ________________

Answers H: **1)** veinticinco / **2)** catorce / **3)** seis / **4)** veintiocho / **5)** trece / **6)** diez / **7)** ocho / **8)** veintiséis - veinte y seis / **9)** treinta / **10)** cero

MI LISTA DE VOCABULARIO

This is a list of the words that you have learned in this unit.

ayudar	(el) documento
bailar	(el) domingo/(los) domingos
buscar	dos
caminar	él/ella
catorce	ellos/ellas
cinco	enseñar
comprar	escuchar
conversar	estudiar
cuatro	(la) fiesta
descansar	(el) gimnasio
(el) día	hablar
diecinueve	(el) hospital
dieciocho	(la) iglesia
dieciséis	(el) jefe/(la) jefa
diecisiete	judío
diez	(el/los) jueves
doce	Júpiter

llegar	quince	uno
(la) luna	regresar	usted/ustedes
(el/los) lunes	(la) responsabilidad	veinte
Marte	(el) sábado/(los) sábados	veinticinco
(el/los) martes	(la) semana	veinticuatro
Mercurio	seis	veintidós
(el) mes	(el) Señor	veintinueve
mirar	siete	veintiocho
(el/los) miércoles	tarde	veintiséis
necesitar	temprano	veintisiete
normalmente	(el) tenis	veintitrés
nosotros/nosotras	(la) Tierra	veintiuno
nueve	tomar	Venus
ocho	trabajar	viajar
once	(el) trabajo	(el/los) viernes
pagar	trece	visitar
(el) planeta	treinta	vosotros/vosotras
practicar	tres	yo
preparar	tú/vos	

UN POCO DE CULTURA

The number of Hispanics / Latinos in the United States

According to the 2000 United States Census Bureau, there are 35,305,818 Hispanics[10] living in the U.S., comprising 12.5% of the U.S. population. Slightly more than half of the Hispanic population (59.7%) was born in the U.S. The reports for 2004 already show that Hispanics number around 40,000,000, evidencing a significant rate of growth in just four years.

Hispanics by Groups

Of that 12.5% recorded in the year 2000, the vast majority were of Mexican descent (7.3%). Several other groups were also represented: Puerto

Ricans (1.2%), Cubans (0.4%) and others (3.6%). More than one third of the Hispanic population (39.2%) was under the age of 21.

Educational Attainment

The educational attainment of Hispanics in the U.S. is lower than that of other ethnic groups and reflects the difficult living conditions and hardships that many experienced during their school years. Reports show that there are more Hispanics without a Bachelor's degree (87.9%) than there are white Americans without a Bachelor's degree (69.4%).

Earnings

Based to the previous information, it is not surprising that Hispanics have a lower income than other groups. Only 9.4% of Hispanics make more than $50,000, compared to the 19.4% of white Americans. Almost one fifth of Hispanics of working age (18-64 years old) live below poverty level[11], compared to 8.2% of white Americans.

Regions

According to the 2000 US Census Bureau, the 10 cities with the highest concentration of Hispanics are: East Los Angeles (97%); Laredo, TX (94%); Brownsville, TX (91%); Hialeah, FL (90%); McAllen, TX (80%); El Paso, TX (77%); Santa Ana, CA (76%); El Monte, CA (72%); Oxnard, CA (66%) and Miami, FL (66%). These reports show that the 10 states with the highest percentages of Hispanic populations are: New Mexico (42.1%), California (32.4%), Texas (32%), Arizona (25.3%), Nevada (19.7%), Colorado (17.1%), Florida (16.8%), New York (15.1%), New Jersey (13.3%), and Illinois (12.3%). Hispanics living in the U.S. live mostly in California (31.1%), Texas (18.9%), New York (8.1%), Florida (7.6%). and Illinois (4.3%).

[Footnotes]

[10] The U.S. Census Bureau does not distinguish between the terms Hispanic and Latino, and it groups foreign-born and U.S.-born Hispanics into the same category.

[11] In 2000, the poverty line for a family of one person was $8,350, of two people $11,250, of three $14,150 and of four $17.050.

RECOMENDACIÓN PARA ESTA UNIDAD

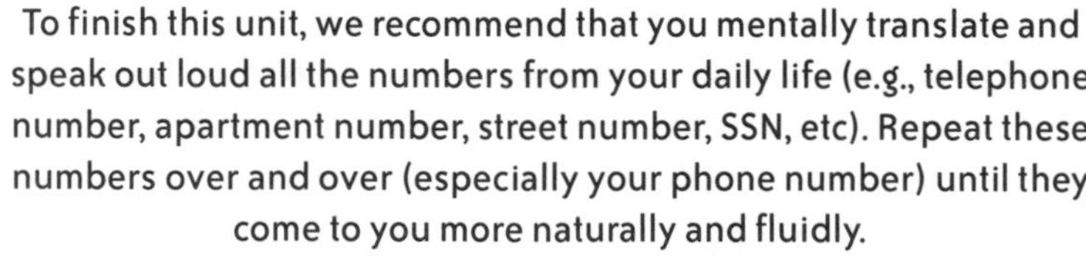

To finish this unit, we recommend that you mentally translate and speak out loud all the numbers from your daily life (e.g., telephone number, apartment number, street number, SSN, etc). Repeat these numbers over and over (especially your phone number) until they come to you more naturally and fluidly.

UNIDAD 10 CONTENIDO

In this unit, you will learn:

1 - How to tell the time

2 - About regular -ER verbs

3 - About regular -IR verbs

4 - The numbers from 31 to 100

5 - Cultural information about the concept of time for Hispanics

LA HORA

(The time)

Peter watches the clock on the wall and realizes it is time for dinner. Do you know how to tell the time in Spanish?

Es[1] la una[2] en punto

Son las cuatro en punto

Son las diez en punto

Es la una y cuarto[3]

Son las tres y cuarto

Son las nueve y cuarto

Es la una y veinticinco[4]

Son las cuatro y diez

Son las nueve y veinte

Es la una y media

Son las cinco y media

Son las once y media

Es la una menos cuarto

Son las siete menos cuarto

Son las tres menos cuarto

Es la una menos veinte

Son las ocho menos diez

Son las doce menos cinco

[Footnotes]

[1] One o'clock is the only hour that uses the verb 'ser' in singular (es) instead of the plural (son).
[2] 'Una' is in feminine because it refers to 'hora,' which is feminine.
[3] People who are used to digital watches prefer to say the number of minutes instead of 'cuarto' and 'media' ('son las cuatro y cuarenta y cinco,' or even 'quedan quince minutos para las cinco').
[4] You can add the word 'minutos' after the number that represents minutes, but not after 'cuarto,' 'en punto,' or 'media.'

Ejercicio A

Select the best answer for each time shown.

1) 3:20
a) Son las tres y veinte
b) Son las tres y dos minutos
c) Quedan 20 para las tres

2) 5:50
a) Son las cinco menos diez
b) Son las seis y cincuenta
c) Son las seis menos diez

3) 1:15
a) Son la una y cuarto
b) Es la una y cuarto
c) Es la una y cuatro

4) 10:30
a) Son las diez y treinta
b) Son las diez y cuarto
c) Son las diez menos cuarto

5) 9:05
a) Son las nueve y cincuenta
b) Son las cinco y nueve
c) Son las nueve y cinco

Answers A: **1)** - a) / **2)** - c) / **3)** - b) / **4)** - a) / **5)** - c)

Ejercicio B

¿Qué hora es? Write down the following times in both analog and digital formats. The first one is done for you.

1) 2:30 *Son las dos y media – Son las dos y treinta*

2) 4:15 ______________________________

3) 7:35 ______________________________

4) 10:55 ______________________________

5) 12:50 ______________________________

6) 1:05 ______________________________

Answers B: **2)** Son las cuatro y cuarto - Son las cuatro y quince / **3)** Son las ocho menos veinticinco (o Quedan 25 para las ocho) - Son las siete y treinta y cinco / **4)** Son las once menos cinco (o Quedan cinco para las once) - Son las diez y cincuenta y cinco / **5)** Es la una menos diez - Son las doce y cincuenta (o Quedan diez para la una) / **6)** Es la una y cinco -Es la una y cinco

EXPRESIONES ÚTILES

[Footnotes]

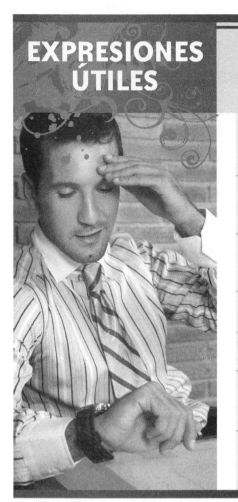

[5] *In México, the expression ¿Qué horas son? is more common.*

¿Qué hora es?[5] *(What time is it?)*	… de la noche *(at night)*
¿Tiene(s) hora? *(Do you have the time?)*	… de la madrugada *(in the morning –between 12:00am and sun rise)*
¿Sabe(s) qué hora es? *(Do you know what time it is?)*	¿A qué hora…..? *((At) what time…?)*
Son las….. *(It is….)*	A las….. *(At….)*
Es la una….. *(It is one….)*	A la una….. *(At one….)*
… de la mañana *(in the morning)*	No tengo reloj *(I don't have a watch)*
… de la tarde *(in the afternoon)*	Mi reloj no funciona *(My watch does not work)*

Ejercicio C

Answer these questions using vocabulary from above.

1) ¿A qué hora almuerzas *(eat lunch)*?

____

____

3) ¿A qué hora regresas a casa?

____

____

2) ¿Tienes hora?

____

____

4) ¿A qué hora preparas la cena?

____

____

Possible Answers C: **1)** Almuerzo a la(s)…. de la tarde / **2)** Sí, son las…. - es la una…. - no tengo reloj - mi reloj no funciona / **3)** Regreso a casa a la(s)… de la noche / **4)** Preparo la cena a la(s)…. de la noche

LOS VERBOS TERMINADOS EN -ER Y -IR

Verbs that end in -ER and -IR have different endings than those that end in -AR, but they are studied together because most -ER and -IR endings are similar (except for the 'nosotros' and 'vosotros' forms). Let's take a look at the conjugation of regular -ER and -IR verbs in the present tense:

BEBER *(to drink)*	**ESCRIBIR** *(to write)*
(yo) beb**o**	(yo) escrib**o**
(tú) beb**es**	(tú) escrib**es**
(él, ella) (usted) beb**e**	(él, ella) (usted) escrib**e**
(nosotros, -as) beb**emos**	(nosotros, -as) escrib**imos**
(vosotros, -as) beb**éis**	(vosotros, -as) escrib**ís**
(ellos, ellas) (ustedes) beb**en**	(ellos, ellas) (ustedes) escrib**en**

Some common regular -ER verbs include:

- aprender *(to learn)*
- beber *(to drink)*
- comer *(to eat)*
- comprender *(to understand)*
- creer *(to believe)*
- leer *(to read)*
- ofender *(to offend)*
- perder *(to lose/to misplace)*
- vender *(to sell)*

Some common regular -IR verbs include:

- escribir *(to write)*
- existir *(to exist)*
- prohibir *(to prohibit)*
- recibir *(to receive)*
- subir *(to go up/to ascend)*
- vivir *(to live)*

Ejercicio D

Match the beginning of each sentence with its logical ending.

1) Yo vivo

2) Los OVNI[6]s *(UFOs)*

3) Mis amigos comen

4) Mis padres no comprenden

5) Ana siempre pierde

6) Vendo un sofá

a) sus llaves *(keys)*

b) por 100 dólares

c) en un apartamento muy bonito

d) no existen

e) español

f) en un restaurante bueno

Answers D: **1)** - c) / **2)** - d) / **3)** - f) / **4)** - e) / **5)** - a) / **6)** - b)

[Footnotes]

[6] *O.V.N.I. stands for Objeto Volador No Identificado (Unidentified Flying Object = UFO).*

Ejercicio E

Complete the following sentences by conjugating the verbs in parentheses.

1) Mis amigos ____________________ (vivir) en España.

2) Los precios del petróleo *(oil)* _____________ (subir) todos los días.

3) Mi hija ____________________ (leer) un libro de Harry Potter.

4) Mi familia y yo ____________________ (comer) a las dos y cuarto.

5) Yo no ____________________ (beber) alcohol.

6) Ustedes ____________________ (vender) muchas cosas.

7) Yo no ____________________ (creer) eso.

8) Tú no ____________________ (comprender) la lección.

9) Antonio ____________________ (escribir) muy bien.

10) Usted ____________________ (aprender) muy rápido.

Answers E: **1)** viven / **2)** suben / **3)** lee / **4)** comemos / **5)** bebo / **6)** venden / **7)** creo / **8)** comprendes / **9)** escribe / **10)** aprende

Ejercicio F

Now translate the previous sentences into English.

1) ____

2) ____

3) ____

4) ____

5) ____

6) ____

7) ____

8) ____

9) ____

10) ____

Answers F: **1)** My friends live in Spain / **2)** The oil prices increase every day / **3)** My daughter reads - is reading a Harry Potter book / **4)** My family and I eat at 2:15pm / **5)** I don't drink alcohol / **6)** You sell a lot of - many things / **7)** I don't think so - I don't believe that / **8)** You don't understand the lesson / **9)** Anthony writes very well / **10)** You learn - are learning very fast

LOS NÚMEROS[7] DEL 31 AL 100

Numbers from 31 to 100

31.	treinta y uno	48.	cuarenta y ocho
32.	treinta y dos	49.	cuarenta y nueve
33.	treinta y tres	50.	cincuenta
34.	treinta y cuatro	51.	cincuenta y uno
35.	treinta y cinco	52.	cincuenta y dos
36.	treinta y seis	53.	cincuenta y tres
37.	treinta y siete	54.	cincuenta y cuatro
38.	treinta y ocho	55.	cincuenta y cinco
39.	treinta y nueve	56.	cincuenta y seis
40.	cuarenta	57.	cincuenta y siete
41.	cuarenta y uno	58.	cincuenta y ocho
42.	cuarenta y dos	59.	cincuenta y nueve
43.	cuarenta y tres	60.	sesenta
44.	cuarenta y cuatro	70.	setenta
45.	cuarenta y cinco	80.	ochenta
46.	cuarenta y seis	90.	noventa
47.	cuarenta y siete	100.	cien

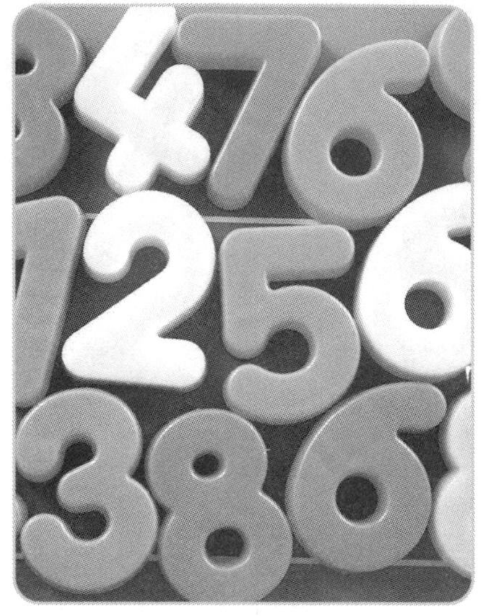

[Footnotes]

[7] In Spanish, the abbreviation of 'number' is Nº (a capital N followed by a small superscript, underlined letter 'o').

** For telephone numbers, many Spanish speakers tend to pair digits (5-39-56-48). If the pair starts with a cero (5-39-**05**-48), then they say 'cero' plus the number.*

Ejercicio G

Match the following numbers with their correct spelling.

1) 37
2) 49
3) 41
4) 65
5) 99
6) 52
7) 72
8) 98
9) 68
10) 83

a) cincuenta y dos
b) sesenta y ocho
c) sesenta y cinco
d) cuarenta y nueve
e) ochenta y tres
f) setenta y dos
g) cuarenta y uno
h) treinta y siete
i) noventa y nueve
j) noventa y ocho

Answers G: **1)** - h) / **2)** - d) / **3)** - g) / **4)** - c) / **5)** - i) / **6)** - a) / **7)** - f) / **8)** - j) / **9)** - b) / **10)** - e)

Ejercicio H

Try to spell out these numbers.

1) 35 ______________________

2) 42 ______________________

3) 49 ______________________

4) 51 ______________________

5) 68 ______________________

6) 73 ______________________

7) 100 ______________________

8) 87 ______________________

9) 90 ______________________

10) 96 ______________________

Answers H: **1)** treinta y cinco / **2)** cuarenta y dos / **3)** cuarenta y nueve / **4)** cincuenta y uno / **5)** sesenta y ocho / **6)** setenta y tres / **7)** cien / **8)** ochenta y siete / **9)** noventa / **10)** noventa y seis

Ejercicio I

Say aloud and then write these telephone numbers. Remember to pair the last six digits. The first one is done for you.

1) 844-0471 *ocho – cuarenta y cuatro – cero cuatro – setenta y uno*

2) 306-5086 ______________________

3) 831-0974 ______________________

4) 623-4692 ______________________

5) your telephone # here ______________________

Answers I: **2)** tres – cero seis – cincuenta – ochenta y seis / **3)** ocho – treinta y uno – cero nueve – setenta y cuatro / **4)** seis – veintitrés – cuarenta y seis – noventa y dos

MI LISTA DE VOCABULARIO

This is a list of the words that you have learned in this unit.

¿a qué hora…? a la una/a las dos	cincuenta (y uno, y dos, y tres, etc)
almorzar	comer
aprender	comprender
beber	creer
(la) cena	cuarenta (y uno, y dos, y tres, etc)
cien	

cuarto	media	sesenta (y uno, y dos, y tres, etc)
de la madrugada	menos	setenta (y uno, y dos, y tres, etc)
de la mañana	noventa (y uno, y dos, y tres, etc)	son las ....
de la noche	ochenta (y uno, y dos, y tres, etc)	subir
de la tarde	ofender	treinta (y uno, y dos, y tres, etc)
en punto	O.V.N.I.	vender
es la una....	perder	vivir
escribir	prohibir	y
existir	¿qué hora es?	
(la) hora	recibir	
leer	(el) reloj	

UN POCO DE CULTURA

The concept of time

The concept of time is very different in Hispanic cultures than in non-Hispanic cultures. In informal situations (e.g., parties, meeting a friend, etc), Hispanic culture does not dictate that you must arrive on time. It is also assumed that there is no specific ending time for such events. Therefore, when you are invited to a party, the invitation will state the starting time, but not the ending time. If you host the party, you will have to stay up until the last guest decides to leave.

Specific activities also fall at different times of the day in Hispanic cultures. For example, in Spain, people eat lunch (the biggest meal) around 2:00pm, a snack around 6:00pm, and then a light dinner around 9:30pm. As a result, restaurants will not open for dinner until 8:00pm or 9:00pm. Prime time television starts at 9:00pm. If you wish to go out at night to a club or to some bars with friends, people do not start crowding these places until around midnight, and start to head home at 4:00am or 5:00am. If you are in the center of Madrid at 2:00am, you might find yourself in the midst of rush hour traffic!

An interesting difference regarding the daily work schedule: in Spain, the split work day is common. Many people leave work around noon to eat lunch at home, and return to work two or three hours later. Thus, stores and museums are often closed between 2:00 and 5:00pm. As a result, people finish working in the early evening, much later than a typical American does. Many people find that this system is beneficial in terms of health and family life, since they eat home-cooked meals, get to see their family frequently, and even have time to take a little nap. In addition, if your children's school also has a split schedule, you can pick them up to eat lunch at home.

In some countries in Latin America, schools can have schedules very different from those in the United States, because there are two shifts for attending school: one starts very early in the morning and the other starts in the afternoon. Schools adopt these shifts because there are many school-aged children in an area, but not enough schools for them all to attend at the same time.

RECOMENDACIÓN PARA ESTA UNIDAD

To finish this unit, we recommend that you follow these suggestions to learn verbal endings. If you are already panicking about how to remember the present-tense regular verbal endings for -AR, -ER, and -IR verbs, wait until you find out that irregular verbs do not follow this pattern or that there are at least thirteen more tenses to study (each one with six different endings)!

Indeed, learning verbal endings is one of the most difficult tasks in Spanish, especially for people whose native language does not have verbal variation. We recommend that, rather than just learning the endings (-o, -as, -a, -amos, etc), you learn an entire verb for -AR (hablo, hablas, habla, hablamos, habláis[8], hablan), an entire verb for -ER (como, comes, come, comemos, coméis, comen) and an entire verb for -IR (vivo, vives, vive, vivimos, vivís, viven). Since it is easier to remember an entire word than random letters, you will find this task much simpler.

Let's try it. Repeat aloud the entire conjugation of HABLAR a few times and then try to conjugate the following verbs: pagar *(to pay)*, nadar *(to swim)*, abandonar *(to abandon)*. You can write them out first if you like. Now try with BEBER: temer *(to fear)* and responder *(to answer/to respond)*. And finally with ESCRIBIR: consumir *(to consume)* and unir *(to unite/to join)*.

[Footnotes]

[8] *If you don't want to learn the 'vosotros' form, just skip it while you recite the conjugation.*

UNIDAD 11

CONTENIDO

In this unit, you will learn:

1 - Expressions and vocabulary related to the weather

2 - The months and seasons

3 - Some names of holidays

4 - Cultural information about Hurricane Mitch

el clima / el tiempo

EL CLIMA/ EL TIEMPO[1]

(The weather)

After an intense first day at work, Peter returns to his apartment to rest. On his way home, he notices dark clouds in the sky and decides to listen to the weather channel on the radio.

La radio[2]:

Hoy *(today)* el tiempo no es muy bueno. Hay nubes en el cielo y hace un poco de fresco. *(Today the weather is not very good. There are clouds in the sky and it is a little cool.)*

También hace viento. Los niveles de contaminación y de alérgenos son altos. *(Also, it is windy. The levels of pollution and allergens are high.)*

Esperamos lluvia para esta noche en la ciudad.
(We expect rain for tonight in the city.)

En las afueras, el cielo está nublado y ya está lloviendo en algunas zonas del norte. *(In the suburbs, the sky is cloudy and it is already raining in some areas of the north.)*

El pronóstico del tiempo para mañana no es mucho mejor:
(The forecast for tomorrow is not much better:)

Cielos nublados, lluvia todo el día, y frío por la noche.
(Cloudy skies, rain all day, and cold at night.)

[Footnotes]

[1] In Spanish, 'tiempo' can mean not only 'time' but also 'weather.'
[2] In some Spanish-speaking countries, the radio (broadcast system) is feminine but the actual radio (machine) is masculine; in others, they are both feminine nouns.

Ejercicio A

From the dialogue, write the translations for these words and expressions. Articles are not needed.

1) it is raining ____________

2) rain ____________

3) forecast ____________

4) clouds ____________

5) cloudy ____________

6) wind ____________

7) cool ____________

8) sky ____________

9) suburbs ____________

10) cold ____________

Answers A: **1)** está lloviendo / **2)** lluvia / **3)** pronóstico / **4)** nubes / **5)** nublado / **6)** viendo / **7)** fresco / **8)** cielo / **9)** afueras / **10)** frío

EXPRESIONES PARA EL TIEMPO

(Weather expressions)

Expresiones con 'hace'

¿Qué tiempo hace? *(How is the weather?)*

Hace[3] frío *(It is cold)*[4]

Hace fresco *(It is cool)*

Hace buen/mal tiempo *(It is a good/bad day)*

Hace calor *(It is hot)*

Hace sol *(It is sunny)*

Hace viento *(It is windy)*

Expresiones con 'está'

¿Cómo está el clima/tiempo? *(How is the weather?)*

Está despejado *(It is a clear day)*

Está nublado *(It is cloudy)*

Está soleado *(It is sunny)*

Está húmedo *(It is humid)*

Está seco *(It is dry)*

Está tormentoso *(It is stormy)*

Expresiones con 'hay'

Hay mucha contaminación *(There is a lot of pollution/it is smoggy)*

Hay neblina *(It is foggy)*

Hay hielo *(It is icy)*

Hay tormenta *(There is a storm)*

Expresiones con otros verbos

Llueve/está lloviendo *(It rains/it is raining)*

Nieva/está nevando *(It snows/it is snowing)*

[Footnotes]

[3] *'Hace' is an expression that does not translate literally (because it means he/she does/makes).*

[4] *If you want to say that something is cold or hot to the touch, say 'está frío,' 'está caliente,' etc; rather than using 'hace.' For now, use 'hace' only for weather expressions.*

Ejercicio B

¿Qué tiempo hace? Describe the weather in your town during the following seasons *(estaciones)*.

1) En la primavera *(spring)*:

hace ______________________

y está ______________________

2) En el verano *(summer)*:

hace ______________________

está ______________________

y hay ______________________

3) En el otoño *(fall)*:

hace ______________________

y está ______________________

4) En el invierno *(winter)*:

hace ______________________

está ______________________

y hay ______________________

Ejercicio C

Match these weather-related terms with their translations. Many are cognates and/or loans.

1) ciclón	a) tornado
2) huracán	b) volcanic eruption
3) tornado	c) barometric pressure
4) ola de calor	d) lava
5) erupción volcánica	e) cyclone
6) presión barométrica	f) meteorology
7) meteorología	g) tectonic plate
8) lava	h) ocean
9) placa tectónica	i) heat wave
10) océano	j) hurricane

Answers C: **1)** - e) / **2)** - j) / **3)** - a) / **4)** - i) / **5)** - b) / **6)** - c) / **7)** - f) / **8)** - d) / **9)** - g) / **10)** - h)

Ejercicio D

Match these weather-related illustrations with their meaning in Spanish.

1) 

2)

3) 

4) 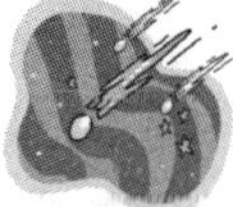

5)

a) nieve

b) tsunami

c) grados[5]

d) lluvia

e) lluvia de meteoros

[Footnotes]

[5] *In Spanish-speaking countries, the Celsius scale (grados centígrados) is more commonly used than the Fahrenheit scale.*

Answers D: **1)** - c) / **2)** - d) / **3)** - a) / **4)** - e) / **5)** - b)

MÁS VOCABULARIO DEL CLIMA

granizo, granizar *(hail, to hail)*

hielo *(ice)*

tormenta/temporal/tempestad *(storm/tempest)*

rayo/relámpago *(lightning)*

trueno *(thunder)*

deslizamiento de tierra *(mudslide/mudflow)*

terremoto *(earthquake)*

mar *(sea)*

montañas *(mountains)*

Ejercicio E

Select the best option to complete these weather-related sentences.

1) El ____ es típico en una tormenta.
a) cielo b) trueno c) ola de calor

2) Un tsunami es una gran ola en el ____.
a) océano b) cielo c) terremoto

3) En un terremoto, las ____ se mueven *(move)*.
a) olas de calor b) erupciones volcánicas
c) placas tectónicas

4) Cuando el cielo está ____, hay muchas nubes.
a) nublado b) despejado c) soleado

5) La ____ es agua que cae *(falls)* del cielo.
a) lava b) nube c) lluvia

6) En Florida hay muchos ____.
a) tornados b) huracanes c) terremotos

7) En California hay muchos ____.
a) tornados b) huracanes c) terremotos

8) En Kansas hay muchos ____.
a) tornados b) huracanes c) terremotos

9) En el hemisferio norte, en verano hace ____.
a) calor b) frío c) fresco

10) En el hemisferio norte, en invierno hace ____.
a) calor b) frío c) fresco

Answers E: **1)** - b) / **2)** - a) / **3)** - c) / **4)** - a) / **5)** - c) / **6)** - b) / **7)** - c) / **8)** - a) / **9)** - a) / **10)** - b)

LOS MESES DEL AÑO *(The months of the year)*

1 **ENERO**	2 **FEBRERO**	3 **MARZO**
4 **ABRIL**	5 **MAYO**	6 **JUNIO**
7 **JULIO**	8 **AGOSTO**	9 **SEPTIEMBRE**
10 **OCTUBRE**	11 **NOVIEMBRE**	12 **DICIEMBRE**

[Footnotes] **Los meses del año son similares en español y en inglés, ¿verdad? This is because they all come from Latin. Some come from the names of gods and goddesses (e.g., marzo, mayo, junio) and others from the names of emperors (e.g., julio, agosto). In Spanish, the months of the year are not capitalized.*

Ejercicio F

¿Cierto *(true)* **o Falso** *(false)***?**

1) En enero está soleado y hace calor en Nueva York — C F

2) En abril y mayo normalmente llueve — C F

3) En julio hace frío en Florida — C F

4) En agosto hace mucho calor en Texas — C F

5) En diciembre hace frío en Chicago — C F

6) Cuando nieva o llueve, está nublado — C F

7) En Argentina es verano cuando en los Estados Unidos es invierno — C F

8) En España es verano cuando en los Estados Unidos es invierno — C F

9) Normalmente nieva en invierno en Nueva York — C F

10) En febrero siempre es invierno en todo el mundo — C F

Answers F: **1)** - F / **2)** - C / **3)** - F / **4)** - C / **5)** - C / **6)** - C / **7)** - C / **8)** - F / **9)** - C / **10)** - F

Ejercicio G

When are the following holidays and events?

1) enero	a) día de la Madre
2) febrero	b) día de la Raza *(Columbus Day)*
3) marzo o abril	c) San Valentín
4) mayo	d) día del Padre
5) junio	e) comienzan las clases en la universidad
6) julio	f) Navidad *(Christmas)*
7) agosto o septiembre	g) Semana Santa *(Easter)*
8) octubre	h) día de la Independencia de Estados Unidos
9) noviembre	i) Año Nuevo *(New Year's)*
10) diciembre	j) día de Acción de Gracias *(Thanksgiving)*

Answers G: **1)** - i) / **2)** - c) / **3)** - g) / **4)** - a) / **5)** - d) / **6)** - h) / **7)** - e) / **8)** - b) / **9)** - j) / **10)** - f)

OTRAS EXPRESIONES

[Footnotes]

[6] The signs of the zodiac signs are capitalized in Spanish.

¿Cuándo es tu cumpleaños? *(When is your birthday?)*	Año bisiesto *(Leap year)*
Mi cumpleaños es el 19 de mayo *(My birthday is on May 19)*	¿Qué signo (del zodíaco) eres? *(What sign (of the zodiac) are you?)*
¿Y el tuyo? *(And yours?)*	Soy….. y tú? *(I am a…. and you?)*
El mío es el 14 de abril *(Mine is April 14)*	Aries[6], Tauro, Géminis, Cáncer, Leo, Virgo, Libra, Escorpio, Sagitario, Capricornio, Acuario, Piscis
¿En qué año naciste? *(What year were you born?)*	

Ejercicio H

¿En qué fecha cae….? ¿Qué día es…? *(What date is ….?)*. **Answer these questions using full sentences. The first one is partially done for you.**

1) ¿Qué día es tu cumpleaños? *Mi cumpleaños es el...* ______

2) ¿Qué día es San Valentín? ______

3) ¿En qué fecha cae Año Nuevo? ______

4) ¿En qué fecha cae el día de Navidad? ______

5) ¿En qué fecha cae el día de la Independencia de EE.UU.[7]? ______

6) ¿Es éste un año bisiesto? ______

7) ¿Qué signo eres? ______

[Footnotes]

[7] *Estados Unidos (United States)*

[8] *In some countries, people say 'uno' and in others, people say 'primero.'*

Answers H: **2)** El día de San Valentín es el 14 de febrero. / **3)** Año Nuevo es el uno[8] de enero. / **4)** El día de Navidad es el 25 de diciembre. / **5)** El día de la Independencia de Estados Unidos es el 4 de julio. / **6)** No, éste no es un año bisiesto. - Sí, éste es un año bisiesto. / **7)** Soy….

MI LISTA DE VOCABULARIO

This is a list of the words that you have learned in this unit.

abril
Acuario
(las) afueras o (los) suburbios
(el) alérgeno
agosto
(el) año
(el) Año Nuevo
Aries
(el) buen tiempo
(el) calor
Cáncer
Capricornio
(el) ciclón
(el) cielo
(la) ciudad
(el) clima
¿cómo está el tiempo?
(la) contaminación
(el) cumpleaños
(el) deslizamiento
despejado
diciembre
(el) día de Acción de Gracias
(el) día de la Independencia
(el) día de la Raza
(el) día de la Hispanidad
(el) día de San Valentín
¿en qué fecha cae...?
enero
(la) erupción volcánica
Escorpio
febrero
(el) fresco
(el) frío
Géminis
(el) grado
granizar/granizo
hace
(el) hielo
hoy
húmedo
(el) huracán
(el) invierno
julio
junio
(la) lava
Leo
Libra
llueve/está lloviendo
(la) lluvia
(el) mal tiempo
mañana
(el) mar
marzo
mayo
mejor
(el) mes
(el) meteorito
(la) meteorología
(la) montaña
(la) Navidad
(la) neblina
nieva/está nevando
(la) nieve
(el) nivel
(el) norte
noviembre
(la) nube

nublado	¿qué día es....?	(el) tifón
(el) océano	¿qué tiempo hace?	todo el día
octubre	(la) radio	(la) tormenta o (la) tempestad
(la) ola de calor	(el) rayo o (el) relámpago	tormentoso
(el) otoño	Sagitario	(el) tornado
Piscis	seco	(el) trueno
(la) placa tectónica	(la) Semana Santa	(el) tsunami
por la mañana	septiembre	un poco de
por la noche	(el) sol	(el) verano
por la tarde	soleado	(el) viento
(la) presión barométrica	Tauro	Virgo
(la) primavera	(el) terremoto	(el) volcán
(el) pronóstico	(el) tiempo	(la) zona

UN POCO DE CULTURA

Hurricane Mitch

In October of 1998, Hurricane Mitch, one of the 10 deadliest hurricanes in history, hit Central America and caused such devastation that these countries have still not completely recovered from it. The surviving population continues to suffer the aftermath of Mitch, including the loss of friends and family members, homes, jobs, crops, businesses and chances for education.

Starting near Jamaica, Mitch caused devastation in every single country in Central America from Panama to Mexico. Its deadliest force fell on Honduras, Nicaragua and Guatemala. Although the final death toll is unknown, the National Hurricane Center (NHC) estimates that between 9,000 and 11,000 people were killed either by the direct hit or by the mudslides and floods caused by the hurricane. Even though some countries took precautions and evacuated people from the coast, they could not completely avoid what came upon them. According to the NHC, 50% of Honduras's crops were lost and a vast number of livestock also perished, causing an increase in unemployment and poverty throughout the country. It is believed that one fifth of the population of Honduras was left homeless. The infrastructure of all these countries was also severely damaged, causing the quick spread of diseases such as cholera and malaria, which further decimated the population. Many countries sent humanitarian help to Central America, but in 1999, the International Monetary Fund estimated the external financing needs of Honduras and Nicaragua over the next few years to be in the range of $1.4 billion.

One of the consequences of this devastation is the high number of children left orphaned and homeless, many of whom survived by begging, selling their bodies, or trafficking drugs. Violence and unemployment are still high in these countries.

Another long-term consequence of the hurricane is that the now-salty soil is too infertile to produce the basic Central American food stuffs: corn, beans, yucca, rice, etc. The fishing industry has also diminished due to the large amounts of garbage left on the waters and the destruction of the natural habitats of fish and shellfish. Clearly, it comes as no surprise that El Salvador, Honduras, and Guatemala have the lowest high school and college graduation rates in all of Central America. Not surprisingly, many Central Americans have tried to cross Mexico in search of a better life in the United States. However, only a few ultimately made it, due to the extortion, rape, robbery, abuses and assaults by Mexican officials and the infamous 'Mara' Mexican gang. Many of these would-be Central American immigrants are indigenous people or farmers who cannot anticipate the conditions awaiting them on the trip.

Right after Mitch hit, and according to an April 2006 article published in Migration Information Source[9], the United States Immigration and Naturalization Service (INS) granted temporary protected status (TPS) to nationals from Honduras and Nicaragua until the year 2007, and to nationals from Guatemala and El Salvador until March of 1999. After two additional major earthquakes in 2001, the TPS for Salvadorans was extended to September of 2007. Quoting data from the 2000 U.S. Census, the article states that there are about 2 million Central Americans living in the U.S., more than half of whom are from El Salvador and Guatemala.

[Footnotes]

[9] *From the Migration Policy Institute, http://www.migrationinformation.org/USFocus/display.cfm?id=385#1*

UNIDAD 11

RECOMENDACIÓN PARA ESTA UNIDAD

To finish this unit, we recommend the movie *El Norte* (1983, USA) by Gregory Nava, and the documentary *De Nadie* (2005, Mexico) by Tin Dirdamal, if you are interested in the struggles of Central Americans crossing the border to the United States. *El Norte* tells the story of a young Mayan woman and her brother who escape political persecution in Guatemala and cross Mexico to reach the U.S. *De Nadie* is a documentary that follows the lives of several Central Americans forced to leave their families for economic reasons and risk their lives in Mexico trying to earn enough money to cross into the U.S.

UNIDAD CONTENIDO

UNIDAD 12

In this unit, you will learn:

1 - Vocabulary related to professions and responsibilities

2 - About irregular verbs in the -'yo'- form

3 - Cultural information about some famous professional Hispanics/Latinos

las profesiones

LAS PROFESIONES

(Professions)

When Ana returns home for the day, her daughter Sofía informs her that she has to prepare for a school presentation about her parents' professions. She shows Ana a picture book with different illustrations.

(el) abogado/
(la) abogada

(el) secretario/
(la) secretaria

(el) enfermero/
(la) enfermera

(el) cocinero/
(la) cocinera

(el) arquitecto/
(la) arquitecta

(el) panadero[1]/
(la) panadera

(el) cajero/
(la) cajera

(el) bombero/
(la) bombera*

(el) jardinero[2]/
(la) jardinera

(el) mesero/
(la) mesera[3]

(el) peluquero/
(la) peluquera

[Footnotes]

[1] *In Spanish, 'pan' means 'bread.'*
[2] *'Jardinero' is also used in baseball for a person in the left, center, or right field positions.*
[3] *Another word for waiter/waitress is 'camarero/a.'*

(la) niñera**

(el) albañil**

(el) policía**

(el) músico**

(el) cura**

(el/la) estudiante

(el/la) dentista

(el/la) soldado

(el / la) intérprete

(el/la) periodista

(el/la) modelo

(el) doctor/(la) doctora

(el) profesor/
(la) profesora[4]

(el) pintor/
(la) pintora

(el) hombre de negocios/(la) mujer de negocios

(el) conductor/
(la) conductora

(el) escritor/
(la) escritora

(el) juez/(la) jueza*

(el) actor/(la) actriz

[Footnotes]

**Some professions are generally used in the masculine form because, they have historically, been performed by men. However, there are less-common feminine versions, as in the case of a female firefighter (la bombera), female judge (la jueza), female clown (la payasa), or female bullfighter (la torera).*

***There are also some names of professions that simply do not exist in the opposite gender, such as babysitter ('la niñera,' but not 'el niñero') or bishop ('el obispo,' but not 'la obispa'). Sometimes, the female version of the word already exists, but it has a completely different meaning, such as 'el músico' (musician), but 'la música' (music); 'el cura' (priest), but 'la cura' (the cure); or 'el policía' (policeman), but 'la policía' (the police).*

[4] In some countries, the words 'profesor' and 'maestro' are synonymous, but in others, 'profesor' is a college professor, whereas 'maestro' is a school teacher.

Ejercicio A

Match these people with the places where they usually work.

1) El abogado — a) en la oficina
2) La doctora — b) en el restaurante
3) El secretario — c) en la panadería
4) La estudiante — d) en la corte[5] *(court)*
5) La mesera — e) en el periódico *(newspaper)*
6) El policía — f) en el mercado *(market)*
7) El panadero — g) en la escuela
8) El cajero — h) en la clínica dental
9) La periodista — i) en el hospital
10) La dentista — j) en la estación de policía[6]

[Footnotes]

[5] *Another word for 'court' is 'juzgado.'*
[6] *Another word for 'police station' is 'comisaría de policía.'*

Answers A: **1)** - d) / **2)** - i) / **3)** - a) / **4)** - g) / **5)** - b) / **6)** - j) / **7)** - c) / **8)** - f) / **9)** - e) / **10)** - h)

Ejercicio B

Conjugate the verbs in parentheses to complete these sentences explaining some of the activities these people do at their jobs.

1) El actor ________________ (actuar) en el teatro *(theater)*.

2) La dentista ________________ (mirar) los dientes *(teeth)* de sus pacientes.

3) El doctor ________________ (trabajar) en el hospital.

4) Nosotros somos cocineros y ________________ (cocinar) *(to cook)* comida mexicana.

5) Las panaderas ________________ (preparar) pan.

6) El estudiante ________________ (estudiar) en la biblioteca.

7) Tú eres bombero y ________________ (apagar) *(to put out)* los incendios *(fires)*.

8) Yo soy abogada y ________________ (trabajar) en la corte.

9) Las profesoras ________________ (enseñar) español.

10) Ustedes son modelos y ________________ (trabajar) para Vogue.

Answers B: **1)** actúa / **2)** mira / **3)** trabaja / **4)** cocinamos / **5)** preparan / **6)** estudia / **7)** apagas / **8)** trabajo / **9)** enseñan / **10)** trabajan

Ejercicio C

Circle the word that DOES NOT relate to these professions.

1) Arquitecta	a) edificio *(building)*	b) planos *(blue prints)*	c) juguetes *(toys)*
2) Cajero	a) dientes	b) mercado	c) dinero *(money)*
3) Jardinero	a) jardín	b) teatro	c) flores *(flowers)*
4) Mesero	a) novela	b) comida	c) restaurante
5) Peluquero	a) pelo *(hair)*	b) peluquería	c) idiomas *(languages)*
6) Niñera	a) jardín	b) bebé	c) juguetes
7) Policía	a) seguridad *(security)*	b) pistola *(gun)*	c) cocina *(kitchen)*
8) Intérprete	a) cuadros *(paintings)*	b) idiomas	c) corte
9) Periodista	a) periódico	b) investigación	c) jardín
10) Soldado	a) pistola	b) guerra *(war)*	c) restaurante
11) Profesor	a) pelo	b) examen	c) estudiante
12) Pintora	a) cuadros	b) novela	c) pintura *(paint)*
13) Escritor	a) pistola	b) libro	c) novela

Answers C: **1)** -c) / **2)** - a) / **3)** - b) / **4)** - a) / **5)** - c) / **6)** - a) / **7)** - c) / **8)** - a) / **9)** - c) / **10)** - c) / **11)** - a) / **12)** - b) / **13)** - a)

LAS RESPONSABILIDADES *(Responsibilites)*

Ana makes a list of the things she does at the office so that her daughter can prepare her presentation.

1) Soy secretaria. Trabajo en el departamento de Recursos Humanos.
2) Ayudo *(I help)* a contratar *(with the hiring)* a personas para nuestra empresa *(company)*.
3) Pongo anuncios *(I post announcements)* de puestos de trabajo *(job positions)* en el periódico *(newspaper)*.
4) Hago *(I do)* entrevistas *(interviews)* a los solicitantes *(applicants)*.
5) Digo *(I say/I tell)* a mi jefe qué *(which)* solicitante me gusta más *(I like the most)* y por qué *(why)*.
6) Ayudo a los nuevos empleados *(new employees)* con sus documentos de contratación *(hiring documents)*.

7) Estoy ocho horas en la oficina y voy *(I go)* a almorzar *(eat lunch)* de 1:00 a 2:00.
8) Escribo cartas *(I write letters)* y mensajes electrónicos *(e-mails)*.
9) Hago fotocopias y mando *(I send)* faxes.
10) Llamo por teléfono y tomo *(I take)* mensajes *(messages)* para otras *(other)* personas.
11) Archivo *(I file)* documentos.
12) Voy a la oficina de correos *(post office)* y envío *(I send)* documentos.
13) Organizo *(I organize)* las cosas de la oficina y actualizo *(I update)* mi agenda de direcciones.
14) Leo *(I read)* las leyes sobre contratación *(hiring laws)*.
15) Preparo cheques para pagar *(to pay)* a los empleados.

Ejercicio D

Using the previous information, complete these sentences.

1) La profesión de Ana es ______________________

2) 'I send' se dice en español ______________ y __________

3) Ana entrevista a los ______________________

4) Ana ayuda a los nuevos ______________________

5) Ana ______________ cheques.

Answers D: **1)** secretaria / **2)** envío - mando / **3)** solicitantes / **4)** empleados / **5)** prepara

VERBOS IRREGULARES EN LA FORMA 'YO'

An irregular verb is one that does not follow the regular conjugation patterns that we have seen so far. Verbs can be irregular in many different ways. In this unit, we are going to take a look at those verbs that are irregular in the first person singular ('yo'). The irregularity differs from verb to verb: some end in -go, others in -oy, and some others are completely unique.

SALIR *(to go out)*	**PONER** *(to put)*	**TRAER** *(to bring)*	**DECIR*** *(to say)*
salgo	**pongo**	**traigo**	**digo**
sales	pones	traes	dices
sale	pone	trae	dice
salimos	ponemos	traemos	decimos
salís	ponéis	traéis	decís
salen	ponen	traen	dicen

VENIR* (to come)	TENER* (to have)	HACER (to do)	DAR (to give)	ESTAR (to be)
vengo	**tengo**	**hago**	**doy**	**estoy**
vienes	tienes	haces	das	estás
viene	tiene	hace	da	está
venimos	tenemos	hacemos	damos	estamos
venís	tenéis	hacéis	dais	estáis
vienen	tienen	hacen	dan	están

IR* (to go)	SER* (to be)	CONOCER (to know)	SABER (to know)	VER (to see)
voy	**soy**	**conozco**	**sé**	**veo**
vas	eres	conoces	sabes	ves
va	es	conoce	sabe	ve
vamos	somos	conocemos	sabemos	vemos
vais	sois	conocéis	sabéis	veis
van	son	conocen	saben	ven

[Footnotes]

*'Decir,' 'venir,' and 'tener' also have another irregularity, but we will see that in another unit

'Ser' and 'ir' have other irregularities. We already learned 'Ser.' We will see 'ir' in a later unit.

Ejercicio E

Select the appropriate verb to complete these sentences in the -'yo'-form.

1) Por las mañanas ______ 'buenos días.'

a) hago b) digo c) veo d) conozco e) sé

2) Por las noches ______ cansado.

a) digo b) soy c) traigo d) estoy e) salgo

3) Los sábados por la noche ______ al cine con mis amigos.

a) hago b) soy c) voy d) tengo e) traigo

4) No ______ a tu hermano.

a) doy b) conozco c) tengo d) pongo e) vengo

5) Yo siempre *(always)* ______ del trabajo a las 6 de la tarde.

a) salgo b) veo c) sé d) soy e) tengo

6) ______ un coche muy bonito.

a) estoy b) soy c) tengo d) hago e) pongo

7) Un viernes sí y otro no *(every other Friday)* ______ mi dinero *(money)* en el banco *(bank)*.

a) pongo b) soy c) digo d) salgo e) hago

Answers E: **1)** - b) / **2)** - d) / **3)** - c) / **4)** - b) / **5)** - a) / **6)** - c) / **7)** - a)

Ejercicio F

Complete the following sentences with the appropriate form of the verb in parentheses.

1) Yo ____________ (estar) en Hawai.

2) Hoy *(today)* yo no ____________ (tener) dinero para el cine.

3) Yo ____________ (venir) a casa tarde.

4) Algunos domingos yo ____________ (ir) a la iglesia.

5) Yo ____________ (poner) sal *(salt)* en la comida.

6) Yo siempre ____________ (hacer) ejercicio físico *(physical exercise)* los lunes.

7) Yo no ____________ (saber) qué hora es, porque no ____________ (tener) reloj.

8) Yo ____________ (ver) a mi novia *(girlfriend)* un día sí y otro no *(every other day)*.

9) Yo ____________ (salir) del trabajo muy tarde.

10) Yo no ____________ (dar) los 'buenos días' nunca *(never)*. ¡Qué grosero! *(How rude!)*

Answers F: **1)** estoy / **2)** tengo / **3)** vengo / **4)** voy / **5)** pongo / **6)** hago / **7)** sé - tengo / **8)** veo / **9)** salgo / **10)** doy

MI LISTA DE VOCABULARIO

This is a list of the words that you have learned in this unit.

(el) abogado/(la) abogada

(el) actor/(la) actriz

actualizar

(la) agenda de direcciones

(el) albañil

almorzar

(el) anuncio

apagar

archivar

(el) arquitecto/(la) arquitecta

(la) biblioteca

(el) bombero/(la) bombera

(el) cajero[7]/(la) cajera

(la) carta

(el) cheque

(la) clínica dental

(la) cocina

cocinar

(el) cocinero/(la) cocinera

(la) comida

(el) conductor/(la) conductora

conocer

contratar

(la) corte

(el) cuadro

dar

decir

(el/la) dentista

(el) diente

(el) dinero

(el) doctor/(la) doctora

(el) edificio

(el) ejercicio físico
(el) enfermero/(la) enfermera
(la) empresa
(la) entrevista
enviar
(el) escritor/(la) escritora
(la) escuela
(la) estación de policía
(el/la) estudiante
(el) examen
(la) flor
grosero
(la) guerra
hacer
(el) hombre/(la) mujer de negocios
(el) hospital
(el) incendio
(el/la) intérprete
(la) investigación
ir
(el) jardín
(el) jardinero/(la) jardinera
(el) juez/(la) jueza
(el) juguete
(la) ley
llamar
(el) maestro/(la) maestra
mandar
(el) mensaje electrónico

(el) mercado
(el) mesero/(la) mesera
(el/la) modelo
(la) niñera
(la) novela
nunca
(el) obispo
(la) oficina de correos
organizar
(el/la) paciente
(el) pan
(la) panadería
(el) panadero/(la) panadera
(el) pelo
(la) peluquería
(el) peluquero/(la) peluquera
(el) periódico
(el / la) periodista
(el) pintor/(la) pintora
(la) pintura
(la) pistola
(el) plano
(el) policía

poner
¿por qué?
(el) profesor/(la) profesora
(el) puesto de trabajo
(el) restaurante
saber
(la) sal
salir
(el) secretario/(la) secretaria
(la) seguridad
siempre
(el) soldado
(el / la) solicitante
(el) teatro
tener
tomar
traer
un día sí y otro no
venir
ver

[Footnotes]

[7] *An ATM is called 'cajero automático.'*

UN POCO DE CULTURA

We believe you are ready to read short paragraphs in Spanish. Here is some information about famous Hispanic/Latino professionals. You do not need to know every single word to understand a sentence, so relax and do your best. Good luck!

Un escritor famoso

Gabriel García Márquez, un escritor *(writer)* hispano famoso, nació *(was born)* en 1928 en Colombia. Él es periodista, novelista y activista político. En 1982 ganó *(won)* el Premio Nóbel de literatura. Es famoso por su realismo mágico *(magical realism)*, donde *(where)* los elementos mágicos aparecen *(appear)* en la vida diaria normal *(normal daily life)*. Su libro más popular es *Cien años de soledad* *(100 Years of Solitude)*.

Una presentadora de televisión famosa

Cristina Saralegui nació en Cuba y emigró *(emigrated)* a Miami en 1960, a la edad de *(at the age of)* 12 años. Se hizo famosa *(she became famous)* en 1989 con su propio *(own)* show de televisión *(El Show de Cristina)*, que es retransmitido en los EE.UU. por Univisión. Ella también tiene un gran negocio de decoración y muebles *(furniture)* para la casa.

Una actriz famosa

Una de las actrices latinas más famosas en Estados Unidos, Jennifer López (J-Lo), es también bailarina, cantante y mujer de negocios de origen puertorriqueño. Jennifer López nació en Nueva York en 1969 y aparece *(appears)* en películas como *My family (1995, USA), Money Train (1995, USA), Selena (1997, USA), The Wedding Planner (2001, USA), y Maid in Manhattan (2002, USA)*. Su primer disco *(her first album)* salió *(was released)* en 1999 pero su primer disco en español salió en 2007. Sus negocios son de perfumes y ropa *(clothes)* principalmente *(mainly)*.

How did you do?

RECOMENDACIÓN PARA ESTA UNIDAD

To finish this unit, we recommend that you read a bilingual book. You should start with a children's book. Later on, you will be able to move on to a young adult bilingual book (such a book on fairy tales or legends, for example) or a children's book written in Spanish only. Visit your local bookstore and browse for some books in the children's section.

UNIDAD 13

CONTENIDO

In this unit, you will learn:

1 - Vocabulary related to hobbies and other activities

2 - About the present progressive

3 - How to ask a question using interrogative words

4 - Cultural information about the currencies of different Spanish-speaking countries

los pasatiempos

LOS PASATIEMPOS

(Hobbies)

The next day, Ana brings Peter some papers he needs to sign. She notices he is distracted.

Ana: ¿Estás bien?

Peter: Sí, lo siento. *(Yes, I am sorry.)* Estoy pensando en mis amigos de Sudamérica. Me pregunto qué están haciendo *(I wonder what they are doing)* en este momento.

Ana: ¿Los echas de menos[1]? *(Do you miss them?)*

Peter: Sí, mucho.

Ana: ¿Y qué crees *(And what do you think)* que está haciendo Federico en este momento?

Peter: Federico.... Uhmm... Seguramente está arreglando su coche. *(He is probably fixing his car.)* A él le gustan mucho los coches y le gusta arreglarlos cuando no funcionan bien *(He loves cars and loves to fix them when they do not run properly.)*

Ana: ¿Dónde arregla los coches? *(Where does he fix the cars?)*

Peter: Ahí mismo en el garaje de su casa. *(Right there in the garage at his house)*

Ana: ¿Cuál es su profesión?

Peter: No tiene profesión definida. Su familia tiene mucho dinero.

Ana: Ahhhhh.... y, ¿cómo lo conoces? *(How do you know him?)*

[Footnotes]

[1] *A more popular expression in Latin America to say that you miss someone is 'extrañar.' Example: Yo extraño a mis amigos (I miss my friends).*

Peter:	Es amigo de un amigo.
Ana:	¿Y qué está haciendo tu amiga Cristina, la actriz?
Peter:	¿Cristina? Uhmmm… probablemente está trabajando *(she is probably working)* en una película *(movie)*.
Ana:	¿Cuántos años hace que es actriz? *(How many years has she been an actress?)*
Peter:	Ella es actriz desde hace cinco años. *(She has been an actress for five years)*
Ana:	¡Qué vidas tan emocionantes! *(What exciting lives!)*
Peter:	Sí, mucho más emocionante que mi vida. Yo trabajo y trabajo, a veces miro partidos de fútbol *(sometimes I watch soccer games)* en la tele, cocino *(cook)*, o hago puzzles[2] *(do puzzles)*.
Ana:	Por favor, no te quejes. ¡¡Yo no tengo tiempo para hacer nada!! *(Please don't complain. I don't have time to do anything!!)*

[Footnotes]

[2] *Another word for 'puzzle' is 'rompecabezas.'*

Ejercicio A

Enlaza *(Match)* **cada** *(each)* **ilustración con una actividad apropiada** *(appropriate activity)*.

1) Federico está arreglando su coche

2) Cristina está actuando

3) Ricardo y Mari Carmen están esquiando

4) Damián y Gabriela están tomando el sol

5) Eva está leyendo

6) Yo estoy cocinando

7) Tú estás mirando la televisión

8) Isabel está haciendo un puzzle

9) Mis amigos están viajando en tren

10) Petra está jugando al tenis

Respuestas A: **1)** - g) / **2)** - i) / **3)** - e) / **4)** - j) / **5)** - a) / **6)** - b) / **7)** - f) / **8)** - d) / **9)** - h) / **10)** - c)

EL PRESENTE PROGRESIVO *(Present progressive)*

To indicate that an action or activity is happening right now, use the present progressive. The present progressive is formed with the present tense of the verb 'estar' and the present participle (gerund) of a verb.

> Yo estoy hablando *(I am talking)*
> Tú estás bebiendo *(You are drinking)*
> ¿Qué está pasando? *(What is happening?)*

To form the present participle, drop the -ar and add -ando; or drop the -er/-ir and add -iendo.

cantar	cant- + -ando	estoy cantando
beber	beb- + -iendo	estoy bebiendo
escribir	escrib- + -iendo	estoy escribiendo

If you have an -ER or -IR verb that has two vowels in a row (ee, ui, ae, etc), change the 'i' from '-iendo' into a 'y.'

leer	le- + -iendo	estoy leyendo
destruir	destru- + -iendo	estoy destruyendo
caer	ca- + -iendo	estoy cayendo

Some common questions in the present progressive:

> What are you doing?
> *¿Qué estás haciendo?*
>
> What is going on?
> *¿Qué está sucediendo? / ¿Qué está pasando?*

UNIDAD 13

Ejercicio B

Traduce *(Translate)* **estas frases usando** *(using)* **el presente progresivo. No olvides** *(Don't forget)* **que el verbo 'estar' debe hacer concordancia con el sujeto** *(must agree with the subject)*.

1) Daniel is eating with *(con)* his parents.

____

2) Dolores and Fernando are living in this apartment.

____

3) Jaime is returning from Mexico now.

____

4) You (tú) are selling your car.

____

5) You (plural) are eating in a very bad restaurant.

____

Respuestas B: **1)** Daniel está comiendo con sus padres. / **2)** Dolores y Fernando están viviendo en este apartamento. / **3)** Jaime está regresando - volviendo de México ahora. / **4)** Tú estás vendiendo tu coche. / **5)** Ustedes están comiendo en un restaurante muy malo.

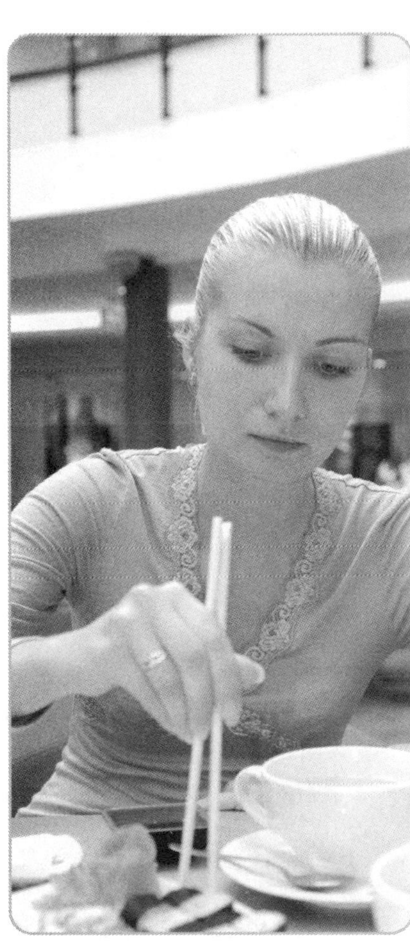

Ejercicio C

¿Qué estás haciendo ahora? *(You do not need to repeat 'estoy' every time you mention an activity, just use commas.)*

Estoy ______________________________

____

____

____

____

OTRAS ACTIVIDADES COMUNES

(Other common activities)

caminar *(to stroll/to walk)*

conducir[3] *(to drive)*

correr *(to run)*

escribir a máquina *(to type)*

hacer deporte *(to do sports)*

ir[4] de compras *(to go shopping)*

ir de vacaciones *(to go on vacation)*

jugar a las cartas *(play cards)*

montar/andar en bicicleta *(to bike)*

nadar *(to swim)*

pasear *(to stroll, to walk)*

pescar *(to fish)*

pintar *(to paint)*

tocar[5] un instrumento *(to play an instrument)*

[Footnotes]

[3] In Latin America, the word 'manejar' (to drive) is more commonly used.
[4] Unlike in English, the present progressive of the verb 'ir' (I am going) is not frequently used in Spanish. The simple present is used instead. Example: I am going to the store = I go to the store = Voy a la tienda.
[5] To play (games, with other people, etc) is 'jugar,' but to play (music, an instrument, etc) is 'tocar.'

Ejercicio D

Completa estas frases con el presente progresivo de los verbos en paréntesis. Don't forget to include and conjugate the verb 'estar.'

1) Marisa ______________ (pintar) un cuadro muy bonito.

2) Adela y Julián ______________ (pescar) en el río *(river)*.

3) Jorge ______________ (tocar) el saxofón.

4) Yo ______________ (jugar) a las cartas en el bar.

5) Ustedes ______________ (pasear) a su perro.

6) Nosotros ______________ (correr) por el parque.

7) Tú ______________ (conducir) tu coche.

Respuestas D: **1)** está pintando / **2)** están pescando / **3)** está tocando / **4)** estoy jugando / **5)** están paseando / **6)** estamos corriendo / **7)** estás conduciendo

HACER PREGUNTAS *(Asking questions)*

The verb 'to ask'[6] in Spanish is 'preguntar.' The word 'question' is 'pregunta.' Therefore, 'to ask a question' *should* be 'preguntar una pregunta,' but to avoid sounding redundant, people say 'hacer una pregunta' *(to 'make' a question)*. The verb 'to answer' can be 'responder' or 'contestar.'

¿Tienes una pregunta?
(Do you have a question?)

Tengo una pregunta.
(I have a question.)

Por favor, conteste la pregunta.
(Please, answer the question.)

Por favor, repita la pregunta.
(Please, repeat the question.)

No comprendo la pregunta.
(I don't understand the question.)

¿Quiere la respuesta en español?
(Do you want the answer in Spanish?)

Inversion

When asking a question, the order of the subject and the verb (S-V) is usually inverted[7] (V-S).

Peter	está	en Madrid
Subject	*Verb*	*Prep. object*

¿Está	Peter	en Madrid?
Verb	*Subject*	*Prep. object*

¿Dónde	está	Peter?
Interrogative	*Verb*	*Subject*

Auxiliary 'do'
In Spanish you do not need to translate the auxiliary 'do' (does, did) that exists in certain questions in English.

Do you live here? / ¿Vives (tú)[8] aquí?

Question mark
In Spanish an inverted question mark is placed at the beginning of the question and a regular one at the end.

¿Quién es esa persona? *(Who is that person?)*

Y tú, ¿qué quieres? *(And you, what do you want?)*

Interrogative words (Q-words)
Here is a list of some useful interrogative words:

¿Qué? *(What?/Which?)*

¿Cuál/es? *(What?/Which?)*

¿Dónde? *(Where?)*

¿Adónde? *(Where to?)*

¿Cuándo? *(When?)*

¿Por qué? *(Why?)*

¿Por cuánto tiempo? *(For how long?)*

¿Para qué? *(For what (purpose)?)*

¿Cómo? *(How?)*

¿Quién/es? *(Who?)*

¿De quién? *(Whose?)*

¿De qué color? *(What color?)*

¿Cuánto/a? *(How much?)*

¿Cuánto tiempo hace? *(How long ago?)*

¿A qué hora? *(At what time?)*

¿Cuántos/as? *(How many?)*

Qué and Cuál
Both ¿Qué? and ¿Cuál? mean 'What?' and 'Which?,' but there are rules for their usage. In general:

—¿Qué? is used to request a definition and/or explanation. In these cases, it means 'What?'

¿Qué es esto? / *(What is this?)*

¿Qué estás comiendo? / *(What are you eating?)*

—When followed by a noun, ¿Qué? can be translated as 'Which?'

¿Qué niño es tu hijo? / *(Which boy is your son?)*

¿Qué casa te gusta más? / *(Which house you like the most?)*

—¿Cuál? also means 'Which?' or 'What?,' but it is not followed by a noun[9] and usually implies a choice among several options.

¿Cuál es tu número de teléfono?
(What is your telephone number?)

¿Cuál es tu casa? / *(Which one is your house?)*

¿Cuáles son tus amigos? / *(Which ones are your friends?)*

¿Cuál quieres? / *(Which one do you want?)*

De quién
Unlike in English, ¿De quién? is followed by the verb.

¿De quién es este apartamento?
(Whose apartment is this?)

[Footnotes]

[6] Careful, because 'to ask for' is 'pedir' (e.g., He is asking for some bread = él está pidiendo algo de pan).
[7] In the Dominican Republic and Puerto Rico, the word order is not inverted (e.g.,¿Qué tú quieres?)
[8] Remember that the subject pronouns are not absolutely necessary all the time, since the ending of the verb tells who the subject is.
[9] In some countries, you will hear ¿Cuál? followed by a noun (e.g., ¿Cuál libro quieres?)

Written accents

Interrogative words always have an accent when used to ask a question (or in indirect speech).

¿Adónde vas? / *(Where are you going?)*
No sé adónde voy / *(I don't know where I am going)*

Cuánto/a and Cuántos/as

¿Cuántos/as? and ¿Cuánto/a? must agree with the noun they refers to (explicit or not).

¿Cuántos libros tienes? / *(How many books do you have?)*
¿Cuántos tienes? / *(How many do you have?)*

Ejercicio E

Selecciona el interrogativo más apropiado para estas preguntas.

1) ¿______ estás? Bien, gracias.

a) Qué | b) Por qué | c) Dónde | d) Cómo

2) ¿______ estás? Estoy en mi casa.

a) Dónde | b) Por cuánto tiempo | c) De quién | d) Qué

3) ¿______ es esta persona? Él es mi padre

a) Por qué | b) Cuántas | c) Quién | d) Dónde

4) ¿______ es tu dirección? Es Calle El Salvador, número 34, piso cuarto A.

a) Cuál | b) Qué | c) Dónde | d) Por cuánto tiempo

5) ¿______ es esta oficina? Esta oficina es del jefe.

a) Cuál | b) De quién | c) Quién | d) Quiénes

6) ¿______ es el concierto? El concierto es a las 3 de la tarde.

a) A qué hora | b) Dónde | c) Qué | d) Cuál

7) ¿______ no vienes a mi casa? Porque *(because)* estoy muy cansado.

a) Cuánto | b) Adónde | c) Por qué | d) Cuántas

8) ¿______ escribes en ese cuaderno *(notebook)*? Yo escribo sobre *(about)* los mayas.

a) Cuánto | b) Qué | c) Cómo | d) A qué hora

9) ¿______ te llamas? Me llamo Imanol.

a) Cómo | b) Dónde | c) De quién | d) De qué color

10) ¿______ es el cielo? El cielo es azul.

a) Cuándo | b) De quién | c) Qué | d) De qué color

Respuestas E: **1)** - d) / **2)** - a) / **3)** - c) / **4)** - a) / **5)** - b) / **6)** - a) / **7)** - c) / **8)** - b) / **9)** - a) / **10)** - d)

Ejercicio F

Enlaza estas preguntas con sus respuestas.

1) ¿Dónde trabajas?	a) Son de Federico
2) ¿Por qué estudias español?	b) Es alto y delgado
3) ¿Quién llama por teléfono?	c) Esta tarde
4) ¿De quiénes son estos coches?	d) En una ciudad cerca de aquí
5) ¿Cómo es tu padre?	e) Porque tengo amigos en Sudamérica
6) ¿Cuándo vienes a mi casa?	f) Tu madre

Respuestas F: **1)** - d) / **2)** - e) / **3)** - f) / **4)** - a) / **5)** - b) / **6)** - c)

Ejercicio G

Traduce estas frases usando los interrogativos.

1) Where are your (tus) parents? __________

2) Who is that man? __________

3) How many cars do you (usted) have? __________

4) What color is her cat? __________

5) What does he need? __________

6) Which one is her car? __________

7) How is his mother? __________

8) Why do they need a pen? __________

9) What time does Peter return from work? __________

10) What time is it? __________

Respuestas G: **1)** ¿Dónde están tus padres? / **2)** ¿Quién es ese hombre? / **3)** ¿Cuántos coches tiene usted? / **4)** ¿De qué color es su gato? / **5)** ¿Qué necesita él? / **6)** ¿Cuál es su coche? / **7)** ¿Cómo está su madre? / **8)** ¿Por qué necesitan ellos un bolígrafo? / **9)** ¿A qué hora regresa Peter del trabajo? / **10)** ¿Qué hora es?

MI LISTA DE VOCABULARIO

This is a list of the words that you have learned in this unit.

¿a qué hora?
¿adónde?
arreglar
(el) bar
(la) bicicleta
caminar
(las) cartas
¿cómo?
con
correr
¿cuál?
¿cuándo?
¿cuánto?/¿cuánta?
¿cuánto tiempo hace?
¿cuántos?/¿cuántas?
¿cuántos años hace?
¿de qué color?
¿de quién?/¿de quiénes?
¿dónde?
echar de menos o extrañar
emocionante
escribir a máquina
esquiar
(el) garaje
hacer deporte
(el) instrumento
ir de compras
ir de vacaciones
jugar
manejar o conducir
montar
nadar
¿para qué?
pasear
pescar
pintar
¿por cuánto tiempo?
¿por qué?
porque
¿qué?
¿qué está pasando?
¿qué está sucediendo?
¿quién?/¿quiénes?
(el) río
(el) saxofón
sobre
tocar un instrumento
tomar el sol
(el) tren
(la) vida

UN POCO DE CULTURA

Currencies

Collecting coins is a popular hobby. Did you know that there are different currencies throughout the Spanish-speaking world?

Europa	Centroamérica y Caribe	Sudamérica
España – **euro**	México – **peso mexicano**	Venezuela – **bolívar**
	Guatemala – **quetzal**	Colombia – **peso colombiano**
	Honduras – **lempira**	Ecuador – **dólar (U.S.)**
	El Salvador – **colón**	Perú – **nuevo sol**
	Nicaragua – **córdoba**	Bolivia – **boliviano**
	Costa Rica – **colón costarricense**	Paraguay – **guaraní**
	Panamá – **balboa**	Chile – **peso chileno**
	Cuba[10] – **peso cubano**	Uruguay – **peso uruguayo**
	Puerto Rico – **dólar (U.S.)**	Argentina – **peso argentino**
	República Dominicana – **peso dominicano**	

[Footnotes]

[10] *In Cuba, the locals use a different currency than the tourists.*

RECOMENDACIÓN PARA ESTA UNIDAD

To finish the unit, we recommend that you focus on what you are doing at different moments of the day, and express what you are doing in Spanish using the present progressive (e.g., ahora estoy leyendo, ahora estoy comprando en el mercado). It is a very simple activity, but helps you practice.

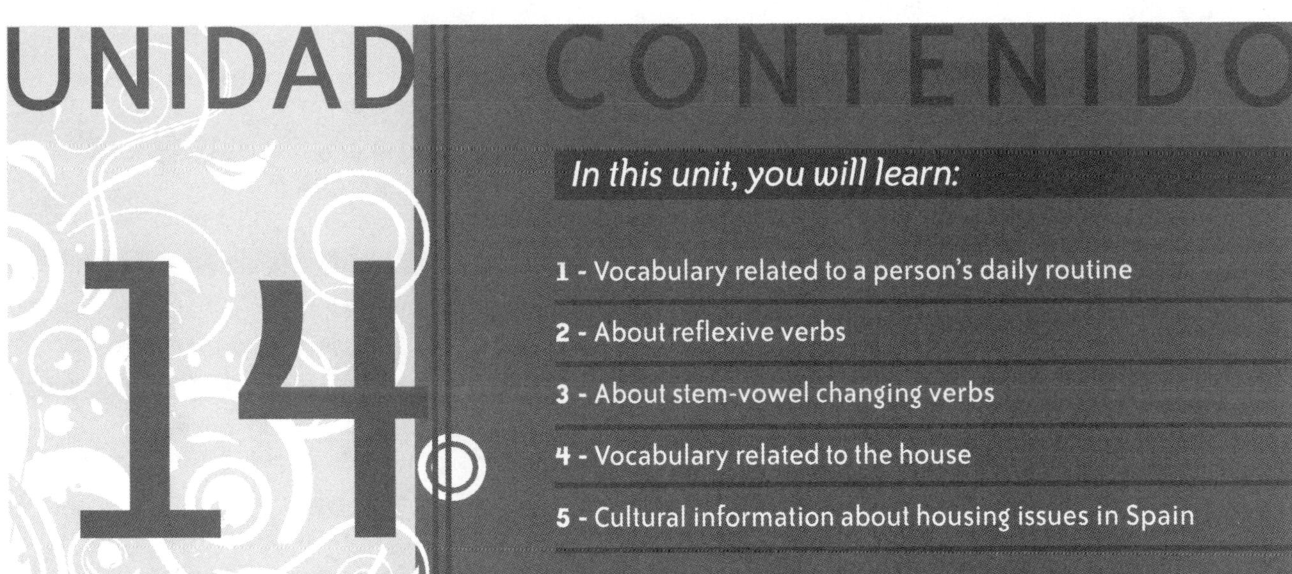

la rutina diaria

LA RUTINA DIARIA

(The daily routine)

Peter is surprised by Ana's comment about having no time for anything. He is wondering how she spends her time outside the office.

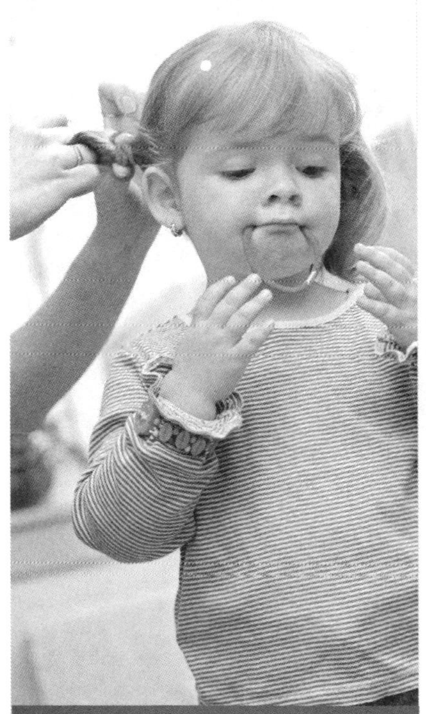

Peter:	¿En serio *(Seriously)* no tienes tiempo para nada *(for nothing)*?
Ana:	Para nada interesante. Paso *(I spend)* todo mi tiempo en mi trabajo *(at work)*, con mis hijos y en mi casa. No tengo tiempo para mí *(for myself)*.
Peter:	¿No vas al cine nunca? *(You never go to the movies?)* ¿No tienes tiempo para un masaje *(massage)*? ¿para salir con *(go out with)* las amigas?
Ana:	No.
Peter:	¡Pero *(But)* eso es horrible! A ver *(Let's see)* …. Cuéntame qué haces un día de la semana típico *(Tell me what you do on a typical week day)*.
Ana:	Me despierto *(I wake up)* a las 6 de la mañana y me levanto *(I get up)* inmediatamente. Me cepillo los dientes *(I brush my teeth)*, me ducho *(I take a shower)*, me pongo maquillaje *(I apply makeup)* y me visto *(and I get dressed)*. Luego *(Then)* preparo el desayuno *(breakfast)* para mis hijas, las despierto *(I wake them up)* y las llevo *(I take them)* a la escuela. Después voy al trabajo *(After that I go to work)*.
Peter:	Bueno, ¿y después del trabajo? *(OK, and after work?)*

Ana:	Después del trabajo, recojo *(I pick up)* a mis hijas del colegio[1] *(school)* y las llevo a casa. Les ayudo *(I help them)* un poco con la tarea *(homework)*, preparo la cena, y después de cenar jugamos *(we play)* un poco o vemos *(we watch)* la televisión. Después se acuestan *(Later they go to bed)*.
Peter:	¿Y qué haces tú cuando ellas se acuestan? *(And what do you do when they go to bed?)*
Ana:	Me cambio de ropa *(I change clothes)* y lavo los platos *(I wash the dishes)*. A veces *(Sometimes)* preparo la comida del día siguiente *(next day)*, pero no siempre *(but not always)*. Después veo la tele un rato *(a little while)* o me acuesto, agotada *(exhausted)*.
Peter:	Sí, ya comprendo. Pero, ¿no te ayuda tu marido? *(doesn't your husband help you?)*
Ana:	Enrique trabaja mucho más que yo. Cuando llega a la casa, se ducha *(he takes a shower)*, cena un poco *(he has some dinner)* y se acuesta, agotado también. Además, él viaja *(he travels)* mucho.
Peter:	Ohhhhh.... ¡Dios mío! *(Oh, my goodness!)*

[Footnotes]

[1] *'Colegio' is another word for school.*

Ejercicio A

Selecciona *(Select)* **la frase** *(phrase)* **para cada ilustración de la rutina.**

1)
a) Ana se cepilla los dientes
b) Ana se despierta
c) Ana se ducha

3)
a) Margarita se pone maquillaje
b) Margarita se levanta
c) Margarita se acuesta

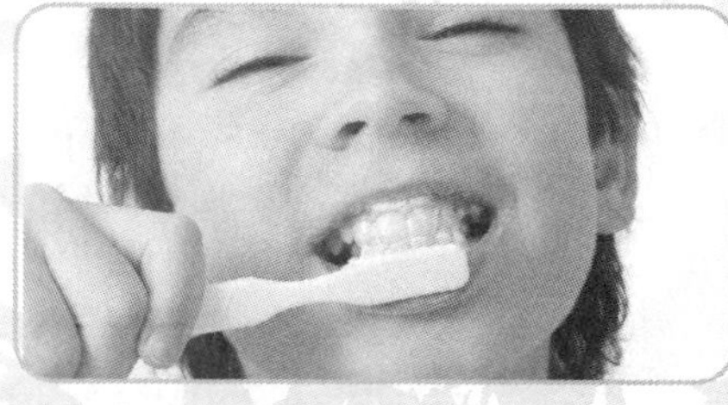

2)
a) Pablo se pone la ropa
b) Pablo se cepilla los dientes
c) Pablo se acuesta

4)
a) Luis se ducha
b) Luis se despierta
c) Luis se viste

Respuestas A: **1)** - b) / **2)** - b) / **3)** - a) / **4)** - c)

LOS VERBOS REFLEXIVOS *(Reflexive verbs)*

With reflexive verbs, the action of the verb reflects back on the subject[2]. This effect is represented by a reflexive pronoun (e.g., levantar<u>se</u>, acostar<u>se</u>, poner<u>se</u>, etc), which is attached to the infinitive. When the reflexive verb is conjugated, the pronoun must agree with the subject:

LEVANTAR<u>SE</u> *(to get up)*	**me** levanto
	te levantas
	se levanta
	nos levantamos
	os levantáis
	se levantan

[Footnotes]

[2] *There are some verbs that are reflexive but do not follow this logic, such as 'quejarse' (to complain).*

Ejercicio B

Ahora enlaza el principio *(beginning)* **de estas frases con el final** *(ending)* **para hablar sobre la rutina de estas personas. Todos son verbos reflexivos.**

1) Rodolfo se

2) Nosotros nos

3) Yo me

4) Mis padres se

5) Tú te

a) ponemos ropa formal para ir a trabajar

b) despiertan muy temprano

c) bañas *(take a bath)* por la mañana

d) acuesta con su esposa a las 10 de la noche

e) cepillo los dientes todos los días

Respuestas B: **1)** - d) / **2)** - a) / **3)** - e) / **4)** - b) / **5)** - c)

Ejercicio C

Traduce estas frases sobre la rutina usando la estructura reflexiva y los verbos en paréntesis. La primera *(first)* **frase ya está hecha** *(is already done).*

1) Ana wakes up early (despertarse) *Ana se despierta temprano*

2) Ana gets up immediately (levantarse) ______

3) Ana brushes her[3] teeth (cepillarse) ______

4) She takes a shower (ducharse) ______

5) She puts on makeup (ponerse) ______

Respuestas C: **2)** Ana se levanta inmediatamente / **3)** Ana se cepilla los dientes / **4)** Ella se ducha / **5)** Ella se pone maquillaje

[Footnotes]

[3] *Since the reflexive verb already tells us that Ana is brushing her own teeth, you should avoid being redundant by writing 'the teeth' instead of 'her teeth.'*

VERBOS DE CAMBIO RADICAL *(Stem-vowel changing verbs)*

Stem-vowel changing verbs (or stem-changing verbs) have a change in the vowel of the verb's root in all persons except for 'nosotros' and 'vosotros.' Stem-vowel changing verbs can have other irregularities as well, such as being reflexive, having an irregular -'yo'-form, etc.

There are three types of root change. You must remember which verbs undergo which change.

1.- The vowel 'o' changes to 'ue':

alm**o**rzar >>>>> alm**ue**rz-

RECORDAR (to remember)	**JUGAR**[4] *(to play)*	**VOLVER** *(to return)*	**PODER** *(to be able)*	**MORIRSE** *(to die)*	**DORMIR** *(to sleep)*
recuerdo	**juego**	**vuelvo**	**puedo**	**me muero**	**duermo**
recuerdas	**juegas**	**vuelves**	**puedes**	**te mueres**	**duermes**
recuerda	**juega**	**vuelve**	**puede**	**se muere**	**duerme**
recordamos	jugamos	volvemos	podemos	nos morimosos	dormimos
recordáis	jugáis	volvéis	podéis	morís	dormís
recuerdan	**juegan**	**vuelven**	**pueden**	**se mueren**	**duermen**

Other **o>ue** stem-vowel changing verbs include:

almorzar *(to eat lunch)*
acostarse *(to go to bed)*
costar *(to cost)*
doler *(to hurt)*

encontrar *(to find)*
llover *(to rain)*
mostrar *(to show)*
mover *(to move)*

probar *(to try/to taste)*
sonar *(to sound)*
soñar *(to dream)*

2.- The vowel 'e' changes to 'ie': t**e**ner >>>>> **tie**n-

PENSAR *(to think)*	**DESPERTARSE** *(to wake up)*	**PERDER** *(to lose)*	**QUERER** *(to want)*	**PREFERIR**[5] *(to prefer)*	**SENTIR** *(to feel)*
pienso	**me despierto**	**pierdo**	**quiero**	**prefiero**	**siento**
piensas	**te despiertas**	**pierdes**	**quieres**	**prefieres**	**sientes**
piensa	**se despierta**	**pierde**	**quiere**	**prefiere**	**siente**
pensamos	nos despertamos	perdemos	queremos	preferimos	sentimos
pensáis	os despertáis	perdéis	queréis	preferís	sentís
piensan	**se despiertan**	**pierden**	**quieren**	**prefieren**	**sienten**

[Footnotes]

[4] *Even though 'jugar' has a 'u' in its root, it used to have an 'o' in its Latin*

[5] *When the root has two or more vowels, the one that changes is the one closest to the end (e.g., prefer-ir > prefier-o).*

Other **e>ie** stem-vowel changing verbs include:

comenzar *(to begin/to start)* **empezar** *(to begin/to start)* **entender** *(to understand)*	**medir** *(to measure)* **mentir** *(to lie)*	**nevar** *(to snow)* **sentarse** *(to sit down)* **venir** *(to come)*

3.- The vowel 'e' changes to 'i'[6]: **decir >>>>> dic-**

DECIR *(to say)*	**SEGUIR** *(to follow)*	**REPETIR** *(to repeat)*	**SERVIR** *(to serve)*	**VESTIRSE** *(to get dressed)*
digo	**sigo**	**repito**	**sirvo**	**me visto**
dices	**sigues**	**repites**	**sirves**	**te vistes**
dice	**sigue**	**repite**	**sirve**	**se viste**
decimos	seguimos	repetimos	servimos	nos vestimos
decís	seguís	repetís	servís	os vestís
dicen	**siguen**	**repiten**	**sirven**	**se visten**

[Footnotes]

[6] *Verbs that have the e>i change are always -ir verbs. However, this does not mean that all -ir verbs have an e>i change.*

Other **e>i** stem-vowel changing verbs include:

conseguir *(to get/to obtain)* **pedir** *(to ask for)*	**reír** *(to laugh)* **sonreír** *(to smile)*

Ejercicio D

Completa estas frases con la forma apropiada de los verbos en paréntesis, que son verbos de cambio radical *(root change)*.

1) El coche ____________________(costar) mucho dinero.

2) Peter ____________________(pensar) en sus amigos de Sudamérica.

3) ¿A qué hora ______________(venir) el tren?

4) Yo no ____________________ (recordar) dónde están mi llaves *(keys)*.

5) Nosotros __________________(despertarse) a las 8 de la mañana.

6) ____________________ (nevar) *(It snows)*

7) Elena ____________________ (acostarse) muy tarde todos las noches.

8) Los chicos ____________________ (vestirse) después de ducharse *(after taking a shower)*.

9) El cliente ____________________ (pedir) comida a la mesera del restaurante.

10) Nosotros no ____________________ (querer) más comida, gracias.

Respuestas D: **1)** cuesta / **2)** piensa / **3)** viene / **4)** recuerdo / **5)** nos despertamos / **6)** Nieva / **7)** se acuesta / **8)** se visten / **9)** pide / **10)** queremos

Ejercicio E

Traduce estas frases usando verbos de cambio radical.

1) Elisa serves the table.

____

2) Manuel does not want (to) sleep.

____

3) My son always returns late.

____

4) I don't sleep very well.

____

Respuestas E: **1)** Elisa sirve la mesa / **2)** Manuel no quiere dormir / **3)** Mi hijo siempre vuelve tarde / **4)** No duermo muy bien

LA CASA
(The house)

This is Ana's house, where she spends all of her time when she is not at work.

sala/salón-comedor

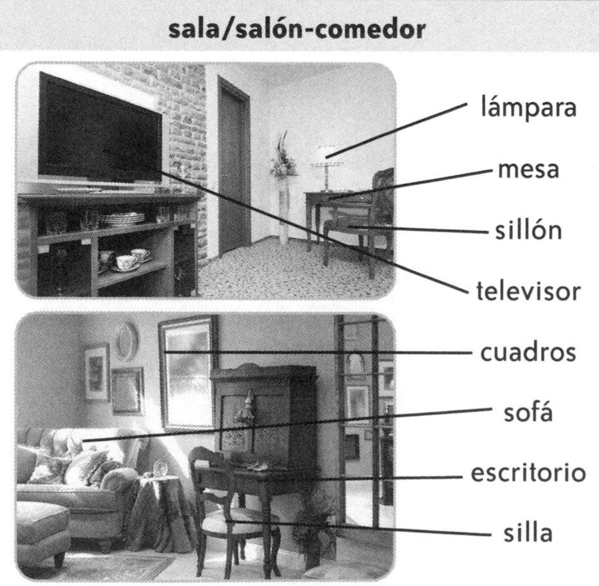

dormitorio[7]

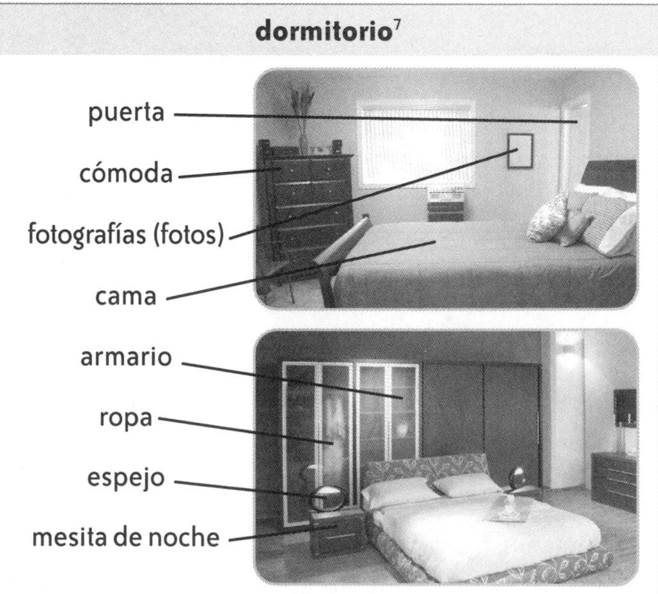

UNIDAD 14

cocina

dormitorio de los niños

cuarto de baño

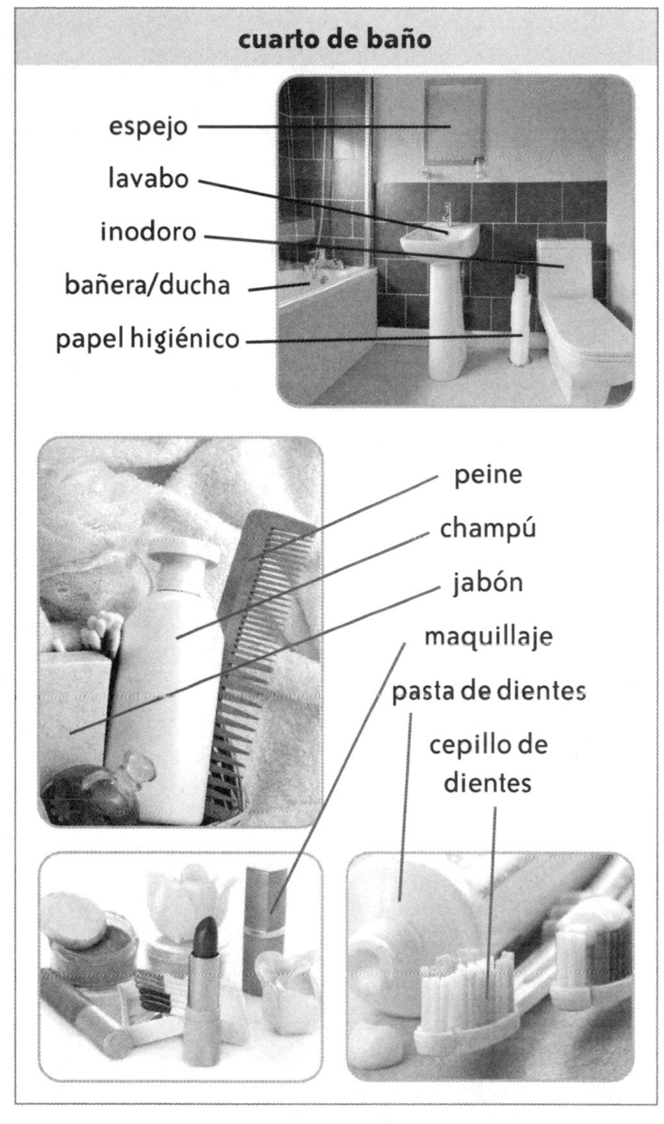

[Footnotes]

[7] *Other words for 'bedroom' are 'habitación,' 'recámara,' 'cuarto,' and 'alcoba.'*

Ejercicio F

Enlaza las actividades con las partes de la casa.

1) Ana lava los platos	a) en su dormitorio
2) Ana duerme	b) frente *(in front of)* al espejo
3) La hija juega con sus juguetes	c) en su cama
4) Ana y su esposo preparan la comida	d) en la cocina
5) Ana se pone maquillaje	e) en el fregadero

Respuestas F: **1)** - e) / **2)** - c) / **3)** - a) / **4)** - d) / **5)** - b)

Ejercicio G

Selecciona la palabra que NO corresponde con las partes de la casa.

1) Cocina:	**2)** Dormitorio:	**3)** Cuarto de baño:	**4)** Sala:	**5)** Casa:
cubiertos	platos	inodoro	lámpara	ático
fregadero	cama	lavavajillas	refrigerador	chimenea
sofá	espejo	lavabo	sillón	coche
microondas	cómoda	espejo	mesa	sótano

Respuestas G: **1)** sofá / **2)** platos / **3)** lavavajillas / **4)** refrigerador / **5)** coche

MI LISTA DE VOCABULARIO

This is a list of the words that you have learned in this unit.

acostar/acostarse
agotado
almorzar
(el) armario
(el) ático
(el) balcón
bañar/bañarse
(la) bañera
(la) cama
cenar
cepillar/cepillarse
cepillo de dientes
(el) champú
(la) chimenea
(el) colegio
comenzar
(la) cómoda
cómodo

conseguir
costar
(el) cuadro
(los) cubiertos
decir
dedicar
(el) desayuno
desde
despertar/despertarse
después
diario
¡Dios mío!
doler
dormir/dormirse
(el) dormitorio
(la) ducha
ducharse
empezar

¿en serio?	morir/morirse	sentarse
encontrar	mostrar	sentir/sentirse
entender	mover/moverse	servir
(la) escuela	(la) muñeca	siempre
(el) espejo	nada	siguiente
(la) estufa	nevar	(la) silla
(el) fregadero	(el) papel higiénico	(el) sillón
frente a	(la) pasta de dientes	(el) sofá
(el) garaje	(el) patio	sonar
(el) horno	pedir	soñar
inmediatamente	(el) peine	sonreír
(el) inodoro	pensar	también
ir	perder	(la) televisión
(el) jabón	(el) piso o (la) planta	(el) televisor[8]
(el) juguete	(el) plato	tener
(la) lámpara	poder	(la) terraza
(el) lavabo	poner/ponerse	(el) tiempo
lavar	preferir	típico
(el) lavavajillas o	probar	un rato
(el) lavaplatos	(la) puerta	(el) vaso
levantar/levantarse	querer	vestir/vestirse
llevar	recoger	volver
llover	recordar	
(el) maquillaje	(el) refrigerador	
(el) masaje	reír/reírse	
medir	repetir	
mentir	(la) rutina	
(la) mesa	(la) sala o (el) salón o	
(la) mesita de noche	(el) salón-comedor	
(el) microondas	seguir	

[Footnotes]

[8] *'Televisor' refers to the actual television set, but 'televisión' refers to the programs you watch on the 'televisor.' You can use the verbs 'mirar'* (to look at) *and 'ver'* (to see) *to talk about watching television* (la tele).

UN POCO DE CULTURA

Housing Issues in Spain

Article 47 of the 1978 Spanish Constitution reads: «Todos los españoles tienen derecho a disfrutar[9] de una vivienda digna y adecuada» *(All Spaniards have the right to worthy and adequate housing).* However, in most Spanish cities, buying an apartment within the city limits is close to impossible for a single person earning an average salary. In 2007 a three bedroom apartment cost between •400,000 and • 700,000 (approx. $530,000 - $940,000[10]). Thirty years ago, a family was usually able to afford a decent dwelling with only one person (the husband / father) working . What has happened during the last 30 years in Spain?

Since 2003, a national organization called Plataforma Por Una Vivienda Digna (http://www.viviendadigna.org) has been protesting and demonstrating against the ridiculous prices that banks, real estate agencies, and construction companies charge for housing. According to them, from 1987 to 2005, home prices have increased 250%. This dire situation has forced younger people to wait longer to purchase their own home, required mortgages lasting 40-50 years, and precipitated the criminal activities related to housing (abuses, fraud, speculation, etc.)

One solution to the problem is renting, which can be between 10% and 50% cheaper than owning, though most Spaniards consider renting a waste of money. Another solution is to live in the suburbs, which most people are doing now, in spite of the two-hour commutes it can require. One consequence of this shift to the suburbs is that many cities' downtown areas have become empty lots taken over by illegal immigrants, drug addicts, and criminals. A consequence of the long commutes is that parents cannot spend as much time at home with their children as they did when transit time was shorter. This change is eroding the traditional Spanish way of life, and affecting other areas of society, such as nutrition, education, and family values. Unfortunately, the housing market is so strong (1/7th of the Gross Domestic Product) that the current conditions will probably continue for a long time, to the detriment of Spanish society and culture. How difficult is it to buy a house in the city where you live? Is possible for a young person to buy a house or a condo by himself/herself?

[Footnotes]

9 The verb 'disfrutar' can mean 'to enjoy', but also can mean 'to have,' 'to possess,' 'to get,' or 'to receive.'

10 At the exchange rate of 1.00 euro = 1.345 U.S. dollars.

RECOMENDACIÓN PARA ESTA UNIDAD

To finish this unit, we recommend that you stay tuned to issues that affect Hispanics/Latinos in your community, such as health care, housing, etc. Good sources of information are the Internet, local newspapers, and Latino USA (National Public Radio). On National Puplic Radio's website, you can access numerous podcasts in English about these issues, as well as the first all-Spanish podcast, *Al Grano con María Hinojosa*, released in June of 2007.

UNIDAD 15

CONTENIDO

In this unit, you will learn:

1 - Vocabulary related to household chores and errands

2 - About expressions of frequency

3 - About the verb 'ir' and the structure 'ir a + infinitive'

4 - Vocabulary related to fun activities

5 - Cultural information about household chores and gender roles

los quehaceres domésticos

LOS QUEHACERES DOMÉSTICOS[1]

(Household chores)

When Peter asks Ana how she spends her weekends, he is again surprised to hear that she still has no time to go out with friends or relax. Then, Ana tells him about the different household chores that each family member does during the weekend.

EL FIN DE SEMANA *(The weekend)*

SÁBADO

Ana — pasar la aspiradora *(vacuum)*, preparar la comida del fin de semana, hacer las camas *(make the beds)*, ayudar a las niñas con su tarea del colegio *(help the girls with their homework)*, limpiar la letrina de Arigato *(clean Arigato's litter box)*

Enrique — lavar la ropa *(do laundry)*, colgar la ropa limpia en el armario *(hang clean clothes in the closet)*, ir al supermercado *(go grocery shopping)*, revisar que los coches están funcionando adecuadamente *(check that the cars are working properly)*

Sofía — barrer el suelo[2] *(sweep the floor)*, quitar la mesa *(clear the table)*, poner los platos en el lavaplatos *(put the dishes in the dishwasher)*, recoger los platos *(put away the dishes)*

[Footnotes]

[1] Other expressions for 'housework' are 'las faenas domésticas' and 'las tareas domésticas.'

[2] Another word for 'suelo' is 'piso.' Whereas the word 'suelo' only means the floor you step on, the word 'piso' can mean both the floor you step on and the floors of a multi-story building. For example, in the elevator, you can ask somebody '¿A qué piso va?' (What floor are you going to?), but you cannot ask '¿A qué suelo va?'

Rosa — **recoger los juguetes** *(put away the toys)*, **ordenar la habitación de las niñas** *(pick up the girls' room)*, **sacudir el polvo** *(dust)*

DOMINGO

Ana — **planchar la ropa** *(iron clothes)*, **preparar la comida de la semana siguiente, limpiar el baño** *(clean the bathroom)*

Enrique — **cortar la hierba o limpiar el jardín** *(mow the lawn or clean the garden)*, **ordenar el garaje** *(pick up the garage)*, **sacar la basura** *(take out the garbage)*

Sofía — **quitar la mesa, poner los platos en el lavaplatos, recoger los platos**

Rosa — **recoger los juguetes, ordenar la habitación, regar las plantas** *(water the plants)*

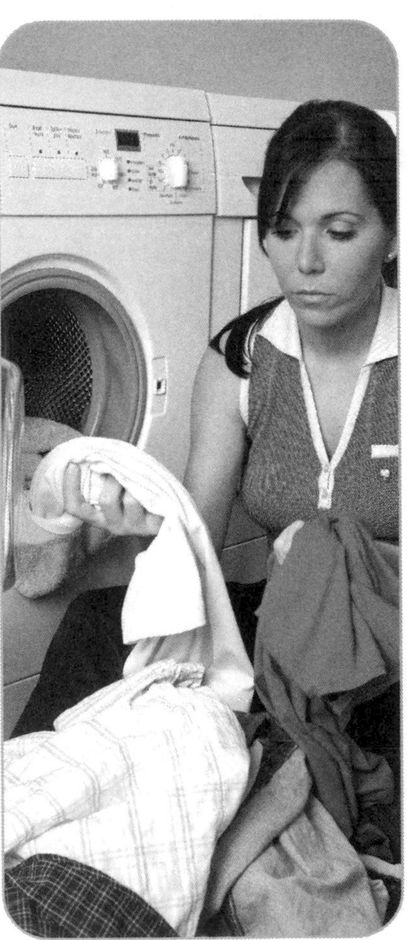

Ejercicio A

Enlaza las acciones con sus elementos para formar quehaceres domésticos.

1) recoger	a) el suelo
2) sacudir	b) la comida
3) quitar	c) la hierba
4) cortar	d) el polvo
5) planchar	e) la aspiradora
6) barrer	f) la mesa
7) preparar	g) la ropa
8) hacer	h) los platos en el lavaplatos
9) poner	i) los juguetes
10) pasar	j) la cama

Respuestas A: **1)** - i / **2)** - d / **3)** - f / **4)** - c / **5)** - g / **6)** - a / **7)** - b / **8)** - j / **9)** - h / **10)** - e

Ejercicio B

Enlaza ahora los quehaceres domésticos con las herramientas *(tools)* **o elementos necesarios** *(necessary elements).*

1) planchar con

2) pasar la aspiradora por

3) lavar la ropa en

4) barrer el suelo con

5) poner los platos en

6) poner la basura en

7) sacudir el polvo de

8) secar la ropa en

a) los muebles *(furniture)*

b) el lavaplatos

c) la secadora *(dryer)*

d) la plancha *(iron)*

e) la alfombra *(carpet)*

f) la escoba *(broom)*

g) la lavadora *(washer)*

h) el cubo *(bucket)* de la basura

Respuestas B: **1)** - d) / **2)** - e) / **3)** - g) / **4)** - f) / **5)** - b) / **6)** - h) / **7)** - a) / **8)** - c)

EXPRESIONES DE FRECUENCIA

The following expressions can be used to indicate how often you do a particular activity. To ask how frequently someone does something, you can ask/say:

¿con qué frecuencia?/
¿cada cuánto tiempo?/
¿cada cuánto?
(how often?)

cada día/todos los días
(every day)

siempre / *(always)*

casi siempre / *(almost always)*

un día sí y otro no
(every other day)

a menudo / *(often)*

frecuentemente/
con frecuencia
(frequently)

muchas veces / *(many times)*

de vez en cuando
(once in a while)

a veces/algunas veces
(sometimes)

un par de veces
(a couple of times)

una vez a la semana/
una vez por semana
(once a week)

dos veces al mes
(twice a month)

tres veces al año
(three times a year)

casi nunca, raras veces
(almost never, rarely)

nunca[3] / *(never)*

[Footnotes]

[3] *When 'casi nunca' or 'nunca' fall after the verb, you must put a 'no' before the verb (no barro el suelo nunca). When 'casi nunca' or 'nunca' go before the verb, it is not necessary to use the 'no' (nunca barro el suelo).*

Ejercicio C

¿Con qué frecuencia....? Completa estas frases con la forma apropiada de los verbos en paréntesis y una expresión de frecuencia (clue provided in English). La primera frase está hecha *(done)*.

1) Ana ___plancha___ (planchar) la ropa ___una vez a la semana___ *(1 x week)*

2) Enrique __________ (sacar) la basura __________ *(every day)*

3) Rosa __________ (regar[4]) las plantas __________ *(2 x month)*

4) Sofía __________ (hacer) las camas __________ *(sometimes)*

5) Ana no __________ (ordenar) el garaje __________ *(almost never)*

6) Rosa no __________ (preparar) la comida __________ *(never)*

7) Sofía y Rosa __________ (recoger) sus juguetes __________ *(often)*

Respuestas C: **2)** saca - todos los días (o cada día) / **3)** riega - dos veces al mes / **4)** hace - a veces (o algunas veces) / **5)** ordena - casi nunca / **6)** prepara - nunca / **7)** recogen - a menudo (o con frecuencia) (o frecuentemente)

[Footnotes] *[4] 'Regar' is a stem-vowel changing verb (e>ie).*

HACER RECADOS[5] *(Running errands)*

In addition to her daily and weekly household chores, Ana explains to Peter that she and her family run a lot of errands in their neighborhood.

Cada 15 días voy al banco a depositar mi cheque.

De vez en cuando Enrique va a la oficina de correos *(post office)* a recoger *(pick up)* un paquete postal.

Dos domingos al mes todos *(we all)* vamos a la iglesia *(church)*.

Una vez al mes Sofía visita a su doctor en el hospital.

Cada semana Enrique va al supermercado a comprar comida.

Una vez al mes voy al estacionamiento *(parking garage)* y pago *(I pay)* mi cuota mensual *(monthly fee)*.

Cuatro veces al mes voy a la tintorería *(dry cleaner's)* para llevar *(take)* mi ropa sucia *(dirty)*.

Nunca tengo tiempo de ir a la peluquería *(hairdresser's)*.

A veces voy a la ferretería *(hardware store)* para comprar herramientas *(tools)*.

[Footnotes] *[5] Another word for 'errand' is 'mandado.'*

Ejercicio D

Responde estas preguntas con frases completas usando *(using)* **la información previa** *(previous)*.

1) ¿Quién paga la cuota del estacionamiento?

____

2) ¿Con qué frecuencia va Ana a la peluquería a cortarse el pelo?

____

3) ¿Cuántas veces al mes va Sofía al hospital?

____

4) ¿Adónde va Ana con su ropa sucia?

____

5) ¿Qué hace Ana en el banco?

____

6) ¿Qué compra Ana en la ferretería?

____

7) ¿Cuándo van todos a la iglesia?

____

8) ¿Qué hace Enrique en la oficina de correos?

____

9) ¿Cada cuánto va Enrique al supermercado?

____

10) ¿A quién visita Sofía en el hospital?

____

Respuestas D: **1)** Ana paga la cuota. / **2)** Ana nunca va a la peluquería. (o Ana no va a la peluquería nunca) (o Ana nunca tiene tiempo de ir a la peluquería.) / **3)** Sofía va al hospital una vez al mes. / **4)** Ana va a la tintorería. / **5)** Ana deposita su cheque. / **6)** Ana compra herramientas. / **7)** Todos van a la iglesia dos domingos al mes. / **8)** Enrique recoge un paquete postal. / **9)** Enrique va al supermercado cada semana. / **10)** Sofía visita a su doctor.

EL VERBO 'IR'

You have probably already noticed the irregular conjugation of the verb 'ir':

IR *(to go)*
voy
vas
va
vamos
vais
van

The verb 'to go' can be used to indicate the action of going somewhere. If you mention where you are going, then you must use the preposition 'a,' followed by the destination. When 'a' is followed by the article 'el,' write the contraction 'al.'

Ana va a la tintorería
Enrique va al supermercado
Yo voy a España

In addition, the verb 'to go' can be used to indicate an immediate future action (I am going to…). It is followed by the preposition 'a' and then a verb in the infinitive.

Yo voy a comer pronto
Tú vas a dormir luego
Nosotros vamos a estudiar

And if you want to indicate an immediate future action and also mention where you are going, both in the same sentence, here is how you do it:

Ana va a la tintorería a llevar su ropa
Ana va a llevar su ropa a la tintorería

Ejercicio E

Escribe los recados que tú tienes que hacer esta semana.
Usa vocabulario de esta unidad y usa el verbo 'ir' en la forma 'yo.'

El martes	El miércoles	El viernes	El fin de semana
______	______	______	______
______	______	______	______
______	______	______	______
______	______	______	______
______	______	______	______
______	______	______	______
______	______	______	______

ACTIVIDADES DE OCIO

(Spare time/fun activities)

Peter suggests that Ana take off a couple of hours a week to do something she likes, so she does not feel so frustrated. Her family can help with the household chores when she is not at home. Her husband and she can take turns at home, so that they can both rest and do fun activities. These are some of the places and activities that Peter suggests to her:

ir a ver una película al cine
(go to see a movie at the movie theater)

salir a un bar o restaurante con amigas
(go out to a bar or restaurant with friends)

pasear por el parque y observar a la gente
(walk in the park and watch people)

visitar a algún amigo en el hospital
(visit a friend at the hospital)

ir al teatro a ver una obra de teatro
(go to the theater to see a play)

ir al salón de belleza a hacerse un masaje, una pedicura o una manicura
(go to the beauty salon to get a massage, a pedicure, or a manicure)

ir a la peluquería a cortarse el pelo
(go to the hairdresser's to get a haircut)

ir a correr[6] al parque / *(go jogging in the park)*

hacer ejercicio en el gimnasio / *(exercise at the gym)*

leer un libro / *(read a book)*

llamar por teléfono a una vieja amiga
(call an old friend)

ir al parque de atracciones con sus hijas
(go to the amusement park with her daughters)

[Footnotes]

[6] *'Correr' can mean both 'running' and 'jogging.' In some countries, the word 'trotar' (to trot) refers to jogging only.*

ir a la piscina pública a nadar
(go to the public swimming pool to swim)

ver su programa de televisión favorito
(watch her favorite television program)

tomar el sol en la terraza
(sunbathe on the balcony)

ir a mirar escaparates
(go window-shopping)

ir al zoológico / *(go to the zoo)*

ir a un museo / *(go to a museum)*

Ejercicio F

¿Qué actividad vas a hacer esta semana?

En mi tiempo libre *(free time)*,
esta semana yo voy a

____

____

____

____

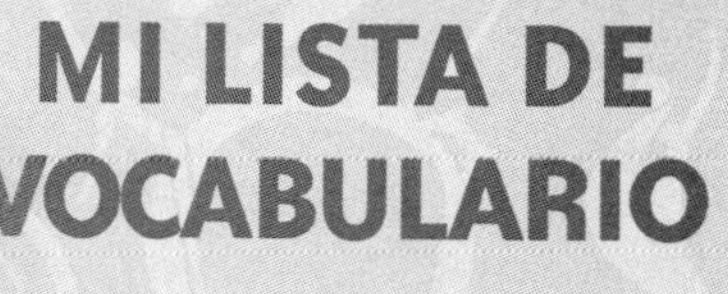

MI LISTA DE VOCABULARIO

This is a list of the words that you have learned in this unit.

a la semana
a menudo
a veces o algunas veces
al año
al día
al mes
(la) alfombra
allá
barrer
(la) basura
¿cada cuánto?/¿con qué frecuencia?
cada día/todos los días
casi nunca
casi siempre
cortar
(la) cuota mensual
de vez en cuando
depositar
(el) escaparate
(la) escoba
(el) estacionamiento
favorito
(la) ferretería
(el) fin de semana
frecuentemente o con frecuencia
hacer ejercicio
(la) herramienta
(la) hierba
(la) iglesia
ir

(la) lavadora
lavar
limpiar
limpio
llamar por teléfono
(la) manicura
(el) masaje
muchas veces
(el) mueble
(el) museo
nunca tengo tiempo de + *infinitivo*
(la) obra de teatro
observar
(el) ocio
ordenar
(el) paquete postal
para
(el) parque
pasar la aspiradora
(la) pedicura
(la) película
(la) piscina[7]
(la) plancha
planchar
previo
(el) programa de televisión
(los) quehaceres domésticos o (las) faenas domésticas
quitar
(el) recado o (el) mandado
recoger
regar
(la) ropa
sacar
sacudir el polvo
(el) salón de belleza
(la) secadora
siempre
siguiente
sucio
(el) suelo o (el) piso
(el) supermercado
(el) tiempo libre
(la) tintorería
un par de veces
una vez
(el) zoológico

[Footnotes]

[7] *Other words for 'piscina' are 'alberca' and 'pileta.'*

UN POCO DE CULTURA

Let's try reading in Spanish again. We think you are now ready for a longer text. Let's try this one on household chores.

Las faenas domésticas, los hombres y las mujeres

Tradicionalmente, los hombres y las mujeres hacen trabajos diferentes. Por ejemplo, las mujeres normalmente cocinan, cuidan *(take care)* a los hijos, y hacen los quehaceres domésticos, mientras que *(whereas)* los hombres trabajan y mantienen económicamente *(support)* a la familia.

Sin embargo *(However)*, con la modernización y la liberación de la mujer, estos papeles *(roles)* tradicionales han cambiado *(have changed)*, especialmente en las ciudades *(cities)* y en las clases sociales media y alta *(middle and high social classes)*, donde las mujeres reciben más educación.

Ahora hay muchos hombres que *(who)* cocinan o son muy activos en la educación de sus hijos, por ejemplo. También hay mujeres que ganan *(earn)* más dinero que sus esposos o toman la decisión de no casarse *(getting married)* o no tener hijos. Estos nuevos papeles cambian *(change)* un poco la dinámica *(dynamics)* de la sociedad *(society)*.

Cuando en una familia, el padre y la madre trabajan fuera *(outside)* de casa, es justo *(it is fair)* que los dos *(both)* compartan *(share)* las faenas domésticas y la atención a los hijos. En estos casos es normal ver a un hombre cocinando, pasando la aspiradora, o acostando a los niños.

A pesar de *(Despite)* todos estos cambios modernos, la tradición es todavía *(still)* muy fuerte. Por ejemplo, si por cualquier razón (médica, social, etc), uno de los padres tiene que estar en la casa, se espera que *(it is expected that)* la esposa deje *(gives up)* su trabajo y se quede *(remains)* en casa. Todavía no es común ver que el esposo se quede en casa y la esposa trabaje fuera de casa.

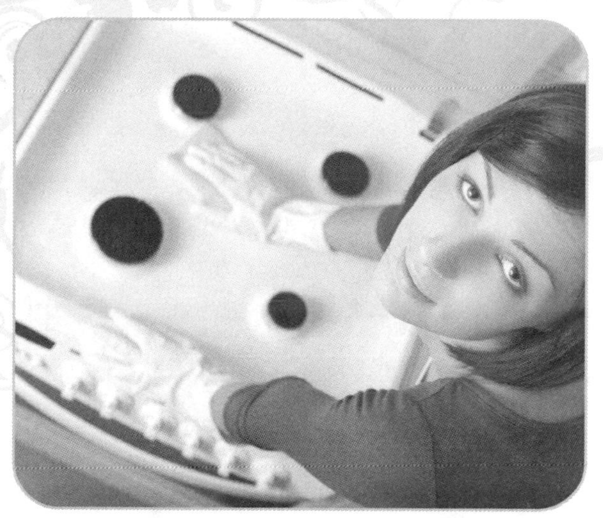

How did you do?
You should already know (or be able to guess) all the vocabulary and grammar that is not translated in the passage. If you did not understand the passage or had to look up many words in the dictionary, you should go back and review the first 13 lessons before continuing to the next unit. Even though you might think that reviewing will slow you down, it will actually help you learn the next lessons faster, and will eventually speed up your progress.

RECOMENDACIÓN PARA ESTA UNIDAD

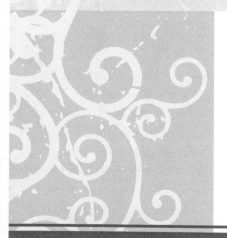

To finish the unit, we recommend that you pay attention this week to the household chores that you and other people around you perform, as well as the errands that you run. If you find a chore, a location, or a tool that is not mentioned in this unit, look it up and add it to your list. Also, try to notice whether these chores are influenced by traditional gender roles.

UNIDAD 16 CONTENIDO EXÁMEN 2

exámen 2

EXÁMEN 2

In this unit, you will find several exercises to practice what you have learned in units 9—15. If you do well in this second exam, go ahead and continue studying the next units. However, if you are not satisfied with your exam results, we recommend that you review the previous seven units before advancing.

Ejercicio A

Selecciona la palabra que NO corresponde con los verbos de los quehaceres domésticos.

1) limpiar
a) el polvo
b) el baño
c) la plancha

2) barrer
a) el suelo
b) el lavavajillas
c) el piso

3) planchar
a) la hierba
b) la ropa
c) la plancha

4) recoger
a) los platos
b) las plantas
c) los juguetes

5) ordenar
a) la habitación
b) el garaje
c) la comida

Respuestas A: **1)** - c) / **2)** - b) / **3)** - a) / **4)** - b) / **5)** - c)

Ejercicio B

Responde estas preguntas con frases completas sobre la frecuencia con la que estas personas hacen sus recados.

1) Félix / 3 x week — ¿Con qué frecuencia va Félix al gimnasio?

____

2) Loreto / Sundays — ¿Con qué frecuencia va Loreto [female] a la iglesia?

____

3) Roberto / 1 x month — ¿Cada cuánto limpia Roberto el jardín de su casa?

____

4) Flor / 2 x year — ¿Cada cuánto tiempo visita Flor [female] a su abuela?

____

5) Jerónimo / every other Saturday — ¿Cada cuánto prepara Jerónimo la comida de la semana?

____

Respuestas B: **1)** Félix va al gimnasio 3 veces por/a la semana / **2)** Loreto va a la iglesia cada domingo / todos los domingos / **3)** Roberto limpia el jardín (de su casa) una vez al mes / **4)** Flor visita a su abuela 2 veces al año / **5)** Jerónimo prepara la comida de la semana un sábado sí y otro no

Ejercicio C

Completa estas frases con la forma apropiada del verbo IR.

1) Azucena ________ al hospital porque está enferma.

2) Laura y María _______ al centro comercial para comprar ropa.

3) Yo no _______ al cine frecuentemente.

4) ¿_____________ tú a la farmacia hoy?

5) Nosotros no _____________ a ese restaurante nunca.

Respuestas C: **1)** va / **2)** van / **3)** voy / **4)** Vas / **5)** vamos

Ejercicio D

Utiliza del 1 al 6 para ordenar cronológicamente las siguientes acciones rutinarias.

___ me visto

___ me voy al trabajo

___ me ducho y me lavo los dientes

___ me despierto

___ me seco *(I dry myself off)*

___ me levanto inmediatamente

Respuestas D: **1)** me despierto / **2)** me levanto... / **3)** me ducho... / **4)** me seco / **5)** me visto / **6)** me voy...

Ejercicio E

Une con una linea el nombre de las personas con la acción que le corresponda

1) Antonio	**a)** se cepillan los dientes tres veces al día
2) Nosotras	**b)** me levanto a las 6 de la mañana
3) Tú	**c)** se pone la ropa rápidamente
4) Ustedes	**d)** te acuestas tarde
5) Yo	**e)** nos duchamos por la noche

Respuestas E: **1)** - c) / **2)** - e) / **3)** - d) / **4)** - c) / **5)** - b)

Ejercicio F

Observa el ejemplo 1 y conjuga correctamente los verbos de cambio radical *(stem-vowel changing verbs)*.

1) Lola / almorzar / 1pm — *Lola almuerza a la una de la tarde*

2) Federico / jugar / fútbol

3) Adela y Paco / despertarse / 8am

4) Nosotros / querer / ir al cine

5) Ustedes / no / servir / comida

Respuestas F: **2)** Federico juega (al) fútbol / **3)** Adela y Paco se despiertan a las 8 de la mañana / **4)** Nosotros queremos ir al cine / **5)** Ustedes no sirven (la) comida

Ejercicio G

Escribe en la linea el nombre de la habitación *(room)* **y el de los objetos que ves en ella.**

1) ______________________

2) ______________________

3) ______________________

4) ______________________

Respuestas G: **1)** SALA: sofá, escritorio, silla, alfombra, cuadros, espejo / **2)** CUARTO DE BAÑO: inodoro, lavabo, espejo, bañera-ducha, papel higiénico / **3)** COCINA: refrigerador, armario, microondas, horno-estufa, fregadero / **4)** DORMITORIO: cama, cómoda, armario, mesita de noche

Ejercicio H

Utiliza el presente progresivo y describe la actividad que están realizando las personas.

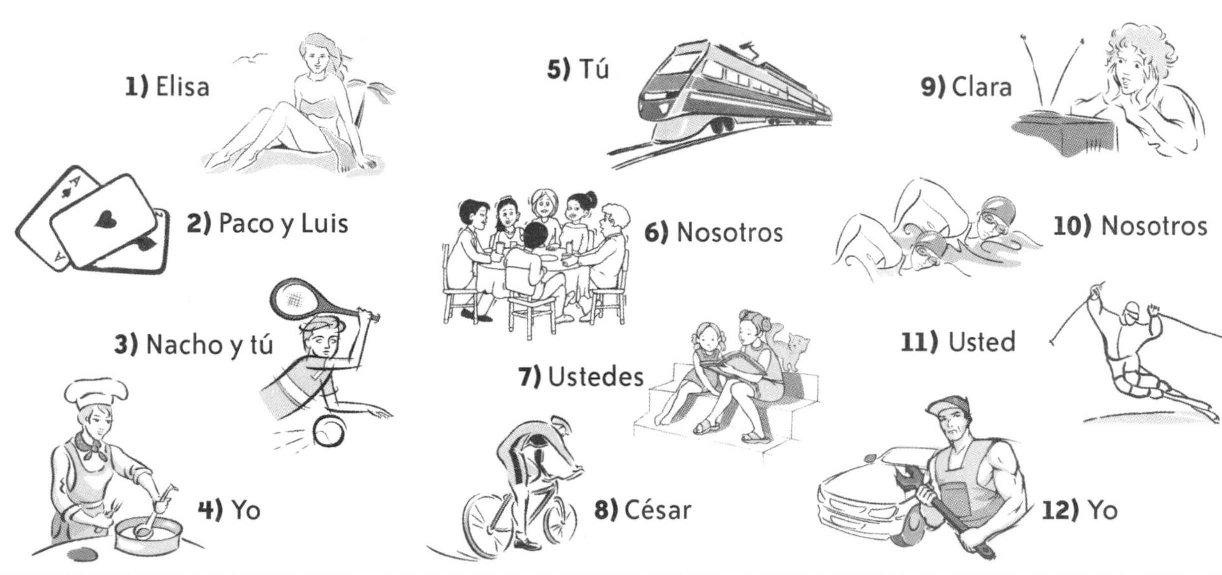

1) Elisa

2) Paco y Luis

3) Nacho y tú

4) Yo

5) Tú

6) Nosotros

7) Ustedes

8) César

9) Clara

10) Nosotros

11) Usted

12) Yo

Respuestas H: **1)** Elisa está tomando el sol / **2)** Paco y Luis están jugando (a las) cartas / **3)** Nacho y tú están jugando tenis / **4)** Yo estoy cocinando / **5)** Tú estás viajando en tren / **6)** Nosotros estamos comiendo en un restaurante / **7)** Ustedes están leyendo libros / **8)** César está montando en bicicleta / **9)** Clara está mirando la tele / **10)** Nosotros estamos nadando / **11)** Usted está esquiando / **12)** Yo estoy arreglando coches

Ejercicio I

Utiliza interrogativos apropiados (¿Dónde? ¿Cuándo? etc.) para traducir las siguientes preguntas.

1) Where is my car?

2) Whose house is that?

3) When do you (tú) return?

4) What's your (formal) name? / or

5) How are you (ustedes)?

6) Does he want this?

7) Do you (tú) live here?

8) What time is it?

9) What time is the movie?

10) Who are those men?

Respuestas I: **1)** ¿Dónde está mi coche - carro? / **2)** ¿De quién es esa casa? / **3)** ¿Cuándo regresas? / **4)** ¿Cómo se llama usted? - ¿Cuál es su nombre? / **5)** ¿Cómo están ustedes? / **6)** ¿Quiere él esto? / **7)** ¿Vives aquí? / **8)** ¿Qué hora es? / **9)** ¿A qué hora es la película? / **10)** ¿Quiénes son esos hombres?

Ejercicio J

Escribe el nombre de las profesiones que ves en las ilustraciones. Incluye el artículo definido (el, la) que corresponda.

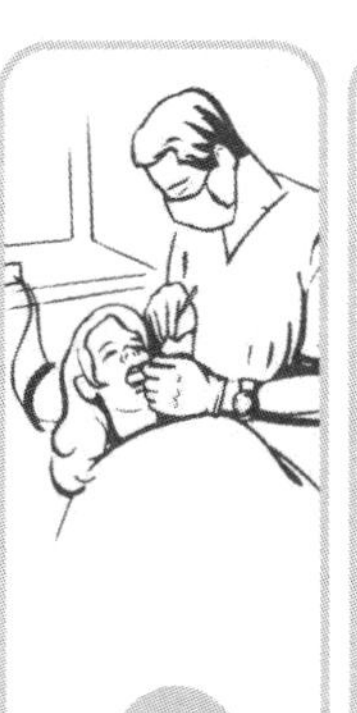

Respuestas J: **1)** el policía / **2)** la jueza / **3)** el panadero / **4)** la estudiante / **5)** el dentista / **6)** la actriz / **7)** el músico

Ejercicio K

Observa el ejemplo 1 y describe la actividad que está realizando cada persona. Utiliza la forma YO irregular de los verbos que están dentro del paréntesis.

1) (traer)

Yo traigo flores.

2) (decir)

Yo _______ 'Hola'.

3) (dar)

Yo _______ un regalo a Juan.

4) (ser)

Yo _______ católico.

5) (ver)

Yo _______ la tele.

Respuestas K: **2)** digo / **3)** doy / **4)** soy / **5)** veo

Ejercicio L

Responde las siguientes preguntas sobre el clima. Usando 'hace', 'está', u otras expresiones.

1) ¿Qué tiempo hace en Chicago en invierno?

____

____

2) ¿Qué tiempo hace en Florida en verano?

____

____

Posibles respuestas L: **1)** En Chicago hace frío y viento, nieva y está nublado / **2)** En Florida hace calor y está soleado, y no llueve mucho

Ejercicio M

Traduce las siguientes palabras relacionadas con el clima. No necesitas artículos.

1) lightning ____________________

2) thunder ____________________

3) ice ____________________

4) earthquake ____________________

5) to hail ____________________

6) cool ____________________

Respuestas M: **1)** rayo - relámpago / **2)** trueno / **3)** hielo / **4)** terremoto / **5)** granizar / **6)** fresco

UNIDAD 16

Ejercicio N

Observa el ejemplo 1 y escribe el mes del año que corresponde a los siguientes días festivos.

1) Día de Acción de Gracias

noviembre

2) Año Nuevo

____

3) Navidad

____

4) Día de la Independencia

____

5) San Valentín

____

6) Tu cumpleaños

____

Respuestas N: **2)** enero / **3)** diciembre / **4)** julio / **5)** febrero

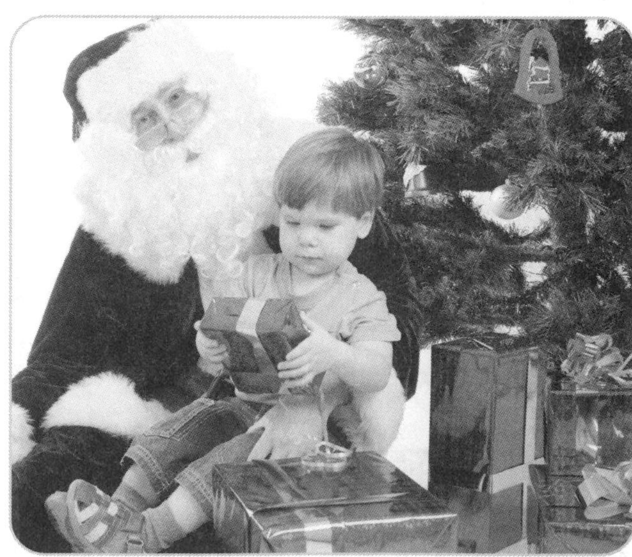

Ejercicio Ñ

¿Qué hora es? Escribe tu respuesta en formato análogo y digital.

1)  ______________________

____

____

2)  ______________________

____

____

3)  ______________________

____

____

Respuestas Ñ: **1)** Son las ocho y cuarto - Son las ocho y quince / **2)** Son las cuatro menos cuarto (or, quedan quince para las cuatro') - Son las tres y cuarenta y cinco / **3)** Es la una en punto

Ejercicio O

Responde estas preguntas con frases completas.

1) ¿Dónde vives?

2) ¿Comprendes la lección?

3) ¿Tienes preguntas?

4) ¿A qué hora regresas a casa del trabajo?

5) ¿Con quién practicas español?

Posibles respuestas O: **1)** Vivo en (plus your address, city, etc) / **2)** Sí, comprendo la lección - No, no comprendo la lección. / **3)** Sí, tengo preguntas - No, no tengo preguntas / **4)** Regreso a casa a las (plus hour) / **5)** Practico español con X - No practico español con nadie

Ejercicio P

Escribe los siguientes números en español.

1) 85 ______________

2) 100 ______________

3) 12 ______________

4) 98 ______________

5) 75 ______________

Respuestas P: **1)** ochenta y cinco / **2)** cien / **3)** doce / **4)** noventa y ocho / **5)** setenta y cinco

UNIDAD 17

UNIDAD 17 CONTENIDO

In this unit, you will learn:

1 - Vocabulary related to sports and other interests

2 - About the structure of 'gustar'

3 - About other verbs with the 'gustar' structure

4 - Cultural information about some famous Hispanic/ Latino sport figures

los deportes

LOS DEPORTES

(Sports)

Peter's suggestions seem interesting. Ana would like to get some exercise, but she does not know what to try.

Peter: Entonces, ¿te gusta la idea de practicar algún deporte? *(So, do you like the idea of doing a sport?)*

Ana: Sí, mucho. Me gusta nadar. Quizás.... *(Yes, a lot. I like to swim. Maybe...)*

Peter: Sí, nadar es bueno, pero la piscina pública está en obras *(but the public swimming pool is under construction)* y no puedes ir ahora *(and you cannot go now)*.

Ana: Oh, sí, es verdad. Tengo que esperar.... También me fascina correr... *(Oh, yes, that's true. I have to wait.... I also love to run....)*

Peter: Correr es muy bueno para el metabolismo *(for the metabolism)* en general. ¿Y qué tal montar en bicicleta? *(And what about riding a bike)* O caminar por el parque? *(Or walking in the park?)* Tu familia puede ir contigo *(Your family can go with you)*

Ana: Sí, suena bien *(that sounds good)*. De hecho *(Actually)*, a mi hija Sofía le gustan las actividades más tranquilas, como el yoga. Quizás *(Maybe)* podemos *(we can)* hacer yoga juntas *(together)* una vez a la semana.

Peter: ¡Buena idea! ¿Ves? *(You see?)* Hay muchas cosas que puedes hacer para entretenerte *(There are many things you can do to entertain yourself)*.

Ana: Sí, tienes razón. *(Yes, you are right.)*

Peter:	Además *(Besides)*, no necesitas practicar un deporte. Puedes entretenerte simplemente caminando por la calle o mirando escaparates *(window shopping)*… nada muy difícil.
Ana:	¡Por supuesto! Gracias por todas tus ideas.

When Ana gets home, she looks at a book she has about sports and the equipment needed to play them.

atletismo
zapatillas deportivas, pista de atletismo

ciclismo
bicicleta, casco

gimnasia
gimnasio

natación
piscina, traje de baño

baloncesto[1]
balón/pelota de baloncesto, cancha de baloncesto, canasta/cesta

esquí
esquís, nieve, botas de esquí

golf
palos, pelotas, campo de golf

patinaje sobre hielo
patines de hielo, pista de hielo

béisbol
bate, pelota de béisbol, guante

fútbol
balón/pelota de fútbol, campo de fútbol, espinilleras

kárate
y otras artes marciales, karategui, cinturón

patinaje sobre ruedas
patines de ruedas

caminar
zapatillas deportivas[2]

fútbol americano
casco, balón de fútbol americano,

[Footnotes]

[1] *Many Spanish-speakers also say 'basketball' or 'basket' with a Spanish pronunciation.*

[2] *There are many other words for 'sneakers,' such as 'zapatos deportivos,' 'playeras,' 'tenis,' etc.*

tenis
raqueta, pelota de tenis, cancha de tenis

voleibol
pelota de voleibol, red

yoga
colchoneta, ropa cómoda

Ejercicio A

Selecciona la palabra que NO corresponde a estos deportes.

1) natación	a) patines	b) agua	c) piscina
2) ciclismo	a) bicicleta	b) casco	c) pelota
3) baloncesto	a) pelota	b) karategui	c) cancha
4) golf	a) palos	b) esquíes	c) pelota
5) atletismo	a) pista	b) zapatillas	c) bicicleta
6) yoga	a) ropa cómoda	b) palos	c) colchoneta
7) patinaje sobre hielo	a) canasta	b) patines	c) pista

Respuestas A: **1)** - a) / **2)** - c) / **3)** - b) / **4)** - b) / **5)** - c) / **6)** - b) / **7)** - a)

Ejercicio B

Enlaza con una línea los deportes con los verbos que le corresponden.

1) natación
2) béisbol
3) yoga
4) patinaje
5) esquí
6) atletismo
7) ciclismo

a) jugar
b) correr
c) esquiar
d) montar
e) nadar
f) patinar
g) hacer

Respuestas B: **1)** - e) / **2)** - a) / **3)** - g) / **4)** - f) / **5)** - c) / **6)** - b) / **7)** - d)

LA ESTRUCTURA 'GUSTAR'

The verb 'gustar' does not follow the conjugation pattern that we have seen so far. Although it is often translated as 'to like,' it functions more along the lines of 'to please.' So when we say 'I like sports' in Spanish, we are actually saying 'sports please me,' where 'sports' is the subject. Let's take a look at the elements of the structure. This type of conjugation also applies to other verbs that we will see in a moment.

1+2 **Preposition plus prepositional pronoun**[3]	3 **Negation**	4 **Indirect object pronoun**	5 **Verb**	6+7 **Subject** (article plus noun) (proper name) (verb) (que + another sentence)
A mí		me		el[4] chocolate *(a noun in singular)*
A ti		te	gusta	
A[5] Peter, a ella/a usted	no	le		nadar *(one or more verbs)*
A nosotros, as		nos		que tú seas de Perú *(a sentence)*
A vosotros, as		os	gustan	
A Peter y a Ana, a ellas/a ustedes		les		los niños *(a noun in plural)*

Ejemplos *(Examples)*:

(A mí) me gusta el fútbol *(I like soccer)*

(A ti) te gustan los deportes *(You like sports)*

A Peter le gusta mirar la tele *(Peter likes to watch TV)*

(A nosotros) nos gusta correr y caminar *(We like to run and to walk)*

¿A ustedes les gustan mis patines nuevos? *(Do you guys like my new skates?)*

A Peter y a Ana les gusta su trabajo *(Peter and Ana like their job)*

[Footnotes]

[3] *This part is a repetition of the pronoun in #4, so it is often omitted unless is needed to clarify or emphasize who is receiving the action.*
[4] *Don't forget the article, even though it is not there in English (e.g., I like children = Me gustan los niños).*
[5] *Don't forget the 'a' (e.g., Peter likes to run = A Pedro le gusta correr).*

Ejercicio C

Enlaza el principio *(beginning)* **de estas frases con el final apropiado.**

1) A Sofía

2) A Ana y a Enrique

3) A mí

4) A ti

5) A nosotros

a) no les gustan las faenas domésticas

b) nos gusta patinar sobre hielo

c) te gusta el fútbol

d) le gusta el yoga

e) me gustan los deportes

Respuestas C: **1)** - d) / **2)** - a) / **3)** - e) / **4)** - c) / **5)** - b)

Ejercicio D

Traduce las siguientes frases.

1) We (masc.) don't like martial arts. ______

2) Fabiana, do you like this racquet? ______

3) I like this golf club a lot. ______

4) What do you (tú) like to do at the gym? ______

5) My friends like to play basketball twice a week. ______

6) Mr. Pérez, do you like the new golf course? ______

7) I don't like it. ______

8) Juliana likes the public swimming pool. ______

9) You (ustedes) like to skate on ice. ______

10) They (fem.) like the basketball court because it is big. ______

Respuestas D: **1)** (A nosotros) no nos gustan las artes marciales. / **2)** Fabiana, ¿te gusta esta raqueta? / **3)** (A mí) me gusta mucho este palo de golf. / **4)** ¿(A ti) qué te gusta hacer en el gimnasio? / **5)** A mis amigos les gusta jugar al baloncesto dos veces a la semana. / **6)** Señor Pérez, (a usted) le gusta el campo de golf nuevo? - el nuevo campo de golf? / **7)** No me gusta. / **8)** A Juliana le gusta la piscina pública. / **9)** A ustedes les gusta patinar sobre hielo. / **10)** A ellas les gusta la cancha de baloncesto porque es grande.

OTROS INTERESES

(Other interests)

Enrique, Ana's husband, also like Peter's suggestions that they try to relax more. He is looking for something to do every once in a while. His daughter brings him a book for ideas.

1) aprender a tocar el piano

6) estudiar historia antigua de Egipto

2) fotografía

7) aprender carpintería

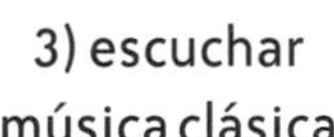

3) escuchar música clásica

8) aprender diseño gráfico

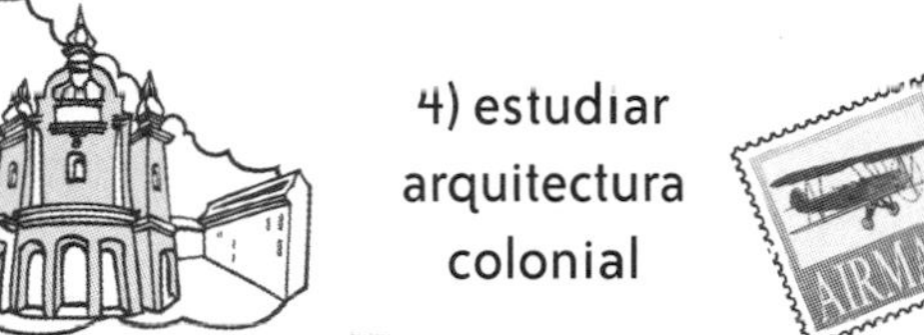

4) estudiar arquitectura colonial

9) coleccionar sellos

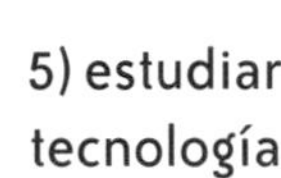

5) estudiar tecnología

10) aprender mecánica

Ejercicio E

Can you tell what these disciplines are in English? Most of them are cognates.

1) ______________________

2) ______________________

3) ______________________

4) ______________________

5) ______________________

6) ______________________

7) ______________________

8) ______________________

9) ______________________

10) ______________________

Respuestas E: **1)** learn how to play the piano / **2)** photography / **3)** listen to classical music / **4)** study colonial architecture / **5)** study technology / **6)** study ancient history of Egypt / **7)** learn carpentry / **8)** learn graphic design / **9)** collect stamps / **10)** learn mechanics

VERBOS CON ESTRUCTURA 'GUSTAR' *(Verbs with the 'gustar' structure)*

Other verbs also use the 'gustar' structure. Here is a list of common ones:

gustar *(to like)* encantar *(to like a lot / to love)* disgustar *(to annoy)*

interesar *(to interest)* fascinar *(to fascinate)* molestar *(to bother)*

doler *(to hurt[6])* caer bien *(to like [a person]/to fit well [clothes]/to sit well [food])*

caer mal *(to dislike [a person]/to fit badly [clothes]/to sit badly [food])*

parecer bien/mal *(to seem OK or not)* emocionar *(to excite)* aburrir *(to bore)*

dar asco *(to disgust)* dar miedo *(to scare)* preocupar *(to worry)*

Ejemplos:

A Ramón le emocionan los animales marinos. Por eso *(that's why)* él estudia biología marina.

A Patricia le aburren las películas. Por eso, ella nunca va al cine.

Me duele[7] la cabeza *(head)*. Por eso, tomo Tylenol.

A mis padres les da asco la cerveza *(beer)*. Por esta razón, ellos siempre beben vino *(wine)*.

[Footnotes]

[6] 'Doler' can only be used when a part of the body is causing pain. When you want to say that somebody hurt you, the verb is not 'doler,' but 'hacer daño' or 'lastimar.'

[7] When indicating that a part of your body hurts, you don't have to say 'my teeth' or 'my head.' Instead, write 'the teeth,' 'the head,' etc. (e.g., My back hurts = Me duele la espalda).

Ejercicio F

Completa estas frases con un elemento de la estructura 'gustar'.

1) Me ________________ bien Federico.

2) A Jaime ________________ encanta la fotografía.

3) A mis padres les ______________ coleccionar sellos.

4) ________ Elena y a José les interesa la mecánica.

5) Me duelen __________________ pies.

Respuestas F: **1)** cae / **2)** le / **3)** fascina, gusta, etc / **4)** A / **5)** los

Ejercicio G

Traduce estas frases usando la estructura 'gustar'. *(Always start with the person).*

1) History bores Ernesto. ______________________________________

2) Studying mechanics is exciting to Gerardo. ______________________________________

3) We (masc.) don't like sports. ______________________________________

4) The theater play seems fine *(use parece bien)* to me. ______________________________________

5) The problems of the world worry you (ustedes). ______________________________________

6) Mexican food disgusts you (usted). ______________________________________

Respuestas G: **1)** A Ernesto le aburre la historia. / **2)** A Gerardo le emociona estudiar mecánica. / **3)** (A nosotros) no nos gustan los deportes. / **4)** (A mí) me parece bien la obra de teatro. / **5)** A ustedes les preocupan los problemas del mundo. / **6)** A usted le da asco la comida mexicana.

Ejercicio H

Ahora completa esto con tu información. Circle the correct verb form that goes with what you write.

1) Me gusta/Me gustan

____

____

2) Me molesta/Me molestan

____

____

3) Me aburre/Me aburren

____

____

4) Me emociona/Me emocionan

____

____

5) Me da miedo/Me dan miedo

____

____

6) Me duele/Me duelen *(+ a body part)*

____

____

7) Me interesa/Me interesan

____

____

8) Me fascina/Me fascinan

____

____

MI LISTA DE VOCABULARIO

This is a list of the words that you have learned in this unit.

aburrir	en
(la) arquitectura colonial	encantar
(las) artes marciales	entretenerse
(el) atletismo	esperar
(el) balón	(la) espinillera
(el) baloncesto/ (el) basketball	(el) esquí
	estar en obras
(el) bate	fascinar
(el) béisbol	(la) fotografía
(las) botas de esquí	(el) fútbol
¡buena idea!	(el) fútbol americano
bueno	(la) gimnasia
(la) cabeza	(el) golf
caer bien/caer mal	(el) guante
(el) campo	gustar
(la) canasta	(la) historia antigua
(la) cancha	(la) idea
(la) carpintería	(el) interés
(el) casco	interesar
(la) cerveza	juntos
(el) ciclismo	(el) kárate
(el) cinturón	(el) karategui
(la) colchoneta	(la) mecánica
coleccionar sellos	(el) metabolismo
contigo	molestar
(la) cultura indígena	montar a caballo
emocionar	(la) natación

(el) palo	(la) pista de hielo	¡tienes razón!
parecer	por eso /por esta razón	(el) traje de baño
(el) patinaje sobre hielo/ sobre ruedas	preocupar	(la) verdad
	público	¿ves?
(los) patines de hielo/de ruedas	quizás	(el) vino
	(la) red	(el) voleibol
(la) pelota	simplemente	(el) yoga
(la) piscina	¡suena bien!	(las) zapatillas deportivas
(la) pista de atletismo	(la) tecnología	

UN POCO DE CULTURA

Deportistas hispanos/latinos famosos

Un boxeador

Óscar de la Hoya, de ascendencia mexicana, nació *(was born)* en Los Ángeles en 1973. Óscar boxea desde pequeño y ha ganado *(has won)* numerosos premios *(prizes)*, incluyendo la medalla de oro *(gold medal)* en los Juegos Olímpicos de Barcelona de 1992. De sus 43 campeonatos *(championships)* profesionales, ha ganado 38. Óscar también es un hombre de negocios y tiene empresas *(companies)* en bienes raíces *(real state)*, ropa *(clothing)*, y programas de televisión.

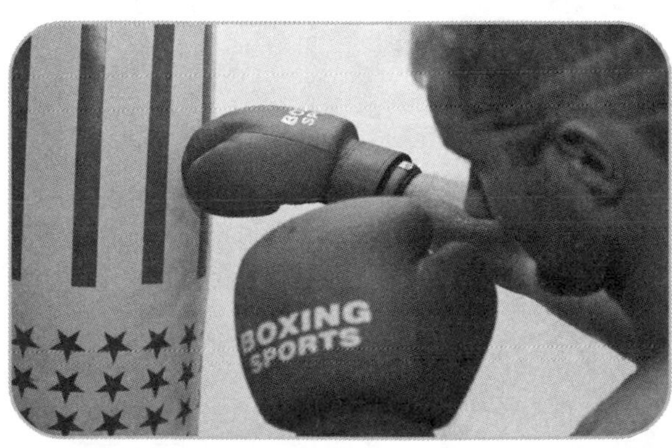

Una tenista

Arantxa Sánchez-Vicario nació en España en 1971. Desde los años 80 ha ganado premios en varios torneos *(championships)* famosos, como el Roland Garros, el Abierto de Australia, Wimbledon, y el Abierto de Estados Unidos. Es la primera y única *(only)* mujer española que fue *(was)* Número 1 en la WTA (Women's Tennis Association). También fue campeona del mundo *(world champion)* en 1994. En el año 2002, Arantxa anunció su retiro *(announced her retirement)* del tenis.

Un jugador de béisbol

Sammy Sosa (Samuel Peralta Sosa), de la República Dominicana, viene de una familia muy grande (siete hermanos) y muy pobre. Es jugador de béisbol (o pelotero) desde pequeño *(since he was a child)* y tuvo *(had)* la oportunidad de jugar con los Chicago Cubs, haciéndose famoso *(becoming famous)* especialmente en 1998, cuando rompió *(broke)* un récord mundial de jonrones[8] *(homeruns)*.

Un jugador de fútbol

Carlos 'El Pibe' Valderrama es un jugador de fútbol colombiano que nació en 1963. Ha jugado *(He has played)* para Francia, España y Estados Unidos. Ha sido *(He has been)* capitán de la selección de Colombia por 11 años.

[Footnotes]

[8] 'Jonrón' (phonetic adaptation of 'homerun') is a popular word in Latino communities in the United States.

RECOMENDACIÓN PARA ESTA UNIDAD

To finish this unit, we recommend that you check out the sports pages of a newspaper from a Spanish-speaking country. Click on this website and select a country: http://www.prensaescrita.com/

Check the 'Deportes' section to see what kind of sports they discuss and whether they report in the same way that United States newspapers do. Read some articles and see how much you understand.

UNIDAD 18

CONTENIDO

In this unit, you will learn:

1 - Vocabulary related to clothes and shopping

2 - Expressions with 'tener'

3 - Vocabulary related to materials, fabrics and designs

4 - Cultural information about Hispanics/Latinos in the fashion industry

la ropa

LA ROPA[1]

(Clothes)

Ana just realized that she has not bought new clothes in a long time, so she is thinking of going to the mall to relax a little while shopping. These are some of the items she sees at the mall for her and for her husband.

camisa de manga larga

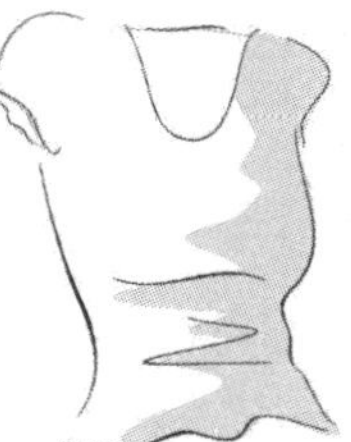

camiseta[2]

medias[4]

blusa

chaqueta[3]

calcetines

camisa de manga corta

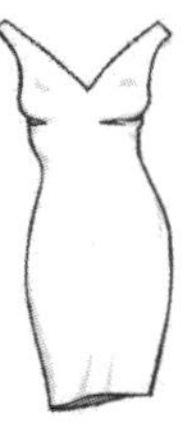

vestido

pantalones largos

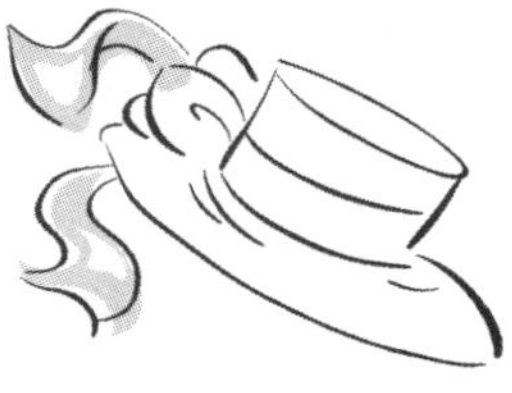
sombrero

abrigo[6]

sostén[7]

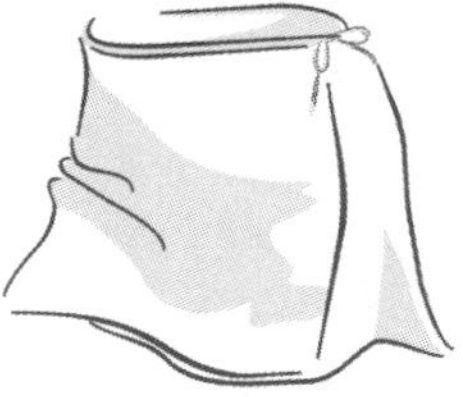
falda

jeans/vaqueros

suéter de cuello alto

bragas[8]

suéter/jersey

guantes

calzoncillos[9]

pantalones cortos

traje de chaqueta

gorra

pijama[5]

impermeable

gorro

esmoquin

vestido de noche

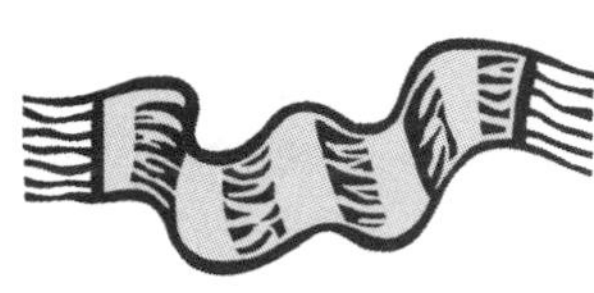
bufanda

[Footnotes]

[1] *Even though in English this word is plural, in Spanish, 'ropa' is a singular word (e.g., esta ropa es bonita* = these clothes are beautiful*).*

[2] *Another word for t-shirt is 'playera.'*

[3] *Other words for jacket are 'chamarra,' 'cazadora,' 'saco,' and 'americana.'*

[4] *In some countries, 'medias' means 'socks,' but in others, 'medias' means 'pantyhose.'*

[5] *'Pijama' is some countries is masculine and in others is feminine. It is also sometimes in the plural (pijamas).*

[6] *Another common word for 'coat' is 'saco.'*

[7] *Other words for 'bra' are 'sujetador' and 'brasier.'*

[8] *Other words for female underwear include 'pantaletas,' 'panties,' 'bombachas,' and 'calzones.'*

[9] *Other words for male underwear include 'shorts' and 'calzones.'*

Ejercicio A

Ana necesita hacer una lista de diferentes prendas de ropa *(clothing items)* **para estaciones** *(seasons)* **y ocasiones diferentes. Let's help her out! Group the items of clothing from the box into different categories. Try not to repeat any.**

suéter	falda	vestido de noche	camiseta
pantalones cortos	abrigo	suéter de cuello alto	traje de chaqueta
guantes	falda y blusa	esmoquin	camisa de manga corta

	Ana	Enrique
1) Tiene una fiesta *(party)* formal:	______	______
2) Tiene que ir *(has to go)* al trabajo:	______	______
3) Tiene calor:	______	______
	______	______
4) Tiene frío:	______	______
	______	______

Respuestas A: **1)** Ana: vestido de noche - Enrique: esmoquin / **2)** Ana: falda y blusa - Enrique: traje de chaqueta / **3)** Ana: falda, camiseta (o camisa de manga corta) - Enrique: camisa de manga corta (o camiseta), pantalones cortos / **4)** Ana or Enrique: suéter, suéter de cuello alto, abrigo, guantes

EXPRESIONES CON 'TENER'

Even though 'tener' means 'to have' and mostly indicates possession, it also has other uses:

tener frío *(to be cold)*

tener calor *(to be hot)*

tener hambre *(to be hungry)*

tener sed *(to be thirsty)*

tener miedo *(to be scared)*

tener sueño *(to be sleepy)*

tener que + infinitive *(to have to + verb)*

tener cuidado *(to be careful)*

tener prisa *(to be in a hurry)*

tener razón *(to be right)*

tener 14 años *(to be 14 years old)*

tener ganas de + infinitive *(to feel like + verb)*

Ejercicio B

Selecciona la mejor expresión para las siguientes situaciones.

1) En Chicago, en enero, Adela…

a) tiene calor	b) tiene frío	c) tiene hambre	d) tiene sed

2) En Miami, en agosto, Roberto…

a) tiene que ir	b) tiene miedo	c) tiene hambre	d) tiene calor

3) En el desierto *(desert)*, yo…

a) tengo sed	b) tengo prisa	c) tengo cuidado	d) tengo 10 años

4) En mi cumpleaños *(birthday)*, yo…

a) tengo 20 años	b) tengo sed	c) tengo calor	d) tengo frío

5) Cuando veo una película de horror, yo….

a) tengo frío	b) tengo miedo	c) tengo prisa	d) tengo que ir

Respuestas B: **1)** - b) / **2)** - d) / **3)** - a) / **4)** - a) / **5)** - b)

EXPRESIONES ÚTILES PARA IR DE COMPRAS

(Useful expressions when shopping)

De la dependienta/el dependiente *(store clerk)*

¿Qué talla usa usted? *(What is your size?)*

¿En qué puedo ayudarle? *(How can I help you?)*

Todo en la tienda está en rebajas *(Everything in the store is on sale)*

¿Le gustaría probarse esta falda? *(Would you like to try on this skirt?)*

No tenemos más de ese tipo *(We don't have anymore like that one)*

¿Desea pagar en efectivo, con cheque o con tarjeta de crédito?
(Do you wish to pay cash, by check or with a credit card?)

Del cliente/De la cliente

¿Me puede mostrar esa blusa, por favor? *(Could you please show me that blouse?)*

¿Podría traerme una talla menos? *(Could you bring me a smaller size?)*

¿De qué (material) está hecho...? *(What material is this made of?)*

¿Se pueden lavar estas camisas? *(Can these shirts be washed?)*

¿Se puede planchar este material? *(Can this material be ironed?)*

Perdón[10], ¿dónde están los probadores? *(Excuse me, where is the fitting room?)*

¿Tiene esta camisa pero con mangas cortas? *(Do you have this shirt but with short sleeves?)*

¿Cuánto cuesta esto? *(How much is this?)*

¿Tienen esta camisa en otro color? *(Do you have this shirt in a different color?)*

Comentarios sobre la ropa

Esta talla es muy grande *(This size is very big)*

La talla mediana es demasiado pequeña *(A medium is too small)*

Esta camisa no me queda bien *(This shirt does not fit me well)*

No me veo bien con este abrigo *(I don't look good in this coat)*

Tengo frío: necesito un suéter *(I am cold. I need a sweater)*

Tengo calor: necesito una camiseta *(I am hot: I need a t-shirt)*

Los pantalones están en la percha[11] *(The pants are on the hanger)*

Tiene una mancha *(It has a stain)*

La cremallera está rota *(The zipper is broken)*

A este abrigo le falta un botón *(This coat is missing a button)*

Este vestido es de seda *(This dress is (made) of silk)*

Sólo se puede lavar en seco *(It can only be dry cleaned)*

El cuello me aprieta un poco *(The neck is a little tight)*

Esta blusa se transparenta *(This blouse is see-through)*

Estos guantes no hacen juego con el abrigo *(These gloves do not match the coat)*

Las mangas me quedan largas *(The sleeves are too long for me)*

[Footnotes]

[10] 'Perdón' is both formal and informal. 'Perdona' or 'disculpa' are informal. 'Perdone' or 'disculpe' are formal. These expressions can be used to call somebody's attention or to apologize.
[11] Another word for hanger is 'gancho.'

Ejercicio C

Selecciona la expresión correcta para cada pregunta.

1) ¿Cómo me quedan estos pantalones?
- a) Las mangas te quedan largas
- b) El cuello te aprieta un poco
- c) Esa talla es muy grande

2) ¿Le gustaría probarse esta falda?
- a) Sí, ¿pero la tiene en otro color?
- b) Sí, ¿cuánto cuestan estos pantalones?
- c) Sí, pero tiene una con mangas cortas

3) ¿Tienes frío?
- a) Sí, necesito unas sandalias *(sandals)*
- b) Sí, necesito una minifalda *(miniskirt)*
- c) Sí, necesito un abrigo

4) ¿Esta chaqueta se puede lavar?
- a) Sí, se puede planchar
- b) No, pero se puede lavar en seco
- c) No, todo en la tienda está en rebajas

5) ¿En qué puedo ayudarle?
- a) Necesito un vestido de noche
- b) No tenemos más de ese tipo
- c) Esa bufanda no hace juego

Respuestas C: **1)** - c) / **2)** - a) / **3)** - c) / **4)** - b) / **5)** - a)

Ejercicio D

Pilar está en la tienda comprando ropa y hablando con la dependienta. Indica el orden correcto de la conversación escribiendo 1, 2, 3, etc. sobre la línea *(on the line provided)*. **Observa el ejemplo 1.**

Pilar's sentences

1 Hola, buenos días.
__ La azul, gracias, pero esta talla es muy pequeña. ¿Tiene esta blusa en una talla más grande?
__ La mediana, por favor.
__ Me queda muy bien. Las mangas son un poco largas, pero está bien. Me la llevo.
__ Necesito una blusa para el trabajo.
__ En efectivo, por favor. Aquí tiene 30 dólares.
__ ¿En rebajas? ¡Qué bien! ¡Qué suerte tengo! ¿Y cuánto cuesta ahora?
__ Muchas gracias y que tenga un buen día.
__ Ésta me gusta mucho. ¿Tiene esta blusa en azul?

The clerk's sentences

__ Sí, la tengo en azul y en verde. ¿Cuál prefiere?

__ Usted también. Adiós.

__ Buenos días. ¿En qué puedo ayudarle?

__ Cuesta 29 dólares, con impuestos *(taxes)* incluidos. ¿Cómo quiere pagar en efectivo, con tarjeta o con cheque?

__ Sí, tengo la talla mediana y la talla grande, ¿cuál necesita usted?

__ Perfecto, la voy a poner en una bolsa *(bag)*. ¿Sabe que esta blusa está en rebajas?

__ Aquí tiene *(here you have)*. ¿Cómo le queda?

__ Gracias, y aquí tiene su cambio: un dólar.

__ Ah, muy bien. Aquí tenemos blusas muy bonitas y formales.

Respuestas D: **1)** Hola... / **2)** Buenos días... / **3)** Necesito... / **4)** Ah, muy bien... / **5)** Esta me gusta... / **6)** Sí, la tengo... / **7)** La azul... / **8)** Sí, tengo... / **9)** La mediana... / **10)** Aquí tiene... / **11)** Me queda... / **12)** Perfecto... / **13)** ¿En rebajas?... / **14)** Cuesta... / **15)** En efectivo... / **16)** Gracias... / **17)** Muchas gracias... / **18)** Usted...

Ejercicio E

Usando las expresiones útiles, traduce las siguientes frases.

1) This skirt is missing a button. ____________________

2) This yellow scarf does not match these pants. ____________________

3) Excuse me, sir. Where is the fitting room? ____________________

4) This new shirt does not look good on me. ____________________

5) The size is too (demasiado) small. ____________________

6) The blue coat has a stain. ____________________

7) Do you (usted) have these jeans in size 6? ____________________

8) Can this material be washed? ____________________

Respuestas E: **1)** A esta falda le falta un botón / **2)** Esta bufanda amarilla no hace juego con estos pantalones / **3)** Perdón, señor, ¿dónde están los probadores - el probador? / **4)** Esta camisa nueva no me queda bien / **5)** La talla es demasiado pequeña / **6)** El abrigo azul tiene una mancha / **7)** ¿Tiene (usted) estos jeans/pantalones vaqueros en la talla 6? / **8)** ¿Se puede lavar este material?

LOS MATERIALES, LAS TELAS Y LOS DISEÑOS

(Materials, fabrics, and designs)

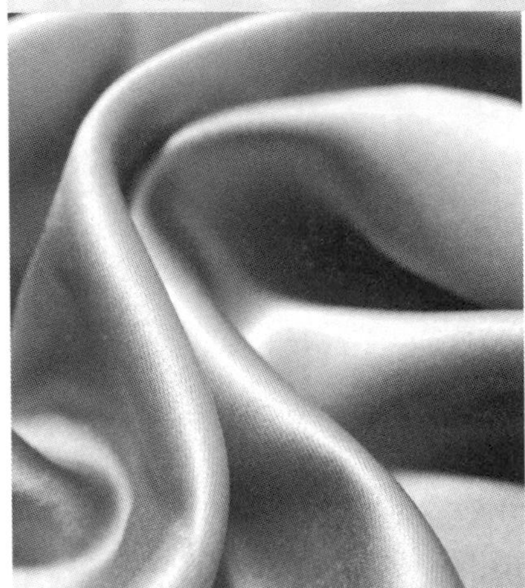

seda[12] *(silk)*

algodón *(cotton)*

poliéster *(polyester)*

cuero *(leather)*

piel vuelta/ante *(suede)*

nilón/nylon *(nylon)*

lana *(wool)*

lino *(linen)*

plástico *(plastic)*

raso *(satin)*

rayón *(rayon)*

terciopelo *(velvet)*

tela vaquera/mezclilla *(denim)*

piel(es) *(fur)*

pana *(corduroy)*

teñido *(dyed)*

desteñido *(faded)*

falso *(fake/imitation)*

roto/desgarrado *(torn)*

a rayas *(striped)*

con lunares *(polka-dotted)*

a cuadros *(checked / plaid)*

estampado *(print)*

liso *(solid)*

pintado a mano *(hand-painted)*

[Footnotes]

[12] *In Spanish, all materials go after the noun with the preposition 'de' (e.g., Silk blouse = blusa de seda).*

Ejercicio F

Traduce estas frases sobre materiales, telas y diseños.

1) My silk dress is very expensive ______________________

2) This belt is (made) of plastic ______________________

3) Velvet is softer than linen ______________________

4) Is this cotton? ______________________

5) I love denim ______________________

Respuestas F: **1)** Mi vestido de seda es muy caro / **2)** Mi cinturón es de plástico / **3)** El terciopelo es más suave que el lino / **4)** ¿Es esto algodón? / **5)** Me encanta la tela vaquera - la mezclilla

MI LISTA DE VOCABULARIO

This is a list of the words that you have learned in this unit.

a cuadros
a rayas
(el) abrigo
(el) algodón
apretar
aquí tiene
barato
(la) blusa
(las) bragas o (las) pantaletas
(la) bufanda
(el) calcetín o (la) media
(los) calzoncillos o (los) calzones
(la) camisa
(la) camiseta o (la) playera
caro
(la) chaqueta
(el) cinturón
con lunares
corto
(la) cremallera
¿cuánto cuesta?
(el) cuello
(el) cuello alto
(el) cuero
demasiado
desteñido
(el) diseño
en rebajas
(el) esmoquin
estampado
(la) falda
falso
(la) fiesta

(la) gorra
(el) gorro
(el) guante
hacer juego con
hecho
(el) impermeable
(el) impuesto
(los) jeans/vaqueros
(la) lana
largo
lavar en seco
¿le gustaría...?
(el) lino
liso
(la) mancha
(la) manga corta/larga
mediana
(la) media
(la) mezclilla o (la) tela vaquera
(la) minifalda
(el) nylon o (el) nilón
(los) pantalones cortos
(los) pantalones largos
(la) percha
perdón
(la) piel
(la) piel vuelta o (el) ante
(el) pijama
pintado a mano

(el) plástico
¿podría...?
(el) poliéster
(el) probador o (los) probadores
probarse
quedar bien / mal
(el) raso
(el) rayón
(la) ropa interior

roto
(la) sandalia
(la) seda
(el) sombrero
(el) sostén
(el) suéter
(la) talla
(la) tela
tener X años
tener calor
tener cuidado
tener frío
tener ganas
tener hambre
tener miedo
tener prisa
tener que + infinitivo
tener razón
tener sed
tener sueño
teñido
(el) terciopelo
(el) tipo
(el) traje de chaqueta
transparentarse
verse bien/mal
(el) vestido
(el) vestido de noche
(el) zapato

UNIDAD 18

UN POCO DE CULTURA

Hispanos/Latinos famosos en el mundo de la moda *(fashion industry)*

Óscar de la Renta

Nacido *(born)* en 1932, de origen dominicano y puertorriqueño pero criado *(but raised)* en España, es probablemente *(probably)* el diseñador de moda *(fashion designer)* hispano más famoso del mundo. En los años 80 se hizo famoso *(became famous)* por diseñar el uniforme de los Boy Scouts de los Estados Unidos. Su línea *(line)* de diseño incluye no sólo *(not only)* ropa, sino también *(but also)* accesorios, perfumes, muebles, joyería *(jewelry)* y gafas/lentes *(glasses)*.

Carolina Herrera

Nació en Venezuela en 1939 y se hizo una diseñadora famosa en los años 80, cuando ya vivía *(when she was living)* en los Estados Unidos, especialmente por diseñar los vestidos de Jacqueline Onassis. Carolina Herrera tiene boutiques por todo el mundo donde vende su ropa y sus perfumes.

Ágatha Ruiz de la Prada

Es una diseñadora de modas española que nació en 1960. Su estilo particular tiene colores vivos *(bright)* y los adornos *(ornaments)* inusuales, como cajas *(boxes)*, soles *(suns)*, y estrellas *(stars)*. Ágatha también diseña muebles para la casa y perfumes.

RECOMENDACIÓN PARA ESTA UNIDAD

To finish this unit, we recommend that you check out the El Corte Inglés website: http://www.elcorteingles.es

El Corte Inglés is an internationally known Spanish department store. At El Corte Inglés, you can find clothes, food, household items, computers... you name it! Check out the fashion *(moda)* section to see the latest trends.

UNIDAD 19

UNIDAD 19

CONTENIDO

In this unit, you will learn:

1 - Vocabulary related to shoes

2 - About the prepositions 'por' and 'para'

3 - Vocabulary related to accessories

4 - About direct object pronouns

5 - Cultural information about the world of fashion models

los zapatos

LOS ZAPATOS

(Shoes)

Enrique is looking at his wife's shoe collection. He does not understand why anyone needs so many shoes but still goes shopping for more.

Enrique: Tienes muchos zapatos...

Ana: No son muchos. Mira *(Look)*, estos zapatos negros son muy bonitos. Los uso en el trabajo *(I use them at work)*.

Enrique: Pero los blancos *(the white ones)* también son para el trabajo, ¿no? *(right?)*

Ana: Sí, pero los llevo con ropa diferente. *(Yes, but I wear them with different clothes)*

Enrique: Y esos zapatos rojos de tacón alto *(high heels)*, ¿para qué son? *(what are they for?)*

Ana: Una amiga me los dio. Son para salir. Quiero ponérmelos pronto. *(A friend gave them to me. They are for going out. I want to wear them soon)*

Enrique: ¿Y por qué tienes 3 pares de botas? *(And why do you have 3 pairs of boots?)*

Ana: Son para situaciones diferentes. Las uso para la lluvia *(rain)* o para la nieve *(snow)*. Aquéllas *(Those over there)* son para otras ocasiones.

Enrique: ¿Y aquellos zapatos sin tacón *(flats)* también son para el trabajo?

Ana: No, aquéllos son para caminar *(for walking)*. Me gustan porque la suela *(sole)* es muy cómoda *(comfortable)*.

Enrique: ¿Cuántos pares *(How many pairs)* de sandalias tienes?

Ana: Bastantes *(Quite a few)*. Necesito este par para cuando hace mucho calor *(when it is very hot)*, uso esas sandalias para ir a los recados *(for running errands)*, y aquéllas…. tú me las regalaste por mi cumpleaños *(you gave them to me for my birthday)*.

Enrique: ¿Yo las compré para ti? *(I bought them for you?)*

Ana: Sí, tú… ¿no lo recuerdas? Hace 3 años. *(Yes, you… don't you remember? 3 years ago)*

Enrique: No lo recuerdo. Mira, esas zapatillas deportivas *(sneakers)* no tienen cordones *(shoelaces)*.

Ana: No los necesitan. Tienen Velcro, ¿ves? *(See?)* Son para correr.

Enrique: Pero tú nunca tienes tiempo para correr *(But you never time for running)*… ¿y por qué necesitas tantos bolsos *(so many bags)*?

Ana: Los tengo porque hacen juego con *(they match)* mis zapatos, con mis cinturones *(belts)*, y con mis joyas *(jewelry)*.

Ejercicio A

¿Para qué quiere Ana tantas cosas? Enlaza cada artículo *(item)* **con su propósito** *(purpose)*.

1) tres pares de botas	a) para el calor y los recados
2) zapatos negros y blancos	b) para salir
3) sandalias	c) para correr
4) zapatos sin tacón	d) para el trabajo
5) zapatillas deportivas	e) para la nieve, la lluvia y otras ocasiones
6) zapatos rojos de tacón alto	f) para caminar

Respuestas A: **1)** - e) / **2)** - d) / **3)** - a) / **4)** - f) / **5)** - c) / **6)** - b)

LAS PREPOSICIONES 'POR' Y 'PARA'

In Spanish, there are two prepositions that translate as 'for' ('por' and 'para'). They are not interchangeable: each is used in specific situations. Let's see the most common uses:

POR

Expresses duration *(for, per)*:

Voy al centro comercial por dos horas

(I am going to the mall for two hours)

Van al cine una vez por semana

(They go to the movies once a week)

Expresses the reason for an action *(for, because of, on account of)*:

No puedo ir a tu casa por la lluvia

(I cannot go to your house because of the rain)

Te regalé las sandalias por tu cumpleaños

(I gave you the sandals for your birthday)

Expresses exchange or interchange *(for)*:

Venden una camisa por $10

(They are selling a shirt for $10)

Hoy trabajo por ti si el viernes trabajas por mí

(Today I'll work for you if on Friday you work for me)

Expresses motion *(through, by, around)*:

Mete los brazos por las mangas

(Put your arms through the sleeves)

Paso por su casa todos los días

(I pass by her house every day)

Expresses the manner or means by which something is done *(by, by means of, through, via)*:

Vienen por tren

(They are coming by train)

Siempre hablamos por Internet

(We always talk via Internet)

Expresses the actor in a passive voice sentence *(by)*:

La película está hecha por Andy García

(The movie was made by Andy García)

El zapato fue usado por Jacqueline Onassis

(The shoe was used by J.O.)

Used in many idioms:

por favor *(please)*

por Dios *(for God's sake)*

por supuesto *(of course)*

por ejemplo *(for example)*

por fin *(finally)*

por lo general *(in general)*

por aquí *(this way)*

por eso *(that's why)*

por la mañana / tarde / noche

(in the morning, afternoon, evening / at night)

PARA

Expresses the purpose of an action or an object *(for, for the purpose of):*

Las zapatillas deportivas son para correr

(The sneakers are for running)

El paraguas es para la lluvia

(The umbrella is for the rain)

Expresses a destination or recipient *(for, to, towards):*

Salgo para Portugal el próximo martes

(I am going to Portugal next Tuesday)

Yo las compré para ti

(I bought them for you)

Expresses deadlines *(by):*

Necesito terminar el proyecto para las 5

(I need to finish the project before 5)

Expresses whom you work for *(for):*

Trabajo para una compañía americana

(I work for an American company)

Expresses opinion or perspective *(for, according to):*

Para mí, este abrigo no te queda bien

(In my opinion, this coat does not fit you well)

Ejercicio B

Escribe 'por' o 'para' según sea necesario *(as needed).*

1) Antonio va caminando _______ su casa en este momento.

2) Mi madre tiene un regalo *(a present)* _______ tu esposa.

3) Necesito terminar este trabajo _______ mañana _______ la mañana *(tomorrow morning).*

4) Estas zapatillas deportivas son _______ caminar _______ el parque _______ las tardes.

5) ¿_______ qué tienes los zapatos _______ toda la casa? Tienes que organizarlos mejor.

6) _______ favor, no compres más zapatos.

7) _______ lo general siempre hacemos juntos los quehaceres domésticos.

8) Hoy yo trabajo _______ ti porque estás enfermo.

9) En el mercado me dieron *(they gave me)* $50 _______ mi silla vieja.

10) Hoy compré *(I bought)* una lámpara _______ mi escritorio.

Respuestas B: **1)** para / **2)** para / **3)** para - por / **4)** para - por - por / **5)** por - por / **6)** por / **7)** por / **8)** por / **9)** por / **10)** para

UNIDAD 19

LOS ACCESORIOS *(Accesories)*

bolso / bolsa[1]

pulsera

reloj

gemelos/ mancuernillas

gafas de sol

cartera / billetera

corbata

cinturón

anillo

paraguas[2]

collar

pendientes / aretes

colgante

gafas[3]

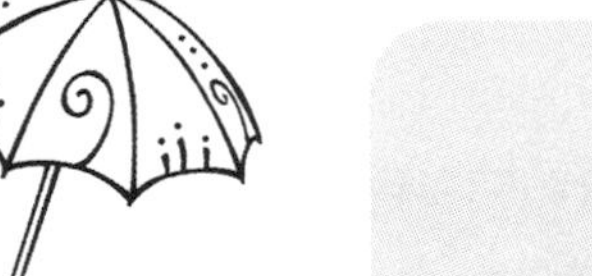

[Footnotes]

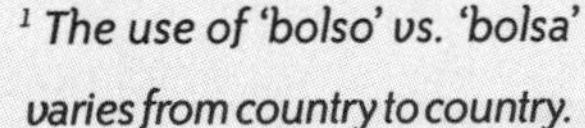
[1] *The use of 'bolso' vs. 'bolsa' varies from country to country.*

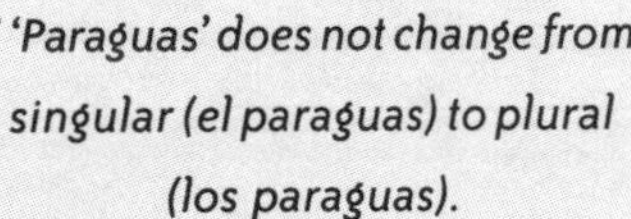
[2] *'Paraguas' does not change from singular (el paraguas) to plural (los paraguas).*

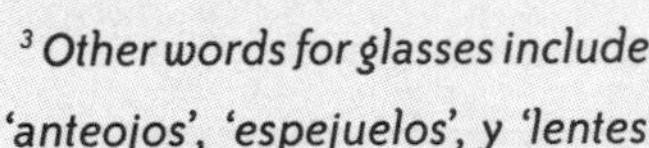
[3] *Other words for glasses include 'anteojos', 'espejuelos', y 'lentes'.*

Ejercicio C

¿Para qué sirven estos accesorios? *(What purpose do these accessories serve?)*

1) El reloj	a) sirve para decorar las manos *(hands)*
2) La cartera	b) los hombres la usan para vestir más formalmente
3) La corbata	c) sirve para indicar la hora
4) El cinturón	d) sirve para poner dentro *(put inside)* cosas personales
5) El bolso	e) sirve para la lluvia
6) El anillo	f) sirve para poner dentro dinero
7) El paraguas[4]	g) sirve para sujetar *(hold in place)* los pantalones

Respuestas C: **1)** - c) / **2)** - f) / **3)** - b) / **4)** - g) / **5)** - d) / **6)** - a) / **7)** - e)

[Footnotes]

[4] *In some countries, the word 'sombrilla' is used for umbrella (for rain), but in others, 'sombrilla' means exclusively beach umbrella or parasol.*

LOS PRONOMBRES DE OBJETO DIRECTO (Direct object pronouns)

A direct object is that part of speech that directly receives the action of the verb. It can be:

an object:

Tengo un bolso aquí

(I have a bag here)

a place:

Visito un museo hoy

(I visit a museum today)

a person:

Veo a Gabriel[5] todos los días

(I see Gabriel every day)

an entire clause:

Veo que tienes ropa bonita

(I see that you have beautiful clothes)

Some verbs do not take direct objects (e.g., I go to the movies).

If you do not want to repeat the direct object over and over (I bought a blouse, I washed the blouse, and I dried the blouse), you can replace it with a direct object pronoun (I bought a blouse, washed it, and dried it). For every direct object, there is a direct object pronoun. These are the direct object pronouns in Spanish:

PRONOMBRES DE OBJETO DIRECTO
me
te
lo / la
nos
os
los / las

[Footnotes]

[5] When the direct object is a person, the personal 'a' is required: Visito a Susana (I visit Susan)

In Spanish, pronouns go before the verb, but after the 'no' (if there is one):

(Yo) los uso en el trabajo

(I use them at work)

(Yo) no lo recuerdo

(I don't remember that)

When the construction is either 1) preposition + infinitive, or 2) positive command, the pronoun is attached to the end of the verb:

Para llevarte al trabajo…

(In order to take you to work…)

¡Mírame!

(look at me!)

When you have a construction with two verbs, and the second verb is an infinitive (comprar) or a gerund (comprando), you have two options. The pronoun can either go before the first verb, or attached to the end of the second verb. Both forms are commonly used:

(Yo) los quiero comprar pronto

(I want to buy them soon)

(Yo) quiero comprarlos pronto

(I want to buy them soon)

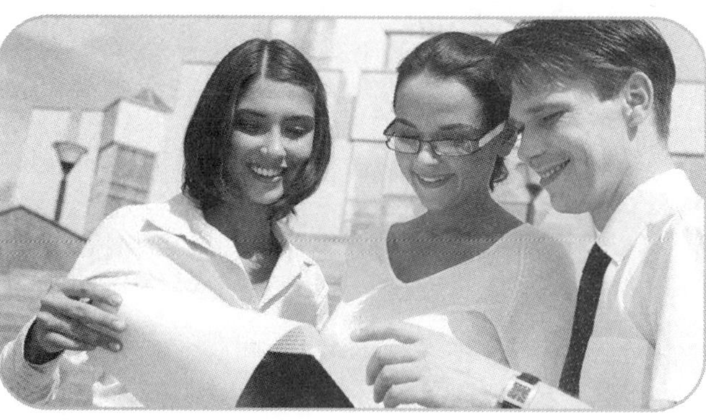

UNIDAD 19

Ejercicio D

Traduce estas frases usando pronombres de objeto directo para los objetos directos subrayados *(underlined)*. **Observa el ejemplo 1.**

1) Tengo muchas sandalias aquí *Las tengo aquí*

2) Emilia compra zapatos en la tienda ____________

3) Tú visitas a tu madre con frecuencia ____________

4) No queremos estos pantalones ____________

5) No quiero usar faldas en el trabajo ____________

or ____________

6) ¿Recuerdas a mi prima? ____________

7) Uso estas zapatillas en casa ____________

8) Jorge lleva un traje a la tintorería ____________

9) Ustedes necesitan estas bufandas hoy ____________

10) Puede tocar la suela *(you can touch the sole)* ____________

or ____________

Respuestas D: **2)** Emilia los compra en la tienda / **3)** Tú la visitas con frecuencia / **4)** No los queremos / **5)** No quiero usarlas en el trabajo - No las quiero usar en el trabajo / **6)** ¿La recuerdas? / **7)** Las uso en casa / **8)** Jorge lo lleva a la tintorería / **9)** Ustedes las necesitan hoy / **10)** Puede tocarla - La puede tocar

Ejercicio E

Traduce estas frases usando pronombres de objeto directo.

1) Alfonso sees me in the mornings

____

2) I visit her every Tuesday

____

3) I give it (masc, sing) to my parents

____

4) They (masc.) buy them (fem, pl.) in the store

____

5) We (fem.) do not need it (fem, sing)

____

Respuestas E: **1)** Alfonso me ve por las mañanas / **2)** (Yo) la visito cada martes / **3)** (Yo) lo doy a mis padres / **4)** Ellos las compran en la tienda / **5)** (Nosotras) no la necesitamos

MI LISTA DE VOCABULARIO

This is a list of the words that you have learned in this unit.

(el) accesorio
(el) anillo
(el) bolso o (la) bolsa
caminar
(la) cartera o (la) billetera
(el) cinturón
(el) colgante
(el) collar
(la) corbata
(el) cordón
(el) cumpleaños
(las) gafas (de sol)
(el) gemelo
(la) joya
lo / la / los / las
me
nos
os
(el) par
para
(el) paraguas
(el) pendiente o (el) arete
por
por aquí
por Dios
por ejemplo
por eso
por fin
por lo general
(el) propósito
(la) pulsera
recordar
regalar
(el) reloj
sin tacón
(la) suela
sujetar
(el) tacón alto / bajo
te
Velcro

UN POCO DE CULTURA

El mundo de las modelos

La industria de la moda y el calzado *(The fashion and shoe industry)* de España es líder *(leader)* y modelo *(role model)* para otros países de habla hispana *(Spanish-speaking countries)*. Los últimos diseños *(The latest designs)* de moda se presentan en la Pasarela Cibeles *(the Cibeles Fashion Show)*, en Madrid, cada *(every)* dos años. Ésta es una

oportunidad de oro *(golden opportunity)* no sólo *(not only)* para los diseñadores de moda *(fashion designers)* sino también *(but also)* para los nuevos modelos *(models)*.

Aunque la estética *(Although aesthetics)* es muy importante en el mundo de la moda, concepto que se refleja *(evidenced)* en la vida diaria *(daily life)* de la gente de las grandes ciudades, la idea de ser y parecer saludable *(looking healthy)* se está haciendo popular últimamente *(is becoming popular lately)*.

En el año 2006 la Comunidad de Madrid prohibió *(prohibited)* a las modelos demasiado delgadas *(too skinny female models)* participar en la Pasarela Cibeles. La Comunidad de Madrid piensa que las adolescentes sufren *(suffer)* de anorexia y bulimia porque quieren parecerse a *(look like)* esas modelos. Ahora la Comunidad de Madrid calcula el índice de masa corporal *(calculates the body mass index)* de cada modelo. Aquellas modelos que no cumplan los requisitos *(who do not meet the requirements)* son descalificadas *(disqualified)*. Por esta razón *(Because of this)*, muchas modelos famosas están enojadas e incluso *(and even)* se niegan *(they refuse)* a trabajar en Madrid. Otros países de Europa están intentando adoptar *(are trying to adopt)* este nuevo sistema para promover *(to promote)* la salud y la belleza natural *(health and natural beauty)*.

Pero las modelos no son sólo caras bonitas que únicamente se preocupan por *(only care about)* trabajar en el mundo de la moda. Esto lo demuestran personas como Inés Sastre.

Inés Sastre

Es una modelo famosa española nacida *(born)* en 1973 que ha ganado *(has won)* muchos premios *(awards)*. En 1996 se hizo famosa *(became famous)* por ser la nueva cara *(new face)* de Trésor, una fragancia de Lancôme. Inés Sastre habla francés, italiano, inglés y español perfectamente, tiene una licenciatura *(B.A.)* en literatura francesa de La Sorbonne y estudios graduados en literatura medieval. Inés ha participado *(has participated)* en muchas películas europeas y una americana, *The Lost City* (USA, 2005) de Andy García. También es embajadora *(ambassadress)* de UNICEF.

RECOMENDACIÓN PARA ESTA UNIDAD

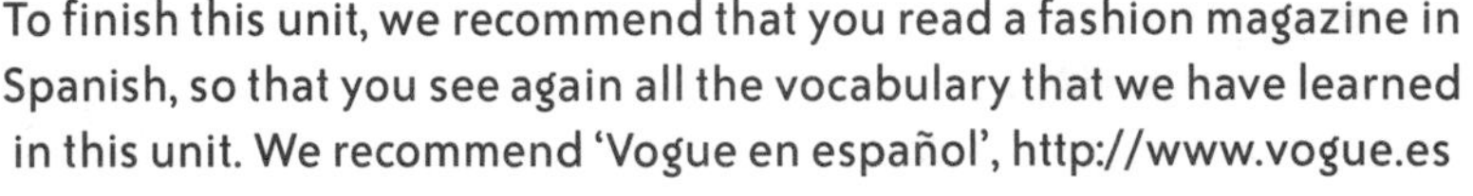

To finish this unit, we recommend that you read a fashion magazine in Spanish, so that you see again all the vocabulary that we have learned in this unit. We recommend 'Vogue en español', http://www.vogue.es

UNIDAD 20

CONTENIDO

In this unit, you will learn:

1 - Vocabulary related to food

2 - About indefinite and negative expressions

3 - How to write a recipe

4 - About the passive 'se'

5 - Cultural information about markets in Spanish-speaking countries

en el mercado

EN EL MERCADO

(At the market)

Enrique and Ana are at the market buying some food for the week.

Ana:	Cielo[1], vamos a la frutería *(fruit stand)*. No tenemos nada de fruta.
Enrique:	Muy bien. Podemos hacer una ensalada de frutas *(fruit salad)* esta noche *(tonight)*.
Ana:	Me parece bien. *(Sounds good to me.)* Entonces necesitamos algunas *(some)* naranjas, manzanas *(apples)*, uvas *(grapes)*, y unas fresas *(strawberries)* también *(also)*.
Enrique:	No olvides *(Don't forget)* el melón ni el mango.
Ana:	Muy bien.

(Enrique talks to the fruit stand clerk:)

Enrique:	Disculpe, señora *(Excuse me, madam)* ¿Me pone *(Could you give me)* dos kilos de naranjas, por favor?
Ana:	Cariño, mientras *(while)* tú estás aquí comprando, yo voy a la carnicería *(meat stand)* porque ahora no hay nadie *(there is nobody)*. ¿Qué hace falta? *(What do we need?)*
Enrique:	Hace falta carne de vaca[2] *(beef)*, pollo *(chicken)* y cerdo *(pork)*. Compra unas chuletas *(chops)* y algunas costillas *(ribs)* también, por favor.
Ana:	Vale[3]. Te veo allá cuando termines. *(I'll see you there when you are finished.)*

(A moment later)

[Footnotes]

[1] 'Cielo' (which means 'sky' or 'heaven') would translate to 'honey' or 'sweetie.' The same with 'cariño,' a few lines below.
[2] Another word for 'beef' is 'carne de res.'
[3] In Spain, 'vale' is the equivalent to 'OK' or 'very well.'

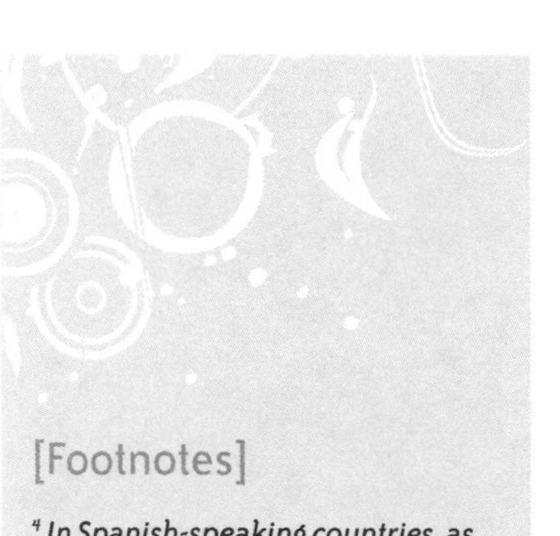

[Footnotes]

[4] In Spanish-speaking countries, as in the U.S., people think of certain fruits—like the tomato—as vegetables.

Enrique:	¡Ya estoy aquí *(Here I am)*! Ya tengo la fruta. Oye *(Listen)*, no tenemos ni tomates[4] ni zanahorias *(carrots)*. Voy a la verdulería *(vegetable stand)* a comprarlos mientras tú esperas aquí *(while you wait here)*.
Ana:	¿Podrías comprar lechuga, pimientos, espinaca, cebollas, y ajo? *(Could you buy lettuce, peppers, spinach, onions, and garlic?)*
Enrique:	Sí, pero… ¿no tienes ninguna cebolla *(any onions)* en casa?
Ana:	No, ni cebollas ni ajo *(neither onions nor garlic)*.
Enrique:	También necesitamos algo de pan *(some bread)*. Voy a comprarlo luego *(later)*.

Ejercicio A

Escribe el vocabulario del diálogo en estas categorías.

Carne *(Meat)*

1) ____________
2) ____________
3) ____________

Fruta *(Fruit)*

1) ____________
2) ____________
3) ____________
4) ____________
5) ____________
6) ____________

Verduras *(Vegetables)*

1) ____________
2) ____________
3) ____________
4) ____________
5) ____________
6) ____________
7) ____________

Otro *(Other)*

1) ____________

Respuestas A: **Carne:** carne de res, pollo, cerdo / **Fruta:** naranjas, manzanas, uvas, fresas, mango, melón / **Verduras:** tomates, zanahorias, lechuga, pimientos, espinaca, cebollas, ajo / **Otro:** pan

Ejercicio B

Completa estas frases seleccionando la palabra más apropiada.

1) Una persona vegetariana no come...

a) verduras b) pan c) carne

2) A Bugs Bunny le gustan mucho las...

a) naranjas b) uvas c) zanahorias

3) A Popeye le encanta la...

a) espinaca b) fresa c) carne de res

4) El vino *(wine)* se hace con *(is made with)*...

a) uvas b) fresas c) verduras

5) California y Florida son estados famosos por sus...

a) panes b) frutas c) carnes

Respuestas B: **1)** - c) / **2)** - c) / **3)** - a) / **4)** - a) / **5)** - b)

MAS VOCABULARIO DE COMIDA

[Footnotes] 5 *Other words for mushrooms are 'hongos' and 'setas.'*
6 *Other words for beans are 'frijoles,' 'habichuelas,' and 'habas.'*

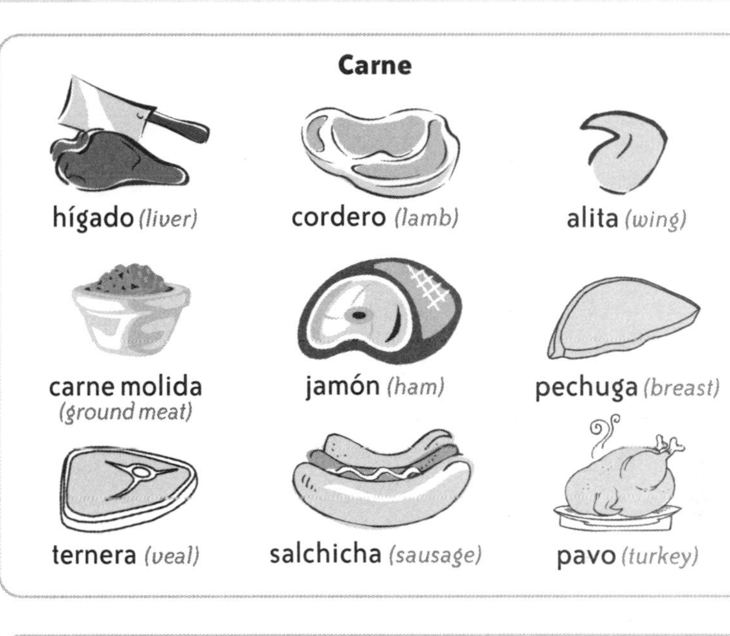

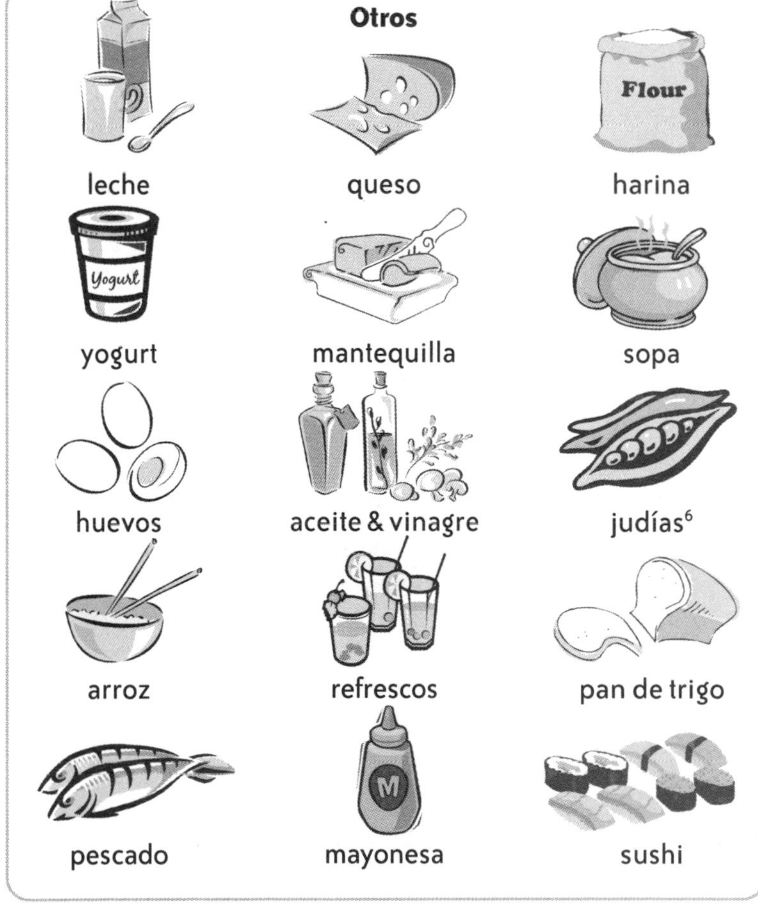

Ejercicio C

Completa estas frases con el <u>nuevo</u> vocabulario de comida.
(Articles might help you select the appropriate word.)

1) La ________________ y el _______________ son dos productos lácteos *(dairy products)*.

2) El ________________ es un cítrico *(citrus fruit)*.

3) No me gusta el pan blanco. Prefiero el pan de ___________ *(wheat)*.

4) El _________________ es una fruta verde por dentro *(inside)* y negra por fuera *(outside)*.

5) No como carne roja. Prefiero otra carne, como *(like)* el ________________.

6) No tengo mucha hambre. Voy a prepararme un sándwich[7] de _____________ y queso.

7) El aliño/aderezo *(dressing)* más común para una ensalada es el aceite y el ____________.

8) ¿Quieres un vaso *(glass)* de _______________ antes de *(before)* ir a dormir?

9) Las gallinas ponen *(lay)* ___________________.

10) ¿Por qué no vamos a un restaurante japonés a comer ______________?

Respuestas C: **1)** leche (o mantequilla), queso (o yogurt) / **2)** limón / **3)** trigo / **4)** aguacate / **5)** pavo / **6)** jamón, pavo, etc / **7)** vinagre / **8)** leche / **9)** huevos / **10)** sushi (o pescado)

[Footnotes]

[7] *'Sándwich' is a loan word from English. Other Spanish words for 'sandwich' are 'emparedado' or 'bocadillo.'*

LAS EXPRESIONES INDEFINIDAS Y NEGATIVAS

(Indefinite and negative expressions)

In Spanish, double (and even triple) negation is possible and grammatically correct. A sentence like 'No quiero nada' *(I don't want nothing)* is perfectly correct.

The following sets of words or expressions can be used in affirmative sentences and negative sentences:

En frases afirmativas	En frases negativas
algo *(something)*	nada *(nothing)*
alguno[8], alguna, algunos, algunas *(some, any)*	ninguno[9], ninguna *(none, any)*
alguien *(somebody, anyone)*	nadie *(nobody, no one)*
siempre *(always)*	nunca *(never)*
o…..o….. *(either…or…)*	(ni)…ni… *(neither…nor…)*
también *(also/too)*	tampoco *(neither/not either)*

En frases afirmativas:

Quiero comprar algo *(I want to buy something)*

¿Quieres alguna fruta? *(Do you want some/ any fruit?)*

¿Quieres alguna? *(Do you want any?)*

Alguien preguntó por ti *(Somebody asked for you)*

Siempre tengo hambre *(I am always hungry)*

Elige: ¿(o) jugo[10] o leche? *(Choose: (either) juice or milk)*

¿Quieres agua también? *(Do you want water too?)*

You can use the word 'también' when you want to express agreement with someone, as long as his or her sentence is affirmative.

Yo quiero una naranja *(I want an orange)*
Yo también *(me too)*
A mí me gustan los limones *(I like lemons)*
A mí también *(me too)*

En frases negativas:

No quiero comprar nada *(I don't want to buy anything)*

¿No quieres ninguna fruta? *(You don't want any fruit?)*

¿No quieres ninguna? *(You don't want any?)*

Nadie preguntó por ti *(Nobody asked for you)*

Nunca tengo hambre *(I am never hungry)*

No elijas (ni) el jugo ni la leche
(Choose neither the juice nor the milk)

¿No quieres agua tampoco? *(You don't want water either?)*

You can place all the negative expressions either in front of the verb or behind. If you place them behind, you need a 'no' in front of the verb:

Nada me gusta/No me gusta nada
(I don't like anything = I like nothing)

Ninguna me gusta/No me gusta ninguna
(I like no one)

Nadie te llamó hoy/No te llamó nadie hoy
(Nobody called you today)

Nunca llueve/No llueve nunca
(It never rains)

Ni la fruta ni la carne se ven bien/
No se ven bien ni la fruta ni la carne
(Neither the fruit nor the meat looks good)

Tampoco quiero ir/No quiero ir tampoco
(I don't want to go either)

You can use the word 'tampoco' when you want to express agreement with someone, as long as his or her sentence is negative.

Yo no quiero una naranja *(I don't want an orange)*

Yo tampoco *(neither do I)*

A mí no me gustan los limones *(I don't like lemons)*

A mí tampoco *(neither do I)*

[Footnotes]

[8] When 'alguno' precedes a masculine, singular noun, it drops the -o (e.g., ¿Quieres algún libro?), but when it stands by itself, it does not (e.g., ¿Te gusta alguno?).

[9] When 'ninguno' precedes a masculine, singular noun, it drops the -o (e.g., ¿No quieres ningún libro?), but when it stands by itself, it does not (e.g., No quiero ninguno). There are no plurals.

[10] In Spain, the word for 'jugo' (juice) is 'zumo.'

Ejercicio D

Selecciona la mejor respuesta para estas frases.

1) ¿Vas al cine frecuentemente?
a) no voy al cine con nadie b) no voy al cine nunca c) no voy al cine tampoco

2) ¿Me llamó alguien hoy?
a) no llamó nadie b) también llamó alguien c) nunca llamó

3) Siempre tengo hambre.
a) yo tampoco b) yo también

4) Nunca quiero trabajar.
a) yo tampoco b) yo también

5) ¿Qué prefieres, leche o agua?
a) no quiero leche o agua b) quiero leche y agua c) no quiero leche ni agua

Respuestas D: **1)** - b) / **2)** - a) / **3)** - b) / **4)** - a) / **5)** - c)

Ejercicio E

Traduce esta conversación entre Federico y su esposa.
(Phrases with * can be written in two different ways. Try both ways to practice.)

1) Federico, we don't have anything in the fridge. ____________________

2) Do you want something from the store? ____________________

3) Yes, thanks. Could you bring *(podrías traer)* some grapes and apples? ____________________

4) We don't have any apples? ____________________

5) No, we don't have any. ____________________

6) How weird! *(Qué raro!)* We always have some. ____________________

7) We don't have any oranges either*. ____________________

8) Yeah, but (pero) we never have any oranges*. ____________________

Respuestas E: **1)** Federico, no tenemos nada en el frigorífico / **2)** ¿Quieres algo de la tienda? / **3)** Sí, gracias. ¿Podrías traer algunas uvas y (algunas) manzanas? / **4)** ¿No tenemos ninguna manzana? / **5)** No, no tenemos ninguna. / **6)** ¡Qué raro! Siempre tenemos algunas. / **7)** Tampoco tenemos ninguna naranja. - No tenemos ninguna naranja tampoco. / **8)** Sí, pero nunca tenemos ninguna naranja - Sí, pero no tenemos ninguna naranja nunca.

UNA RECETA[11] *(A recipe)*

Enrique is trying to prepare gazpacho, a Spanish tomato-based cold soup. He is following a cookbook recipe.

Gazpacho andaluz[12]

Ingredientes:
1 kg. de tomates maduros *(ripe)*
1/2 cebolla
1/2 pepino
1 pimiento verde pequeño
3 rebanadas gruesas *(thick slices)* de pan duro *(hard bread)*
1 diente *(clove)* de ajo
1 huevo
aceite, vinagre, perejil *(parsley)* y sal *(salt)*

Primero se pelan *(peel)* los tomates, se cortan *(cut)* en pedazos *(pieces)*, y se ponen *(put)* en una batidora/licuadora *(blender)*. Luego se hace lo mismo *(the same)* con el pepino, el pimiento, y el ajo.
Más tarde se añaden *(add)* 2 vasos *(glasses)* de agua fría. Se tritura *(blend)* todo y se ponen las rebanadas de pan duro en el líquido también unos minutos.
Después se añaden 2 cucharadas *(spoonfuls)* de aceite de oliva *(olive)*, una de vinagre, un poco de perejil, un poco de sal, y la yema *(yolk)* del huevo. Finalmente se tritura todo y se añaden unos cubitos de hielo *(ice cubes)* para enfriarlo.

[Footnotes]
[11] *'Receta' can also mean 'prescription.'*
[12] *From Andalucía (southern Spain).*

EL 'SE' PASIVO *(Present progressive)*

The passive 'se' is generally used for giving instructions, as an alternative to commands (e.g., 'tomatoes are cut' versus 'cut the tomatoes'). You will encounter this structure frequently in Spanish. The pronoun 'se' always goes before the verb. The verb agrees with the subject, which follows it.

Se cortan los tomates
(tomatoes are cut)

Se corta el tomate
(the tomato is cut)

Ejercicio F

Completa esta receta de la tortilla española *(Spanish potato omelet)* **con la forma apropiada de los verbos que observas entre paréntesis. *(Remember: the word 'todo' is singular.)***

1) Se _______________ (pelar) 4 patatas medianas y media cebolla.

2) Se _______________ (cortar) las patatas en pedazos finos *(fine pieces)*.

3) Se _______________ (freír[13]) *(fry)* las patatas y la cebolla.

4) Se _______________ (colar[14]) *(drain)* todo para eliminar el aceite.

5) En otro recipiente *(container)*, se _______________ (batir) 4 huevos.

6) Se _______________ (mezclar) *(mix)* todo junto *(all together)*.

7) Se _______________ (añadir) sal.

8) Se _______________ (echar) *(pour)* todo en la sartén *(frying pan)* a fuego mediano *(medium heat)*.

9) Cuando el fondo *(bottom)* está hecho, se _______________ (freír) el otro lado.

10) Se _______________ (usar) un plato *(plate)* para darle la vuelta a la tortilla *(to turn the omelet)*.

Respuestas F: **1)** pelan / **2)** cortan / **3)** fríen / **4)** cuela / **5)** baten / **6)** mezcla / **7)** añade / **8)** echa / **9)** fríe / **10)** usa

[Footnotes]

[13] *'Freír' is an e>i stem-vowel changing verb.*
[14] *'Colar' is an o>ue stem-vowel changing verb.*

MI LISTA DE VOCABULARIO

This is a list of the words that you have learned in this unit.

(el) aceite
(el) aceite vegetal/de maíz/de oliva
(el) aguacate
(el) ajo
(el) aliño o (el) aderezo
(la) alita
algo
alguien
algún/a/os/as
alguno/a
añadir

(el) arroz
(el) brócoli
(la) carne de vaca/res
(la) carne molida
(la) carnicería
(la) cebolla
(el) cerdo
(la) cereza
(el) champiñón o (la) seta o (el) hongo
(la) chuleta
cielo

(la) ciruela
cítrico
colar
(el) cordero
(el) cubito de hielo
(la) cucharada
dar la vuelta
después
(el) diente de ajo
duro
echar
(la) ensalada
(el) espárrago
(la) espinaca
(el) fondo
freír
(la) fresa
(la) fruta
(la) frutería
(el) queso
(la) harina
(el) hígado
(el) huevo
(el) jamón
(la) judía o (el) frijol[15]
(el) kilo
(la) leche
(la) lechuga
(el) limón
maduro

(el) maíz
(el) mango
(la) mantequilla
(la) manzana
(la) mayonesa
me parece bien
(el) melocotón o (el) durazno
(el) melón
nada
nadie
(la) naranja
ni...ni...
ningún/a
ninguno/a
o...o...
(el) pan
(la) patata o (la) papa
(el) pavo
(la) pechuga
pelar
(el) pepino
(la) pera
(el) perejil
(el) pescado
(el) pimiento
(la) piña
(el) plátano o (la) banana
(el) pollo
(el) producto lácteo
¿qué hace falta?

qué raro
(el) queso
(la) rebanada
(la) receta
(el) recipiente
(el) refresco
(la) sal
(la) salchicha
(el) sándwich
siempre
(la) sopa
(el) sushi
también
tampoco
(la) ternera
todo junto
(el) tomate
(la) tortilla
(el) trigo
triturar
(la) uva
(el) vaso
(la) verdulería
(el) vinagre
(la) yema del huevo
(el) yogurt
(la) zanahoria

[Footnotes]

[15] *In Mexico, the stress of the word 'frijol' is on the last syllable, but in Colombia, it falls on the second to last (thus the written accent on the 'i').*

UN POCO DE CULTURA

Los mercados y el regateo

En los países de habla hispana, los lugares *(places)* donde se venden ciertos *(certain)* productos tienen un nombre derivado del producto más la terminación *(ending)* '-ería'. Por ejemplo, en la lechería se vende leche (y probablemente otros productos lácteos), y en la papelería se vende papel (y probablemente otros artículos de oficina). Los profesionales que trabajan en estos lugares también tienen un nombre derivado del producto más la terminación '-ero/a'. Por ejemplo, el carnicero es el hombre que vende carne en la carnicería, y el pescadero es el hombre que vende pescado en la pescadería, y así *(and so on)*.

El concepto de estos pequeños negocios *(businesses)* especializados en algunos productos es muy antiguo *(old)*. Muchas veces, estos establecimientos *(establishments)* se unen *(join each other)* para crear *(to create)* un 'mercado', donde hay muchos puestos *(stands)* diferentes convenientemente localizados cerca los unos de los otros *(conveniently located close to each other)*. Los mercados son establecimientos muy interesantes porque normalmente venden productos frescos *(fresh)* y permiten la práctica del regateo *(bargaining)*.

Regatear *(to bargain)* es negociar el precio *(price)* de un producto entre el vendedor *(seller)* y el comprador *(customer)*. Es una práctica que todavía *(still)* existe en muchos mercados y se espera *(it is expected)* que el comprador no acepte el producto al precio anunciado *(advertised price)*. Sin embargo *(however)*, esta práctica está desapareciendo *(disappearing)* hoy en día *(nowadays)* y ahora los productos tienen precios fijos *(fixed prices)*.

También la estructura de los mercados es diferente ahora: antes *(before)*, cada persona o familia tenía *(had)* su negocio particular dentro del *(inside)* mercado, pero ahora es común que una gran compañía posea *(a large company owns)* todos los negocios y venda toda clase *(all kinds)* de productos en un lugar *(place)*, como la compañía Walmart en Estados Unidos, por ejemplo.

RECOMENDACIÓN PARA ESTA UNIDAD

To finish this unit, we recommend that you explore the Internet and find a recipe (in Spanish) for a typical dish from a Spanish-speaking country (e.g., paella, ajiaco, arroz con pollo, mondongo, ropa vieja, arroz con gandules, cocido, etc.). Some will use the passive 'se' in the instructions, but others will use either infinitives or commands. To practice 'se,' we recommend the 'Comida Latina' section of Contacto Magazine http://www.contactomagazine.com

UNIDAD 21

CONTENIDO

In this unit, you will learn:

1 - How to order in a restaurant

2 - About indirect object pronouns

3 - About double object pronouns

4 - Cultural information about restaurants and the concept of 'la sobremesa'

en el restaurante

EN EL RESTAURANTE

(At the restaurant)

Peter, while exploring his new neighborhood, sees a Colombian restaurant and decides to try the food. The menu sounds familiar to him because he visited Colombia once.

MENÚ

Aperitivos *(Appetizers)*

Maduros *(Fried sweet plantains)*

Empanada de carne *(Meat-filled turnover)*

Aborrajados *(Fried plantains with cheese)*

Patacones *(Twice-fried plantain patties)*

Arepa de queso *(Cheese-filled fried corn pancake)*

Papa rellena *(Beef stuffed potato)*

Platos principales *(Main dishes)*

Bandeja paisa[1]: Bistec, arroz, huevo frito *(fried)*, fríjoles, chicharrón *(deep-fried pork rind)* y arepa

Chuleta valluna[2]: Chuleta de lomo *(tenderloin)* de cerdo, arroz y patacones

Arroz con pollo: Pollo, arroz, ensalada y maduros

Ropa vieja: Carne de res desmechada *(shredded)*, arroz y maduros

Churrasco[3]: Carne de res con salsa *(sauce)* chimichurri[4], tostones y yuca *(yucca)*

Sancocho de pescado: Sopa de pescado *(Fish soup)* con yuca, plátanos verdes y maíz

Tamal valluno: Tamal de cerdo envuelto en hojas de plátano *(wrapped in banana leaves)*

Cazuela de mariscos: Sopa espesa *(thick)* de mariscos *(shellfish)* con maduros

Ajiaco: Sopa de pollo con papas, maíz y aguacate

Sobrebarriga *(beef skirt)* **a la criolla** *(creole)*: Carne de res con salsa criolla, arroz y ensalada

Ceviche peruano: Mariscos marinados *(marinated)* en limón con cilantro y yuca

Postres *(Desserts)*

Flan *(Vanilla-egg custard)*

Tres leches[5] *(Cake of three milks)*

Bebidas *(Drinks)*

Jugos (con leche o con agua)
Jugo de mora *(Blackberry juice)*
Jugo de lulo *(Lulo juice)*
Jugo de guanábana *(Soursop juice)*
Jugo de maracuyá *(Passion fruit juice)*
Jugo de piña
Jugo de mango

Refrescos *(Sodas)*
Pony Malta *(Malt)*
Colombiana *(Champagne flavored soda)*
Coca-cola, Pepsi-cola, Sprite
Fanta de manzana, Fanta de naranja

Vinos *(Wines)*

Cervezas *(Beers)*

Café *(Coffee)*
Café colombiano

[Footnotes]

[1] People from Medellín, Colombia are called 'paisas.' Thus, this dish is typical of Medellín. The word 'bandeja' literally means 'tray.' Items are displayed separately on this tray/dish.

[2] The word 'valluno/a' means 'del valle' (of the valley), referring to Valle del Cauca, on the Pacific coast, where the city of Cali is located.

[3] 'Churrasco' is a term that refers to grilled beef: a thick cut of steak (Argentina, Bolivia, Uruguay, Paraguay), tenderloin steak (Nicaragua, Cuba), skirt or flank steak (Puerto Rico), think cut of steak (Chile), etc.

[4] The Argentinean chimichurri sauce is made of chopped parsley, dried oregano, pepper, garlic, salt, paprika, olive oil and vinegar, all ingredients typical of the Spanish and Italian cuisines.

[5] The three milks are: evaporated milk, condensed milk, and either whole milk or cream.

Ejercicio A

¿Qué les recomiendas a estas personas? Observa el menú del restaurante colombiano y recomienda algunos platos a estas personas.

1) Ana María no come carne de res y a ella no le gustan los plátanos. ¿Qué aperitivo le recomiendas?

Le recomiendo ______________________________

2) A Diego no le gusta el pollo ni la carne de res. ¿Qué platos principales le recomiendas?

Le recomiendo ______________________________

3) Arturo y Juana son alérgicos *(allergic)* a las frutas tropicales. ¿Qué bebida les recomiendas?

Les recomiendo ______________________________

4) A mí me encantan el pescado y los mariscos. ¿Qué platos principales me recomiendas?

Te recomiendo ______________________________

5) Nosotros no bebemos alcohol. ¿Qué bebidas nos recomiendas?

A ustedes les recomiendo ______________________________

Respuestas A: **1)** la arepa / **2)** la chuleta valluna, el sancocho de pescado, la cazuela de mariscos, el ceviche peruano y el tamal vallino / **3)** los refrescos, el café, el vino y la cerveza / **4)** el sancocho de pescado, la cazuela de mariscos y el ceviche peruano / **5)** los jugos, los refrescos y el café

Ejercicio B

Si tú visitaras *(If you visited)* **el restaurante colombiano, ¿qué platos pedirías** *(would you order)***?**

Yo pediría *(I would order)*

____

____

porque me gusta/gustan *[select one]*

____

____

pero *(but)* no pediría

____

____

porque no me gusta/gustan *[select one]*

____

____

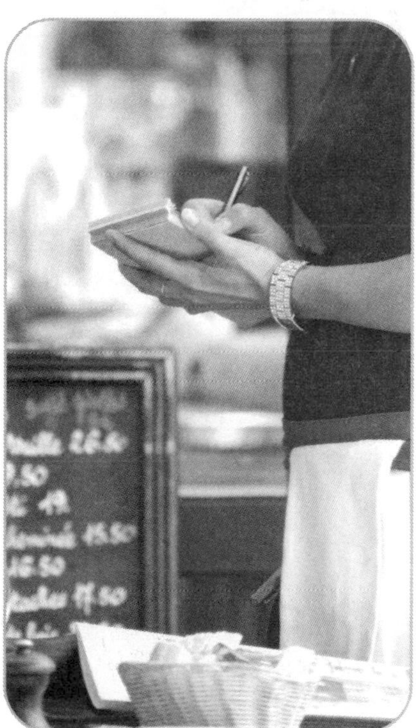

Ejercicio C

Traduce estas frases típicas de restaurante.

1) The meat is wrapped in banana leaves.

____

2) Do you (ustedes) have fish soup today?

____

3) I don't like pork.

____

4) Could you bring me *(Podría usted traerme)* a glass of passion fruit juice, please?

____

5) I don't want dessert, thanks.

____

6) Is this beer Colombian?

____

7) What appetizers do you (ustedes) have today?

____

Respuestas C: **1)** La carne está envuelta en hojas de plátano. / **2)** ¿Tienen sancocho - sopa de pescado hoy? / **3)** No me gusta el cerdo. / **4)** ¿Podría traerme un vaso de jugo de maracuyá, por favor? / **5)** No quiero postre, gracias. / **6)** ¿Es esta cerveza colombiana? / **7)** ¿Qué aperitivos tienen hoy?

FRASES ÚTILES *(Useful phrases)*

Del cliente

¿Qué recomienda usted? *(What do you recommend?)*

¿Es picante? *(Is it spicy?)*

Mi comida está fría *(My food is cold)*

Me falta... *(I am missing...)*

Esta carne está cruda/no está hecha *(This meat is raw/is underdone)*

Todo estaba delicioso *(Everything was delicious)*

Mis felicitaciones a la cocinera/al cocinero *(My compliments to the cook)*

Mi cuchara y mi cuchillo están sucios *(My spoon and my knife are dirty)*

La cuenta, por favor *(The check, please)*

¿Me trae cubiertos por favor? *(Could you bring me silverware?)*

Creo que hay un error en la cuenta *(I think there is an error in the bill)*

Voy a dejar $10 de propina *(I am going to leave a $10 tip)*

Del mesero		
Buen provecho *(Enjoy your food)*	¿Le gustaría probar...? *(Would you like to try...?)*	Aquí tiene su cuenta *(Here is the check)*
¿De qué sabor lo quiere? *(What flavor would you like?)*	¿Cómo está todo? *(How is everything?)*	¿Necesita cambio? *(Do you need change?)*
El plato especial del día es... *(The daily special is...)*	¿Necesita algo más? *(Do you need anything else?)*	No aceptamos cheques personales *(We don't take personal checks)*

Ejercicio D

Enlaza estas frases típicas de un restaurante con las respuestas apropiadas.

1) ¿De qué sabor lo quiere?
2) ¿Le gustaría probar el pescado?
3) ¿Cómo está todo?
4) Aquí tiene su cuenta
5) Esta carne está cruda
6) Me falta un cuchillo
7) Mi cuchara está sucia

a) ¡Oh, mi cartera está en el coche!
b) Ahora le traigo uno
c) No, gracias. Hoy quiero carne
d) Ahora le traigo una limpia
e) De fresa, por favor
f) Muy bueno, gracias
g) Ahora la llevo a la cocina otra vez

Respuestas D: **1)** - e) / **2)** - c) / **3)** - f) / **4)** - a) / **5)** - g) / **6)** - b) / **7)** - d)

LOS PRONOMBRES DE OBJETO INDIRECTO *(Indirect object pronouns)*

An indirect object is a part of speech that indirectly receives the action of the verb. The indirect object usually refers to a person, and it is often located after the direct object.

Marta da un libro a su hermana
(Marta gives a book to her sister)

Yo recomiendo el pescado a Felipe
(I recommend the fish to Felipe)

Some verbs do not require an indirect object (e.g., I ran a mile).
When using a gustar-like structure, the indirect object is always present.

Me encanta el ceviche
(I love ceviche = Ceviche is pleasing to me)

A Luis le gusta la fruta
(Luis likes fruit = Fruit is pleasing to him)

When you do not want to repeat the indirect object over and over, you can replace it with an indirect object pronoun (she gave Yolanda the book, told her how much she loved her, and promised her to…). For every indirect object, there is an indirect object pronoun. These are the indirect object pronouns in Spanish:

PRONOMBRES DE OBJETO INDIRECTO	me te le nos os les

In Spanish, pronouns go before the verb, but after the 'no' (if there is one).

Yo le recomiendo la arepa
(I recommend the arepa to him)
Yo no le recomiendo la sopa
(I do not recommend the soup to her)

When the construction is either 1) preposition + infinitive, or 2) positive command, the pronoun is attached to the end of the verb.

Para recomendarte algo...
(In order to recommend something to you...)

Tráigale algo
(Bring him something)

When you have a construction with two verbs, and the second verb is an infinitive (comprar) or a gerund (comprando), you have two options. The pronoun can either go before the first verb, or attached to the end of the second verb. Both forms are commonly used:

Diana te quiere preparar la comida
(Diana wants to prepare the food for you)

Diana quiere prepararte la comida
(Diana wants to prepare the food for you)

Ejercicio E

Re-escribe estas frases sustituyendo el objeto indirecto subrayado *(underlined)* **por el pronombre de objeto indirecto. Para el último ejercicio, escribe las dos posibilidades.**

1) Jaime recomienda el cerdo a Jessica
Jaime le recomienda el cerdo

2) Tú das al mesero la propina
____

3) Nosotras preparamos la comida para ti
____

4) Ellos no traen la cuenta a nosotros
____

5) Yo no recomiendo a ellos nada del menú
____

6) Voy a llevar el almuerzo a ti
__________ or __________

Respuestas E: **2)** Tú le das la propina / **3)** Nosotros te preparamos la comida / **4)** Ellos no nos traen la cuenta / **5)** Yo no les recomiendo nada del menú / **6)** Te voy a llevar el almuerzo - Voy a llevarte el almuerzo

LOS DOS PRONOMBRES JUNTOS

(Both pronouns together)

When a sentence has both an indirect object pronoun and a direct object pronoun, the indirect object pronoun always precedes the direct object pronoun:.

Tú me los das *(You give them to me)*
Ella te la envía *(She sends it to you)*
Ella quiere comprártela *(She wants to buy it for you)*

If both pronouns start with the letter 'l' (e.g., yo le lo doy), change the indirect object pronoun to 'se.'

Ellos le los preparan ===> Ellos se los preparan
(They prepare them for him)
Beto les lo recomienda ===> Beto se lo recomienda
(Beto recommends it to them)

PRONOMBRES DE OBJETO INDIRECTO	PRONOMBRES DE OBJETO DIRECTO
me	me
te	te
le	lo/la
nos	nos
os	os
les	los/las

Ejercicio F

Completa estas frases escribiendo los pronombres de objeto indirecto y objeto directo. La primera está hecha. *(Remember that the indirect goes first and might change to 'se'.)*

1) María prepara la comida para sus hijas.

María _se_ _la_ prepara.

2) El mesero trae la cuenta a nosotros.

El mesero _____ _____ trae.

3) Los clientes piden la cuenta al mesero.

Los clientes _____ _____ piden.

4) Yo recomiendo el jugo de lulo a ti.

Yo _____ _____ recomiendo.

5) Ustedes quieren comprar esta fruta para ella.

Ustedes _____ _____ quieren comprar.

or Ustedes quieren comprár_______.

Respuestas F: **2)** nos la / **3)** se la / **4)** te lo / **5)** se la / -sela

MI LISTA DE VOCABULARIO

This is a list of the words that you have learned in this unit.

alérgico
(el) aperitivo
(la) bebida
¡buen provecho!
(el) café
(el) cambio
(la) cerveza
(el) cheque personal
criollo
crudo
(el) cubierto
(la) cuchara
(el) cuchillo
(la) cuenta
dejar
delicioso
envuelto
(el) error
espeso
frito
guanábana
(la) hoja de plátano
(el) jugo
le
les
(la) lógica
(el) lomo
(el) lulo
(el) maracuyá
(el) marisco
me
me falta
(el) menú
(la) mora
nos
os
pedir
picante
(el) plato principal
(el) postre
probar
(la) propina
recomendar
(el) refresco
relleno
(el) sabor
(la) salsa
según
sucio
te
(el) tenedor
útil
(el) vino
(la) yuca

UN POCO DE CULTURA

Los restaurantes

Pedir *(to order)* en un restaurante de los Estados Unidos y pedir en un restaurante de otro país, incluyendo *(including)* los países de habla hispana *(Spanish-speaking)* tiene semejanzas *(similarities)* y diferencias. Una semejanza es que muchas personas hacen negocios *(do business)* durante el almuerzo *(lunch)* o la cena *(dinner)*. Otra semejanza es que hay diferentes categorías de restaurantes, unos más caros que otros, unos más elegantes que otros, etc.

Las diferencias son muchas. Por ejemplo, en muchos países hispanos se cena *(people have dinner)* muy tarde, entre las 9:00 y las 10:00 de la noche. Otra diferencia es que la comida completa *(complete meal)* puede consistir de varios platos uno detrás de otro *(several courses, one after another)*, más postre, café y licor. Otra diferencia es que es normal ver a la gente fumar *(smoking)* en los cafés, restaurantes y bares. También puede ser normal tirar *(throw)* basura en el suelo del bar. En algunos países, además *(in addition)*, no es tradicional dejar propina *(leaving a tip)* porque los camareros reciben un sueldo *(salary)* normal como cualquier otro *(any other)* profesional. Para saber cómo comportarte *(how to behave)*, haz lo que hagan los demás *(do as others do)*. Una costumbre típica de los países hispanos es la sobremesa.

La sobremesa

La sobremesa es una costumbre importante en la cultura hispana. Los hispanos aprecian *(appreciate)* la comida y el tiempo dedicado *(dedicated)* a la comida. Comer dentro de *(inside)* un coche, por ejemplo, mientras *(while)* la persona conduce *(drives)* al trabajo o a la casa, es una idea loca *(insane)* para un hispano. La filosofía es disfrutar *(enjoy)* no sólo de la comida, sino también del momento de la digestión. La sobremesa es ese momento después de *(after)* comer cuando una persona charla *(chats)* con la familia y los amigos mientras *(while)* toma el postre, el café o fuma un cigarrillo *(cigarette)*.

RECOMENDACIÓN PARA ESTA UNIDAD

Para finalizar esta unidad, te recomendamos que visites un restaurante hispano e intentes *(try)* pedir *(to order)* tu comida en español (si el mesero /la mesera habla español). Pide *(Order)* comida nueva para ti. ¡Explora lo desconocido! *(Explore the unknown!)*

UNIDAD 22

CONTENIDO

In this unit, you will learn:

1 - Vocabulary related to music and dancing
2 - About the verbs 'saber' and 'conocer'
3 - About the personal 'a'
4 - The numbers from 100 to 10,000
5 - Cultural information about the influences on Latin music

el baile

EL BAILE

(Dance)

Ana is trying to find something fun that she and her husband can enjoy together once in a while. She is thinking of signing up for dancing classes, but does not know whether Enrique would be interested.

Ana: Cielo, pienso que deberíamos *(I think we should)* tomar clases de baile.
Enrique: ¿Clases de baile? ¿Por qué?
Ana: Porque es una forma *(way)* de hacer ejercicio pero también es divertido *(fun)*.
Enrique: No sé *(I don't know)*… Yo no sé bailar muy bien. Soy un poco patoso/torpe *(clumsy)*, ya lo sabes *(you know that)*.
Ana: Noooooo… vas a hacerlo muy bien, ya verás *(you'll see)*. ¿Qué baile te gustaría aprender *(would you like to learn)*?
Enrique: No sé. ¿Cuál te gusta a ti? *(Which one do you like?)*
Ana: A mí me gustan la salsa, el merengue, y la cumbia.
Enrique: Ah, pues a mí me gustan los bailes de salón *(ballroom dances)*: el vals, el bolero, la balada… algo tranquilo *(something calm)*.
Ana: Ah, pero esos bailes son tan aburridos *(boring)*…
Enrique: Quizás *(Maybe)*, pero son fáciles de aprender *(easy to learn)*.
Ana: ¿Por qué dices eso? El merengue es muy fácil.
Enrique: Ah, pero todas esas vueltas *(all those turns)*… me mareo *(I get dizzy)*.

Ana: ¡No seas ridículo! El vals también tiene muchas vueltas.

Enrique: ¿Pero tú sabes bailar algo?

Ana: No, por eso *(that's why)* quiero tomar clases. ¡Venga! *(C'mon!)* Vamos a tomar una clase divertida…. ¿Salsa?

Enrique: Vale. Supongo que puedo intentarlo, pero no te prometo nada. *(OK. I suppose I can try it, but I can't promise you anything.)*

Ana: Ah, ¡qué bien! ¡Gracias, eres maravilloso *(you are wonderful)*!

Enrique: Sí, sí… maravilloso. Cuando te pise *(When I step on your foot)*, vas a ver lo maravilloso que soy *(you'll see how wonderful I am.)*

Ana: No, hombre, no seas pesimista.

Enrique: ¿Conoces alguna academia donde podamos ir? *(Do you know of an academy where we could go?)*

Ana: No, pero conozco a un instructor de baile. Él puede recomendarnos algún sitio. *(No, but I know a dance instructor. He can recommend a place to us.)*

Ejercicio A

¿De qué hablan Enrique y Ana? Contesta estas preguntas con frases completas.

1) ¿Qué quiere hacer Ana para divertirse *(to have fun)*?

____

2) ¿Qué bailes le gustan a Ana?

____

3) ¿Qué bailes le gustan a Enrique?

____

4) ¿Qué piensa Ana sobre *(about)* los bailes que sugiere *(suggests)* Enrique?

____

5) ¿Qué piensa Enrique sobre los bailes que sugiere ella?

____

6) Al final *(finally)*, ¿qué clase deciden *(decide)* tomar juntos *(together)*?

____

7) ¿Conoce Ana *(Does Ana know)* alguna academia?

____

Respuestas A: **1)** Ana quiere tomar clases de baile / **2)** A Ana le gustan la salsa, el merengue y la cumbia / **3)** A Enrique le gustan los bailes de salón: el vals, el bolero y la balada / **4)** Ella piensa que son aburridos / **5)** Él piensa que son difíciles (porque hay muchas vueltas y se marea) / **6)** Ellos deciden tomar (juntos) la clase de salsa / **7)** No, ella no conoce ninguna academia (pero conoce a un instructor de baile)

Ejercicio B

¿Cómo se dicen las siguientes expresiones en español? Consulta el diálogo.

1) Don't be ridiculous

____

2) I suppose...

____

3) I think we should...

____

4) I don't know

____

5) I can't promise you anything

____

6) It is fun

____

7) You'll see

____

Respuestas B: **1)** No seas ridículo / **2)** Supongo que... / **3)** Pienso que deberíamos... / **4)** No sé / **5)** No te prometo nada / **6)** Es divertido / **7)** Ya verás

INSTRUMENTOS MUSICALES

(Musical instruments)

piano

saxofón

bajo

órgano

violín

batería

guitarra

tambor

flauta

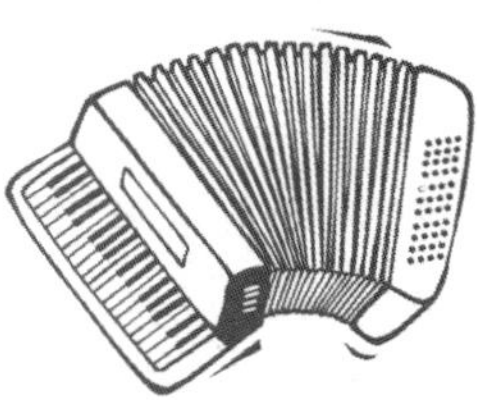
acordeón

clarinete

congas

MÁS VOCABULARIO DE BAILES Y MÚSICA

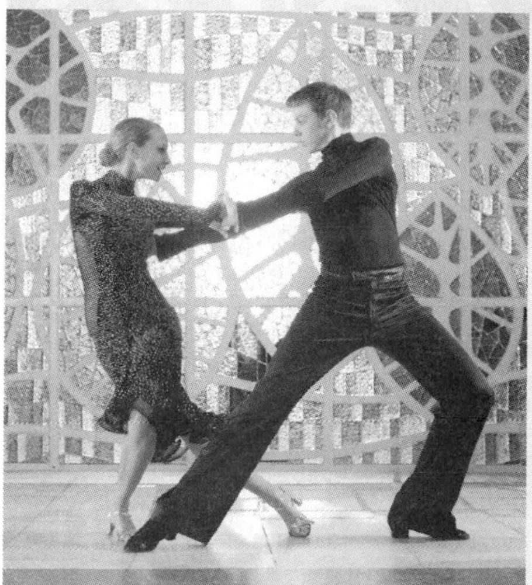

cha-cha-chá	twist	pop
rumba	ballet	blues
mambo	bossa nova	hip-hop
flamenco	rock	bachata
swing	jazz	vallenato
polca	milonga	heavy metal

LOS VERBOS 'SABER' Y 'CONOCER'

You already saw how to conjugate the verbs 'saber' *(to know)* and 'conocer' *(to know)* when we studied irregular 'yo'-form verbs. Here are the conjugations again:

CONOCER *(to know)*	**SABER** *(to know)*
conozco	sé
conoces	sabes
conoce	sabe
conocemos	sabemos
conocéis	sabéis
conocen	saben

Both verbs mean 'to know,' but they are used for different purposes.

Conocer
is used with people, places or things that you are familiar with or know of.

Conozco a tu hermano
(I know your brother)

¿Conoces alguna academia de baile?
(Do you know of a dance academy?)

¿Conoces la última canción de Shakira?
(Have you heard Shakira's latest song?)

When you use it with people, you must include the preposition 'a' (called the 'personal a'), to distinguish people from places.

¿Conoces a Sydney? *(Do you know Sydney?)*
[Sydney is a person]

¿Conoces Sydney? *(Do you know Sydney?)*
[Sydney is a place]

Saber
refers to knowledge or memorization of information, or to a skill that you learned (to play an instrument, to speak a foreign language, to dance, etc.).

¿Sabes la última canción de Shakira?
(Do you know [by heart] Shakira's latest song?)

No sé nada *(I don't know anything)*

Sé bailar *(I know how to dance or I can dance)*

Ellos saben tocar la flauta
(They know how to play the flute)

No sé a qué hora es el concierto
(I don't know what time the concert is)

¿Sabes quién viene a bailar?
(Do you know who is coming to dance?)

Ejercicio C

Encierra con un círculo *(around)* **la mejor opción para estas frases.**

1) ¿Sabes/Conoces algún restaurante peruano en Nueva York?

2) Yo no sé/conozco qué es la lambada.

3) No sé/conozco.

4) ¿Tu hermana sabe/conoce tocar el piano?

5) Nosotros no sabemos/conocemos cómo usar un acordeón.

6) ¿Quién es esa mujer? No la sé/conozco.

7) Mis amigos saben/conocen la ciudad de Chicago.

8) ¿Sabes/Conoces el poema de Rubén Darío titulado *(titled)* 'Margarita'?

9) Sí, pero no lo sé/conozco de memoria.

10) Ese hombre está mirándote. ¿Lo sabes/conoces de algo? *(Do you know him from somewhere?)*

Respuestas C: **1)** Conoces / **2)** sé / **3)** sé / **4)** sabe / **5)** sabemos / **6)** conozco / **7)** conocen / **8)** Conoces / **9)** sé / **10)** conoces

Ejercicio D

Traduce estas frases al español. Usa el 'a' personal cuando sea necesario.

1) Do you (tú) know Carlos?

____

2) Do you (usted) know how to play the bass?

____

3) I know this man. He is a great dancer *(bailarín[1])*.

____

4) I don't know her in person, but I know who she is.

____

5) You guys know what the name of this dance is?

____

Respuestas D: **1)** ¿Conoces a Carlos? / **2)** ¿Sabe usted (cómo) tocar el bajo? / **3)** Conozco a este hombre. Es un gran bailarín. / **4)** No la conozco en persona, pero sé quién es. / **5)** ¿Saben ustedes cuál es el nombre de este baile? / ¿Saben ustedes cómo se llama este baile?

[Footnotes]

[1] The feminine of 'bailarín' is 'bailarina' (as in 'bailarina de ballet'). When talking about flamenco dancers, however, the terms 'bailador' and 'bailadora' are used.

LOS NÚMEROS DEL 100 AL 10.000

(Numbers from 100 to 10,000)

Numbers from 100 to 900	
100	cien
101	ciento uno
102	ciento dos
114	ciento catorce
135	ciento treinta y cinco
167	ciento sesenta y siete
200	doscientos
300	trescientos
400	cuatrocientos
500	quinientos
600	seiscientos
700	setecientos
800	ochocientos
900	novecientos

Numbers from 1.000 to 10.000	
1.000[2]	mil
1.001	mil uno
1.002	mil dos
1.030	mil treinta
1.100	mil cien
1.140	mil ciento cuarenta
1.520	mil quinientos veinte
1.903	mil novecientos tres
2.000	dos mil
3.000	tres mil
10.000	diez mil

[Footnotes]

[2] *In Spain, thousands are denoted by a period instead of by a comma. In contrast, decimals are denoted by a comma. Examples: One thousand four hundred = 1.400; the value of Pi = 3,14.*

Ejercicio E

Selecciona los dígitos que corresponden con estos números.

	a)	b)	c)
1) dos mil ocho	a) 2.080	b) 2.008	c) 2.800
2) mil seiscientos veinte	a) 1.620	b) 1.206	c) 1.602
3) novecientos cuatro	a) 409	b) 904	c) 494
4) siete mil doscientos treinta y tres	a) 7.023	b) 7.233	c) 7.323
5) nueve mil novecientos nueve	a) 9.090	b) 9.990	c) 9.909

Respuestas E: **1)** - b) / **2)** - a) / **3)** - b) / **4)** - b) / **5)** - c)

Ejercicio F

Escribe los siguientes números en español.

1) 1.995

2) 6.502

3) 9.004

4) 7.713

5) 1.035

Respuestas F: **1)** Mil novecientos noventa y cinco / **2)** Seis mil quinientos dos / **3)** Nueve mil cuatro / **4)** Siete mil setecientos trece / **5)** Mil treinta y cinco

Ejercicio G

Escribe cuánto cuestan los siguientes instrumentos y clases de baile. Observa el ejemplo 1.

1) $ 4,314

1) *El violín y el saxo cuestan cuatro mil trescientos catorce dólares*

2) ______________________

3) ______________________

4) ______________________

5) ______________________

2) Cha-cha: 100 •/week

3) Tango: $140/month

4) 1,209 •

5) Mambo: $153/month

Respuestas G: **2)** La clase de cha-cha-chá cuesta cien euros a la semana / **3)** La clase de tango cuesta ciento cuarenta dólares al mes / **4)** La guitarra cuesta mil doscientos nueve euros / **5)** La clase de mambo cuesta ciento cincuenta y tres dólares al mes

MI LISTA DE VOCABULARIO

This is a list of the words that you have learned in this unit.

aburrido
(la) academia
(el) acordeón
(la) bachata
(el) bailador/(la) bailadora
(el) bailarín/(la) bailarina
(el) baile (de salón)
(el) bajo
(la) balada
(el) ballet
(la) batería
(el) blues
(el) bolero
(la) bossa nova
(el) cha-cha-chá
cien
ciento...
cinco mil
(el) clarinete
(la) conga
conocer
costar
cuatro mil
cuatrocientos
(la) cumbia
deberías
decidir
diez mil
divertido
divertirse
(el) dólar
dos mil
doscientos
(el) euro
fácil (de aprender)
(el) flamenco
(la) flauta
(la) forma
(la) guitarra
(el) heavy metal
(el) hip-hop
(el) instructor/(la) instructora
(el) instrumento musical
intentar
(el) jazz
juntos
(el) mambo
maravilloso
marearse
(el) merengue
mil
(la) milonga
(la) música
novecientos
nueve mil
ocho mil
ochocientos
(el) órgano
patoso/torpe
(el) piano
(la) polca
(el) pop
por lo menos
prometer
quinientos
ridículo
rock (clásico, n'roll)
(la) rumba
saber

(la) salsa	(el) sitio	trescientos
(el) saxofón	sugerir	(el) twist
seis mil	swing	(el) vallenato
seiscientos	(el) tambor	(el) vals
setecientos	tranquilo	(el) violín
siete mil	tres mil	(la) vuelta

UN POCO DE CULTURA

Las influencias en la música hispana/latina

La música de los hispanos/latinos tiene varias influencias. Una influencia es la de Europa, especialmente de España, donde se usa la guitarra mucho. La música de España también está influida por otras músicas, como la música de los gitanos *(gypsies)*, los árabes *(Arabs)*, los celtas *(Celts)* y otros. La música latina también tiene influencias de otros países europeos, como la influencia italiana en el tango argentino, por ejemplo.

Otra influencia muy importante viene de África. Esta influencia es evidente en los ritmos *(rhythms)* del mambo y del merengue, y se representa muy bien con los sonidos *(sounds)* de los tambores, las maracas y las congas.

Otra influencia viene de las culturas indígenas de América, como podemos ver en la música del vallenato de Colombia. Sus instrumentos musicales todavía *(still)* se usan para tocar música en América Central y América del Sur. En Bolivia, por ejemplo, se usa la zampoña *(panpipe)*, una flauta múltiple hecha de bambú *(made of bamboo)*. Otra influencia viene de los Estados Unidos. La salsa, por ejemplo, es un baile creado por *(created by)* los latinos de Nueva York. El pop en español de muchos países también está claramente *(clearly)* influenciado por la música rock y pop de Estados Unidos.

RECOMENDACIÓN PARA ESTA UNIDAD

Para finalizar esta unidad, te recomendamos que visites un lugar de baile latino (discoteca, club, etc.) para observar salsa, merengue, y otros bailes. Si tienes interés, también puedes tomar clases de baile en una academia. Además *(Besides)*, allí puedes conocer a personas hispanas/latinas y puedes practicar tu español también.

UNIDAD 23

CONTENIDO

In this unit, you will learn:

1 - Vocabulario relacionado con las relaciones románticas *(romantic relationships)*

2 - Sobre estructuras recíprocas *(reciprocal structures)*

3 - Sobre expresiones con 'hace'

4 - Información cultural sobre bodas *(weddings)*

las relaciones románticas

LAS RELACIONES ROMÁNTICAS

(Romantic relationships)

Cuando Peter está en casa, recibe *(he receives)* **una llamada de teléfono** *(a telephone call)* **de su padre. Su padre le dice que quiere divorciarse de** *(to get a divorced from)* **su esposa después de** *(after)* **40 años de matrimonio** *(marriage)*. **Peter está muy sorprendido** *(surprised)* **y afligido** *(distraught)*. **Al día siguiente, su jefe habla con él.**

Antonio Pérez: Peter, ¿qué tal va todo?

Peter: Todo va bien, señor Pérez.

Antonio Pérez: Pregunto porque hoy lo veo un poco triste.

Peter: Bueno.... He recibido *(I have received)* malas noticias *(bad news)* de casa.

Antonio Pérez: Oh, ¡cuánto lo siento! Escuche *(Listen)*, si necesita tomarse unos días libres *(days off)*... sin problema, ¿eh?

Peter: Muchas gracias, señor Pérez, pero no hace falta *(there is no need)*. Se trata de mis padres. No comprendo lo que está pasando *(what's going on)*. Mi padre dice *(says)* que él y mi madre van a divorciarse *(are getting divorced)*. Yo sé que mis padres se aman *(love each other)* mucho.

Antonio Pérez: ¿Sí? ¡Qué triste! *(How sad!)* Aquí en España el divorcio *(divorce)* no es común en esa generación. ¿En su país es algo común?

Peter: Sí... bastante común *(very common)*, pero... no entiendo por qué. Mis padres se quieren *(love each other)*, se llevan bien *(get along with each other)*, se cuidan el uno al otro *(take care of each other)*....

Antonio Pérez:	A esa edad *(At that age)*… ¿quién sabe *(who knows)*? Quizás *(Maybe)* ya están cansados *(tired)* y no se soportan *(they can't stand each other)*.
Peter:	No creo *(I don't think so)*. Simplemente no entiendo qué está ocurriendo.
Antonio Pérez:	¿Ellos nunca se pelean *(fight)*?
Peter:	No, nunca se pelean. Si discuten *(If they have a discussion)*, se hablan con respeto *(they talk to each other with respect)*.
Antonio Pérez:	Si tienen problemas, deben *(must)* hablar con un psicólogo o un consejero matrimonial *(marriage counselor)* antes de *(before)* divorciarse, pienso yo *(I think)*.
Peter:	Sí, eso pienso yo también. Debo *(I must)* hablar con mi madre para averiguar *(to find out)* qué está pasando.
Antonio Pérez:	Sí, hable con ella. ¡Pobrecita! *(Poor thing!)* Tómese el resto del día libre *(off)* a ver si se siente mejor mañana *(to see if you feel better tomorrow)*.
Peter:	Muchas gracias. Ahora me voy, entonces *(I am leaving then)*. Y perdone.
Antonio Pérez:	No hay de qué *(Don't mention it)*. Cuídese *(Take care)*.

Ejercicio A

¿Qué ocurre? Responde estas preguntas con frases completas.

1) ¿Quién llama por teléfono a Peter?

____

2) ¿Qué quiere el padre de Peter?

____

3) ¿A Peter le gusta la noticia *(news)*?

____

4) El señor Pérez sugiere que ellos hablen con…

____

5) ¿Qué va a hacer Peter? ______________________________

Posibles respuestas A: **1)** El padre de Peter lo llama por teléfono. / **2)** Él va a divorciarse de su esposa. / **3)** A Peter no le gusta la noticia. (Él está sorprendido y afligido.) / **4)** … un psicólogo o un consejero matrimonial / **5)** Peter va a hablar con su madre./Peter va a tomar el resto del día libre.

ACCIONES RECÍPROCAS *(Reciprocal actions)*

When two or more people do something to each other, this reciprocity is indicated by the pronoun 'se' (e.g., casarse, divorciarse, odiarse, hablarse, etc.) and sometimes also by the expression 'el uno al otro[1]' (to one another). The subject must be plural (two people) and the pronoun must agree with it. These are the only three possible pronouns:

PRONOMBRES RECÍPROCOS
—
—
—
nos
os
se

Examples:

Mis padres <u>se aman</u> *(My parents love each other)*

Jorge y José Luis <u>se escriben</u> *(Jorge and José Luis write to each other)*

Nosotros <u>nos besamos</u> *(We kiss each other)*

Ustedes <u>se ven</u> frecuentemente *(You guys see each other frequently)*

[Footnotes]

[1] The expression 'el uno al otro'/'la una a la otra'/'los unos a los otros'/'las unas a las otras' can only be used in conjunction with a reciprocal 'se' construction.

Ejercicio B

Lee el diálogo entre Peter y su jefe otra vez, localiza *(locate)* **los verbos en construcciones recíprocas, y escríbelos aquí. Observa el ejemplo 1.**

1) *van a divorciarse*

2) ________

3) ________

4) ________

5) ________

6) ________

7) ________

8) ________

9) ________

10) ________

Respuestas B: **2)** se aman / **3)** se quieren / **4)** se llevan bien / **5)** se cuidan el uno al otro / **6)** no se soportan/ **7)** nunca se pelean / **8)** nunca se pelean / **9)** se hablan con respeto / **10)** divorciarse

Ejercicio C

Traduce estas frases al español usando verbos en construcción recíproca.

1) Nacho and Juliana write to each other every week.

____

2) Luis and Merche[2] don't fight frequently.

____

3) My mother and I tell (use *contar)* each other our problems.

____

4) We (masc.) see each other at church every Sunday.

____

5) You guys fall in love (use *enamorarse)* every time you see each other.

____

6) Daniel and Luisa say goodbye (use *despedirse)* at the station *(estación)*.

____

Respuestas C: **1)** Nacho y Juliana se escriben cada semana - todas las semanas / **2)** Luis y Merche no se pelean frecuentemente. / **3)** Mi madre y yo nos contamos nuestros problemas. / **4)** (Nosotros) nos vemos en la iglesia cada domingo - todos los domingos. / **5)** Ustedes se enamoran cada vez que se ven. / **6)** Daniel y Luisa se despiden en la estación.

[Footnotes]

[2] *'Merche' is a nickname for Mercedes.*

MAS VOCABULARIO SOBRE RELACIONES ROMÁNTICAS

novio[3]

boda

padrino de bodas

damas de honor

novia

anillo de boda/alianza

madrina de bodas

pareja

banquete

besarse

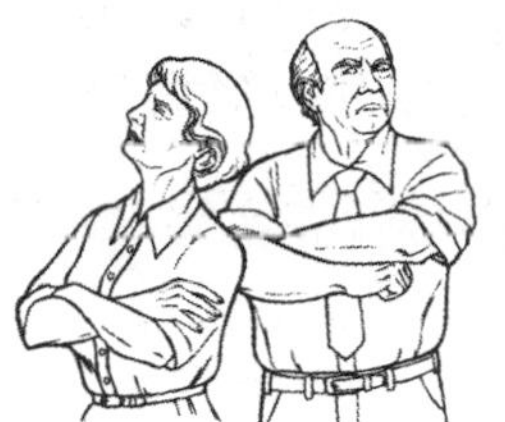
pegarse

comprometerse

enamorarse

¿me quieres/me amas? *(do you love me?)*

te amo/te quiero *(I love you)*

matrimonio[4] *(marriage)*

amar/querer *(to love)*

lío/aventura *(affair)*

separarse *(to get separated)*

acostarse con *(to sleep with)*

bendición *(blessing)*

tener relaciones sexuales *(to have sexual relations)*

salir con *(to date/to go out with)*

casarse por lo civil/por el juzgado *(to get married in court)*

casarse por la iglesia *(to get married in church)*

divorciarse *(to get divorced)*

enfadarse/enojarse *(to get mad at each other)*

vivir juntos *(to live together)*

[Footnotes]

[3] *If the couple is engaged, the words 'enamorado/a' or 'prometido/a' are used in some countries. When a couple is living together but not married, you might hear the word 'compañero' o 'pareja' (partner).*

[4] *In some Spanish-speaking countries, 'matrimonio' also means 'wedding.'*

Ejercicio D

Elige la mejor respuesta a estas frases.

1) Felipe, yo te quiero mucho. Y tú, ¿_____?

a) te quiero	b) me quieres	c) nos queremos

2) Fue *(It was)* una _____ muy bonita con la novia y su vestido blanco, la iglesia.... Ahhhhh.

a) dama de honor	b) aventura	c) boda

3) Los padres de Roberto ya no se quieren más y van a _____.

a) casarse	b) divorciarse	c) enamorarse

4) Es normal que una _____ tenga dificultades *(has difficulties)* durante su matrimonio.

a) pareja	b) novio	c) madrina de bodas

5) A Eva y a Lucho no les gusta _____ en público. Son muy tímidos *(shy)*.

a) divorciarse	b) separarse	c) besarse

Respuestas D: **1)** - b) / **2)** - c) / **3)** - b) / **4)** - a) / **5)** - c)

LOS PROBLEMAS MATRIMONIALES

(Marriage problems)

Cuando Peter regresa a casa, habla por teléfono con su madre. Ella le explica un poco los problemas que tiene con su esposo. Al día siguiente, Peter ve a su jefe.

Antonio Pérez: Ah, Peter. ¿Se encuentra mejor *(Are you feeling better)*? ¿Habló usted con su familia?

Peter: Sí. Parece que *(It seems that)* mis padres tienen problemas desde hace mucho tiempo *(for a long time)*.

Antonio Pérez: Ah, ¡qué pena! *(How sad!)* ¿Está deprimida *(depressed)* su madre?

Peter: No, está bien, pero está harta de *(fed up with)* mi padre desde hace varios años. No soporta vivir con él. *(She can't stand living with him.)* Dice que fuma en la casa y por eso ella tiene alergias *(allergies)*...

Antonio Pérez: ¿Y qué responde él?

Peter: No le hace caso. *(He doesn't pay her any attention.)*

Antonio Pérez: Ya veo. *(I see.)*

Peter: También dice que él no le ayuda *(helps)* con los quehaceres domésticos y ella entonces *(then)* no quiere hacer nada tampoco. Cosas así… *(Things like that…)*

Antonio Pérez: Sí, comprendo. Parece que ya no se aguantan. *(It looks like they can't stand each other anymore.)*

Peter: Eso parece. *(So it seems.)*

Antonio Pérez: ¿Van a ver a un consejero matrimonial?

Peter: No, porque mi padre dice *(says)* que entonces *(then)* él tiene que cambiar *(change)* su forma de vida. ¡Es increíble! *(It is incredible!)*

Antonio Pérez: Su padre es un poco testarudo *(stubborn)*, ¿no?

Peter: Bastante. *(A lot.)* Me pregunto que harán con Pluto. *(I wonder what they will do with Pluto.)*

Antonio Pérez: ¿Pluto?

Peter: El perro de ellos… *(Their dog…)*

Ejercicio E

Escribe los problemas que tiene la madre de Peter con el padre de Peter.

Ella dice que él ______________________

y por eso ella ______________________

También dice que él ______________________

y entonces ella ______________________

Respuestas E: **1)** fuma en la casa - tiene alergias / **2)** no le ayuda con los quehaceres domésticos - no quiere hacer nada tampoco

EXPRESIONES DE TIEMPO CON 'HACE'

(Time expressions with 'hace')

You have already seen the word 'hace' in different contexts: as the third person singular of the verb 'hacer' *(to do)* (e.g., Peter hace la cama), and in expressions of weather (e.g., hace frío). Now we are going to use 'hace' to express duration of an action in the present:

> **¿Cuánto (tiempo) hace que** + *verb in present*
> ¿Cuánto tiempo hace que sales con él?
> *(How long have you been dating him?)*

> **¿Hace cuánto (tiempo) que** + *verb in present*
> ¿Hace cuánto que estás divorciada?
> *(For how long have you been divorced?)*

To answer, you can also switch the order of the elements:

> **Hace + *amount of time* + que** + *verb in present*
> Hace 2 meses que salgo con Ismael
> *(I have been dating Ismael for two months)*

> *Verb in present* **desde hace + *amount of time***
> Salgo con Ismael desde hace 2 meses
> *(I have been dating Ismael for two months)*

Ejercicio G

Traduce estas frases al español usando la expresión 'hace' en dos construcciones.
(Try not to translate word for word/literally. Instead, use the structures you just learned.)
Observa el ejemplo 1.

1) I have been divorced for four years.

Hace cuatro años que estoy divorciado. / Estoy divorciado/a desde hace cuatro años.

2) Elisa has been going out with Daniel for three years.

____

3) We (masc.) have been having problems for six months.

____

4) How long have you (usted) known your husband?

____

5) How long have you (tú) had this affair with him?

____

Respuestas G: **2)** Elisa sale/está saliendo con Daniel desde hace tres años. *and* Hace tres años que Elisa sale/está saliendo con Daniel. / **3)** (Nosotros) tenemos/estamos teniendo problemas desde hace seis meses. *and* Hace seis meses que tenemos/estamos teniendo problemas. / **4)** ¿Hace cuánto (tiempo) que conoce (usted) a su esposo? *and* ¿Cuánto (tiempo) hace que conoce (usted) a su esposo? / **5)** ¿Hace cuánto (tiempo) que tienes esta aventura con él? *and* ¿Cuánto (tiempo) hace que tienes esta aventura con él?

MI LISTA DE VOCABULARIO

This is a list of the words that you have learned in this unit.

acostarse con
aguantar o soportar
(la) alergia
amarse
(el) anillo (de compromiso/de bodas)
antes de
(la) aventura o (el) lío
averiguar
(el) banquete
(la) bendición
besarse
(la) boda
casarse (por lo civil) (por el juzgado)
casarse (por la iglesia)
comprometerse
(el) consejero matrimonial
contarse
cuánto tiempo hace que
cuidarse
(la) dama de honor
deber
dejar de
deprimido
desde hace
despedirse
(la) dificultad
discutir
divorciarse
el uno al otro/la una a la otra
los unos a los otros/las unas las otras
enamorarse
encontrarse
enfadarse
¡es increíble!
escribirse
eso parece
estar de acuerdo
estar enamorado
fumar
hablarse
hace cuánto (tiempo) que
hace X que
hacer caso a
harto de
llevarse bien
(la) madrina de bodas
matrimonial
(el) matrimonio
¿me quieres?
(la) noticia
(el) novio/(la) novia
(el) padrino de bodas
(la) pareja

pasar/ocurrir
pegarse
pelearse
¡pobrecito!
pronto
(el) psicólogo/(la) psicólogo
¡qué pena!
quererse
recíproco
(la) relación (amorosa/ sexual)
(el) respeto
responder
romántico
salir con
separarse
soportarse
te amo/te quiero
testarudo
verse
vivir juntos
y cosas así

UN POCO DE CULTURA

Las bodas *(Weddings)*

Las bodas en los distintos *(different)* países de habla hispana comparten *(share)* muchos elementos en común, especialmente porque son celebraciones católicas *(Catholic)*, pero también hay pequeñas diferencias.

Diferencias

En algunos países existe la costumbre *(custom)* de entregar *(give)* un anillo de compromiso *(engagement ring)*, pero en otros países esto no se hace.

En unos países hay dos padrinos y dos madrinas durante la boda, mientras que en otros, sólo hay un padrino y una madrina (normalmente el padre de la novia y la madre del novio).
También *(Also)*, en algunos lugares *(some places)* es común llevar el anillo de boda en el dedo anular izquierdo *(left ring finger)*, mientras que en otros, el anillo va en el dedo anular derecho *(right ring finger)*.
En algunos países, durante la boda, la liga *(garter)* de la novia *(bride)* se corta en pedazos *(is cut in pieces)* y se vende *(is sold)* entre los invitados *(guests)*, mientras que *(whereas)* en otros países se cortan la ropa interior *(underwear)* de la novia y la corbata del novio *(the groom's tie)*.

Similitudes

Las bodas hispanas modernas, sin embargo *(however)*, todavía *(still)* conservan muchos elementos en común. Por ejemplo, si te casas por la iglesia católica, tienes que tomar *(you must take)* un cursillo *(course)* prematrimonial gratuito *(free)*.
Otra similitud *(similarity)* es que la novia tira su ramo de bodas *(throws her wedding bouquet)* hacia *(towards)*

las mujeres solteras invitadas a la boda. Esta costumbre significa que la afortunada que lo atrape *(the lucky one who catches it)* se va a casar al año siguiente *(next year)*.

Costumbres tradicionales

Muchas costumbres tradicionales están desapareciendo *(are disappearing)* un poco en las bodas modernas, como la costumbre mozárabe *(Mozarabic)* de las arras. En esta tradición el novio da 13 monedas de plata *(silver coins)* a la novia durante la ceremonia de la boda como señal de compromiso *(a pledge)*, y ella se las da de vuelta *(she returns them to him)*. El intercambio *(The exchange)* de las arras significa que los novios van a compartir bienes y suerte *(share their fortune)*.
Otra tradición que se está perdiendo *(is getting lost)* es la del ajuar *(trousseau or hope chest)*. El ajuar es la colección de bienes *(goods, possessions)* que la novia aporta *(contributes)* al matrimonio *(marriage)*. Normalmente en el ajuar hay ropa interior, bordados *(embroidery)*, y otras cosas para la casa que la novia ha hecho y coleccionado *(has made and collected)* por varios años para este propósito *(purpose)*. Muchas veces, aparte *(besides)* del ajuar, la familia de la novia da una dote *(dowry)* al novio, o sea *(that is)*, una cantidad de dinero y bienes *(amount of money and possessions)*.

RECOMENDACIÓN PARA ESTA UNIDAD

Para finalizar esta unidad, te recomendamos que leas anuncios en español de personas que buscan pareja para relaciones románticas. Aquí encontrarás *(Here you will find)* más vocabulario relacionado con este tema y también estarás informado sobre la vida de los latinos en busca de amor *(in search of love)*. Entra en la página de Univision.com http://www.univision.com/portal.jhtml y haz clic[5] en el icono de Foros que está arriba. Luego haz clic en el enlace *(link)* de 'Vida y Salud' (bajo Categorías principales) y luego selecciona la categoría que te guste dentro de 'Foros de Amor y Romance'.

También tienes información general sobre bodas en http://www.bodas.net/. Puedes leer distintas secciones para practicar tu vocabulario.

[Footnotes]

[5] *Another word for 'to click' is 'pinchar'.*

UNIDAD 24 CONTENIDO

EXÁMEN 3

exámen 3

EXÁMEN 3

En esta unidad vas a encontrar varios ejercicios para practicar lo que has aprendido en las unidades 17–23. Si el resultado del exámen es satisfactorio, puedes comenzar a estudiar las últimas ocho unidades. Sin embargo, si no estás satisfecho/a con los resultados del examen, recomendamos que repases las unidades 17–23 antes de continuar.

Ejercicio A

Observa las ilustraciones y completa estas frases sobre lo que estas personas están haciendo. Usa verbos en estructura recíproca. Observa el ejemplo 1.

1) Ellos *se pelean* ________

2) Nosotros ________

3) Ustedes ________

4) Ellos ________

5) Ellos ________

Respuestas A: **2)** nos escribimos / **3)** se casan / **4)** se aman - se quieren - se enamoran / **5)** se despiden - se dicen adiós

Ejercicio B

Escribe el sustantivo *(noun)* **que mejor describe estas ilustraciones. Incluye el artículo definido (el, la, los, las).**

1) ______

2) ______

3) ______

4) ______

5) ______

Respuestas B: **1)** el anillo de bodas - la alianza / **2)** la novia / **3)** las damas de honor / **4)** la iglesia / **5)** el banquete

Ejercicio C

Responde estas preguntas sobre tu vida usando la expresión de tiempo 'hace'.

1) ¿Hace cuánto tiempo que estudias español?

______

2) ¿Hace cuánto que conduces *(drive)*?

______

3) ¿Cuánto tiempo hace que conoces a tu mejor amigo?

______

4) ¿Cuánto hace que vives en esta ciudad?

______

5) ¿Hace cuánto tiempo que no comes tu comida favorita?

______

Respuestas C: Hace X días/meses/años que.... + verb in present *or* verb in present + desde hace X días/meses/años

Ejercicio D

Completa estas frases escribiendo la forma correcta del verbo 'saber' o del verbo 'conocer'.

1) Pablo, ¿tú ______ bailar merengue? No, no ______ .

2) Isabel ______ a un instructor de baile muy bueno que ______ bailar todo.

3) Nosotros no ______ ese club de baile.

4) Edgar, ¡¡vamos a cantar la última canción de Carlos Vives!! ¿La ______ de memoria?

5) Ustedes no ______ el precio de este curso de salsa, ¿verdad?

Respuestas D: **1)** sabes - sé / **2)** conoce - sabe / **3)** conocemos / **4)** sabes / **5)** saben

Ejercicio E

Escribe el nombre de cinco tipos de música o bailes hispanos/latinos. Utiliza el artículo determinado (el, la).

1) ______________________

2) ______________________

3) ______________________

4) ______________________

5) ______________________

Posibles respuestas E: la salsa, el merengue, la cumbia, el tango, el vallenato, el mambo, el flamenco, la rumba, la bachata, el cha-cha-chá...

Ejercicio F

Escribe estos números en español.

1) 342 ______________________

2) 5.467 ______________________

3) 9.505 ______________________

4) 8.991 ______________________

5) 4.003 ______________________

Respuestas F: **1)** trescientos cuarenta y dos / **2)** cinco mil cuatrocientos sesenta y siete / **3)** nueve mil quinientos cinco / **4)** ocho mil novecientos noventa y uno / **5)** cuatro mil tres

Ejercicio G

Escribe el nombre de estos instrumentos musicales. Utiliza el artículo determinado (el, la).

1)

2)

3)

4)

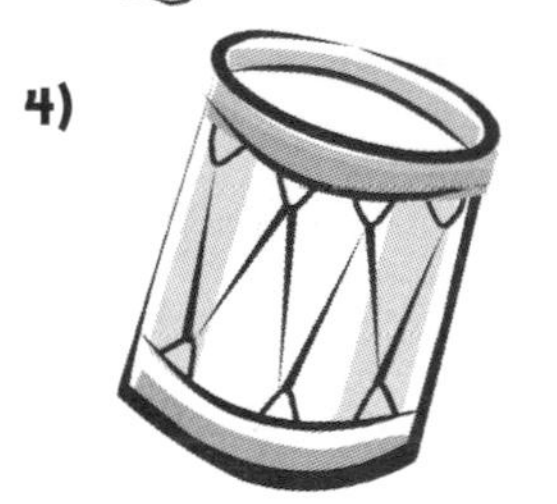

5)

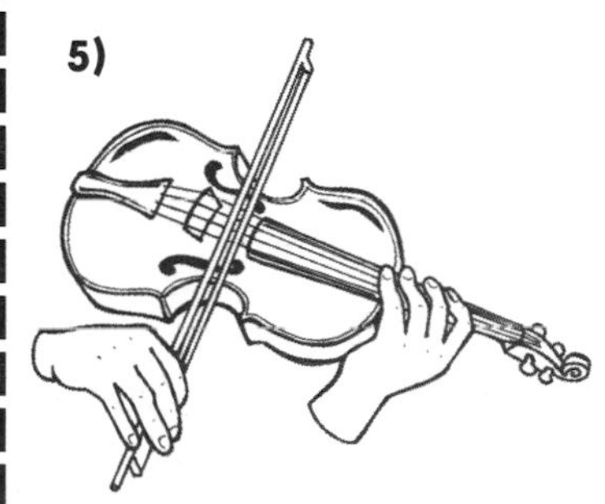

Respuestas G: **1)** el saxofón / **2)** la guitarra / **3)** la flauta / **4)** el tambor / **5)** el violín

Ejercicio H

Ordena las frases del diálogo entre un mesero y su cliente en un restaurante. Observa el ejemplo 1.

1 Buenos días, señor. ¿Qué desea tomar?
___ Yo creo que voy a probar las costillas.
___ Sí, claro. Aquí está el menú. Nuestra especialidad son los camarones al ajillo.
___ Muy bien, señor, ahora le traigo sus costillas. Vienen con puré de papas y espárragos.
___ Buenos días. De momento una coca-cola, gracias. ¿Tiene un menú?
___ Gracias, pero a mí no me gusta el marisco. ¿Tienen carne de res?
___ Ah, muy bien. Me encantan los espárragos.
___ Sí, una carne maravillosa de primera calidad. ¿Desea bistec, chuletas, costillas…?

Respuestas H: **2)** Buenos días… / **3)** Sí, claro… / **4)** Gracias… / **5)** Sí, una carne… / **6)** Yo creo… / **7)** Muy bien… / **8)** Ah, muy bien…

Ejercicio I

Reescribe estas frases usando el pronombre de objeto indirecto y el pronombre de objeto directo en la misma frase. Observa el ejemplo 1.

1) Ricardo da un regalo a su novia
Ricardo se lo da

2) Asunción ofrece una copa de vino a Eva
___

3) El mesero sirve la comida a ti
___

4) Ustedes traen el menú a nosotros
___

5) Mi novia prepara las chuletas para mí
___

Respuestas I: **2)** Ricardo se la ofrece / **3)** El mesero te la sirve / **4)** Ustedes nos lo traen / **5)** Mi novia me las prepara

Ejercicio J

Completa este párrafo sobre la comida con expresiones indefinidas y negativas de la tabla. No se pueden repetir.

algunas
ni
alguien
siempre
nunca
o
ninguna
ni

Julián tiene _________________ (**1**) naranjas en casa, pero no tiene _________________ (**2**) manzana. Necesita ir al mercado, pero *(but)* _________________ (**3**) tiene tiempo de ir porque (**4**) _________________ está trabajando. Por eso, normalmente va su esposa _________________ (**5**) su hijo mayor. Desgraciadamente *(Unfortunately)* _________________ (**6**) su esposa _________________ (**7**) su hijo mayor pueden ir hoy, porque los dos están fuera de la ciudad. Julián necesita que _________________ (**8**) compre más fruta hoy. ¿Qué puede hacer?

Respuestas J: **1)** algunas / **2)** ninguna / **3)** nunca / **4)** siempre / **5)** o / **6)** ni / **7)** ni / **8)** alguien

Ejercicio K

Completa esta receta de sopa de lentejas usando la construcción del 'se' pasivo. Observa el ejemplo 1. ***(Stem-vowel changing verbs are noted for you so you remember to make the change. Remember that 'todo' is singular.)***

1) Primero se ponen (poner) las lentejas a remojar *(soak)* unas horas en agua con sal.

2) Después _________________ (pelar) 4 patatas medianas y _________________ (cortar) en pedazos pequeños.

3) Entonces _________________ (echar) las lentejas en otro recipiente con agua limpia y sal, junto con *(along with)* las patatas, y _________________ (poner) todo a fuego mediano.

4) Mientras tanto *(In the meantime)*, en una sartén _________________ (freír, e>i) cebolla y ajo usando aceite de oliva.

5) Cuando la cebolla y el ajo están dorados *(golden)*, _________________ (echar) todo en el recipiente de las lentejas.

6) Si quiere un poco de carne, salchicha, por ejemplo, también _________________ (añadir) ahora.

7) Finalmente _________________ (cocer, o>ue) todo a fuego medio durante 35 ó 45 minutos.

Respuestas K: **2)** se pelan - se cortan / **3)** se echan - se pone / **4)** se fríen - se echa / **5)** se echa / **6)** añade / **7)** se cuece

Ejercicio L

Completa las siguientes frases con 'por' o 'para' en la descripción de lo que pasa en un restaurante.

1) El cliente viene al restaurante ____________ almorzar.

2) El mesero le ofrece al cliente algo _______ beber, ______ ejemplo, vino o agua.

3) El cliente, ___________ lo general, pide bebida y luego pide su comida.

4) El mesero escribe la orden ____________no olvidar *(not to forget)* nada.

5) El cliente puede estar en el restaurante _______ una o dos horas, depende, pero no mucho tiempo más _________-que hay más personas esperando ___________ sentarse a comer.

6) Después de comer, el cliente sale _________ su casa _____________ descansar _______ la tarde.

7) El mesero tiene que limpiar todas las mesas _________ las 8 de la tarde _________ si viene alguien pronto ________ cenar.

Respuestas L: **1)** para / **2)** para - por / **3)** por / **4)** para / **5)** por - por - para / **6)** para - para - por / **7)** para - para - por

Ejercicio M

Escribe frases usando el pronombre de objeto directo que corresponde a los objetos de las ilustraciones. Observa el ejemplo 1.

1) Diego / querer *Diego lo quiere*

2) David / comprar ____________________

3) Nosotros / llevar ____________________

4) Ustedes / pagar ____________________

5) Tú / necesitar ____________________

Respuestas M: **2)** David la compra / **3)** (Nosotros) las llevamos / **4)** Ustedes los pagan / **5)** (Tú) los necesitas

Ejercicio N

Escribe el nombre de las prendas de ropa que llevan estas personas.

1) Arturo lleva

2) Gloria y Beatriz llevan

3) Tú llevas

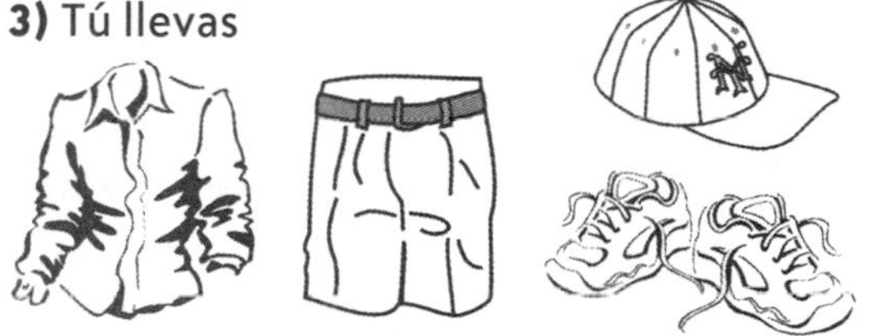

Respuestas N: **1)** Arturo lleva un suéter de cuello alto, un impermeable, (unos) pantalones largos, y (unas) botas / **2)** Gloria y Beatriz llevan (unas) sandalias y (unos) trajes de baño / **3)** Tú llevas una camisa de manga larga, (unos) pantalones cortos, un gorro, y (unas) zapatillas deportivas

Ejercicio Ñ

Usa expresiones con 'tener' y describe cómo se sienten estas personas. Observa el ejemplo 1.

1) Yo *tengo sed* ________

2) Tú ________

3) Nerea ________

4) Nosotros ________

5) Ustedes ________

Respuestas Ñ: **2)** Tú tienes calor / **3)** Nerea tiene frío / **4)** Nosotros tenemos hambre / **5)** Ustedes tienen miedo

Ejercicio O

Traduce estas frases con la estructura gustar. Observa el ejemplo 1.

1) We are interested in sports

A nosotros nos interesan los deportes

2) You (tú) like that girl

____

3) Soraya does not like this food

____

4) They (fem.) love their house

____

5) You (usted) are fascinated by the Caribbean

____

6) My head (cabeza) hurts

____

Respuestas O: **2)** (A ti) te gusta esa chica / **3)** A Soraya no le gusta esta comida / **4)** A ellas les encanta su casa / **5)** A usted le fascina el Caribe / **6)** (A mí) me duele la cabeza

UNIDAD 25

CONTENIDO

En esta unidad vas a aprender:

1 - Vocabulario relacionado con el cuerpo humando *(the human body)*

2 - Sobre el imperativo de tú *(informal commands)*

3 - Sobre el verbo 'doler' *(to hurt)*

4 - Información cultural sobre el sistema de salud *(health care system)* de Venezuela

el cuerpo humano

EL CUERPO HUMANO

(The human body)

Ana lleva *(takes)* **a su hija Sofía al hospital para su revisión mensual** *(monthly checkup)*. **Sofía no tiene buena salud** *(health)*: **tiene diabetes. La doctora primero hace un examen general para ver si** *(if)* **todo está bien.**

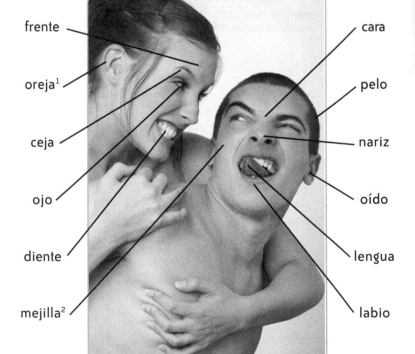

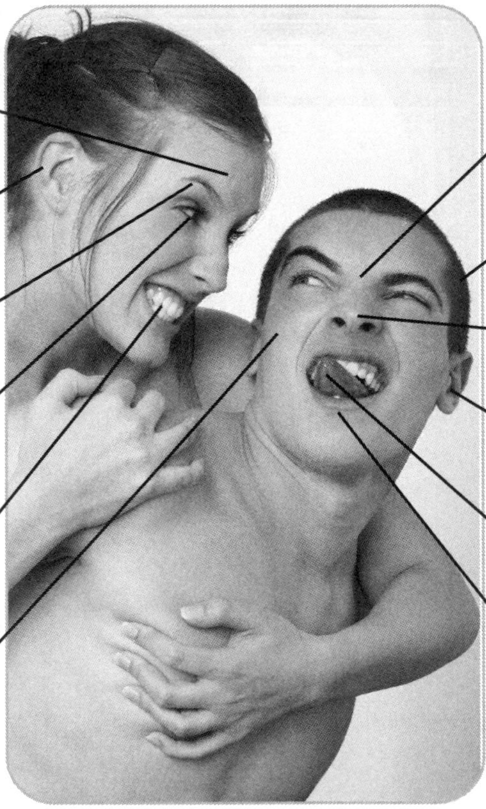

[Footnotes]

[1] *The outer ear and the inner ear have different words in Spanish: 'oreja' and 'oído,' respectively.*

[2] *Other words for 'cheek' are 'carrillo' and 'cachete.'*

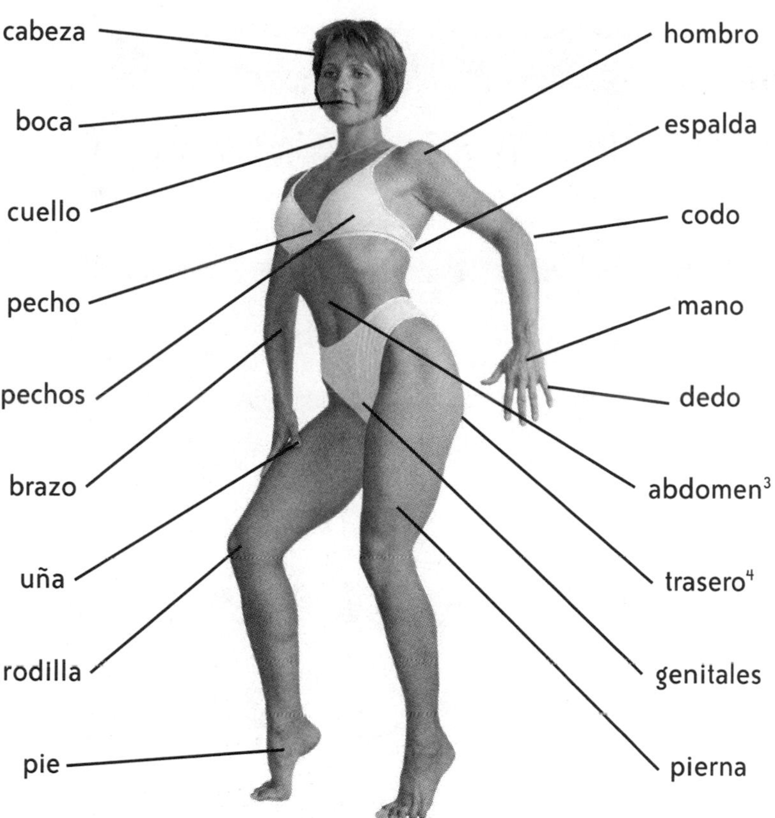

[Footnotes]

[3] *Other words referring to the abdominal area are 'barriga,' 'panza,' 'tripa,' 'estómago,' and 'vientre.'*

[4] *Other words that mean 'behind' or 'rear' are 'pompas,' 'culo,' 'nalgas,' 'asentaderas,' and 'fondillo.'*

La doctora le hace algunas preguntas básicas a Sofía y le da órdenes *(orders)* **para que ella mueva** *(moves)* **su cuerpo.**

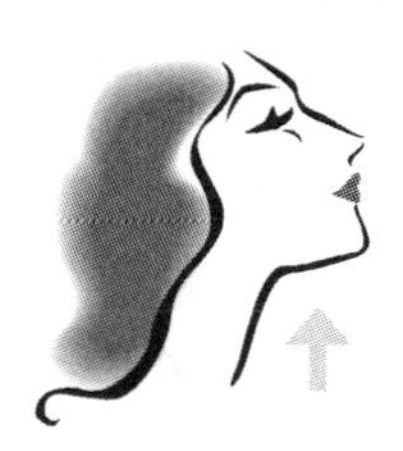
levanta la[5] cabeza

di 'aaaaaaa'

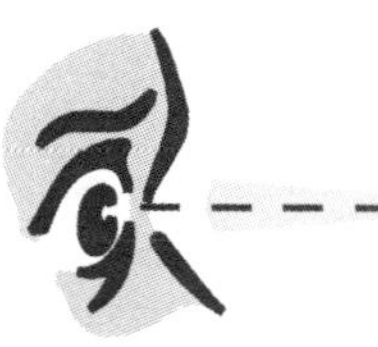
sigue la luz *(light)*

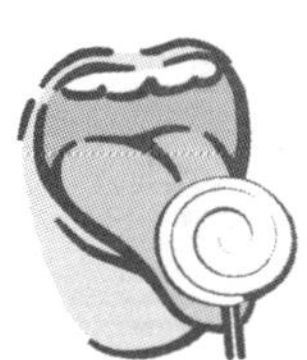
saca la lengua

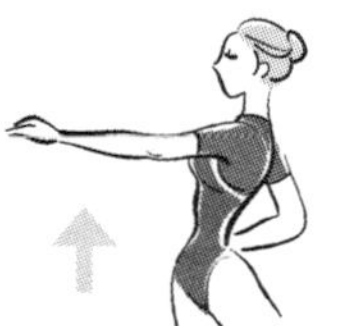
sube el brazo

mueve los dedos

baja la pierna

siéntate

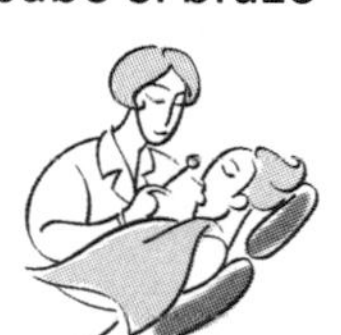

cierra los ojos

aprieta[6] mi mano

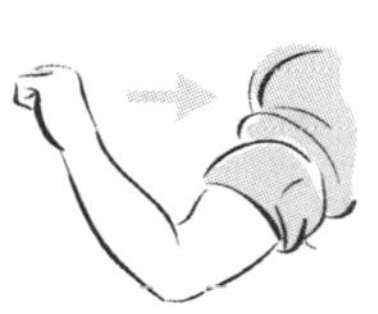
dobla el brazo

levántate[7]

abre la boca

empuja mi mano

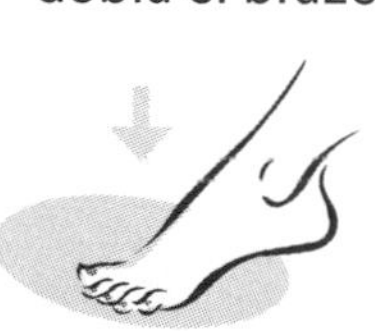
pon el pie aquí

tose

[Footnotes]

[5] *In Spanish, often, instead of using the possessive adjectives with body parts (e.g., levanta tu cabeza), the definite article is used (levanta la cabeza).*

[6] *'Apretar' has several meanings, including 'to press,' 'to push,' and 'to squeeze.'*

[7] *Other words for getting up are 'pararse' and 'ponerse de pie'. The informal commands would be 'párate' and 'ponte de pie'.*

Ejercicio A

Enlaza las siguientes partes del cuerpo con un verbo apropiado.

1) boca	a) escuchar
2) ojos	b) sentarse *(to sit down)*
3) oídos	c) caminar
4) manos	d) pensar *(to think)*
5) piernas	e) respirar *(to breathe)*
6) pecho	f) hablar
7) trasero	g) tocar *(to touch)*
8) cabeza	h) mirar

Respuestas A: **1)** - f) / **2)** - h) / **3)** - a) / **4)** - g) / **5)** - c) / **6)** - e) / **7)** - b) / **8)** - d)

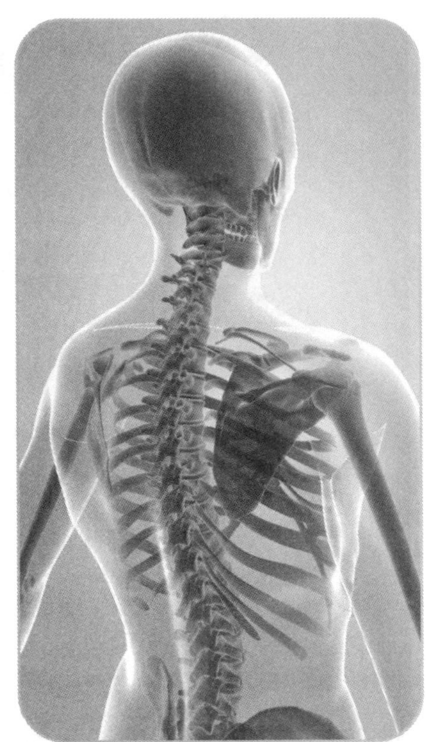

Ejercicio B

Completa estas frases con una palabra apropiada del cuerpo humano.

1) El final *(The end)* de los brazos son las________.

2) Una persona dobla *(bends)* la pierna por *(by)* la ________________.

3) La parte exterior del oído es la ___________.

4) El final de las piernas son los ____________.

5) En la cara tenemos dos ____________, una ____________ y una ______________.

6) La __________ es un poco de pelo que tenemos encima del *(above)* ojo.

7) El cuerpo está unido a *(is joined to)* la cabeza por el ___________.

8) Las mujeres tienen _____________ pero los hombres no.

9) Los __________________ son las partes privadas *(private)* de una persona.

10) En total tenemos 20 ________ en el cuerpo.

11) Dentro de la boca está la _____________.

12) En la punta *(tip)* del dedo está la _________.

Respuestas B: **1)** manos / **2)** rodilla / **3)** oreja / **4)** pies o dedos / **5)** ojos, cejas, mejillas - nariz - boca / **6)** ceja / **7)** cuello / **8)** pechos / **9)** genitales / **10)** dedos / **11)** lengua / **12)** uña

Ejercicio C

Repasa *(Review)* **las órdenes que la doctora dio** *(gave)* **a Sofía. Ahora imagina que** **<u>tú</u> estás en la oficina del doctor. Haz** *(Do)* **las siguientes acciones tú mismo** *(yourself)*.

1) Dobla[8] la pierna

2) Siéntate

3) Pon un dedo en un ojo

4) Cierra la boca

5) Abre los ojos

6) Di 'hola'

7) Sube las cejas

8) Mueve los pies

9) Levanta la mano

10) Tose

[Footnotes]

[8] *Other word for 'to turn' or 'to bend' are 'torcer,' 'flexionar,' and 'girar.'*

Respuestas C: These sentences are asking you to..... **1)** bend your leg / **2)** sit down / **3)** put a finger to one eye / **4)** close your mouth / **5)** open your eyes / **6)** say 'hola' / **7)** raise your eyebrows / **8)** move your feet / **9)** raise your hand / **10)** cough

EL IMPERATIVO DE 'TÚ'

(Informal commands)

When giving orders to a child or to somebody you know well (a friend or a relative), you can use informal commands. This is how you do it:

		Positive commands	Negative commands
-AR verbs	levantar	levant**a**	**no** levant**es**
-ER/-IR verbs	toser	tos**e**	**no** tos**as**

There are several <u>irregular forms</u>:

-Poner: **pon/no pongas**
Pon el dedo sobre la nariz *(Put your finger on your nose)*

-Decir: **di/no digas**
Di la verdad *(Tell the truth)*

-Venir: **ven/no vengas**
Ven por aquí, por favor *(Come this way, please)*

-Salir: **sal/no salgas**
Beatriz, sal de tu casa *(Beatriz, leave your house)*

-Ir: **ve/no vengas**
Ve al hospital *(Go to the hospital)*

-Tener: **ten/no tengas**
Ten paciencia *(Have patience/Be patient)*

-Hacer: **haz/no hagas**
Haz esto *(Do this)*

When you have a <u>pronoun</u>, you treat it differently depending on whether the command is affirmative or negative: you must attach it to the end of the positive command, but place it in front of the negative command.

Di**me** la verdad *(Tell me the truth)*
No **me** digas mentiras *(Don't tell me lies)*

Muéve**los**[9] *(Move them)*
No **los** muevas *(Don't move them)*

Pon**la** allá *(Put it there)*
No **la** pongas allá *(Don't put it there)*

When you have a <u>stem-vowel changing verb</u>, you keep the change.

Cerrar (e>ie) - **Cie**rra los ojos *(Close your eyes)*
Mover (o>ue) - **Mue**ve la cabeza *(Move your head)*

[Footnotes]

[9] *After attaching the pronoun, if the stressed syllable is the third one from the end, it is necessary to write an accent on the vowel of that syllable: levántate, muévela, tíralos, ciérralos, etc.*

UNIDAD 25

Ejercicio D

Sofía tiene algunos comentarios para su doctora y ella responde con órdenes. Escribe las órdenes de la doctora usando el imperativo de tú. Observa el ejemplo 1.
(Pay attention: #6 and #7 have pronouns, and #8 and #9 are negative.)

Sofía		**Doctora**
1) Doctora, siempre tengo sed *(I am always thirsty)*.	(Beber)	Bebe agua.
2) Me duele la cabeza a veces.	(Tomar)	________ un Tylenol.
3) No tengo más insulina.	(Ir)	________ a la farmacia.
4) Necesito más jeringuillas *(syringes)*.	(Comprar)	________ más.
5) Necesito información sobre la diabetes.	(Leer)	________ este libro.
6) No conozco a otros niños con diabetes.	(Buscar / los)	________ en Internet.
7) Necesito una cita *(appointment)* pronto.	(Hacer / la)	________ con mi secretaria.
8) Estoy gorda.	(No comer)	________ tanto.
9) Me gustan mucho los refrescos.	(No beber)	________ refrescos con azúcar.
10) Me gusta comer mucho.	(Cuidar)	________ tu dieta. Es importante.

Respuestas D: **2)** Toma / **3)** Ve / **4)** Compra / **5)** Lee / **6)** Búscalos / **7)** Hazla / **8)** No comas / **9)** No bebas / **10)** Cuida

LOS ORGANOS Y LOS HUESOS

(Organs and bones)

En la oficina de la doctora hay un libro muy interesante con dibujos del cuerpo humano. A Sofía le gusta la medicina y quiere ser doctora cuando sea mayor *(when she grows up)*.

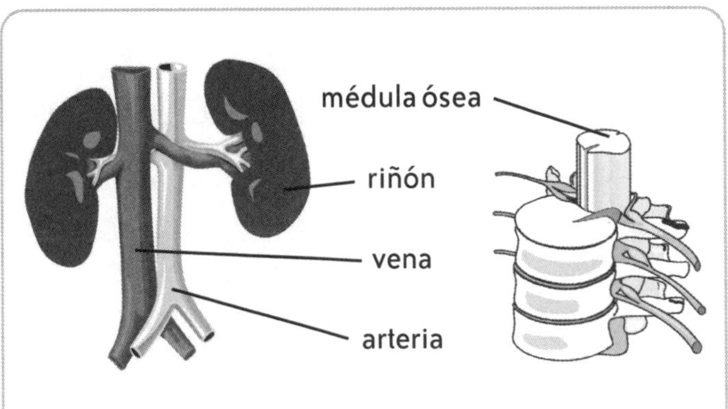

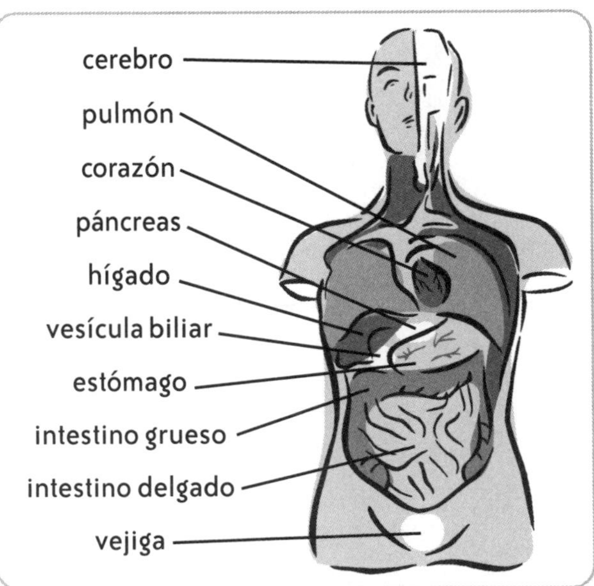

Sofía también encuentra un dibujo con algunos huesos del cuerpo.

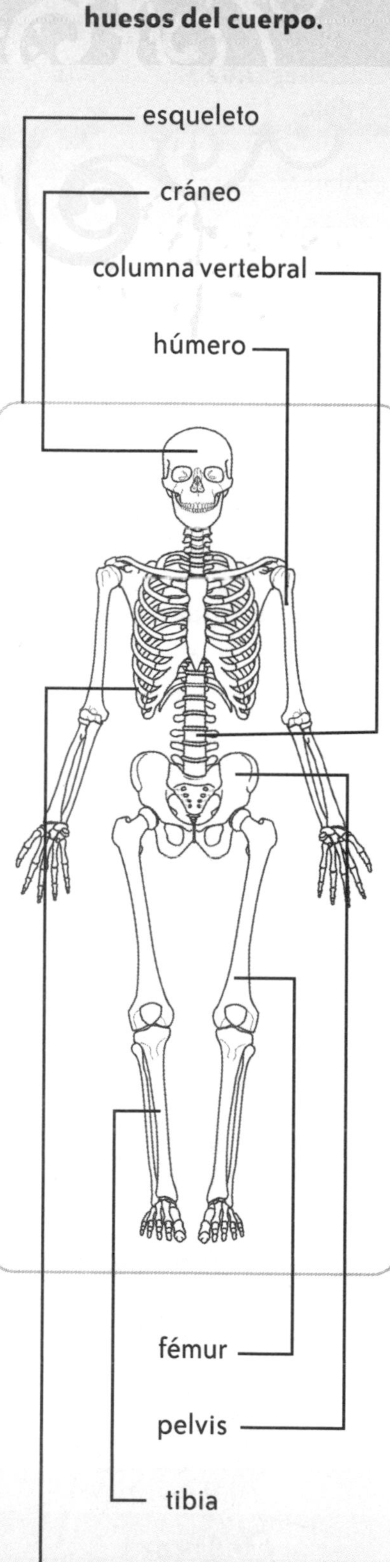

Ejercicio E

Enlaza estos órganos con su función principal.

1) Cerebro	a) almacenar *(collect)* la orina *(urine)*
2) Estómago	b) controlar todo el cuerpo y pensar
3) Riñones	c) llevar la sangre *(blood)*
4) Vejiga	d) digerir *(digest)* la comida
5) Arterias y venas	e) respirar
6) Corazón	f) filtrar *(filter)* la sangre
7) Pulmones	g) palpitar[10]

Respuestas E: **1)** - b) / **2)** - d) / **3)** - f) / **4)** - a) / **5)** - c) / **6)** - g) / **7)** - e)

[Footnotes] [10] *Another word for 'to beat' is 'latir.' 'Latido del corazón' is a heartbeat.*

Ejercicio F

Escribe el nombre de los siguientes huesos de acuerdo a *(according to)* **su descripción. Escribe también los artículos (el, la, los, las).**

1) Es un hueso en el brazo: ________________

2) Es el hueso más largo del cuerpo y está en la pierna: ________________

3) Es el conjunto *(group)* de todos los huesos del cuerpo: ________________

4) Es el hueso que protege *(protects)* el cerebro: ________________

5) Son los huesos que protegen los pulmones y el corazón: ________________

6) Es el conjunto de huesos que tiene muchas vértebras *(vertebrae)*: ________________

Respuestas F: **1)** el húmero / **2)** el fémur / **3)** el esqueleto / **4)** cráneo / **5)** las costillas / **6)** la columna vertebral

EL VERBO 'DOLER' *(The verb 'doler')*

The verb 'doler' is used to indicate that a part of the body hurts, but it is not used to say that somebody hurt us. As we already saw, 'doler' is a stem-vowel changing verb and it also has a gustar-like structure, so the part of the body that hurts usually goes at the end and determines whether the verb is singular or plural.

(A ti) te duelen los pies *(Your feet hurt)*
A Antonio le duele la espalda *(Antonio's back hurts)*

Otras expresiones con doler

¿qué te duele? *(what hurts?)*
¿te duele algo? *(does something hurt?)*
me duele la cabeza *(my head hurts)*
me duelen las piernas *(my legs hurt)*
cuando hago esto, me duele *(when I do this, it hurts)*
no me duele nada *(nothing hurts)*

Ejercicio G

Escribe frases completas con los siguientes elementos. Observa el ejemplo 1.

1) Eusebio / doler / costillas *A Eusebio le duelen las costillas.*

2) Margarita / doler / pies ______

3) nosotros / doler / cabeza ______

4) ustedes / doler / tobillo *(ankle)* ______

5) yo / doler / garganta *(throat)* ______

6) tú / doler / dedos ______

7) Clara y Gaby / doler / oídos ______

Respuestas G: **2)** A Margarita le duelen los pies. / **3)** (A nosotros) nos duele la cabeza. / **4)** A ustedes les duele el tobillo. / **5)** (A mí) me duele la garganta. / **6)** (A ti) te duelen los dedos. / **7)** A Clara y a Gaby les duelen los oídos.

MI LISTA DE VOCABULARIO

This is a list of the words that you have learned in this unit.

(el) abdomen	bajar
abrir	(la) boca
apretar	(el) brazo
(la) arteria	(la) cabeza

(la) cara
(la) ceja
(el) cerebro
cerrar
(la) cita
(el) codo
(la) columna vertebral
(el) conjunto
controlar
(el) corazón
(la) costilla
(el) cráneo
(el) cuello
(el) cuerpo
(el) dedo
(la) diabetes
(el) diente
digerir
doblar
doler
empujar
(la) espalda
(el) esqueleto
(el) estómago
(el) fémur
filtrar
(la) frente
(la) garganta
(los) genitales
(el) hígado

(el) hombro
humano
(el) húmero
(el) intestino delgado/grueso
(la) jeringuilla
(el) labio
(la) lengua
levantar
(la) luz
(la) médula ósea
(la) mejilla o (el) carrillo
mensual
(la) nariz
(el) oído
(el) ojo
(la) oreja
(la) orina
(el) páncreas
palpitar o latir
(el) pecho
(los) pechos
(la) pelvis
(el) pie
(la) pierna
privado
proteger
(la) punta
respirar
(la) revisión
(el) riñón

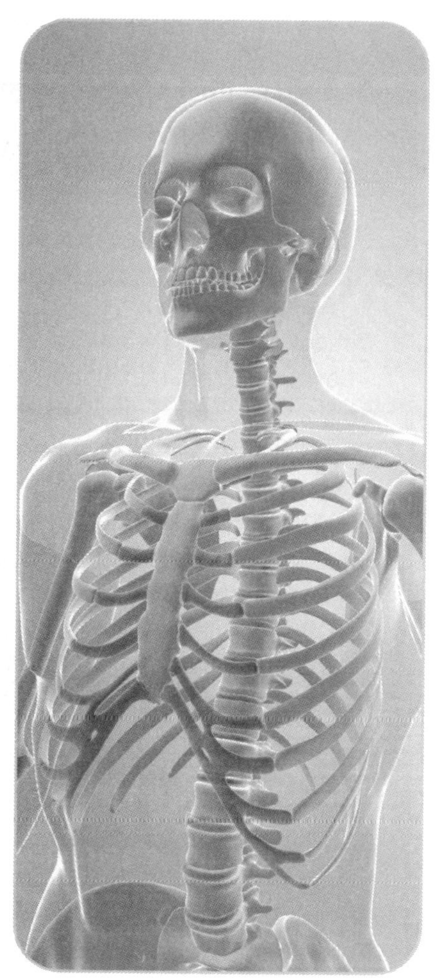

(la) rodilla
sacar
(la) salud
(la) sangre
subir
(la) tibia
(el) tobillo
toser
(el) trasero o (las) nalgas
(la) uña
(la) vejiga
(la) vena
(la) vesícula biliar

UN POCO DE CULTURA

El sistema de salud *(health care system)* de Venezuela

Venezuela, como otros países latinoamericanos (Argentina, Costa Rica, Cuba, y Uruguay), tiene un sistema dual de salud: Por una parte *(On one hand)*, hay un sistema público de salud obligatorio *(obligatory)* que el Estado provee a la población *(population)* a través del Instituto Venezolano de Seguro Social (IVSS); y por otra parte hay un sistema de salud privado voluntario que usan las pocas personas que se lo pueden permitir *(who can afford it)* y que viven en las ciudades donde hay clínicas privadas.

El sistema público de salud es totalmente gratuito *(free)* y los venezolanos no necesitan pagar al médico ni tampoco pagar por los exámenes, pruebas, o resultados de laboratorio. Sin embargo *(However)*, el sistema depende de los fondos *(funds)* económicos del Estado y de las cotizaciones de la población *(contributions from the population)*. Como *(Since)* Venezuela sufre una crisis económica, el sistema de salud actual es deficiente. Por ejemplo, no hay suficiente dinero para tener muchas ambulancias, ni existen clínicas en todos los barrios y las zonas rurales del país. Tampoco hay dinero para tener muchas medicinas en el hospital, ni para pagar bien a los médicos, ni para comprar equipos quirúrgicos *(surgical)* o diagnósticos modernos. Por eso, aunque *(although)* es un sistema gratuito para todos los venezolanos, hay muchos habitantes que no pueden recibir estos beneficios y están desprotegidos *(unprotected)*.

En otros países de Latinoamérica también existe este sistema dual, pero si los países están en crisis, también hay muchos ciudadanos desprotegidos. Según la Comisión Económica para América Central y el Caribe (CEPAL)[11], solamente 9% de los habitantes de Nicaragua tienen algún tipo de seguro médico (16% in Bolivia, 18% in Ecuador, 19% in El Salvador). El resto de la población está desprotegida.

El Instituto Venezolano del Seguro Social (IVSS) fue creado a mitad del siglo XX pero está siendo reformado continuamente *(is under continuous reform)*. Esta entidad *(entity)*, además de proveer *(besides providing)* un sistema público de salud, también ofrece otros servicios sociales, como subsidio de desempleo *(unemployment benefits)*, de jubilación *(retirement benefits)*, de incapacidad *(disability benefits)*, de maternidad, etc. El sistema de seguro social se está reevaluando porque la población de Venezuela está envejeciendo *(getting older)*, ya que la expectativa de vida *(life expectancy)* es más larga y nacen menos niños *(fewer children are being born)* que antes. Además, más trabajos están siendo realizados *(are being created)* por computadoras o máquinas *(machines)* y no por trabajadores contribuyentes *(tax-paying workers)*.

El gobierno está recibiendo ayuda de otros países (como Cuba, por ejemplo) y está intentando *(trying)* adoptar poco a poco un sistema de seguro social similar al de España, Argentina, Costa Rica, y Chile, que está basado en un modelo alemán del siglo XIX mezclado *(mixed)* con un modelo británico posterior.

[Footnotes] [11] *Data from a website article published on March 22, 2006 on http://www.eclac.cl (Press Releases).*

RECOMENDACIÓN PARA ESTA UNIDAD

Para finalizar esta unidad, te recomendamos algunos lugares en Internet donde puedes aprender palabras relacionadas con la salud. Por ejemplo, en la página: http://www.fundamind.org.ar/aprender/glosario.asp hay un glosario de términos *(terms)* en español ordenados alfabéticamente, con su traducción al inglés, y también con una definición o explicación breve en español.

UNIDAD 26

CONTENIDO

En esta unidad vas a aprender:

1 - Vocabulario relacionado con enfermedades y síntomas *(diseases and symptoms)*

2 - Sobre las frases con 'si' *('if' clauses)*

3 - Vocabulario relacionado con tratamientos y medicamentos *(treatments and medicines)*

4 - Sobre los mandatos formales *(formal commands)*

5 - Información cultural sobre la diabetes en los hispanos/latinos de EE.UU.

enfermedades y condiciones

ENFERMEDADES Y CONDICIONES[1]

(Diseases and conditions)

La doctora le ha prestado *(has loaned)* **a Sofía el libro de medicina** *(medicine)* **ilustrado que tiene en su oficina del hospital para que** *(so that)* **Sofía lea** *(reads)* **un poco sobre** *(about)* **la diabetes. Sofía mira el libro en su casa.**

sarampión *(measles)*
varicela *(chicken pox)*
rubéola *(rubella)*
resfriado *(cold)*
gripe[2] *(flu)*
bronquitis *(bronchitis)*
infección *(infection)*
S.I.D.A. *(A.I.D.S.)*
obesidad *(obesity)*
síndrome de Down *(Down syndrome)*
asma *(asthma)*
labio leporino y paladar hendido *(cleft lip and palate)*
aborto espontáneo *(miscarriage)*
enfermedad de transmisión sexual *(sexually transmitted disease)*

ansiedad *(anxiety)*
intoxicación *(food poisoning)*
envenenamiento *(poisoning)*
depresión *(depression)*
embarazo *(pregnancy)*
sinusitis
tuberculosis
cáncer
hepatitis
herpes
artritis
eccema
tétanos
osteoporosis
alergias
cirrosis

[Footnotes]

[1] Some diseases and conditions have both a medical name and a more commonly-used term. Some examples are: 'artritis' and 'reuma' for rheumatoid arthritis; 'herpes zoster' and 'culebrilla' for herpes zoster or shingles; and 'afta,' 'candidiasis,' 'úlceras bucales,' 'llagas,' or 'algodoncillo' for thrush.
[2] Both 'gripe' and 'gripa' are used for 'flu.'

Ejercicio A

Enlaza estas enfermedades con los órganos o partes del cuerpo que afectan principalmente.

1) paladar hendido	a) nariz
2) artritis	b) todo el cuerpo
3) bronquitis	c) hígado
4) labio leporino	d) articulaciones *(joints)*
5) sinusitis	e) piel *(skin)*
6) obesidad	f) boca
7) diabetes	g) sistema inmunológico *(immune system)*
8) hepatitis	h) labio *(lip)*
9) SIDA	i) pulmones
10) eccema	j) páncreas

Respuestas A: **1)** - f) / **2)** - d) / **3)** - i) / **4)** - h) / **5)** - a) / **6)** - b) / **7)** - j) / **8)** - c) / **9)** - g) / **10)** - e)

SÍNTOMAS *(Symptoms)*

fiebre

cansancio

frecuencia al orinar

caída de pelo

inflamación

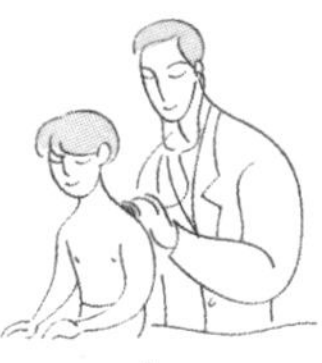
tos

falta de apetito

estreñimiento

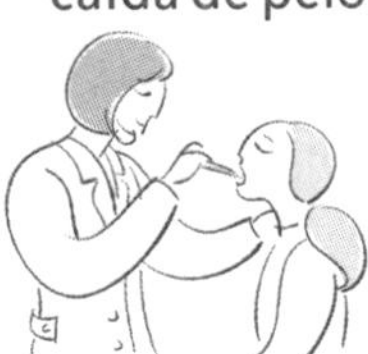
boca seca

ojos llorosos

dolor

deshidratación

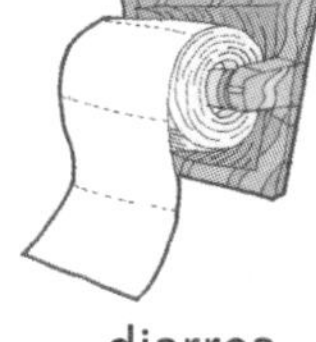
diarrea

temblores

estornudo

herida

aumento de peso

vista nublada

hemorragia

ataque al corazón

mareo

náusea[3]

congestión nasal

falta de sueño

acidez

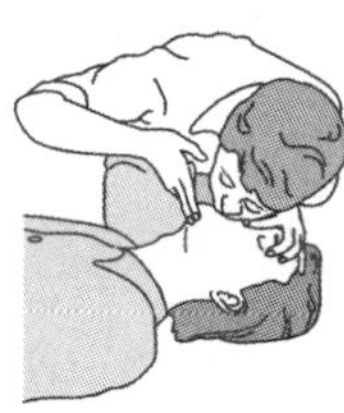
falta de aire

vómito

fractura

sueño

gases

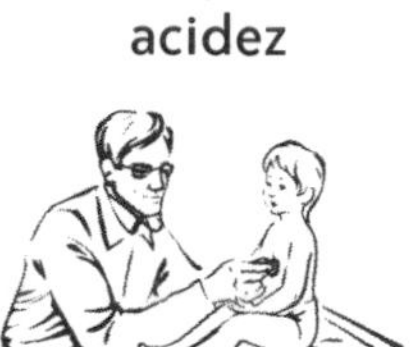
palpitaciones

pérdida de conciencia

[Footnotes] [3] *Other words for nausea are 'basca,' 'asco,' and 'arcadas.'*

Ejercicio B

Escribe algunos síntomas típicos de cada una de estas enfermedades/condiciones.

1) Resfriado ______________________________

2) Insolación *(heat stroke)* ______________________________

3) Osteoporosis ______________________________

4) Enfermedad coronaria ______________________________

5) Alergia ______________________________

Posibles respuestas B: **1)** tos, fiebre, dolor, congestión, ojos llorosos, estornudos, falta de apetito, etc. / **2)** mareo, vómito, náuseas, pérdida de conciencia, cansancio, deshidratación, etc. / **3)** fractura de hueso, cansancio, dolor, etc. / **4)** ataque al corazón, palpitaciones, cansancio, etc. / **5)** ojos llorosos, estornudos, congestión, etc.

FRASES CON 'SI' *('If' clauses)*

The conjunction 'if' can be used in a variety of clause combinations to express conditionality or hypothetical situations. These are some common combinations:

-'If' clause with verb in present tense + verb in present tense:

Si tengo problemas, te llamo
(If I have problems, I'll call you)[4]

-'If' clause with verb in present tense + verb in future:

Si comes eso, vas a ponerte enfermo
(If you eat that, you are going to get sick)
Si comes eso, te pondrás enfermo
(If you eat that, you will get sick)

[Footnotes] [4] *In English, the second clause is in future tense.*

-'If' clause with verb in present tense + command:

Si tienes fiebre, ve al doctor
(If you have a fever, go to the doctor)

-'If' clause with verb in past subjunctive + verb in conditional:

Si tuvieras un resfriado, estornudarías
(If you had a cold, you would sneeze)

Just as in English, if the order of the clauses is inverted, the comma is not needed.

Si tengo problemas, te llamo

Te llamo si tengo problemas

Ejercicio C

Traduce las siguientes frases usando la conjunción 'si'.

1) If you (usted) smoke so much, you are going to have lung cancer soon.

____

2) Dolores, if your son smokes, talk to him.

____

3) If you (ustedes) have diabetes, don't eat sweets (dulces).

____

4) She is going to get fat (engordar) if she eats so much.

____

5) They (fem.) are going to lose weight (adelgazar) if they take these drugs[5].

____

Respuestas C: **1)** Si usted fuma tanto, va a tener cáncer de pulmón pronto. / **2)** Dolores, si tu hijo fuma, habla con él. / **3)** Si ustedes tienen diabetes, no coman dulces / **4)** Ella va a engordar si come tanto. / **5)** Ellas van a adelgazar si toman estas drogas/medicinas.

[Footnotes]

[5] When the word 'drug' refers to medication, it can be translated as 'medicamento' or 'medicina. When it refers to illicit drugs, such as cocaine, marijuana, etc., you use the word 'droga.'

LOS TRATAMIENTOS Y LOS MEDICAMENTOS *(Treatments and medicines)*

El libro de Sofía también tiene una lista de tratamientos y medicamentos para las enfermedades y condiciones que sufren los humanos.

quimioterapia *(chemotherapy)*

fisioterapia/terapia física *(physical therapy)*

inyecciones de insulina *(insulin shots)*

vitaminas y minerales *(vitamins and minerals)*

descanso absoluto *(full rest)*

pastilla, píldora *(pill, tablet)*

compresa de agua caliente *(hot water compress)*

vacuna *(vaccination)*

inhalador *(inhaler)*

mantener el... elevado *(keep the... elevated)*

evitar... *(avoid...)*

transplante *(transplant)*

acupuntura *(acupuncture)*

radiación *(radiation)*

hormonas *(hormones)*

antibiótico *(antibiotic)*

cirugía *(surgery)*

aspirina *(aspirin)*

antidepresivo *(antidepressant)*

penicilina *(penicillin)*

diálisis *(dialysis)*

rehabilitación *(rehabilitation)*

Ejercicio D

Enlaza las siguientes enfermedades o condiciones con sus tratamientos o medicamentos más típicos.

1) diabetes
2) dolor de garganta *(throat)*
3) depresión
4) cáncer
5) menopausia *(menopause)*
6) torcedura *(sprain)* de tobillo
7) infección
8) cirrosis
9) labio leporino y paladar hendido
10) asma

a) hormonas
b) antidepresivos
c) fisioterapia
d) penicilina
e) insulina/diálisis
f) quimioterapia/radiación
g) gárgaras *(gargle)* de agua con sal
h) evitar el alcohol/transplante
i) inhalador
j) cirugía

Respuestas D: **1)** - e) / **2)** - g) / **3)** - b) / **4)** - f) / **5)** - a) / **6)** - c) / **7)** - d) / **8)** - h) / **9)** - j) / **10)** - i)

EL IMPERATIVO DE 'USTED'

(Formal commands)

When giving a command to someone you do not know, to an older person, or to someone who outranks you (e.g., your boss), you must use a formal command: the 'usted' form for one person and the 'ustedes' form for more than one person. This is how you do it:

		Positive commands	Negative commands
-AR verbs	levantar	levant**e**/levant**en**	**no** levant**e**/**no** levant**en**
-ER/-IR verbs	toser	tos**a** / tos**an**	**no** tos**a**/**no** tos**an**

-Señor Ramírez, coma menos comidas grasas *(Mr. Ramírez, eat fewer fatty foods)*

-Señorita García, no tome tanto alcohol *(Ms. García, don't drink so much alcohol)*

-Señores Domínguez, vengan a las tres *(Mr. and Mrs. Domínguez, come at 3:00pm)*

If you compare the formal command with the informal command from last unit, you will notice that sometimes they only differ by one letter (tose = informal/tosa = formal). Although this might seem like a minor difference, addressing somebody as 'tú' when you are supposed to use the 'usted' form is considered rude, particularly when giving orders. So, make sure you use the appropriate ending. For formal commands, this is the opposite letter of the infinite ending (AR = -e; ER/IR = -a).

There are some irregular forms:

(Ir): **vaya/no vaya**
Vaya al doctor mañana *(Go to the doctor's tomorrow)*

(Ser): **sea/no sea**
Sea más responsable *(Be more responsible)*

All verbs that are irregular in the 'yo' form are irregular as commands: **tenga, diga, venga, ponga, etc.**

When your command requires a pronoun, you attach it to the end of the positive command, but in front of the negative command.

Pónga**la**[6] allá *(Put it there)*
No **la** ponga allá *(Don't put it there)*

Siénte**se** aquí *(Sit down here)*
No **se** siente aquí *(Don't sit here)*

Ábra**la** *(Open it)*
No **la** abra *(Don't open it)*

Stem-vowel changing verbs keep their change in the command:

Cerrar (e>ie) / C**ie**rre los ojos *(Close your eyes)*
Mover (o>ue) / M**ue**va la cabeza *(Move your head)*

Verbs that end in -car, -gar, and -zar require a small spelling change to maintain the same sound as in the infinitive:

Buscar / Bus**que** un hospital cercano
(Look for a nearby hospital)

Tragar / Tra**gue** esta pastilla *(Swallow this pill)*

Empezar / Empie**ce** su tratamiento
(Start your treatment)

[Footnotes]

[6] *If the stress of the word falls onto the third to last syllable after attaching a pronoun, write an accent mark on the vowel of that syllable. Example: compre + las = cómprelas.*

Ejercicio E

Completa estas órdenes de un doctor a sus pacientes usando el imperativo de usted (singular y plural) de los verbos en paréntesis.

1) Don[7] Cristóbal, __________ (dejar) de fumar *(quit smoking)*.

2) Doña Remedios, __________ (tomar) su medicina a la hora apropiada.

3) Don Fermín y Don Ricardo, __________ (ir) a hacerse unos rayos X *(X-rays)*.

4) Señor Palacios, __________ (sentarse) allá, por favor.

5) Señora Chávez, no __________ (ponerse) la vacuna de la gripe todavía *(yet)*.

6) Don Ramón y Doña María, no __________ (empezar) a quejarse *(to complain)*.

7) Señores Ramírez, __________ (tener) más paciencia con los resultados.

8) Señorita Marín, __________ (comer) más fruta fresca.

9) Don Jenaro, __________ (correr) un poco por las mañanas.

10) Don Aurelio y Doña Petra, no __________ (ser) tan pesimistas.

Respuestas E: **1)** deje / **2)** tome / **3)** vayan / **4)** siéntese / **5)** se ponga / **6)** empiecen / **7)** tengan / **8)** coma / **9)** corra / **10)** sean

[Footnotes]

[7] *'Don' and 'Doña' are formal titles for men and women, respectively. These titles mean that the verb must be in the 'usted' form. The difference between 'don' and 'señor,' both of which mean 'mister,' is that 'don' goes with the first name of the person (Don Fernando) but 'señor' goes with the last name (señor Rodríguez).*

Ejercicio F

Reescribe estas frases usando el pronombre de objeto directo en vez del objeto directo subrayado *(underlined)*. **Recuerda** *(Remember)* **la posición de los pronombres con el imperativo. Observa el ejemplo 1.**

1) Compre estas medicinas.
Cómprelas

2) Lea estos libros.
____

3) Tómese la temperatura.
____

4) Opérese el tumor.
____

5) Póngase las vacunas.
____

6) No beba refrescos.
____

7) No coma grasa *(fat)*. __________

Respuestas F: **2)** Léalos / **3)** Tómesela / **4)** Opéreselo / **5)** Póngaselas / **6)** No los beba / **7)** No la coma

MI LISTA DE VOCABULARIO

Ésta es una lista de las palabras que has aprendido en esta unidad.

(el) aborto espontáneo
(la) acidez
(la) acupuntura
adelgazar
(la) ansiedad
(el) antibiótico
(el) antidepresivo
(la) articulación
(la) artritis
(el) asma
(la) aspirina
(el) ataque al corazón
(el) aumento de peso
(la) boca seca
(la) bronquitis
(la) caída de pelo
(el) cáncer
(el) cansancio
(la) cirrosis
(la) cirugía
(la) compresa
(la) congestión
(la) depresión
(el) descanso
(la) deshidratación
(la) diabetes
(la) diálisis
(la) diarrea
(el) dolor
(el) eccema
(el) embarazo
(la) enfermedad (coronaria, de transmisión sexual, etc.)
engordar
(el) envenenamiento
(el) estornudo
(el) estreñimiento
evitar

(la) falta de apetito/sueño/aire	(el) medicamento o (la) medicina	(el) sarampión
(la) fiebre	(el) mareo	(el) SIDA
(la) fisioterapia	(la) náusea	(el) síndrome (de Down, etc.)
(la) fractura	(la) obesidad	(el) síntoma
(la) garganta	(los) ojos llorosos	(la) sinusitis
(los) gases	orinar	(el) sistema inmunológico
(la) gripe	(la) osteoporosis	(el) sueño
(la) hemorragia	(el) paladar hendido	(los) temblores
(la) hepatitis	(las) palpitaciones	(el) tétanos
(la) herida	(la) pastilla o (la) píldora	(la) torcedura o (el) esguince
(el) herpes	(la) penicilina	(la) tos
(las) hormonas	(la) pérdida de peso/	(el) transplante
(la) infección	conciencia	(el) tratamiento
(la) inflamación	(la) piel	(la) tuberculosis
(el) inhalador	prestar	(la) vacuna
(la) insolación	(la) quimioterapia	(la) varicela
(la) intoxicación	(la) radiación	(la) vista nublada
(la) inyección	(la) rehabilitación	(las) vitaminas y
(el) labio	(el) resfriado	(los) minerales
(el) labio leporino	(la) rubéola	(el) vómito

UN POCO DE CULTURA

La diabetes de los hispanos/latinos que viven en EE.UU.

Las investigaciones sobre la población hispana[8] de los Estados Unidos muestran *(show)* que los hispanos son más propensos *(prone)* a ciertas enfermedades que los blancos no hispanos. Las razones *(reasons)* pueden ser genéticas; alimenticias *(food-related)*, por el alto consumo de carbohidratos o grasa animal; geográficas, por exposición a pesticidas o por vivir en zonas de baja calidad del agua potable *(drinking water)*; y sociales, por falta de ejercicio, acceso restringido *(restricted)* al sistema de salud, bajos ingresos *(low income)* para pagar medicinas, barreras de lenguaje *(language barriers)*, etc.

Una de estas enfermedades es la diabetes. Una persona con diabetes no tiene o tiene poca insulina, que es una hormona necesaria para convertir la glucosa en energía. Cuando la glucosa no se puede convertir en energía, entra *(enters)* a la sangre y la envenena *(poisons)* poco a poco. Hay dos tipos de diabetes: la diabetes de tipo 1 aparece en la niñez *(childhood)* o adolescencia, y la diabetes del tipo 2 aparece en la edad adulta y está conectada *(is connected)* a la calidad del alimento *(food)* que consumimos y a los hábitos alimenticios y físicos. La diabetes es un catalizador *(catalyst)* para otras condiciones o enfermedades, como enfermedades de corazón, obesidad, hipertensión, colesterol alto, problemas visuales, problemas con los riñones, y mala circulación. En este momento, la diabetes es la causa número seis de muerte *(sixth leading cause of death)* en los Estados Unidos.

Los hispanos/latinos de EE.UU. tienen el doble de probabilidades de desarrollar *(develop)* diabetes que los blancos no hispanos[9]. Según el censo del año 2000, al 25% de los mexicanos y el 25% de los puertorriqueños de más de 65 años se les diagnosticó *(were diagnosed)* diabetes, mientras que solamente el 12.5% de los blancos no hispanos se les diagnosticó esta enfermedad. Entre la población de edad media (45 a 64 años), el 14% de los mexicanos y el 17.5% de los puertorriqueños se les diagnosticó diabetes, comparado con el 7.5% de los blancos no hispanos. Los números muestran *(show)* claramente la gran diferencia entre hispanos y no hispanos. Uno de los factores de riesgo *(risk factors)* de la diabetes es la obesidad. Según el mismo censo *(According to the same census)*, más del 30% de los mexicanos y el 27% de los puertorriqueños entre 45 y 64 años de edad se consideran obesos, comparado con el 23% de los blancos no hispanos. Esto explica en parte el número tan elevado de diabéticos hispanos.

Otras enfermedades que afectan mucho a los hispanos de EE.UU., aparte de *(besides)* la diabetes y la obesidad, incluyen el asma, el virus del SIDA *(HIV)* y la hipertensión, especialmente a los hispanos de origen puertorriqueño y mexicano.

[Footnotes]

[8] The Center for Disease Control and Prevention makes no distinction between US-born Hispanics (or Latinos) and foreign-born Hispanics.

[9] Data from the Centers for Disease Control and Prevention, part of the U.S. Department of Health and Human Services, http://www.cdc.gov/NCHS/data/hpdata2010/chcsummit.pdf.

RECOMENDACIÓN PARA ESTA UNIDAD

Para finalizar esta unidad, te recomendamos una página de Internet en español con información sobre partes del cuerpo, enfermedades, y tratamientos: http://www.nlm.nih.gov/medlineplus/spanish/healthtopics.html

También existen diccionarios etimológicos en línea *(online)* donde puedes encontrar el origen de algunos términos médicos: http://etimologias.dechile.net/

Si estás interesado en leer artículos sobre salud, te recomendamos la página de la American Heart Association (http://www.americanheart.org/). Recuerda hacer clic en 'En español' en el menú de la izquierda.

UNIDAD 27 CONTENIDO

En esta unidad vas a aprender:

1 - Vocabulario relacionado con viajar *(traveling)*

2 - Sobre el modo subjuntivo en general *(the subjunctive mode)*

3 - Sobre el subjuntivo con verbos de voluntad *(volition)* y verbos de recomendación

4 - Información cultural sobre el impacto del turismo en el medio ambiente *(environment)*

viajar

VIAJAR

(Traveling)

Peter está en la oficina de Ana, visitándola por un momento. Encima del escritorio de Ana hay un libro de información turística sobre Sudamérica.

Peter: Ah, qué fotos tan bonitas…

Ana: Sí, muy bonitas. Enrique y yo estamos pensando en ir de viaje *(are thinking of going on a trip)* por Sudamérica para las vacaciones *(vacation)* de agosto[1].

Peter: ¡Estupendo! *(Great!)* ¿Y adónde les gustaría ir?

Ana: No sé todavía. *(I don't know yet.)* Tú conoces bien Sudamérica porque has viajado *(you have traveled)* mucho, ¿verdad? ¿Por qué no me sugieres *(suggest)* algún sitio *(place)* interesante?

Peter: Ah, pero hay tantos sitios…. Vamos a ver *(Let's see)*… recomiendo que vayan *(I recommend that you guys go)* a Perú y visiten Machu Picchu[2], unas ruinas incas *(Inca ruins)* maravillosas.

Ana: Ah, claro *(of course)*. A ver si hay una foto aquí en el libro…. Sí, mira, aquí está. ¡Qué lugar *(place)* tan espectacular! Me encanta. Quiero que Enrique vea *(I want Enrique to see)* esta foto porque este sitio es impresionante *(impressive)*.

Peter: Sí, lo es. Les aconsejo que se queden *(I advise you to stay)* en Perú dos semanas, que viajen *(to travel)* a varios sitios arqueológicos *(archeological sites)* y que conozcan *(to get to know)* a la gente local. Los peruanos son muy buena gente *(good people)*.

[Footnotes]

[1] In Spain, most people are entitled to a month of vacation during the summer, usually in July or August.
[2] Also spelled: Machu Pichu.

Ana: Y, además de *(besides)* Machu Picchu, ¿qué nos recomiendas que hagamos *(what do you recommend that we do)* en dos semanas?

Peter: Les sugiero que vayan *(I suggest you go)* a ver las líneas *(lines)* de Nazca.

Ana: ¿Y eso qué es?

Peter: Son unas líneas que los indígenas de Perú marcaron *(marked)* en el suelo *(ground)* hace 2.000 años aproximadamente *(approximately)*.

Ana: ¿Y qué tienen de interesante?

Peter: Las líneas forman figuras geométricas y figuras de animales, pero son tan grandes que sólo se puede apreciar *(you can only appreciate)* el dibujo *(drawing)* desde el aire *(from the air)*. Es necesario que ustedes alquilen *(rent)* un helicóptero o avioneta *(small plane)*.

Ana: Ay, es bueno que me digas todo esto *(it is good that you are telling me all this)*. ¡Qué bien! Ahora estoy muy entusiasmada con *(excited about)* el viaje *(trip)*.

Peter: También es muy importante que hablen con los incas que todavía *(still)* viven en Perú. Son una civilización increíble *(incredible)*.

Ana: ¡Fantástico *(Fantastic)*! ¡A Perú me voy, entonces *(I am headed to Peru, then!)*

Ejercicio A

Responde estas preguntas con frases completas.

1) ¿Por qué está Ana mirando un libro de América del Sur?

____

2) ¿Qué país le recomienda Peter?

____

3) ¿Por qué sabe Peter tanto *(so much)* de Sudamérica?

____

4) ¿Quién va con Ana en el viaje, cuándo van, y por cuánto tiempo?

____

5) ¿Cuáles son los dos lugares que recomienda Peter para que ellos visiten?

____

6) ¿Qué civilización pre-colombina vive todavía en Perú?

____

7) ¿Cómo se siente Ana sobre el viaje?

____

Posibles respuestas A: **1)** Ana está mirando un libro de Sudamérica porque quiere ir de vacaciones en agosto. / **2)** Peter le recomienda Perú. / **3)** Peter sabe mucho de Sudamérica porque ha viajado mucho. / **4)** Enrique va con Ana en el viaje. Van en (las vacaciones de) agosto. Van por dos semanas. / **5)** Peter recomienda (que ellos visiten) Machu Picchu y las líneas de Nazca. / **6)** Los incas todavía viven en Perú. / **7)** Ana está - se siente muy entusiasmada.

UNIDAD 27

INTRODUCCIÓN SUBJUNTIVO

(Introduction to the subjunctive)

The subjunctive is not a verbal tense, but rather a mode (like the imperative that we use for commands). In other words, it is used when you want to convey non-factual information. For example, if I were to recommend that you do something, the verb 'to do' would be in the subjunctive mode, because it has not happened yet and it might never happen. However, the verb 'to recommend' would be in the indicative mode (which is the normal, factual mode we have seen so far), because it is a fact that I am making a recommendation. There are many verbs and structures that require or trigger subjunctive. We will see some in this unit and also in the next units.

As with the formal command, the subjunctive is formed with the opposite vowel to that of the infinitive (AR verbs = -e, ER/IR verbs = -a):

HABLAR *(to speak)*	**COMER** *(to eat)*
habl**e**	com**a**
habl**es**	com**as**
habl**e**	com**a**
habl**emos**	com**amos**
habl**éis**	com**áis**
habl**en**	com**an**

*-IR verbs have the same endings as -ER verbs

The irregular verbs in the subjunctive are the same as the irregular verbs in the formal commands: **vaya, sea, tenga, diga, vea, conozca, ponga, sepa, traiga, etc.**

Again, stem-vowel changing verbs keep their changes: c**e**rrar = c**ie**rre.

And verbs ending in -car, -gar, and -zar have a spelling change in the subjunctive: buscar = bus**que**, llegar = lle**gue**, comenzar = comien**ce**.

To remember which verbs and structures trigger subjunctive, you can learn to use this little tool:

WEIRDO

W = verbs that express Wish *(I want, I wish...)*

E = verbs that express Emotion *(I am sorry that, I am happy that...)*

I = Impersonal expressions *(it is necessary that, it is important that...)*

R = verbs that make Recommendations *(I recommend, I suggest...)*

D = verbs that express doubt or denial *(I doubt that, I deny...)*

O = expressions with 'Ojalá' *(God willing, I wish...)*

Examples:

-Elena quiere que Javier **llegue** a tiempo
*(Elena wants Javier to **arrive** on time)*

-Ellos sugieren que nosotros **vayamos** al cine
*(They suggest that we **go** to the movies)*

One rule must be met when using the subjunctive in these structures: the subject of the first verb MUST be different than the subject of the second verb:

-(**Yo**) quiero que (**tú**) vayas
*(**I** want that **you** go = **I** want **you** to go)*

-(—) Es necesario que **ellos** vengan a la fiesta
*(**It** is necessary that **they** come to the party)*

Remember that 'que' joins the two clauses, so it will always be present (except for in the 'ojalá' structure), even though it might not translate in English.

Quiero **que** vayas *(I want you to go)*
Ojalá (**que**) mis amigos me visiten
(I wish my friends would visit me)

If the subjects of both verbs are the same, then you do not need the 'que' or the subjunctive; just use the infinitive for the second verb, like in English.

Claudia **quiere ir** *(Claudia **wants to go**)*
[Claudia is the one wanting and also the one going, so it is the same subject]

Ejercicio B

Completa estas frases del diálogo entre Enrique y Ana con la forma del subjuntivo de los verbos en paréntesis. *(Don't look at the original dialogue until you are done with the exercise!)*

1) Recomiendo que ustedes __________ (ir) a Perú y __________ (visitar) Machu Picchu.

2) Quiero que Enrique ______________ (ver) esta foto.

3) Les aconsejo que (ustedes) ______________ (quedarse) en Perú dos semanas, que ____________ (viajar) a varios lugares arqueológicos y que _________ (conocer) a la gente local.

4) ¿Qué nos recomiendas que (nosotros) ______________ (hacer) en dos semanas?

5) Les sugiero que (ustedes) ___________ (ir) a ver las líneas de Nazca.

6) Es necesario que (ustedes) ___________ (alquilar) un helicóptero o avioneta.

7) Es bueno que (tú) me ___________ (decir) todo esto.

8) Es muy importante que (ustedes) ____________ (hablar) con los incas.

Respuestas B: **1)** vayan - visiten / **2)** vea / **3)** se queden - viajen - conozcan / **4)** hagamos / **5)** vayan / **6)** alquilen / **7)** digas / **8)** hablen

Ejercicio C

Traduce estas frases usando el subjuntivo en el segundo verbo.

1) I recommend that you (ustedes) look at these photos.

____

2) Eduardo suggests that I go to South America.

____

3) It is important that we (fem.) do not bother (use *molestar*) the local people.

____

4) I wish (use *desear*) you (tú) to travel a lot.

____

5) It is good that the Inca still *(todavía)* have their customs (costumbres).

____

Respuestas C: **1)** Recomiendo que ustedes miren estas fotos. / **2)** Eduardo sugiere que yo vaya a Sudamérica. / **3)** Es importante que (nosotras) no molestemos a la gente local. / **4)** Deseo que (tú) viajes mucho. / **5)** Es bueno que los incas todavía tengan sus costumbres.

SUBJUNTIVO (con verbos de voluntad) *(with verbs of volition)*

When using a verb of volition (a verb that expresses will or desire) in the first clause, use the subjunctive in the second clause if each clause has a different subject. Verbs of volition include:

querer *(to want)*	**desear** *(to wish)*
preferir *(to prefer)*	**necesitar** *(to need)*

-Yo quiero que Eva venga pronto *(I want Eva to come soon)*

If both clauses have the same subject, do not use 'que' or the subjunctive; conjugate the first verb, then use the infinitive for the second verb.

-Eva quiere venir pronto *(Eva wants to come soon)*

Ejercicio D

Traduce estas frases usando el subjuntivo cuando sea necesario.

1) Noelia wants Fernando to buy the ticket *(boleto)* soon.

____

2) They (masc.) prefer that you (tú) do not smoke in the museum.

____

3) We (masc.) want to travel around *(alrededor de)* the world.

____

4) My parents want us (masc.) to buy that house.

____

5) I want my friends to enjoy *(disfrutar de)* the trip.

____

Respuestas D: **1)** Noelia quiere que Fernando compre el boleto pronto. / **2)** Ellos prefieren que (tú) no fumes en el museo. / **3)** (Nosotros) queremos viajar alrededor del mundo. / **4)** Mis padres quieren que (nosotros) compremos esa casa. / **5)** (Yo) quiero que mis amigos disfruten del viaje.

SUBJUNTIVO (con verbos de recomendación) *(with verbs of recommendation)*

When using a verb of recommen-dation (a verb that makes a suggestion or offers advice) in the first clause, use the subjunctive in the second clause if each clause has a different subject. Verbs of recommendation include:

recomendar *(to recommend)*

aconsejar *(to advise)*

sugerir *(to suggest)*

exigir *(to demand)*

decir *(to tell)*

pedir *(to ask for/to request)*

prohibir *(to prohibit)*

permitir *(to permit/to allow)*

-Mis amigos sugieren que Gerardo vigile sus maletas
(My friends suggest that Gerardo watches his suitcases)
-Laura dice que (nosotros) seamos puntuales
(Laura tells us to be punctual)

If the subject of the second clause is not expressed, use the infinitive for the second verb.

-Mis amigos sugieren vigilar las maletas
(My friends suggest watching the suitcases)

Ejercicio E

Traduce las siguientes frases usando el subjuntivo cuando sea necesario.

1) My friends suggest that I go to Argentina.

____

2) I recommend that you (tú) buy a ticket soon.

____

3) My job demands that I travel once a year to Madrid to practice my Spanish.

____

4) Anita and Pablo advise taking a lot of pictures.

____

5) We (fem.) prohibit Susana to swim in the Caribbean.

____

Respuestas E: **1)** Mis amigos sugieren que (yo) vaya a Argentina. / **2)** (Yo) recomiendo que (tú) compres un boleto pronto. / **3)** Mi trabajo exige que yo viaje una vez al año a Madrid para practicar mi español. / **4)** Anita y Pablo aconsejan tomar/sacar muchas fotos. / **5)** (Nosotras) prohibimos que Susana nade en el Caribe.

UNIDAD 27

MI LISTA DE VOCABULARIO

Ésta es una lista de las palabras que has aprendido en esta unidad.

aconsejar	(la) costumbre
(el) aire	desear
alquilar	(el) dibujo
apreciar	entusiasmado
aproximadamente	(el) espacio
(la) avioneta	estupendo
(el) boleto o (el) pasaje o (el) billete	exigir

fantástico	prohibir
helicóptero	recomendar
inca	(la) ruina
increíble	sacar o tomar fotos
impresionante	(el) sitio o (el) lugar
indígena	(el) suelo
(la) línea	sugerir
maravilloso	(las) vacaciones
marcar	vamos a ver
ojalá	viajar
pensar en + infinitivo	(el) viaje
permitir	

UN POCO DE CULTURA

El turismo y el medio ambiente *(environment)*

Si bien es verdad *(Even though it is true)* que el turismo reaviva *(revives)* la economía de un país y tiene otros beneficios sociales, también es cierto *(it is also true)* que pone en peligro *(endangers)* el medio ambiente cuando no está controlado.

Cada día unas 2.500 personas visitan Machu Picchu, unas ruinas incas que se encuentran en Perú, Sudamérica. Estos turistas tocan las ruinas *(touch the ruins)*, pisan *(step on)* el suelo, generan basura *(create garbage)*, hacen ruido *(make noise)*, y usan los recursos naturales *(use the natural resources)*. Debido a *(Due to)* la gran cantidad *(quantity)* de gente que pasa por las ruinas y también a los deslizamientos de tierra o aludes de lodo y piedra *(mudslides)*, Machu Picchu corre peligro *(is in danger)*. Además, esta zona es el hábitat natural de numerosos animales (como osos, cóndores, y vicuñas), algunos de los cuales están en peligro de extinción; y también de flora única, como cierta especie de orquídeas *(orchids)*.

La UNESCO declaró Machu Picchu como Patrimonio de la Humanidad *(World Heritage Site)* en 1981. Por muchos años UNESCO declaró que estaba en peligro y pidió *(it requested)* al gobierno peruano reducir *(to reduce)* el número de visitantes *(visitors)* y poner más cuidado *(and to take better care)* en la preservación de la ciudadela *(citadel)*. El gobierno peruano no quería perder turismo ni dinero, por lo tanto *(consequently)*, tomó varias iniciativas *(initiatives)* para preservar Machu Picchu, como prohibir los vuelos de helicóptero por encima de *(over)* la ciudadela e imponer ciertas reglas *(rules)* a los turistas.

El gobierno peruano pide *(requests)* que los visitantes no contaminen el medio ambiente, que no enciendan fogatas *(bonfires)*, que no destruyan *(destroy)* las instalaciones públicas como los baños, que no maten *(kill)* a los animales de la zona, que no toquen *(touch)* las plantas, que paguen *(pay)* su boleto, que obedezcan *(obey)* a las autoridades peruanas, que no coman en las ruinas, que no traigan *(bring)* o dejen *(leave)* basura, que no tomen fotografías de los nativos sin *(without)* permiso, y otras reglas que se pueden encontrar en http://www.enjoy-machu-picchu.org/

Gracias a los esfuerzos *(efforts)* del gobierno peruano, la UNESCO declaró en 2007 que Machu Picchu ya no estaba en peligro y la eliminó de su lista de patrimonio en riesgo *(in danger/at risk)*.

En julio de 2007, por voto popular mundial, Machu Picchu fue elegida *(elected)* como una de las nuevas siete maravillas del mundo *(marvels of the world)*.

[Footnotes] [3] *Also spelled Cuzco.*

RECOMENDACIÓN PARA ESTA UNIDAD

Para finalizar esta unidad, te recomendamos que veas la película *Diarios de motocicleta* (2004, coproducción Argentina, USA, etc.). Esta película, que relata la vida de Ernesto 'Che' Guevara cuando era joven, muestra a Ernesto y su amigo Alberto en un viaje por Sudamérica (en motocicleta y a pie). Los países que más se muestran son Argentina, Chile, y Perú. En Perú, visitan Cusco y Machu Picchu y hablan con los incas que viven allá.

También te recomendamos que leas artículos sobre el polémico tema del derecho a la propiedad *(right to ownership)* de los artefactos que Hiram Binham excavó y extrajo *(excavated and extracted)* de Machu Picchu y envió *(shipped)* a la Universidad de Yale, donde todavía están.

UNIDAD 28

CONTENIDO

En esta unidad vas a aprender:

1 - Vocabulario relacionado con el aeropuerto *(airport)*

2 - Sobre el subjuntivo con expresiones impersonales *(impersonal expressions)*

3 - Sobre el subjuntivo con 'ojalá'

4 - Sobre el subjuntivo con verbos de emoción *(verbs of emotion)*

5 - Información cultural sobre la seguridad pública *(public safety)* en los países hispanos

el aeropuerto

EL AEROPUERTO

(The airport)

Enrique tiene que salir de viaje de negocios *(business trip)* **para Venezuela este fin de semana. Ana habla con él antes de que se vaya** *(before he leaves)*.

Ana: Espero[1] que *(I hope that)* tengas un buen viaje. Esos viajes transatlánticos pueden ser tan largos….

Enrique: Sí, lo sé. Siento mucho irme ahora *(I am very sorry to leave now)*, porque tengo muchas cosas que hacer *(many things to do)* en la oficina.

Ana: Pero es importante que vayas, ¿no? *(But it is important that you go, isn't it?)* Eso significa *(That means)* que tus jefes confían en ti *(trust you)*, ¿verdad? *(right?)*

Enrique: Sí, es bueno que ellos me manden *(it is good that they send me)* para hacer estas cosas. Ojalá que todo salga bien *(I hope everything turns out well)* y me suban el sueldo pronto *(and that they raise my salary soon)*.

Ana: Ah, sí, es necesario que se den cuenta de que *(it is necessary that they realize that)* tú eres imprescindible *(indispensable)* para la compañía *(company)*.

Enrique: ¿A qué hora sale mi vuelo? *(What time does my flight leave?)*

Ana: Uhm…aquí está en el correo electrónico *(here is the e-mail)*: a las 4 de la tarde por la puerta de embarque *(boarding gate)* 23. Es esencial que lleves *(It is essential that you have)* todos los papeles en regla *(in order)*. ¿Tienes el pasaporte *(passport)* y el visado *(visa)*?

Enrique: Dudo que pidan *(I doubt they'll ask for)* visado para los turistas de España. Aquí está mi pasaporte.

[Footnotes]

[1] *The verb 'esperar' means both 'to wait' and 'to hope'*

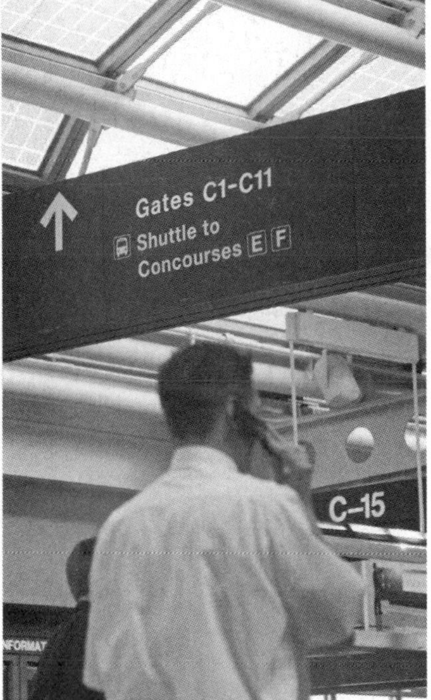

Ana: ¿Tienes el billete[2] de avión *(plane ticket)*?

Enrique: No, pero la azafata de tierra[3] *(airline attendant)* me dijo que los pasajeros *(passengers)* tienen que ir al mostrador de la aerolínea *(airline counter)* para recoger *(to pick up)* su billete.

Ana: ¿Entonces no sabes si tienes asiento de ventanilla o pasillo *(window or aisle seat)*?

Enrique: Todavía no. *(Not yet.)* Ojalá que *(I wish)* me den un asiento al lado de *(next to)* la ventana. Me gusta mirar afuera *(outside)*.

Ana: Sí, es mucho mejor.

Enrique: ¿Dice el mensaje a qué terminal tengo que ir? *(Does the message say which terminal I have to go to?)*

Ana: Sí, a la terminal cuatro. ¿En Venezuela son muy estrictos en la aduana *(customs)*?

Enrique: No sé… ¿por qué?

Ana: Porque pensé que a lo mejor querías llevarte un chorizo… *(because I thought that maybe you wanted to take a sausage with you)*.

Enrique: No, gracias. Sólo son tres días *(It is only three days)*. Estaré bien. *(I will be fine.)* Estoy seguro de que la comida en Venezuela es estupenda. *(I am sure the food in Venezuela is great.)*

Ana: Vale. *(OK.)* Ten cuidado *(Be careful)* en la zona de recogida de equipajes *(baggage claim)*, porque hay muchos robos *(thefts)*. Y fíjate bien *(pay attention)* en las pantallas *(monitors)* de salidas *(departures)* y llegadas *(arrivals)* para ver si tu vuelo está retrasado *(is delayed)* o está cancelado *(is canceled)*.

[Footnotes]

[2] *Another word for ticket is 'boleto.'*
[3] *In Spanish, 'azafata de tierra' refers to the person who works at the airline counter; 'azafata de vuelo' refers to a flight attendant. Other words for 'flight attendant' are 'aeromozo/a' y 'asistente de vuelo' y 'sobrecargo'.*

Ejercicio A

Responde estas preguntas con frases completas.

1) ¿Por qué es importante que Enrique vaya a Venezuela?

____

2) ¿Qué espera Enrique que ocurra *(What does Enrique hope happens)* después del viaje?

____

3) ¿Qué tipo de asiento desea Enrique?

____

4) ¿En qué parte del aeropuerto va a tener problemas Enrique si lleva *(carries)* un chorizo?

____

5) ¿Es necesario que Enrique tenga visado?

____

Posibles respuestas A: **1)** Es importante que Enrique vaya a Venezuela porque eso significa que sus jefes confían en él. / **2)** Enrique espera que sus jefes le suban el sueldo. / **3)** Enrique desea un asiento de ventanilla. / **4)** Enrique va a tener problemas en la aduana. / **5)** No, no es necesario que Enrique tenga visado (porque él es de España).

UNIDAD 28

Ejercicio B

Escribe el nombre de los siguientes objetos y personas que están en un aeropuerto. Las palabras están en el diálogo.

1)
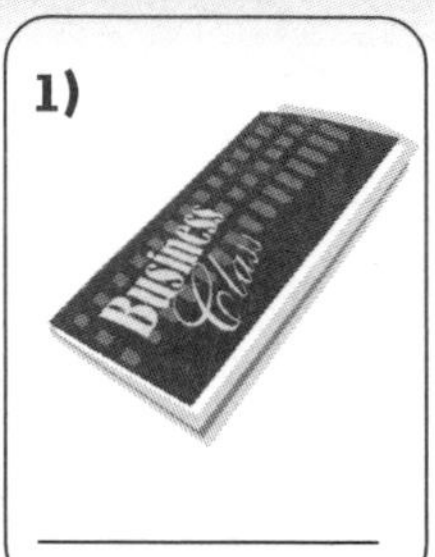

____

2)

____

3)

____

4)
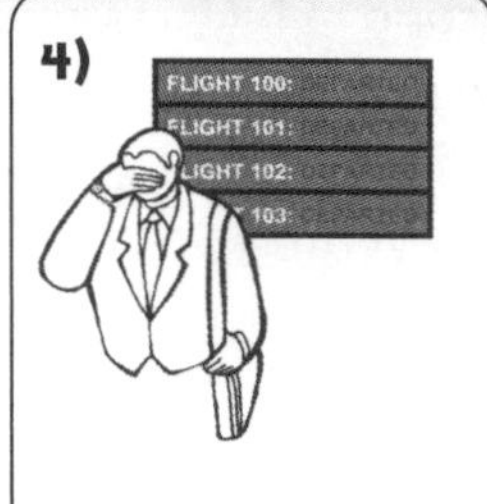

____

5)

____

6)

____

7)

____

8)

____

9)
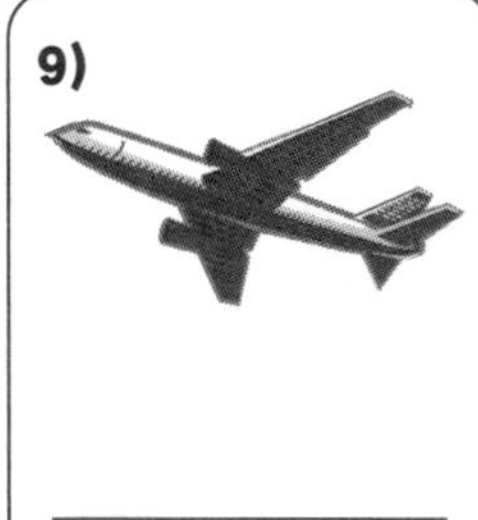
____

10)

____

Respuestas B: **1)** billete / **2)** azafata / **3)** mostrador de la aerolínea / **4)** pantalla de salidas y llegadas / **5)** aduana / **6)** zona de recogida de equipajes / **7)** puerta de embarque / **8)** pasaporte / **9)** avión / **10)** pasajeros

EL SUBJUNTIVO (con expresiones impersonales) *(with impersonal expressions)*

When you have an impersonal expression in the first clause, use the subjunctive in the second clause if a subject is stated. Impersonal expressions include:

es bueno *(it is good)*
es fácil *(it is easy)*
es importante *(it is important)*
es mejor *(it is better)*
es extraño *(it is strange)*
es probable *(it is probable)*
es posible *(it is possible)*
es necesario *(it is necessary)*
es difícil *(it is difficult)*

-Es probable que Enrique no necesite visado para ir a Venezuela
(It is probable that Enrique does not need a visa to go to Venezuela)

If you have an impersonal expression that conveys certainty, do not use the subjunctive in the second clause.

es obvio *(it is obvious)*
es verdad *(it is true)*
es cierto *(it is true)*
es evidente *(it is evident)*
es seguro *(it is sure/certain)*

-Es obvio que Enrique no sabe todavía qué asiento tiene
(It is obvious that Enrique does not know yet what seat he has)

-Es seguro que los jefes de Enrique le van a subir el sueldo
(It is certain that Enrique's bosses will raise his salary)

If the subject of the second clause is not expressed, use the infinitive for the second verb.

-Es posible viajar a Venezuela sin visado
(It is possible to travel to Venezuela without a visa)

Ejercicio C

Completa estas frases sobre el tema de viajar con el infinitivo, el indicativo (presente), o el subjuntivo de los verbos en paréntesis.

1) Es importante que usted no ______________ (viajar) solo.

2) Es probable que ellos ____________ (conocer) otras culturas interesantes.

3) ¿Crees que es posible ______________ (ser) un turista respetuoso *(respectful)*?

4) No es necesario que Victoria ______ (traer) *(to bring)* su pasaporte.

5) Es evidente que nosotros ____________ (ir) de vacaciones frecuentemente.

6) Es necesario que ustedes _______________ (hacer) cola *(stay in line)* en el mostrador de la aerolínea para conseguir su boleto.

7) Es muy importante que los pasajeros extranjeros *(foreign)* ___________ (mostrar) *(show)* sus pasaportes en la zona de control de pasaportes.

Respuestas C: **1)** viaje / **2)** conozcan / **3)** ser / **4)** traiga / **5)** vamos / **6)** hagan / **7)** muestren

EL SUBJUNTIVO (con ojalá)

'Ojalá' is a word of Arabic origin used to express a wish or a hope. A sentence with 'ojalá' *(I wish/I hope/God willing)* always triggers subjunctive. The 'que' can be omitted.

Ojalá que tengas un buen viaje /
Ojalá tengas un buen viaje
(I hope you have a good trip)

Ejercicio D

En el diálogo, Enrique dice dos frases con 'ojalá'. Escribe las frases aquí. Luego escribe la traducción en inglés.

1) ____________________

Traducción: ____________________

2) ____________________

Traducción: ____________________

Respuestas D: **1)** Ojalá que todo salga bien y (ojalá) que me suban el sueldo pronto./I hope everything turns out right and that they raise my salary soon. / **2)** Ojalá que me den un asiento al lado de la ventana./I hope they give me a seat next to the window.

Ejercicio E

Traduce las siguientes frases al español usando ojalá o expresiones impersonales. Usa el subjuntivo cuando sea necesario.

1) It is necessary that you (tú) go to the airport two hours before *(antes de)* your flight.

____

2) I hope the flight is not canceled.

____

3) It is evident that the flight is delayed.

____

4) I hope the flight attendant gives me an aisle seat.

____

5) It is very important to have all the documents in order.

____

Respuestas E: **1)** Es necesario que vayas al aeropuerto dos horas antes de tu vuelo. / **2)** Ojalá que el vuelo no esté cancelado. / **3)** Es evidente que el vuelo está retrasado. / **4)** Ojalá que el/la asistente de vuelo me dé un asiento de pasillo. / **5)** Es muy importante tener todos los documentos en regla.

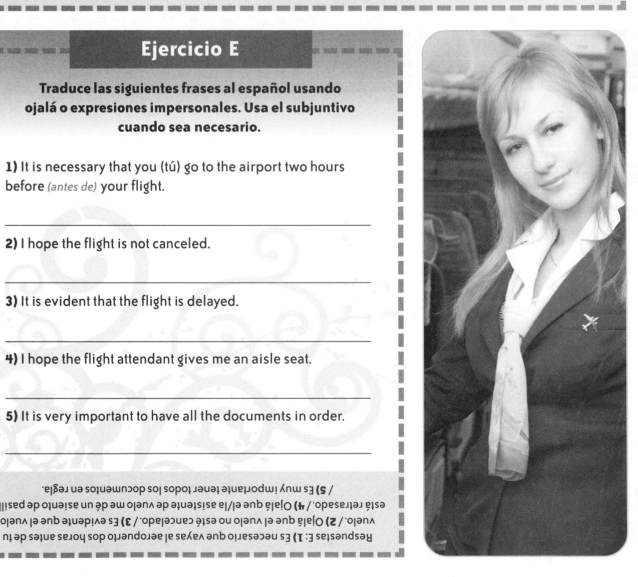

SUBJUNTIVO (con verbos de emoción) *(with verbs of emotion)*

When you have a verb that expresses feelings or emotion in the first clause, use the subjunctive in the second clause if the subjects are different. Verbs of emotion include:

alegrarse de *(to be glad)*
estar contento de *(to be happy about)*
esperar *(to hope)*
lamentar *(to regret)*
sentir *(to be sorry about)*
tener miedo de *(to be afraid of)*
temer *(to be afraid of/to fear)*

-Me alegro de que mi jefe confíe en mí
(I am happy that my boss trusts me)

If the subject of both clauses is the same, use the infinitive for the second verb.

-Espero ir a Perú pronto
(I hope to go to Peru soon)

Ejercicio F

Completa estas frases que dicen los pasajeros en el aeropuerto, usando subjuntivo cuando sea necesario.

1) Espero que (ellos) no ________________ (perder) mi equipaje *(baggage)*.

2) Lamento que la pantalla de salidas y llegadas no ________________ (funcionar) *(function)*.

3) (Yo) siento mucho que el vuelo ________________ (estar) retrasado.

4) Lamento ________________ (viajar) con poco dinero.

5) Mi esposa teme que alguien me ________________ (robar) *(to steal)* mi maleta.

Respuestas F: **1)** pierdan / **2)** funcione / **3)** esté / **4)** viajar / **5)** robe

MI LISTA DE VOCABULARIO

Ésta es una lista de las palabras que has aprendido en esta unidad.

(la) aduana	(el) billete o (el) boleto
(la) aerolínea	cancelar
(el) aeropuerto	(el) chorizo
afuera	cierto
alegrarse de	(la) compañía o (la) empresa
(el) asiento de ventanilla / de pasillo	confiar en

(el) correo electrónico	(la) maleta	(la) salida
darse cuenta de	(el) mensaje	seguro
dudar	(el) mostrador	sentir
en regla	necesario	subir
(el) equipaje	obvio	(el) sueldo
esencial	ojalá	temer
esperar	(la) pantalla o (el) monitor	tener miedo de
evidente	(el) pasaporte	(la) terminal
extranjero	(el) pasajero/(la) pasajera	todavía no
extraño	(el/la) piloto	verdad
funcionar	posible	¿verdad?
hacer cola	probable	(el) visado
imprescindible	(la) puerta de embarque	(el) vuelo
irse	retrasar	(la) zona de recogida de equipaje
lamentar	respetuoso	
(la) llegada	robar	
llevar	(el) robo	

UN POCO DE CULTURA

Seguridad[4] en las calles

Los países de habla hispana son famosos por su alto índice de delincuencia *(crime rate)*. Los robos *(thefts)*, especialmente a los turistas y viajeros *(travelers)* en general, son muy comunes. Desafortunadamente *(Unfortunately)*, muchos de los delitos *(petty crimes)* no se denuncian *(are not reported)* a la policía, por lo que las estadísticas *(statistics)* de delincuencia son en realidad más altas de lo que el gobierno pueda reportar al público.

Los crímenes o delitos graves también tienen índices altos y siguen subiendo *(continue rising)*. Según la BBC[5], Guatemala tiene el índice más alto (55) en Latinoamérica. En 2001, por ejemplo, el índice de Venezuela era del 33 y el de los Estados Unidos era del 5.6[6]. BBC y PROVEA[7] están de acuerdo *(agree)* en que los factores obvios que están relacionados con el índice de delincuencia y criminalidad incluyen la pobreza *(poverty)*, la desigualdad *(inequality)*, el acceso *(access)* a drogas, y el acceso a armas. Como ejemplos de la criminalidad en Latinoamérica, vamos a hablar un poco de los 'pirañas' y el secuestro express.

Pirañas

En Perú hay dos clases de pirañas: las pirañas (peces) *(fish)* y los pirañas (delincuentes juveniles). Los pirañas son jóvenes *(young people)* entre 9 y 20 años que van en grupo y asaltan *(assault)* y roban rápida y eficazmente *(efficiently)* a cualquier *(any)* persona en cualquier momento, incluso a plena luz del día *(even in plain daylight)*.

Secuestro Express

Caracas, la capital de Venezuela, es una de las ciudades más peligrosas *(dangerous)* del continente americano, con más de 2.000 homicidios al año. Un ejemplo de crimen típico de Venezuela es el 'secuestro express'[8]. Es un tipo de secuestro *(kidnapping)* en el que los secuestradores *(kidnappers)* mantienen a la víctima

cautiva *(keep the victim captive)* por un período desde unas horas a un par de días, mientras *(while)* ellos van de cajero en cajero *(from ATM to ATM)* sacando *(withdrawing)* todo el dinero de la víctima y usando sus tarjetas de crédito *(credit cards)*.

[Footnotes]

[4] *'Seguridad' means both 'security' and 'safety.'*
[5] *According to an article published on November 14, 2002 by BBCMundo.com.*
[6] *Information taken from the FBI statistics, http://www.fbi.gov/ucr/cius_01/xl/01tbl01.xls.*
[7] *Information taken from the PROVEA 2001-2002 Annual Report, http://www.derechos.org.ve/.*
[8] *In other countries, such as Colombia, 'secuestro express' is called 'paseo millonario'.*

RECOMENDACIÓN PARA ESTA UNIDAD

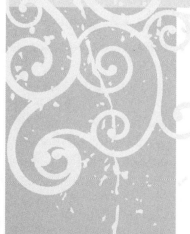

Para finalizar esta unidad, te recomendamos que veas las siguientes películas que muestran la vida criminal en Latinoamérica: *Rodrigo D* (1990, Colombia) y *La vendedora de rosas* (1998, Colombia) de Víctor Gaviria; *Sicario* (1994, Venezuela) de José Ramón Novoa; *Pizza, birra y faso* (1998, Argentina) de Adrián Caetano y Bruno Stagnaro; *Ratas, ratones, rateros* (1999, Ecuador) de Sebastián Cordero; y *Secuestro Express* (2005, Venezuela) de Jonathan Jakubowicz.

Estas películas son difíciles de comprender, porque los personajes *(characters)* utilizan mucho lenguaje callejero o jerga callejera *(slang)*. Además *(Besides)*, son películas muy duras de ver *(hard to watch)*, porque muestran una realidad sucia *(dirty)*, pobre *(poor)*, violenta, y triste a la que *(to which)* muchas personas, incluso niños, están expuestas constantemente *(are constantly exposed)*.

UNIDAD 29

CONTENIDO

En esta unidad vas a aprender:

1 - Vocabulario relacionado con las vacaciones *(vacation)*

2 - Sobre el pretérito *(preterite)*—verbos regulares

3 - Los números a partir del 10.000 *(from 10,000 on)*

4 - Sobre el pretérito—verbos irregulares

5 - Información cultural sobre lugares turísticos para visitar en Latinoamérica

de vacaciones

DE VACACIONES[1]

(On vacation)

Es viernes. Peter y Ana no tuvieron *(didn't have)* **mucho tiempo para hablar durante las horas de trabajo, pero después de trabajar** *(after work)*, **fueron** *(they went)* **a un bar para tomarse una cerveza** *(beer)* **y charlar un rato** *(chat for a while)* **antes de irse cada uno a su casa.**

Ana: Peter, quiero agradecerte *(I want to thank you for)* tus consejos *(advices)* sobre cómo disfrutar *(enjoy)* mejor del tiempo. Enrique y yo estábamos *(were)* tan agobiados *(overwhelmed)* con todas las responsabilidades.

Peter: No hay de qué. *(You're welcome.)* ¡El problema es que ahora yo quiero irme de vacaciones!

Ana: Te comprendo. Y tú siempre vas a lugares tan interesantes. ¿Adónde fuiste *(Where did you go)* de vacaciones la última vez *(last time)*?

Peter: Uhm…¿la última vez? Fui *(I went)* a Costa Rica durante las vacaciones de Navidad *(Christmas)*.

Ana: ¡Qué envidia! *(I am so jealous!*. Cuéntame qué hiciste. *(Tell me what you did.)*

Peter: Ecoturismo. Allí se preocupan *(There they worry about)* y cuidan *(and take care of)* sus zonas naturales. El ecoturismo es una manera *(way)* de conocer y aprender, pero sin dañar el medio ambiente *(but without damaging the environment)*.

Ana: ¡Qué bien! ¿Y qué hiciste durante tu estancia? *(And what did you do during your stay?)*

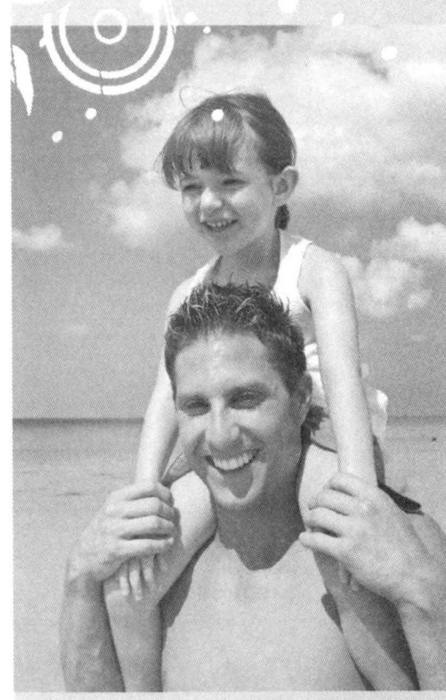

[Footnotes]

[1] *'Vacaciones' is always plural.*

Peter:	Visité parques y playas *(beaches)*, tomé fotos, aprendí *(I learned)* un poco sobre la flora y fauna de la región, y hablé con los ticos. Nos divertimos mucho. *(We had a great time)*
Ana:	¿Quiénes son los ticos?
Peter:	Oh, un 'tico' es una persona de Costa Rica, un costarricense.
Ana:	¡Ah, mira, hoy aprendí una palabra nueva!
Peter:	¡Pura vida![2]

[Footnotes]

[2] People in Costa Rica use the expression ¡pura vida! in different circumstances, but it often means 'great!' or something similar.

Ejercicio A

Escoge la palabra que NO corresponde a estas preguntas.

1) Una palabra/expresión originaria de Costa Rica es:

a) pura vida b) tico c) ecoturismo

2) Algo que hizo Peter durante su estancia en Costa Rica:

a) sacó fotos b) exploró la capital c) habló con los nativos

3) El ecoturismo es turismo, pero cuidando *(taking care of)*…

a) el idioma español b) las plantas c) los animales

4) En Costa Rica se preocupan mucho por…

a) la Navidad b) la flora c) la fauna

Respuestas A: **1)** - c) / **2)** - b) / **3)** - a) / **4)** - a)

EL PRETÉRITO —verbos regulares

(The preterite (or preterit) —regular verbs)

In Spanish, there are two simple past tenses: the preterite and the imperfect. In this unit, we will study the preterite, which is mainly used to talk about actions that began and were completed in the past. Time adverbs and expressions (yesterday, last year, two months ago, etc.) frequently accompany the preterite. Here is how to form the preterite of regular verbs:

HABLAR *(to speak)*	**COMER** *(to eat)*
habl**é**	com**í**
habl**aste**	com**iste**
habl**ó**	com**ió**
habl**amos**	com**imos**
habl**asteis**	com**isteis**
habl**aron**	com**ieron**

*-IR verbs have the same endings as -ER verbs

Ejemplos:

Visité parques y playas

Tomé fotos

Aprendí un poco sobre la flora y fauna de la región

Hablé con los ticos

In general, stem-vowel changing verbs do not change in preterite (alm**o**rzar = alm**o**rcé). However, -IR verbs do change, but only in the third person singular and plural. The changes are o>u and e>i. Example: PEDIR: yo pedí, tú pediste, él p**i**dió, nosotros pedimos, vosotros pedisteis, ellos p**i**dieron.

There are some spelling changes in the 'yo' form of verbs ending in -car, -gar, and -zar (buscar = bus**qué**, llegar = lle**gué**, empezar = empe**cé**).

Ejercicio B

Completa estas frases sobre viajes con el pretérito de los verbos en paréntesis.

1) Cristina _______________ (esperar) muchas horas en el aeropuerto.

2) Antonio _______________ (viajar) a Chile el mes pasado.

3) Yo _______________ (llegar) muy cansado al hotel.

4) Mis compañeros de viaje _______________ (tomar) fotos de las pirámides *(pyramids)*.

5) Yo _______________ (empezar) a empacar[3] *(to pack)* para el viaje una semana antes *(before)*.

[Footnotes]

[3] *Another word for 'to pack' is 'hacer las maletas.'*

Respuestas B: **1)** esperó / **2)** viajó / **3)** llegué / **4)** tomaron / **5)** empecé

Ejercicio C

Traduce estas frases al español usando el pretérito.

1) My friends (fem.) traveled to Mexico last (pasado) summer.

____

____

2) My parents slept (o>u) during the trip.

____

____

3) I arrived late to the airport and missed my flight.

____

____

4) Did you (tú) buy your ticket yet (ya)?

____

____

5) The trip lasted (use *durar*) five hours.

____

____

Respuestas C: **1)** Mis amigas viajaron a México el verano pasado/el pasado verano. / **2)** Mis padres durmieron durante el viaje. / **3)** Llegué tarde al aeropuerto y perdí mi vuelo. / **4)** ¿Compraste tu billete ya? / **5)** El viaje duró cinco horas.

NÚMEROS DESDE EL 10.000

(Numbers from 10,000 on)

Numeros desde el 10.000	
10.000	diez mil
20.000	veinte mil
30.000	treinta mil
40.623	cuarenta mil seiscientos veintitrés etc.
100.000	cien mil
200.000	doscientos mil
345.050	trescientos cuarenta y cinco mil cincuenta
406.004	cuatrocientos seis mil cuatro etc.
1.000.000	un millón
2.000.000	dos millones
3.954.320	tres millones novecientos cincuenta y cuatro mil trescientos veinte
10.000.000	diez millones
100.000.000	cien millones
1.000.000.000	mil millones
30.000.000.000	treinta mil millones
500.000.000.000	quinientos mil millones
1.000.000.000.000	un billón[4] etc.

[Footnotes]

[4] *A 'billón' has represented the amount of a million millions (1.000.000.000.000) since the 15th century in Spain, Latin America, and some European countries. However, in the 17th century, in countries like the United States and Brazil, 'billón' came to mean a thousand millions (1.000.000.000). Be careful when translating and interpreting the words 'billón' and billion.*

Ejercicio D

Escribe los números de estas frases.

1) La velocidad de la luz *(speed of light)* es de... 299.792.458 m/s.[5]

____

2) El área total de la Tierra *(Earth)* es aproximadamente de... 510.000.000 km^2.

____

3) La distancia entre la Tierra y el Sol es de... 149.597.871 km.

____

Respuestas D: **1)** doscientos noventa y nueve millones setecientos noventa y dos mil cuatrocientos cincuenta y ocho... / **2)** quinientos diez millones... / **3)** ciento cuarenta y nueve millones quinientos noventa y siete mil ochocientos setenta y un...

[Footnotes]

[5] *'m/s' stands for 'metros por segundo'* (meters per second).

EL PRETÉRITO —verbos irregulares

(The preterite —irregular verbs)

Some verbs are irregular in the preterite. You must learn them by heart. Here are some common ones:

PODER *(to be able)*	**PONER** *(to put)*	**SABER** *(to know)*	**TENER** *(to have)*	**ESTAR** *(to be)*
pude pudiste pudo pudimos pudisteis pudieron	puse pusiste puso pusimos pusisteis pusieron	supe supiste supo supimos supisteis supieron	tuve tuviste tuvo tuvimos tuvisteis tuvieron	estuve estuviste estuvo estuvimos estuvisteis estuvieron

DECIR *(to say)*	**TRAER** *(to bring)*	**VENIR** *(to come)*	**HACER** *(to do)*	**QUERER** *(to want)*
dije dijiste dijo dijimos dijisteis dijeron	traje trajiste trajo trajimos trajisteis trajeron	vine viniste vino vinimos vinisteis vinieron	hice hiciste hizo hicimos hicisteis hicieron	quise quisiste quiso quisimos quisisteis quisieron

DAR *(to give)*	**SER**[6] *(to be)*	**IR** *(to go)*
di diste dio dimos disteis dieron	fui fuiste fue fuimos fuisteis fueron	fui fuiste fue fuimos fuisteis fueron

[Footnotes]

[6] 'Ser' and 'Ir' have the same form in the preterite. Whereas the preterite of 'ir' (I went) is very common, the preterite of 'ser' (I was) is not commonly used; the imperfect tense is preferred. We will see the imperfect tense in the next unit.

Ejercicio E

Completa estas frases sobre los viajes de Peter con el pretérito de los verbos en paréntesis. Consulta las tablas de los verbos regulares y de los verbos irregulares.

1) Peter y sus amigos ______________ (ir) a Costa Rica para hacer ecoturismo.

2) Peter ______________ (ver) la flora y fauna de Costa Rica.

3) Después de su viaje, él ____________ (ir) a Madrid para comenzar su trabajo nuevo.

4) En Costa Rica, Peter ____________ (hacer) ecoturismo y le ______________ (gustar) mucho.

5) Peter ______________ (traer) muchos recuerdos *(souvenirs)* de Centroamérica.

6) En total, él ______________ (estar) 10 días en Costa Rica.

7) El guía *(The guide)* en Costa Rica ____________ (dar) un buen tour a Peter.

Respuestas E: **1)** fueron / **2)** vio / **3)** fue / **4)** hizo - gustó / **5)** trajo / **6)** estuvo / **7)** dio

Ejercicio F

Traduce estas frases sobre vacaciones usando el pretérito regular y el irregular.

1) My friends spent (use *pasar)* their vacation in Chile.

____

2) My cousin and his girlfriend gave money to the poor children.

____

3) My parents said that they waited for three hours to enter the Alhambra in Granada.

____

4) Were you (tú) in the Yucatan peninsula last month?

____

5) We (fem.) went to Europe three years ago (hace + *period of time*)

____

Respuestas F: **1)** Mis amigos pasaron sus vacaciones en Chile. / **2)** Mi primo y su novia dieron dinero a los niños pobres. / **3)** Mis padres dijeron que (ellos) esperaron (por) tres horas para entrar en la Alhambra de Granada. / **4)** ¿Estuviste (tú) en la península de Yucatán el mes pasado? / **5)** (Nosotras) fuimos a Europa hace tres años.

MI LISTA DE VOCABULARIO

Ésta es una lista de las palabras que has aprendido en esta unidad.

agobiado	cuidar
agradecer	dañar
(el) billón	de vacaciones
(la) cerveza	disfrutar
charlar	divertirse
(el) consejo	durar

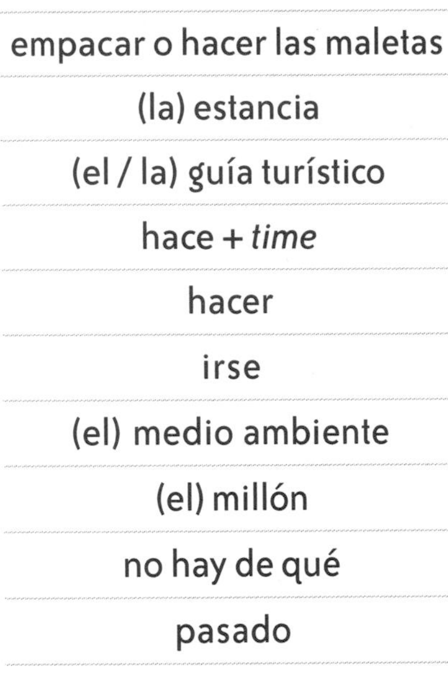

(el) ecoturismo
empacar o hacer las maletas
(la) estancia
(el / la) guía turístico
hace + *time*
hacer
irse
(el) medio ambiente
(el) millón
no hay de qué
pasado

(la) pirámide
(la) playa
preocuparse de
¡pura vida!
¡qué envidia!
(el) rato
(el) recuerdo
tico
traer
(las) vacaciones
ya

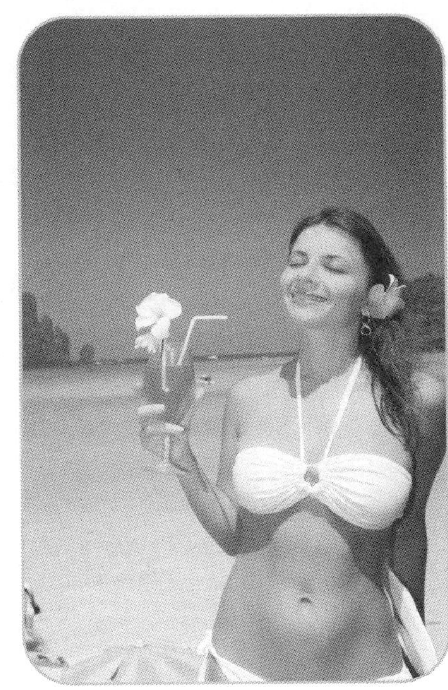

UN POCO DE CULTURA

Lugares turísticos para visitar en Latinoamérica

Las cataratas de Iguazú *(Iguazu[7] Falls)*
Las cataratas de Iguazú están localizadas *(are located)* en la frontera *(border)* de Brasil y Argentina, cerca de la frontera de Paraguay. Tienen más de 200 saltos de agua *(waterfalls)* de hasta *(of up to)* 82 metros de altura *(in height)*, mucho más grandes que las cataratas del Niágara. Las cataratas son una de las principales *(main)* atracciones turísticas de Argentina no sólo por su apariencia magnífica *(magnificent appearance)*, sino también porque los turistas pueden pasear *(ride)* en lancha *(motorboat)*, caminar por los senderos *(trails)*, o viajar en el 'tren ecológico' para disfrutar *(enjoy)* más de cerca esta atracción natural. En la película *The Mission* (1986, USA) aparecen las cataratas de Iguazú.

Las pirámides *(pyramids)* **de México**

Las pirámides de Cholula (en Puebla), de Teotihuacán (a 40 kilómetros de la capital), y de Chichén Itzá (en la península de Yucatán) fueron construidas *(were built)* y modificadas por *(modified by)* varias civilizaciones nativas americanas a lo largo de los siglos *(for centuries)*.

La pirámide de Cholula es la pirámide más grande del mundo y la segunda más alta del mundo[8]. Su construcción empezó *(started)* en el siglo II a.C. *(antes de Cristo = before Christ)*.

La pirámide del Sol, en Teotihuacán, es la segunda pirámide más grande de México y mira *(faces)* hacia el punto exacto *(towards the exact point)* donde el sol se pone *(the sun sets)* el 13 de agosto. Los visitantes *(Visitors)* pueden subir a la cima *(to the top)* después de subir 248 escalones empinados *(after climbing 248 steep steps)*. Cerca *(Nearby)* está la pirámide de la Luna, de menor tamaño *(size)*. Las pirámides fueron construidas con propósitos religiosos *(religious purposes)* para hacer ritos en lo alto *(on the top)* de la pirámide y ofrecerlos *(offer them)* a los dioses *(gods)*.

La pirámide maya en Chichén Itzá (El Castillo o Templo de Kukulcán) da una sombra *(shadow)* con forma de serpiente emplumada *(feathered serpent)* a la salida y puesta del sol *(sunrise and sunset)* en los equinoccios de primavera y otoño. Dentro de la pirámide está el trono *(throne)* de jaguar de Kukulcán, el dios en forma de serpiente emplumada. En la cultura azteca, Kukulcán se llama Quetzalcoatl, la serpiente emplumada. En julio de 2007, la pirámide de Chichén Itzá fue elegida como una de las nuevas siete maravillas del mundo.

[Footnotes]

[7] *In Guaraní, a native language of that area, 'Iguazú' means 'great or big water.'*
[8] *The tallest pyramid is Keops in Egypt.*

RECOMENDACIÓN PARA ESTA UNIDAD

Para finalizar esta unidad, te recomendamos que visites la página de Internet de http://www.world-turism.org, donde puedes encontrar artículos relacionados con turismo. Haz clic en 'español' en el menú de la esquina superior izquierda. También puedes hacer clic en el mapa del mundo para visitar las páginas oficiales de turismo de cada país de habla hispana (bajo la sección 'Actividades y proyectos por país').

Otra página interesante es http://www.turismojusto.org, una organización española cuyo lema *(whose motto is)* es «Cuando viajes piensa en ellos» *(When you travel, think of them)*. Esta organización promueve el turismo responsable y solidario donde se respeta y se ayuda a los países menos desarrollados *(less-developed countries)*.

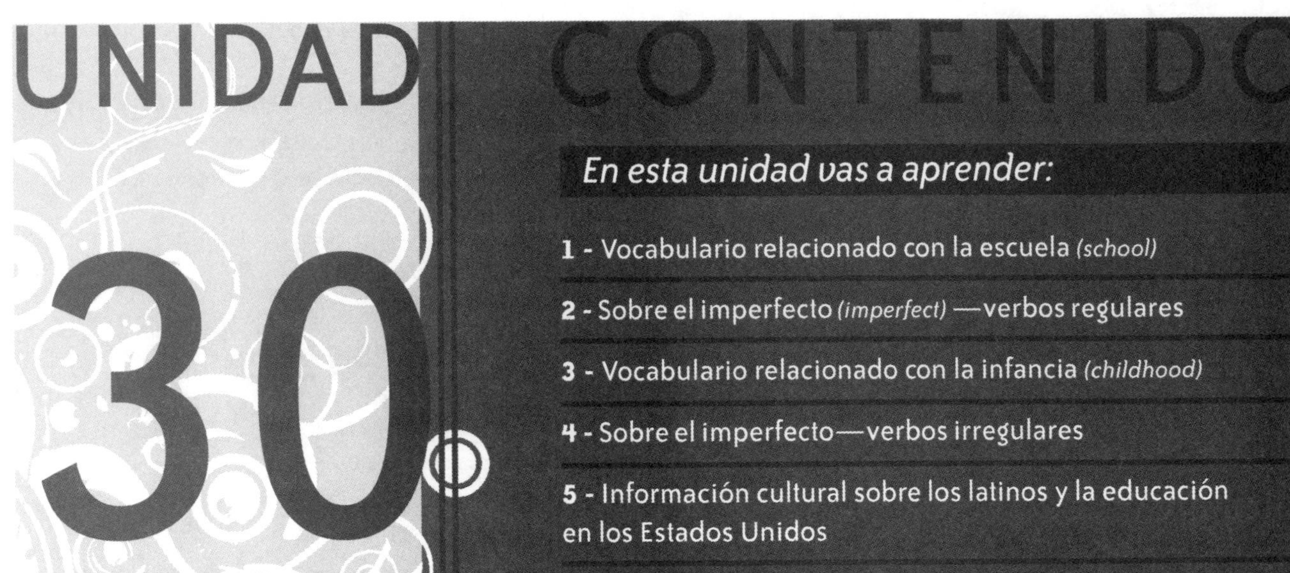

la escuela

LA ESCUELA

(School)

Peter y Ana están hablando sobre aquellos tiempos cuando iban *(they used to go)* **a la escuela.**

Ana:	Peter, ¿y cómo es que *(how is it that)* hablas español tan bien? ¿Lo aprendiste en el colegio[1]?
Peter:	No, lo aprendí en la preparatoria.
Ana:	¿Qué es la preparatoria?
Peter:	Oh, perdón. ¿Cómo se dice en España la escuela antes de la universidad? Lo olvidé *(I forgot)*.
Ana:	¿Bachillerato[2]?
Peter:	Sí, eso *(that's it)*. Gracias. En el bachillerato tomé español por cuatro años y luego tomé español en la universidad. También tenía *(I had)* amigos latinos y practicaba *(I used to practice)* con ellos. Y en mis viajes por Latinoamérica también lo usé *(I also used it)*.
Ana:	Eso explica *(That explains)* porqué hablas tan bien. Yo también tomé inglés en el bachillerato y en la universidad, pero nunca aprendí a hablar bien. Éramos tantos *(There were so many)* en clase…
Peter:	Ah, sí… El problema de tener educación casi gratis *(almost free)* es la masificación. En mi clase de la universidad éramos *(there were)* 25, así que *(so)* siempre practicaba con mis compañeros de clase *(classmates)* o con los profesores.
Ana:	Sí, vosotros no tenéis masificación, pero también es verdad *(but it is also true)* que mucha gente no puede asistir a *(a lot of people cannot attend)* la universidad porque es muy cara *(expensive)*, ¿verdad?

[Footnotes]

[1] 'Colegio' is another word for 'escuela.' It translates as 'school,', not 'college.'
[2] When Ana went to high school, 'bachillerato' was four years in length, like it is in the United States (9th to 12th grade). However, in the current Spanish educational system, 'bachillerato' is only two years (11th and 12th grades). Before that, there is the ESO (Educación Secundaria Obligatoria), which is mandatory.
[3] Another word for 'subject' is 'materia.'

Peter: Sí, es verdad. El costo es muy alto y muchas personas no consiguen *(get)* su diploma.

Ana: ¿Y cómo eran tus profesores? *(And what were your teachers like?)*

Peter: Tenía *(I used to have)* una profesora que siempre empezaba *(always began)* la clase conversando informalmente sobre cualquier cosa *(about anything)*. Me gustaba mucho ella. *(I liked her a lot.)* Era *(She was)* de Puerto Rico y yo iba *(I used to go)* a su clase cinco veces a la semana.

Ana: Yo tenía un profesor británico que era muy grosero *(rude)* y nunca quería *(never wanted)* hacer nada divertido *(fun)*. No me gustaba para nada *(at all)*. Creo que no me gustan mucho las lenguas extranjeras por su culpa. *(I think I don't like foreign languages much because of him.)*

Peter: ¿Qué? ¿Le echas la culpa al profesor? *(What? You blame the teacher?)*

Ana: No te rías! *(Don't laugh!)* Es verdad. *(It is true.)*

Peter: Dime, Ana, ¿aprendiste inglés británico o inglés americano?

Ana: Aprendí inglés británico, porque la mayor parte de *(most of)* los profesores y los libros eran de Inglaterra *(England)*. También había cursos de inglés en el extranjero *(There were also courses abroad)*, pero nunca fui. ¿Y tú?

Peter: No, yo tampoco *(neither did I)*. En aquella época *(In those times)* esos cursos eran muy caros *(expensive)* y mi familia no tenía mucho dinero.

Ana: Oye *(Listen)*, ¿y qué asignaturas[3] *(subjects)* eran tus favoritas?

Peter: Me gustaban el inglés, la biología, y las ciencias sociales, pero odiaba *(I hated)* las matemáticas.

Ana: ¿De verdad? *(Really?)* Mi clase favorita era la clase de arte. Hacíamos esculturas y pintábamos. *(We used to make sculptures and paint.)*

Peter: Ah, qué tiempos.... *(Ah, those were the days....)*

30

Ejercicio A

Responde estas preguntas con frases completas.

1) ¿Con quién practicaba Peter su español cuando estaba en la universidad?

____

2) ¿Por qué Ana nunca aprendió a hablar bien inglés?

____

3) ¿Cómo era el profesor británico de Ana?

____

4) ¿Qué asignatura odiaba Peter cuando era pequeño?

____

5) ¿Cuál era la clase favorita de Ana?

____

Respuestas A: **1)** Peter practicaba con sus compañeros de clase, con los profesores, y con los amigos latinos. / **2)** Ana nunca aprendió - Ana no aprendió nunca a hablar bien inglés porque eran muchos en su clase - porque no le gustaba el profesor. / **3)** El profesor británico de Ana era muy grosero (y nunca quería hacer nada divertido). / **4)** (Él) odiaba las matemáticas. / **5)** La clase favorita de Ana era la clase de arte.

EL IMPERFECTO —verbos regulares e[4] irregulares

The second type of simple past tense is the imperfect (el imperfecto). This tense is mainly used to talk about actions that happened habitually in the past *(I used to go to the beach every summer, I always sat at the back of the room, etc.)* and to describe *(the class was big, there were 25 people, the day was sunny, etc.)*. Here is how to form the regular imperfect tense:

CANTAR *(to sing)*	**COMER** *(to eat)*
cant**aba**	com**ía**
cant**abas**	com**ías**
cant**aba**[5]	com**ía**
cant**ábamos**	com**íamos**
cant**abais**	com**íais**
cant**aban**	com**ían**

*-IR verbs have the same endings as -ER verbs

There are only three irregular verbs:

SER *(to be)*	**IR** *(to go)*	**VER** *(to see)*
era	iba	veía
eras	ibas	veías
era	iba	veía
éramos	íbamos	veíamos
erais	ibais	veíais
eran	iban	veían

[Footnotes]

[4] When the word after the conjunction 'y' starts with 'i' or 'hi,' the conjunction turns into an 'e' to facilitate pronunciation.

[5] As you can see, the 'yo' form and the 'él' form are the same, so make sure you always clarify who the subject is when there is a possibility of confusion.

Stem-vowel changing verbs do not change in the imperfect: (alm**o**rzar = alm**o**rzaba)

Ejercicio B

Completa estas frases sobre el diálogo con el imperfecto de los verbos en paréntesis.

1) Los libros de inglés de Ana __________________ (ser) de Inglaterra.

2) La profesora de Peter __________________ (ser) de Puerto Rico.

3) A Ana no le __________________ (gustar) el profesor británico.

4) A Peter le __________________ (gustar) el inglés y las ciencias sociales.

5) Peter __________________ (ir) a su clase cinco veces a la semana.

6) Peter __________________ (tener) una profesora muy simpática.

7) __________________ (haber)[6] muchos estudiantes en la clase de Ana.

8) Peter __________________ (practicar) español con sus compañeros.

9) Los cursos en el extranjero __________________ (ser) caros y la familia de Peter no __________________ (tener) mucho dinero.

10) Cuando Peter ______________ (estar) en la universidad, aprendió mucho.

Respuestas B: **1)** eran / **2)** era / **3)** gustaba / **4)** gustaban / **5)** iba / **6)** tenía / **7)** Había / **8)** practicaba / **9)** eran / tenía / **10)** estaba

[Footnotes]

[6] The verb 'haber' is always in the singular ['hay' (present), 'hubo' (preterite), 'había' (imperfect), etc.].

LA INFANCIA / LA NIÑEZ

(Childhood)

¿Qué hacías cuando eras pequeño/a?

jugar a las canicas[7]

estudiar

explorar el barrio

pelearse con los hermanos

ver dibujos animados[8] en la televisión

ayudar a mamá

fingir estar enfermo para no ir a clase

jugar videojuegos

hacer la tarea[9]

salir con los amigos

leer historietas[10]

dibujar y pintar

Ejercicio C

Completa estas frases con el vocabulario anterior *(previous)* **sobre la infancia y con el imperfecto cuando sea necesario.**

1) Cuando era pequeño, no me gustaba ________________ del colegio.

2) Para no ir *(In order not to go)* al colegio __________ *(I pretended)* estar enfermo.

3) Mis amigos y yo siempre __________________ a las canicas.

4) Cuando estaba en casa, ______________ historietas.

5) Como era un niño muy bueno, siempre _________________________ con sus faenas domésticas.

Respuestas C: **1)** hacer la tarea/salir con los amigos / **2)** fingía / **3)** jugábamos / **4)** leía / **5)** ayudaba a mi mamá

[Footnotes]

[7] *Another word for 'marbles' is 'bolitas.'*

[8] *Another word for 'cartoons' is 'caricaturas.'*

[9] *Another word for 'homework' is 'deberes.'*

[10] *'Tiras cómicas', 'cómics' or 'historietas' are used in Latin America. Another word for comics is 'Tebeos', used mainly in Spain.*

Ejercicio D

Traduce estas frases sobre la infancia, usando el imperfecto para los verbos subrayados *(underlined)*.

1) When I was a child, I liked to go to the swimming pool.

____

2) When my parents were young, they used to go to church every Sunday.

____

3) There were many people in my class.

____

4) My family used to visit my uncles every Christmas

____

5) Did your (tu) family have money when you were in school?

____

Respuestas D: **1)** Cuando era niño/a (or pequeño/a), me gustaba ir a la piscina. / **2)** Cuando mis padres eran jóvenes, iban a la iglesia cada domingo. / **3)** Había mucha gente/muchas personas en mi clase. / **4)** Mi familia visitaba a mis tíos cada Navidad. / **5)** ¿Tenía tu familia dinero cuando tú estabas en la escuela/el colegio?

Ejercicio E

¿Qué hacías tú cuando eras pequeño/a? Escribe aquí sobre tu infancia.

Yo ______________________________

____

____

MI LISTA DE VOCABULARIO

Ésta es una lista de las palabras que has aprendido en esta unidad.

(la) asignatura o (la) materia	(el) compañero de clase
(el) arte	cuando era pequeño/a / cuando era niño/a
(el) bachillerato o (la) preparatoria	(la) culpa
(la) canica	(el) curso
caro	¿de verdad?
(las) ciencias sociales	dibujar

(los) dibujos animados	gratis	para nada
divertido	grosero	pintar
echar la culpa a	(la) infancia o (la) niñez	¡qué tiempos!
en el extranjero	(la) lengua extranjera	(la) tarea
(la) época	(las) matemáticas	(el) tebeo o (el) cómic
(la) escuela o (el) colegio	(la) mayoría de	(el) videojuego
fingir	olvidar	

UN POCO DE CULTURA

La educación de los hispanos/latinos en los Estados Unidos

El tema de la educación en los Estados Unidos es muy controvertido *(controversial)*. Mientras que *(Whereas)* las universidades son famosas en el mundo por ofrecer una educación de alta calidad *(high quality)*, las escuelas de bachillerato y escuelas de educación primaria tienen muy mala reputación en general. Uno de los factores que contribuyen a esta diferencia en calidad es el dinero. Las universidades son financiadas por los estudiantes, por una gran variedad de instituciones, muchas veces por el estado, e incluso por el gobierno federal. Sin embargo *(However)*, las escuelas dependen mucho del dinero de los impuestos recogidos *(the taxes collected)* en el barrio *(neighborhood)* donde se localizan. Como consecuencia, muchos adolescentes, especialmente en los barrios pobres, no se gradúan del bachillerato. Los estados con niveles más bajos de graduación de la preparatoria son: Texas (77%), West Virginia (78%), Louisiana (79%), Alabama (80%), y South Carolina (81%). Es obvio que los estados del sur necesitan mucha ayuda en el tema de la educación en general. Según Educational Testing Service (ETS), una compañía que crea exámenes estandarizados como GRE, TOEFL, AP y SAT, Estados Unidos ha caído *(has slipped)* hasta la posición número 10 (en el mundo) en cuanto a niveles de graduación de la preparatoria[11].

Existe también una gran disparidad *(disparity)* entre los estudiantes. Hay una gran diferencia entre los niveles *(levels)* de educación de los hispanos/latinos de Estados Unidos y los no-latinos. Según la oficina del censo de los Estados Unidos *(U.S. Census Bureau)*, 9 de cada 10 jóvenes blancos no-latinos se gradúan de la preparatoria (89.4%), comparado con 6 de cada 10 jóvenes latinos (57%). En cuanto a *(In terms of)* estudios superiores, 3 de cada 10 blancos no-latinos se gradúan de la universidad (30%), comparado con 1 de cada 10 latinos (11.4%). De acuerdo con el NCES[12], los latinos tienen niveles de retención y suspensión/expulsión más altos que los de los blancos no-latinos. También es importante destacar *(to note)* que las latinas entre 15 y 19 años tienen niveles más altos de embarazo *(pregnancy)* que las chicas de su edad *(age)* de otros grupos étnicos, lo que *(which)* también contribuye al problema de graduación.

Hay muchos factores que contribuyen a estas diferencias entre latinos y no-latinos. De acuerdo con *(according to)* un artículo publicado en 1996[13], algunos factores incluyen:
-fondos inadecuados para las escuelas
-tratamiento *(treatment)* inapropiado del bilingualismo
-segregación de los latinos a escuelas pobres de barrios pobres
-falta de *(lack of)* representación para los latinos
-cambios *(changes)* constantes en las leyes sobre acción afirmativa *(affirmative action)*
-falta de participación de los latinos en programas preescolares
-responsabilidades de los adolescentes latinos de ayudar a sus familias
A pesar de *(Despite)* la mala calidad de educación que muchos latinos reciben en los Estados Unidos, a veces sobresalen *(stand out)* personas que dejan una gran huella *(leave a mark/make a difference)* en la historia de la educación, como Jaime Escalante.

Jaime Escalante
Jaime A. Escalante, boliviano de origen, fue profesor de matemáticas en una escuela preparatoria *(high school)* en Los Ángeles, California, y también profesor de cálculo en East Los Ángeles College. Se hizo famoso por su capacidad de aumentar *(He became famous for his ability to raise)* notablemente el número de estudiantes que aprobaron *(passed)* los exámenes de Advanced Placement (AP) de cálculo de ETS en los años 80. Por su esfuerzo *(effort)* y dedicación recibió varios premios *(awards)* y condecoraciones, como la Medalla Presidencial de Excelencia en Educación y el Premio Andrés Bello de la Organización de los Estados Americanos. También fue locutor *(newscaster)* del programa FUTUROS de la PBS.
A Jaime Escalante se le atribuyen dos citas *(quotes)*:
«El día en que alguien abandona la escuela se está condenando a un futuro de pobreza.»
(The day someone quits school he is condemning himself to a future of poverty.)
«La determinación + la disciplina + el trabajo duro = el camino al éxito.» *(Determination + discipline + hard work = the path to success.)*

[Footnotes]

[11] *Source: http://www.ets.org/Media/Education_Topics/pdf/onethird.pdf*
[12] *National Center for Education Statistics, http://nces.ed.gov/pubs2003/hispanics/*
[13] *«Our nation on the fault line» (Sept. 1996). Hispanic American Education, http://ed.gov/pubs/FaultLine/call.html*

RECOMENDACIÓN PARA ESTA UNIDAD

Para finalizar esta unidad, te recomendamos que veas la película *Stand and Deliver* (1988, USA) de Ramón Menéndez, inspirada en el trabajo de Jaime Escalante.

También recomendamos dos películas que muestran los problemas que afrontan muchos latinos y latinas cuando tienen que tomar la decisión de ir a la universidad o no. Una película es *Real Women Have Curves* (2002, USA) de Patricia Cardoso. La otra película es el capítulo 16 (*The Fighting Fridas)* de la serie de televisión *American Family: Journey of Dreams* (2002–2004, USA) de Gregory Nava.

UNIDAD 31 CONTENIDO

En esta unidad vas a aprender:

1 - Vocabulario relacionado con leyendas *(legends)*

2 - Sobre la diferencia entre el imperfecto y el pretérito

3 - Información cultural sobre leyendas de los países de habla hispana

las leyendas

LA LLORONA

(The Weeping Woman)

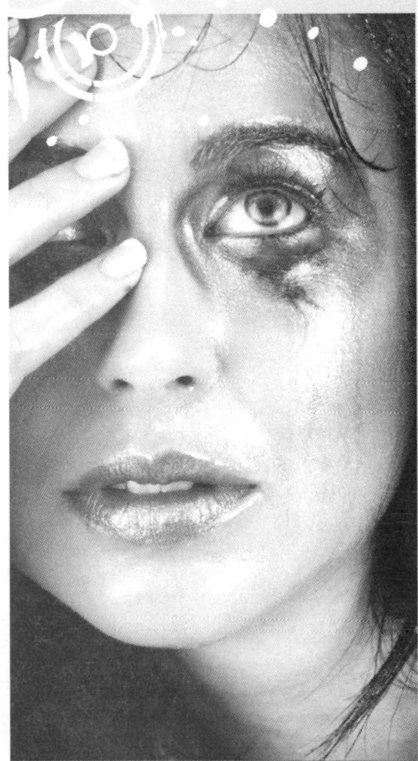

El señor Pérez, el jefe de Ana, sale de la oficina para almorzar en una cafetería cercana *(nearby)*. **Allí ve a Ana, que** *(who)* **está leyendo un libro sobre leyendas** *(legends)*.

Antonio Pérez: Hola, Ana. ¿Cómo está usted?

Ana: Bien, gracias. Aquí, almorzando un poco. ¿Quiere usted sentarse? *(Would you like to sitt?)*

Antonio Pérez: Gracias. ¿Y este libro tan interesante?

Ana: Ah, estoy buscando alguna historia *(story)* interesante para contarles *(to tell)* a mis hijas cuando se vayan a la cama *(when they go to bed)*. Ya les conté *(I already told them)* todas las historias que sé: cuentos de hadas *(fairy tales)*, fábulas *(fables)*, mitos *(myths)*....

Antonio Pérez: Ah, ya veo. ¿Y ahora está buscando una leyenda interesante?

Ana: Sí, en efecto *(that's right)*, pero no veo ninguna buena *(I don't see any good one)* en este libro.

Antonio Pérez: Ana, ¿conoce usted la leyenda de la Llorona *(the Weeping Woman)*?

Ana: No, ¿de qué trata? *(what is it about?)*

Antonio Pérez: Es la historia de una mujer muy hermosa que tiró *(threw)* sus hijos al agua *(water)*. Arrepentida *(Repentant)*, los buscó *(she looked for them)*, pero nunca los encontró *(never found them)*. Y así murió *(And so she died)*, buscando a sus hijos. La leyenda dice que si caminas cerca del agua por la noche es posible que veas a la

Llorona vagando *(wandering)*, llorando, gritando *(shouting)*, y buscando a sus bebés ahogados *(drowned)*.

Ana: ¡¡Ah, pero ésa es una leyenda terrible!! ¡Qué triste! La Llorona es como *(like)* el hombre del saco *(the bogeyman)*.

Antonio Pérez: Sí, quizás necesitamos buscar otra. No queremos que las niñas tengan pesadillas *(nightmares)*.

PRETÉRITO vs. IMPERFECTO

Since both the preterite and the imperfect tenses are past tenses, it is sometimes difficult to decide which one to use in a specific context. Here is some information that might help you decide[1]:

PRETÉRITO
For actions that started and completed, or for a sequence of completed actions: —El mes pasado vi a Irene.*(Last month I saw Irene.)* —Ayer estudié, miré la tele, y me acosté pronto.*(Yesterday I studied, watched TV, and went to bed early,)*
For actions in the past that only happened once:—Cuando era pequeño, fuimos a la playa.*(When I was a child, we went to the beach.)*
For changes in emotional, mental. or physical conditions: —Alberto se puso enfermo.*(Albert got sick.)*
For actions that interrupt longer actions: —El teléfono sonó cuando estaba en la ducha.*(The phone rang when/while I was in the shower.)*

[Footnotes]

[1] These are guidelines for usage, not rules, and that's why the difference between the preterite and the imperfect is so difficult sometimes.

IMPERFECTO
For actions that describe what was happening at a specific moment, or for a sequence of these actions: —Estábamos mirando los pájaros. *(We were looking at the birds.)* —De niña, siempre miraba la tele y jugaba con mis hermanos.*(As a child, I always watched TV and played with my sibling.s)* or *(As a child, I would watch TV and play with my siblings.)*
For habitual actions: —Cuando era pequeño, íbamos a la playa. *(When I was a child, we used to go to the beach.)*
For descriptions of emotional, mental .and physical conditions: —Dolores se sentía mal y tenía fiebre. *(Dolores was feeling sick and had a fever.)*
For longer actions that are interrupted by shorter actions: —Tomaba un examen cuando Eva me llamó.*(I was taking an exam when Eva called me.)*
For non-actions or long-standing emotions: —Yo quería ir.*(I wanted to go.)*
For descriptions:—La casa era grande y tenía muchas ventanas.*(The house was big and had many windows.)*
For age and time:—Eran las 2:00 de la tarde.*(It was 2:00 in the afternoon.)* —Cuando Ernesto tenía 20 años, se casó. *(When Ernest was 20 years old, he got married.)*

Ejercicio A

Selecciona la opción correcta (pretérito o imperfecto) para estas frases sobre la Llorona.

1) La Llorona *(quiso/quería)* mucho a sus hijos. ____________________

2) Un día, la Llorona *(tiró/tiraba)* a sus hijos al agua del río. ____________________

3) Los niños *(se ahogaron/se ahogaban)* *(drowned)*. ____________________

4) Cuando la Llorona *(fue/era)* joven, *(fue/era)* muy guapa. ____________________

5) Su esposo *(se fue/se iba)* con otra mujer. ____________________

Respuestas A: **1)** quería / **2)** tiró / **3)** se ahogaron / **4)** era/era / **5)** se fue

Ejercicio B

Ahora completa esta historia sobre la leyenda de la Llorona con el pretérito o el imperfecto de los verbos en paréntesis.

Hace mucho, mucho tiempo, había *(there was)* una chica joven y bonita que ______________ (1. vivir) en Tenochtitlán con su familia. Siempre ______________ (2. vestirse) de blanco y ______________ (3. llevar) su hermoso pelo negro en dos grandes trenzas *(braids)*. Su nombre ______________ (4. ser) Cihuacoatl.

Un día, a la edad de 15 años, Cihuacoatl ______________ (5. ver) a un príncipe azteca *(Aztec prince)* hermoso *(handsome)* y valiente, e inmediatamente se enamoró *(fell in love)* de él. Los jóvenes ______________ (6. casarse) *(got married)* y tuvieron dos hijos gemelos preciosos. Desgraciadamente *(Unfortunately)*, con el tiempo, el joven príncipe dejó de amar *(stopped loving)* a su esposa y la ______________ (7. abandonar). Ella, desesperada *(desperate)*, lo buscó *(looked for him)* y lo buscó, sin suerte *(without any luck)*.

Un día, mientras *(while)* Cihuacoatl ______________ (8. caminar) por la orilla de un río *(river bank)*, vio a su hermoso[2] príncipe en la otra orilla *(bank)*. A su lado *(At his side)* ______________ (9. ir) una joven bella que reía y le hacía compañía *(kept him company)*. Cihuacoatl ________ (10. ponerse) furiosa *(got furious)* y lo llamó a gritos *(yelled his name)*, pero él la ignoró. En un momento de furia, ella le preguntó si no quería ver a sus bebés tampoco y entonces los ______________ (11. arrojar) *(threw them)* a las aguas *(waters)* del río. La fuerte corriente *(strong current)* los arrastró *(dragged them)* río abajo. En ese momento, Cihuacoatl ______________ (12. darse) cuenta de *(she realized)* su error y ______________ (13. correr) *(ran)* a lo largo de *(along)* la orilla en busca de *(in search of)* sus bebés, pero no los pudo encontrar *(but she could not find them)*. Los buscó toda la noche, llamándolos a gritos, pero nunca los ______________ (14. encontrar). A la mañana siguiente *(Next morning)*, unos hombres ______________ (15. encontrar) a Cihuacoatl muerta *(dead)* cerca de la orilla.

La leyenda dice que si sales de noche y pasas cerca de un río o algún lugar con agua, es posible que escuches los gritos *(shouts)* de la 'la Llorona' *(the Weeping Woman)*, que todavía vaga *(still wanders)* buscando a sus bebés.

[Footnotes]

[2] *For literary effect, adjectives sometimes precede rather than follow the nouns they modify.*

Respuestas B: **1)** vivía / **2)** se vestía / **3)** llevaba / **4)** era / **5)** vio / **6)** se casaron / **7)** abandonó / **8)** caminaba / **9)** iba / **10)** se puso / **11)** arrojó / **12)** se dio / **13)** corrió / **14)** encontró / **15)** encontraron

UNIDAD 31

EL DORADO ('The Gilded One')

Ana y el señor Pérez continúan su conversación sobre leyendas.

Ana: ¿Y no sabe usted otra leyenda para mis hijas?

Antonio Pérez: Uhm...vamos a ver...¿y qué tal la leyenda del Dorado?

Ana: Ay, sí, ésa es perfecta. ¿Por qué no me la cuenta? Usted las cuenta tan bien.... *(You tell them so well....)*

Antonio Pérez: Gracias. Pues todo empezó con una ceremonia religiosa *(religious ceremony)* en la que *(in which)* un cacique *(tribe chief)* se cubría *(was covered)* con polvo de oro *(gold dust)* y por eso lo llamaban 'el dorado' *(the gilded one)*. Más tarde, la leyenda pasó de boca en boca *(was passed on by word of mouth)* y al final 'el dorado' era toda una ciudad hecha de oro *(an entire city made of gold)* que estaba perdida en la selva *(lost in the jungle)*. ¡Imagínese! *(Imagine that!)*

Ana: Sí... Es una leyenda colombiana, ¿verdad?

Antonio Pérez: En efecto. *(That's right.)*

Ejercicio C

Completa estas frases sobre el Dorado con el pretérito o el imperfecto de los verbos en paréntesis.

1) El señor Pérez ________________ (decidir) contar la leyenda a Ana.

2) Mientras él ________________ (contar) la leyenda, Ana ______________ (escuchar).

3) Cuando él ________________ (terminar), ________________ (ser) las 3:00 de la tarde.

4) Después de almorzar, Ana y el señor Pérez ________________ (regresar) a la oficina.

5) A Ana le ________________ (gustar) mucho la historia de El Dorado.

Respuestas C: **1)** decidió / **2)** contaba / escuchaba / **3)** terminó / eran / **4)** regresaron / **5)** gustó

Ejercicio D

Elige un verbo de la tabla y completa estas frases sobre la leyenda del Dorado con la forma correcta del pretérito o el imperfecto.

saltar *(to jump)*	tener *(to have)*	ofrecer *(to offer)*
llegar *(to arrive)*	ver *(to see)*	ser *(to be)*

1) Los indios muiscas *(The Chibcha)* __________ una ceremonia religiosa muy interesante.

2) En esta ceremonia, el cacique ___________ al agua totalmente cubierto de polvo de oro *(covered by gold dust)*.

3) Los muiscas también *(also)* ___________ joyas *(jewels)* y regalos *(gifts)* a la diosa *(goddess)* de la laguna *(lagoon)*.

4) Cuando los españoles _________ y _______ la ceremonia, sintieron mucha codicia *(greed)*.

5) Después de algunos años, la legenda ______________ totalmente diferente a la legenda original.

Respuestas D: **1)** tenían / **2)** saltaba / **3)** ofrecían / **4)** llegaron / vieron / **5)** era

Ejercicio E

Ahora completa la historia del Dorado con el pretérito o el imperfecto de los verbos en paréntesis.

Hace mucho tiempo, los muiscas que vivían en Colombia ________________ (1. tener) un rito religioso *(religious ritual)* que pasó después a la historia *(history)* como *(as)* la famosa leyenda de El Dorado.

En esta ceremonia, los indígenas ______________ (2. llevar) al cacique en balsa *(raft)* hasta el centro de la laguna *(center of the lagoon)* Guatavita. El cacique ________________ (3. estar) cubierto de polvo de oro *(covered in gold dust)*. Entonces *(Then)*, el cacique ________________ (4. arrojar) *(threw)* ofrendas de piedras preciosas *(offerings of precious stones)* y oro a la diosa de la laguna y luego saltaba *(he jumped)* al agua. La ceremonia terminaba con música y baile durante toda la noche. Con este rito, los muiscas ________________ (5. honrar) *(honored)* a la diosa de la laguna y quedaban bajo su protección *(remained under her protection)*.

La historia que corría de boca en boca hablaba del oro y las joyas que los muiscas tenían. Al final la historia era muy diferente y decía que el Dorado ________________ (6. ser) una ciudad toda hecha de oro *(made of gold)*: calles de oro, edificios de oro, oro por todas partes *(everywhere)*. Muchos europeos ________________ (7. decidir) ir a explorar América para ver si podían encontrar la ciudad perdida de 'El Dorado', pero nunca pudieron encontrarla. Los españoles intentaron drenar *(tried to drain)* la laguna Guatavita muchas veces, pero nunca ________________ (8. conseguir) mucho *(never found much)*.

El rito de ofrecer el oro a la diosa de la laguna con el tiempo ________________ (9. transformarse) en *(turned into)* una historia trágica de amor[3]. En esta historia, un cacique muisca descubrió *(found out)* que su esposa lo ________________ (10. engañar) *(was cheating on him)* con un guerrero de su ejército *(warrior from his army)*. Furioso, ________________ (11. matar) *(he killed)* al guerrero y luego mandó arrojar *(ordered to throw)* a su esposa infiel *(unfaithful)* y a su hija pequeñita a la laguna de Guatavita. Su esposa imploró perdón *(begged for pardon)*, pero el cacique no la escuchó. Las dos *(Both)* ________________ (12. ahogarse) *(drowned)* en la laguna. Después de un tiempo, el cacique ________________ (13. arrepentirse) *(regretted)* de su acto cobarde *(cowardly act)* e intentó encontrar *(tried to ask for)* el perdón de su esposa. Por eso, él ______________ (14. organizar) una ceremonia anual en la que él ________________ (15. arrojar) joyas y piedras preciosas a la laguna para pedirle perdón a su esposa y a su hijita.

[Footnotes] [3] *Eventually, this indigenous religious ceremony disappeared as such, conveniently as the Catholic religion was spreading among the natives.*

Respuestas E: **1)** tenían / **2)** llevaban / **3)** estaba / **4)** arrojaba / **5)** honraban / **6)** era / **7)** decidieron / **8)** consiguieron / **9)** se transformó / **10)** engañaba / **11)** mató / **12)** se ahogaron / **13)** se arrepintió / **14)** organizó/ organizaba / **15)** arrojaba

MI LISTA DE VOCABULARIO

Ésta es una lista de las palabras que has aprendido en esta unidad.

a lo largo de	(la) historia
(el) agua	(la) historia
ahogarse	honrar
arrastrar	(el) hombre del saco
arrepentido	ignorar
arrojar	¡imagínese!/¡imagínate!
(la) balsa	implorar
(el) cacique/(la) cacica	(la) laguna
cercano	(la) leyenda
(la) ceremonia	llorar
(la) codicia	(el) mito
contar	muisca
(la) corriente	(la) orilla
(el) cuento de hadas	(la) pesadilla
darse cuenta de	(la) piedra preciosa
de boca en boca	(el) polvo de oro
descubrir	(el) príncipe/(la) princesa
desesperado	(el) regalo
desgraciadamente	(el) río
dorado	(el) rito o (el) ritual
drenar	saltar
en efecto	(la) selva
engañar	sin suerte
(la) fábula	(la) suerte
(la) furia	tirar
gritar	transformarse
(el) grito	(la) trenza
hacer compañía	vagar

UN POCO DE CULTURA

Mitos y leyendas

La literatura refleja *(reflects)* la cultura y la historia de un pueblo. Todos los países tienen leyendas, unas más famosas que otras. Entre *(Among)* las leyendas mexicanas más famosas está la leyenda de la Virgen de Guadalupe[4].

La diferencia entre una leyenda y un mito *(myth)* es que la leyenda es un relato *(narration)* originalmente basado *(originally based)* en un hecho real *(real fact)* con personajes *(characters)* reales, que se ha transformado con el tiempo. Por su parte, el mito es un relato totalmente ficticio *(fictitious)* donde los personajes son supernaturales (dioses, semidioses, héroes, etc.). Los mitos más comunes son aquéllos que intentan explicar el origen de las cosas, animales, y personas que nos rodean *(surround us)*: el origen del sol, la luna, y la tierra; el origen de una civilización, de un dios, de un animal, de los humanos, etc. Entre los mitos más famosos del mundo hispano están el mito del origen de la civilización azteca, el de la civilización inca, y el de la civilización maya.

[Footnotes]

[4] *Although the story of the apparition of the Virgin of Guadalupe to Juan Diego is generally considered a legend, some Catholics may disagree with this classification.*

RECOMENDACIÓN PARA ESTA UNIDAD

Para finalizar esta unidad, te recomendamos que leas un libro de leyendas. Los libros publicados por NTC normalmente están en un nivel de comprensión adecuado para ti en este momento, y algunos tienen un glosario y preguntas de comprensión al final de cada leyenda. Aquí hay algunos ejemplos:

-*Leyendas cubanas*. Autora: Olympia González. Editorial: NTC.
-*Rimas y leyendas*. Autor: Gustavo Adolfo Bécquer. Editorial: Austral.
-*Leyendas de Puerto Rico*. Autora: Adela Martínez Santiago. Editorial: McGraw Hill.
-*Leyendas mexicanas*. Autores: Genevieve Barlow y William Stivers. Editorial: NTC.
-*Leyendas latinoamericanas*. Autores: Genevieve Barlow. Editorial: NTC
-*De oro y esmeraldas: Mitos, leyendas y cuentos populares de Latinoamérica*. Autora: Lulu Delacre. Editorial: Scholastic. *[advanced level]*

UNIDAD 32

UNIDAD 32 CONTENIDO

EXÁMEN 4

exámen 4

EXÁMEN 4

En esta última unidad vas a encontrar varios ejercicios para practicar lo que has aprendido en las unidades 25–31. Con este examen has terminado este libro. ¡Enhorabuena! *(Congratulations!)*

Ejercicio A

Escribe el nombre de los órganos, huesos y partes del cuerpo que se muestran en esta ilustración.

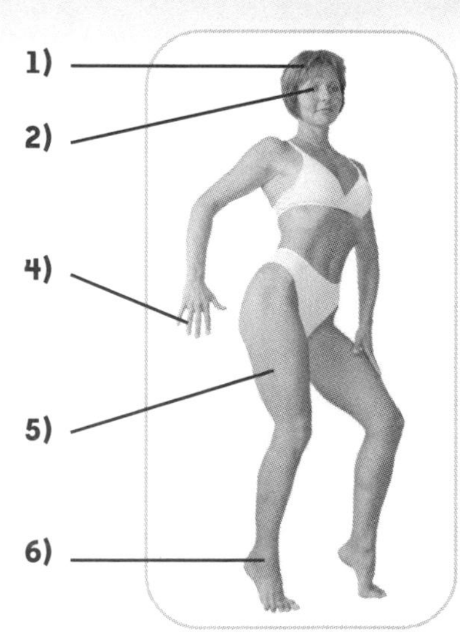

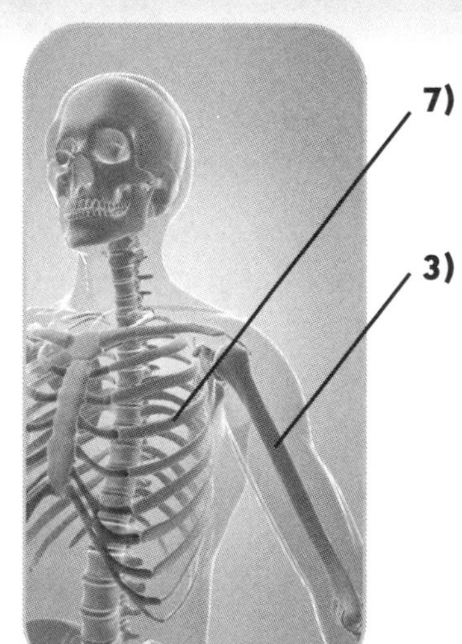

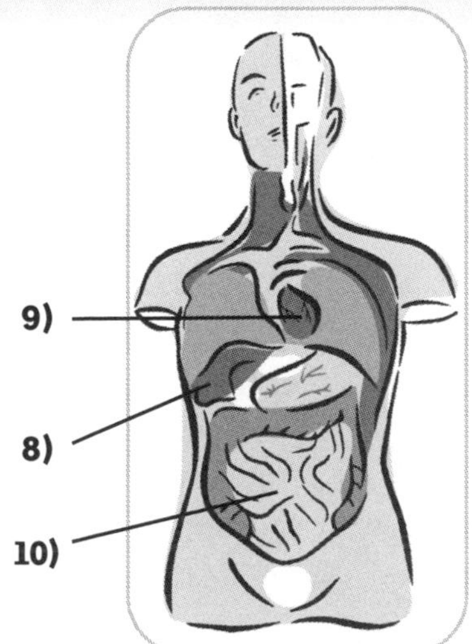

Respuestas A: **1)** cabeza / **2)** ojo / **3)** húmero / **4)** dedo / **5)** pierna / **6)** tobillo / **7)** costillas / **8)** hígado / **9)** corazón / **10)** intestino delgado

Ejercicio B

Un doctor en un hospital tiene dos pacientes: un niño y un adulto. Escribe estas órdenes para los dos pacientes, una con el imperativo de tú y otra con el imperativo de usted. Observa el ejemplo 1.

	NIÑO	ADULTO
1) Subir el brazo	Sube el brazo	Suba el brazo
2) Abrir la boca		
3) Caminar		
4) Toser		
5) Levantarse		
6) Vestirse		
7) Decir «ahhhhh»		
8) No cerrar los ojos		
9) Cerrarlos		
10) No cerrarlos		

Respuestas B: **2)** abre la boca / abra la boca / **3)** camina / camine / **4)** tose / tosa / **5)** levántate / levántese / **6)** vístete / vístase / **7)** di «ahhhh» / diga «ahhhh» / **8)** no cierres los ojos / no cierre los ojos / **9)** ciérralos / ciérrelos / **10)** no los cierres / no los cierre

Ejercicio C

El doctor acaba de examinar *(just examined)* **a su paciente y ahora le va a explicar su situación médica. Escribe frases de 'si' con futuro inmediato (voy a + infinitivo) usando los siguientes elementos. Observa el ejemplo 1.**

1) fumar / cáncer Señor Díaz, si fuma tanto, va a tener cáncer de pulmón

2) beber alcohol / cirrosis ______

3) comer azúcar / diabetes ______

4) no hacer ejercicio / engordar ______

5) no cuidarse / enfermarse ______

Posibles respuestas C: **2)** Señor Díaz, si bebe mucho alcohol, va a tener cirrosis / **3)** Si come tanto azúcar, va a tener diabetes / **4)** si no hace más ejercicio, va a engordar / **5)** Si no se cuida, va a enfermarse (or 'se va a enfermar')

Ejercicio D

Javier es hipocondríaco y siempre piensa que está enfermo. Traduce estas frases que le dice al doctor, usando el verbo doler y la estructura 'gustar'. Observa el ejemplo 1.

1) Doctor, my back hurts all the time

Doctor, me duele la espalda todo el tiempo

2) My feet hurt when I walk

____

3) My eyes also hurt

____

4) It hurts here, is this normal?

____

5) Right now, my arms are hurting

____

Respuestas D: **2)** Me duelen los pies cuando camino / **3)** Me duelen los ojos también / **4)** Me duele aquí, ¿es esto normal? / **5)** Ahora mismo, me duelen/me están doliendo los brazos

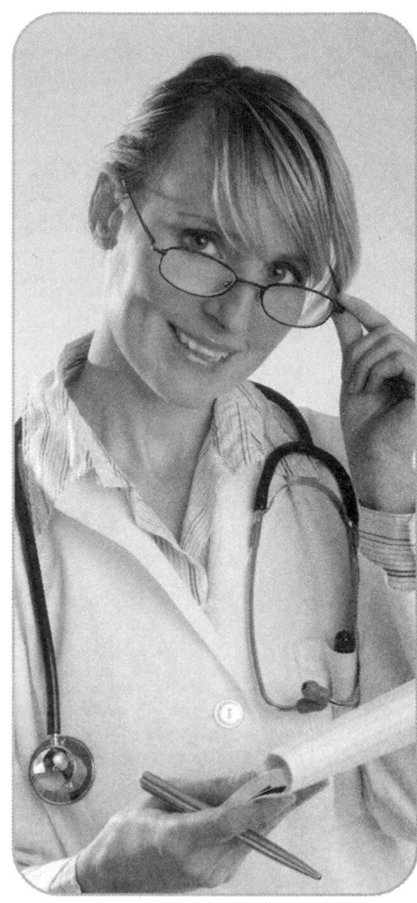

Ejercicio E

Completa estas frases sobre viajes con el subjuntivo, indicativo (presente), o infinitivo de los verbos en paréntesis.

1) Ojalá que el boleto del avión no ________________ (costar) mucho dinero.

2) Mi amigo Julián y yo queremos ________________ (viajar) a Bolivia y a Ecuador.

3) Es importante ________________ (tener) todos los documentos en regla.

4) Mi padre recomienda que nosotros ________________ (ir) en tren.

5) Es obvio que nosotros no ________________ (poder) ir de vacaciones este año.

6) Siento mucho que tú no ________________ (venir) con nosotros a Guatemala.

7) Quiero que mi esposa ________________ (ver) las pirámides de México.

8) Fernando también quiere ________________ (ver) las ruinas incas.

9) Es evidente que el turismo ________________ (afectar) negativamente al medio ambiente.

10) Ojalá que los turistas ________________ (ser) más responsables.

Respuestas E: **1)** cueste / **2)** viajar / **3)** tener / **4)** vayamos / **5)** podemos / **6)** vengas / **7)** vea / **8)** ver / **9)** afecta / **10)** sean

Ejercicio F

Escribe los siguientes números en español.

1) 489.002 ____________________

2) 1.394.000 ____________________

3) 10.772.054 ____________________

Respuestas F: **1)** cuatrocientos ochenta y nueve mil dos / **2)** un millón trescientos noventa y cuatro mil / **3)** diez millones setecientos setenta y dos mil cincuenta y cuatro.

Ejercicio G

Completa este mito sobre el origen de los incas usando el pretérito o el imperfecto de los verbos en paréntesis.

Hace muchos siglos, los hombres vivían como animales: se alimentaban con *(used to eat)* frutas de los árboles y peces de los ríos, y ______________ (1. vestirse) con pieles *(fur)* o andaban desnudos *(naked)*.

Un día, el dios Sol *(the Sun god)* ______________ (2. enviar) *(sent)* a su hijo Manco Cápac y a su hija Mama Ocllo para enseñarles *(to teach)* a los humanos a cultivar maíz *(to grow corn)*, a construir *(build)* casas, y a darle gracias a él *(praise him)*. El dios Sol les ______________ (3. dar) una vara *(stick)* de oro a sus hijos y les dijo *(told them)*: «Caminen en cualquier dirección y donde encuentren *(wherever you find)* un lugar donde sea posible hundir *(sink)* la vara en el suelo *(ground)*, funden un reino *(found a kingdom)*. Sean sabios *(Be wise)* y justos *(just)* con su gente».

Los hermanos ______________ (4. salir) del lago *(lake)* Titicaca y ______________ (5. caminar) por mucho tiempo. Siempre que ellos

______________ (6. detenerse) *(stopped)* para descansar o dormir, intentaban *(tried)* hundir la vara, pero la vara nunca se hundía. Un día, Manco Cápac y su hermana ______________ (7. llegar) al valle de Cusco, un lugar hermoso y fértil. Allí, ellos ______________ (8. hundir) la vara, y la vara ______________ (9. desaparecer) en la tierra. Contentos *(Happy)*, ______________ (10. decidir) fundar allí su imperio *(empire)*: el gran imperio de los incas.

Respuestas G: **1)** se vestían / **2)** envió / **3)** dio / **4)** salieron / **5)** caminaron / **6)** se detenían / **7)** llegaron / **8)** hundieron / **9)** desapareció / **10)** decidieron

APÉNDICE A

TIEMPOS VERBALES EN ESPAÑOL

FORMAS NO CONJUGADAS

Infinitivo cantar / comer
Gerundio (Part. de presente) cantando / comiendo
Participio (de pasado) cantado / comido

MODO INDICATIVO

PRESENTE

canto	como
cantas	comes
canta	come
cantamos	comemos
cantáis	coméis
cantan	comen

PRETERITO IMPERFECTO

cantaba	comía
cantabas	comías
cantaba	comía
cantábamos	comíamos
cantabais	comíais
cantaban	comían

PRETERITO

canté	comí
cantaste	comiste
cantó	comió
cantamos	comimos
cantasteis	comisteis
cantaron	comieron

PRETERITO PERFECTO

he cantado	he comido
has cantado	has comido
ha cantado	ha comido
hemos cantado	hemos comido
habeis cantado	habeis comido
han cantado	han comido

PLUSCUAMPERFECTO	
había cantado	había comido
habías cantado	habías comido
había cantado	había comido
habíamos cantado	habíamos comido
habíais cantado	habíais comido
habían cantado	habían comido

PRETERITO ANTERIOR	
hube cantado	hube comido
hubiste cantado	hubiste comido
hubo cantado	hubo comido
hubimos cantado	hubimos comido
hubisteis cantado	hubisteis comido
hubieron cantado	hubieron comido

FUTURO SIMPLE	
cantaré	comeré
cantarás	comerás
cantará	comerá
cantaremos	comeremos
cantaréis	comeréis
cantarán	comerán

FUTURO PERFECTO	
habré cantado	habré comido
habrás cantado	habrás comido
habrá cantado	habrá comido
habremos cantado	habremos comido
habreis cantado	habreis comido
habrán cantado	habrán comido

CONDICIONAL SIMPLE	
cantaría	comería
cantarías	comerías
cantaría	comería
cantaríamos	comeríamos
cantaríais	comeríais
cantarían	comerían

CONDICIONAL PERFECTO	
habría cantado	habría comido
habrías cantado	habrías comido
habría cantado	habría comido
habríamos cantado	habríamos comido
habríais cantado	habríais comido
habrían cantado	habrían comido

MODO SUBJUNTIVO

PRESENTE	
cante	coma
cantes	comas
cante	coma
cantemos	comamos
cantéis	comáis
canten	coman

PRETERITO IMPERFECTO	
cantara	comiera
cantaras	comieras
cantara	comiera
cantáramos	comiéramos
cantarais	comierais
cantaran	comieran

PRETERITO PERFECTO	
haya cantado	haya comido
hayas cantado	hayas comido
haya cantado	haya comido
hayamos cantado	hayamos comido
hayaís cantado	hayaís comido
hayan cantado	hayan comido

PRETERITO PLUSCUAMPERFECTO	
hubiera cantado	hubiera comido
hubieras cantado	hubieras comido
hubiera cantado	hubiera comido
hubiéramos cantado	hubiéramos comido
hubierais cantado	hubierais comido
hubieran cantado	hubieran comido

MODO IMPERATIVO

TU / VOSOTROS	
canta	come
no cantes	no comas
cantad	comed
no cantéis	no comáis
	irregulars:
	haz
	no hagas, etc

USTED / USTEDES	
cante	coma
no cante	no coma
canten	coman
no canten	no coman
	irregulars:
	hagan
	no hagan, etc

[Notes]

En algunos países, la forma 'vos' se usa en vez de 'tú' y los verbos también son un poco diferentes. ejemplo:tú quieres ir a jugar = vos querés ir a jugarEspaña es el único país en donde se usa la forma 'vosotros' como plural de 'tú'.

NOTAS

NOTAS

NOTAS

NOTAS

NOTAS

PHOTOGRAPHY CREDITS

This book uses images from the following photographers and agencies

Page	Credit
19	©Nyul | Dreamstime.com
22	©Nyul | Dreamstime.com
26	©Yuri Arcurs | Dreamstime.com
27	©Franz Pfluegl | Dreamstime.com
28	©Andres Rodriguez | Dreamstime.com
32	©Nyul | Dreamstime.com
34	©Pavel Losevsky | Dreamstime.com
36	©Yuri Arcurs | Dreamstime.com
37	©Andres Rodriguez | Dreamstime.com
38	©Andres Rodriguez | Dreamstime.com
39	©Tomasz Trojanowski | Dreamstime.com
40	©Monkey Business Images | Dreamstime.com
41	©Andres Rodriguez | Dreamstime.com
44	©Yuri Arcurs | Dreamstime.com
46	©Carlo Dapino | Dreamstime.com
48	©Ron Chapple Studios | Dreamstime.com
49	©Yuri Arcurs | Dreamstime.com
53	©Nyul | Dreamstime.com
54	©Nyul | Dreamstime.com
59	©Choi Chee Seng | Dreamstime.com
61	©Gatto | Dreamstime.com
62	©Dimitris Kolyris | Dreamstime.com
67	©Dmitriy Shironosov | Dreamstime.com
68	©Masta4650 | Dreamstime.com
69	©Franz Pfluegl | Dreamstime.com
70	©Dmitry Ersler | Dreamstime.com
71	©Zdenka Micka | Dreamstime.com
76	©Monkey Business Images | Dreamstime.com
77	©Monkey Business Images | Dreamstime.com
78	©Wojciech Gajda | Dreamstime.com
85	©Diana Lundin | Dreamstime.com
86	©Sonya Etchison | Dreamstime.com
87	©Kamil Okac | Dreamstime.com
87	©matias nirenstein | Stock.xchng
87	©Photos of Puerto Rico.com
88	©Mwproductions | Dreamstime.com
97	©Dmitriy Shironosov | Dreamstime.com
99	©Yuri Arcurs | Dreamstime.com
100	©Dmitriy Shironosov | Dreamstime.com
102	©Yuri Arcurs | Dreamstime.com
104	©Orange Line Media | Dreamstime.com
106	©Dmitriy Shironosov | Dreamstime.com
108	©János Gehring | Dreamstime.com
109	©Alex Brosa | Dreamstime.com
111	©Eastwest Imaging | Dreamstime.com
112	©Monika Adamczyk | Dreamstime.com
114	©Magdalena Sobczyk | Dreamstime.com
117	©Stanislav Perov | Dreamstime.com
118	©Christian Wheatley | Dreamstime.com
119	©Jason Stitt | Dreamstime.com
122	©Yvanovich | Dreamstime.com
123	©Christopher Halloran | Dreamstime.com
125	©Michael Zysman | Dreamstime.com
129	©Dana Bartekoske | Dreamstime.com
133	©Bora Ucak | Dreamstime.com
134	©Greenstockcreative | Dreamstime.com
137	©Andrejs Pidjass | Dreamstime.com
138	©Roxana González | Dreamstime.com
139	©Monkey Business Images | Dreamstime.com
143	©Kornilovdream | Dreamstime.com
144	©Valentin Mosichev | Dreamstime.com
145	©Arpad Nagy-bagoly | Dreamstime.com
146	©Erik Reis | Dreamstime.com
146	©Uros Kovandzic | Dreamstime.com
146	©Elena Volkova | Dreamstime.com
146	©Aida Ricciardiello | Dreamstime.com
150	©Masta4650 | Dreamstime.com
150	©Igor Terekhov | Dreamstime.com
150	©Baloncici | Dreamstime.com
150	©Lorraine Kourafas | Dreamstime.com
150	©Robert Nolan | Dreamstime.com
151	©Stephen Coburn | Dreamstime.com
151	©Irina Drazowa-fischer | Dreamstime.com
151	©David Hughes | Dreamstime.com
151	©Vnlit | Dreamstime.com
151	©Monika Adamczyk | Dreamstime.com
151	©Monika Adamczyk | Dreamstime.com
151	©Alexey Petrunin | Dreamstime.com
151	©Piotr Antonów | Dreamstime.com
152	©Erik Reis | Dreamstime.com
156	©Ginasanders | Dreamstime.com
161	©Deklofenak | Dreamstime.com
163	©Tomasz Trojanowski | Dreamstime.com
164	©Mykola Velychko | Dreamstime.com

165	© Dmitriy Shironosov | Dreamstime.com
167	© David Hughes | Dreamstime.com
167	© Lorraine Kourafas | Dreamstime.com
167	© Baloncici | Dreamstime.com
167	© Stephen Coburn | Dreamstime.com
168	© Laurent Hamels | Dreamstime.com
168	© Andrey Kiselev | Dreamstime.com
172	© Jason Stitt | Dreamstime.com
175	© Diego Cervo | Dreamstime.com
178	© Julia Pivovarova | Dreamstime.com
180	© Kristian Sekulic | Dreamstime.com
181	© Wannous | Dreamstime.com
181	© Evgeniy Gorbunov | Dreamstime.com
182	© Chad Mcdermott | Dreamstime.com
182	© Mike Thomas | Dreamstime.com
186	© Kristian Sekulic | Dreamstime.com
187	© Dmitriy Shironosov | Dreamstime.com
188	© Konstantin Sutyagin | Dreamstime.com
189	© Andres Rodriguez | Dreamstime.com
190	© Anikasalsera | Dreamstime.com
	© Les Cunliffe | Dreamstime.com
	© Cheryl A. Meyer | Dreamstime.com
	© Zoran Simin | Dreamstime.com
	© Nikola Hristovski | Dreamstime.com
	© Dmitry Maslov | Dreamstime.com
191	© Nikola Hristovski | Dreamstime.com
192	© Shariff Che' Lah | Dreamstime.com
193	© Shariff Che' Lah | Dreamstime.com
193	© Denis Pepin | Dreamstime.com
194	© Pavel Kruglov | Dreamstime.com
195	© Nicholas Sutcliffe | Dreamstime.com
199	© Dmitriy Shironosov | Dreamstime.com
201	© Ekaterina Solovieva | Dreamstime.com
202	© Eastwest Imaging | Dreamstime.com
207	© Yuri Arcurs | Dreamstime.com
209	© Monika Adamczyk | Dreamstime.com
210	© Sebastian Czapnik | Dreamstime.com
212	© Monkey Business Images | Dreamstime.com
213	© Andrea Skjold | Dreamstime.com
213	© Joe Gough | Dreamstime.com
214	© Roxana González | Dreamstime.com
214	© Marina Nabatova | Dreamstime.com
214	© James Camp | Dreamstime.com
214	© Elena Weber | Dreamstime.com
215	© Flynt | Dreamstime.com
218	© Monkey Business Images | Dreamstime.com
220	© Eastwest Imaging | Dreamstime.com
221	© Eastwest Imaging | Dreamstime.com
222	© Oleg Filipchuk | Dreamstime.com
225	© Oleg Filipchuk | Dreamstime.com
227	© Asian | Dreamstime.com
228	© Oleg Filipchuk | Dreamstime.com
	© Miroslav Tolimir | Dreamstime.com
	© Konstantin Sutyagin | Dreamstime.com
	© Pavel Burovnikov | Dreamstime.com
	© Asian | Dreamstime.com
229	© Vojtech Vlk | Dreamstime.com
231	© Frenk And Danielle Kaufmann | Dreamstime.com
238	© Andrey Stratilatov | Dreamstime.com
239	© Marco Scisetti | Dreamstime.com
240	© Yvanovich | Dreamstime.com
243	© Invictus999 | Dreamstime.com
244	© Ron Chapple Studios | Dreamstime.com
246	© Franz Pfluegl | Dreamstime.com
248	© Laurent Hamels | Dreamstime.com
249	© Roman Sika | Dreamstime.com
250	© Sebastian Kaulitzki | Dreamstime.com
255	© Sebastian Kaulitzki | Dreamstime.com
267	© Pavel Losevsky | Dreamstime.com
269	© Marion Wear | Dreamstime.com
270	© Ron Chapple Studios | Dreamstime.com
272	© Henrischmit | Dreamstime.com
	© Trevor Harwood | Dreamstime.com
273	© Bryan Busovicki | Dreamstime.com
275	© Chad Mcdermott | Dreamstime.com
277	© Bartosz Ostrowski | Dreamstime.com
	© Pavel Losevsky | Dreamstime.com
278	© Serghei Starus | Dreamstime.com
281	© Dariusz Miszkiel | Dreamstime.com
282	© Martin Purmensky | Dreamstime.com
285	© Tomasz Trojanowski | Dreamstime.com
286	© Nikola Hristovski | Dreamstime.com
288	© Kristian Sekulic | Dreamstime.com
	© Edurivero | Dreamstime.com
289	© Irina Shoyhet | Dreamstime.com
291	© Vanessa Van Rensburg | Dreamstime.com
297	© Luba V Nel | Dreamstime.com
301	© IÑigo Quintanilla | Dreamstime.com
302	© Haak78 | Dreamstime.com
303	© Mm72 | Dreamstime.com
304	© Roman Sika | Dreamstime.com
	© Sebastian Kaulitzki | Dreamstime.com
306	© Dušan Zidar | Dreamstime.com
307	© Suerolopez | Dreamstime.com